Inside World War One?

Studies of the German Historical Institute London

GENERAL EDITOR: Andreas Gestrich

Making and Breaking the Rules
Discussion, Implementation, and Consequences of Dominican Legislation
Edited by Cornelia Linde

The War of the Spanish Succession
New Perspectives
Edited by Matthias Pohlig and Michael Schaich

Bid for World Power?
New Research on the Outbreak of the First World War
Edited by Andreas Gestrich and Hartmut Pogge von Strandmann

The Consumer on the Home Front
Second World War Civilian Consumption in Comparative Perspective
Edited by Hartmut Berghoff, Jan Logemann, and Felix Römer

Dilemmas of Humanitarian Aid in the Twentieth Century
Edited by Johannes Paulmann

Political Languages in the Age of Extremes
Edited by Willibald Steinmetz

The Voice of the Citizen Consumer
A History of Market Research, Consumer Movements, and the Political Public Sphere
Edited by Kerstin Brückweh

The Holy Roman Empire 1495–1806
Edited by R. J. W. Evans, Michael Schaich, and Peter H. Wilson

Unemployment and Protest
New Perspectives on Two Centuries of Contention
Edited by Matthias Reiss and Matt Perry

Removing Peoples
Forced Removal in the Modern World
Edited by Richard Bessel and Claudia B. Haake

Wilhelmine Germany and Edwardian Britain
Essays on Cultural Affinity
Edited by Dominik Geppert and Robert Gerwarth

The Diplomats' World
A Cultural History of Diplomacy, 1815–1914
Edited by Markus Mösslang and Torsten Riotte

European Aristocracies and the Radical Right 1918–1939
Edited by Karina Urbach

The Street as Stage
Protest Marches and Public Rallies since the Nineteenth Century
Edited by Matthias Reiss

Monarchy and Religion
The Transformation of Royal Culture in Eighteenth-Century Europe
Edited by Michael Schaich

Science across the European Empires, 1800–1950
Edited by Benedikt Stuchtey

The Postwar Challenge
Cultural, Social, and Political Change in Western Europe, 1945–1958
Edited by Dominik Geppert

Writing World History, 1800–2000
Edited by Benedikt Stuchtey and Eckhardt Fuchs

Britain and Germany in Europe, 1949–1990
Edited by Jeremy Noakes, Peter Wende, and Jonathan Wright

The Mechanics of Internationalism
Culture, Society, and Politics from the 1840s to the First World War
Edited by Martin H. Geyer and Johannes Paulmann

Inside World War One?
The First World War and its Witnesses

EDITED BY

RICHARD BESSEL AND
DOROTHEE WIERLING

GERMAN HISTORICAL INSTITUTE LONDON

OXFORD
UNIVERSITY PRESS

Great Clarendon Street, Oxford, OX2 6DP,
United Kingdom

Oxford University Press is a department of the University of Oxford.
It furthers the University's objective of excellence in research, scholarship,
and education by publishing worldwide. Oxford is a registered trade mark of
Oxford University Press in the UK and in certain other countries

Published in the United States
by Oxford University Press Inc., New York

© The German Historical Institute London 2018

The moral rights of the authors have been asserted
Database right Oxford University Press (maker)

First published 2018

All rights reserved. No part of this publication may be reproduced, stored in
a retrieval system, or transmitted, in any form or by any means, without the
prior permission in writing of Oxford University Press, or as expressly permitted
by law, by licence, or under terms agreed with the appropriate reprographics
rights organization. Enquiries concerning reproduction outside the scope of the
above should be sent to the Rights Department, Oxford University Press, at the
address above

You must not circulate this book in any other form
and you must impose this same condition on any acquirer

British Library Cataloguing in Publication Data
Data available

Library of Congress Cataloging in Publication Data
Data available

Library of Congress Control Number: 2017954011

ISBN 978–0–19–882059–8

1 3 5 7 9 10 8 6 4 2

Typeset by John Waś, Oxford
Printed in Great Britain
on acid-free paper by
Biddles Ltd, King's Lynn

Links to third party websites are provided by Oxford in good faith and
for information only. Oxford disclaims any responsibility for the materials
contained in any third party website referenced in this work

Foreword

Worldwide, the centenary of the First World War unleashed an astonishing wave of academic and public interest in what can, in George Kennan's famous words, still be perceived as the twentieth century's 'seminal catastrophe'. Research and publications not only revisited old debates such as the question of German 'war guilt', but also covered new ground. New research on the global dimensions of the war was especially interesting and fruitful. Non-European powers and the theatres of war outside Europe received much more attention than had been the case in older research, and the war experiences of non-European soldiers on the battlefields of Europe and in other parts of the world at last received the attention they deserved.

It is particularly in this field of the war experiences of soldiers on the front and the civilian populations at home that rich new material has been unearthed and new research initiated over the past years. Many private collections were handed over to museums and archives, and the new opportunities created by the Internet have allowed private individuals and institutions to make many of these collections publicly available across the globe. However, this new or—in the case of Europe—partly renewed interest in war experiences needs to be accompanied by deliberations on cross-cultural comparisons of such sources and their wider impact on the study of the world war.

This volume is dedicated to the insights that can be gained from analysing such material and to the methodological problems connected with its interpretation. It is the outcome of an exciting conference which Dorothee Wierling initiated as part of her Gerda Henkel Visiting Professorship, and which was organized jointly by the German Historical Institute London and the London School of Economics and Political Science in the academic year 2013/14.

The conference, held at the German Historical Institute London in October 2014, was co-convened by Richard Bessel and Dorothee Wierling as well as Heather Jones and Sönke Neitzel from the LSE. Our combined and very special thanks go to the

Gerda Henkel Foundation, whose generous support of the Visiting Professorship made this conference possible. I am very grateful to all contributors for their co-operation and to Richard Bessel and Dorothee Wierling, who took on the task of editing this volume. At Oxford University Press I should like to thank the Delegates for accepting this volume for publication, the anonymous reviewers for their careful reading of the manuscript and valuable comments and suggestions, and Sarah Holmes and Hollie Thomas for their support in the final editing and production of the book. Finally, special thanks also go to all members of staff at the German Historical Institute who helped organize the conference, and to Angela Davies, who helped revise the essays and saw the volume through the publication process.

Andreas Gestrich

London
October 2017

Contents

Introduction

1. Inside World War One? Ego Documents and the
   First World War   3
   RICHARD BESSEL AND DOROTHEE WIERLING

Part I. Invasion and Occupation

2. Registers of Everyday Life in Warsaw during the
   First World War: The Uses and Limitations of Ego
   Documents   29
   ROBERT BLOBAUM

3. Measuring Lost Time: Civilians' Diaries in Occupied
   Belgium   57
   SOPHIE DE SCHAEPDRIJVER

4. Ego Documents from the Invasion of East Prussia,
   1914–1915   83
   ALEXANDER WATSON

Part II. Soldiers, Doctors, and Nurses

5. 'It was more than madness . . .': Perceptions of War
   among Slovenian Soldiers, 1914–1918   105
   PAVLINA BOBIČ

6. The Thin White Line: Experience and Memory of
   the Alpine Front in the First World War   119
   ROBERTA PERGHER

7. Counter-Narratives of the Great War? War Accounts of Nurses in Austro-Hungarian Service 143
   Christa Hämmerle

8. Front Experience and Psychological Problems: The Voices of Doctors and Patients in Case Studies and Patient Files 167
   Andrea Gräfin von Hohenthal

Part III. War beyond Europe

9. Inside the Ottoman Army: Two Armenian Officers Tell their Story 195
   Mustafa Aksakal

10. Uncovering the Colonial Cultures and Encounters of the British Empire during the First World War 207
    Anna Maguire

Part IV. Uses of Ego Documents

11. Publishing Ego Documents as War Propaganda 231
    Gerd Krumeich

12. A *Vita Nova*: The Construction of a War. Life Experience in Italian First World War Autobiographical Writing 249
    Marco Mondini

13. Alloying Dissent with Patriotism: Dragiša Vasić in Yugoslav Siberia 273
    John Paul Newman

14. The Apotheosis of the Unknown Soldier: Officers, Soldiers, and the Writing of the Great War in Russia 291
    Joshua Sanborn

15. 'Emplotting the Witness': Henri Barbusse and Marc
    Bloch   305
    LEONARD V. SMITH

Notes on Contributors   317

Index   321

Introduction

1
Inside World War One?
Ego Documents and the First World War

RICHARD BESSEL AND DOROTHEE WIERLING

In mid November 1914 Stefan Schimmer, a German farmer who had been sent to the Vosges front, wrote to his wife after two weeks on the front line: 'Those who remain at home cannot imagine it at all. There is no day, no night, no Sunday, no workday.'[1] Like hundreds of thousands of other soldiers, Schimmer had been torn abruptly from his civilian existence and cast into an environment where the familiar rhythms of his life were suspended. In mid April 1915 the French soldier Marcel Papillon wrote to his parents from the front at Bois-le-Prêtre ('Priest's Wood', near Pont-à-Mousson): 'We have experienced a terrible week. It is shameful, dreadful; it is impossible to get an idea of such carnage. One can never escape such a hell. The dead cover the ground. The Boche and Frenchmen are piled together on top of each other, in the mud.'[2] Like hundreds of thousands of other soldiers, Papillon had witnessed scenes hitherto unimaginable. The belief that those who remained at home, those who had not experienced what he had witnessed at the front, 'cannot imagine it at all', that 'it is impossible to get

---

[1] 'Die nur zuhause sind, können es sich gar nicht vorstellen. Es gibt keinen Tag, keine Nacht, keinen Sonntag und keinen Werktag': Briefe unseres Großvaters Stefan Schimmer aus dem Weltkrieg 1914/15, Abschrift von Peter Högler, Oellingen 1979 (typescript, Bibliothek für Zeitgeschichte, Stuttgart, letter dated 15 Nov. 1914); quoted in Peter Knoch, 'Erleben und Nacherleben: Das Kriegserlebnis im Augenzeugenbericht und im Geschichtsunterricht', in Gerhard Hirschfeld, Gerd Krumeich, and Irena Renz (eds.), *Keiner fühlt sich hier mehr als Mensch . . .: Erlebnis und Wirkung des Ersten Weltkriegs* (Essen, 1993), 201.

[2] 'C'est honteux, affreux; c'est impossible de se faire une idée d'un pareil carnage. Jamais on ne pourra sortir d'un pareil enfer. Les morts couvrent le terrain. Boches et Français sont entassés les uns sur les autres, dans la boue': Marthe Joseph Lucien and Marcel Papillon, '*Si je reviens comme je l'espère': lettres du front et de l'arrière, 1914–1918* (Paris, 2003), 124 (13 Apr. 1915); quoted in John Horne, 'Entre expérience et mémoire: les soldats français de la Grande Guerre', *Annales: Histoire, Sciences Sociales*, 60/5 (2005), 903–19, at 908–9.

an idea of such carnage', was widely shared—and neatly frames the subject of this book. How can we get 'inside the First World War'; how can we understand and appreciate the perceptions and experiences of those who lived through it?

The challenge posed by this question is all the more difficult and important since the First World War was a watershed in modern European and indeed world history. The experience of warfare during the 1914–18 conflict was something hitherto unimaginable to most of those who had been plunged into it. The language that described nineteenth-century warfare could not adequately portray a war that 'was entirely different, a war of masses, fought by conscript armies'.[3] It was, at least on the Western Front, industrialized warfare on a colossal scale—warfare that seemed to be dominated by metal and machines (even if much of the experience of the war in fact involved horses and mud), and that seemed to justify Max Weber's description of the First World War as a 'machine war', the first technical–industrial mass war.[4] Death and injury were caused, to an overwhelming degree, by impersonal (industrial) weaponry, in the first instance by artillery and the machine-gun, rather than by hand-to-hand combat. Combat became anonymous. Soldiers were, quite literally, blown to bits. Tens of thousands of soldiers could be cut down in a matter of hours by the use of the new machines for killing. There was no precedent for this sort of warfare, with perhaps the partial exception of the American Civil War. How could it be described, and how could those who read or heard the descriptions possibly understand what it had meant to those who had experienced it?

In his study of French trench newspapers, Stéphane Audoine-Rouzeau observed of attitudes towards the home front that 'the worst ordeal for the soldiers was that of not being understood. . . . the incomprehension and ignorance of the rear, of everything that was tragic in front-line life, were immense.'[5] Indeed, they could not really be understood, for those on the home front, at least in the west, had little or no comprehension of what combatants had experienced. And now these accounts are read by people (ourselves)

---

[3] Jay Winter and Antoine Prost, *The Great War in History: Debates and Controversies, 1914 to the Present* (Cambridge, 2005), 84.
[4] Jörn Leonhard, *Die Büchse der Pandora: Geschichte des Ersten Weltkriegs* (Munich, 2014), 146.
[5] Stéphane Audoin-Rouzeau, *Men at War 1914–1918: National Sentiment and Trench Journalism in France during the First World War* (Providence, RI, 1992), 112.

who can barely appreciate what their authors endured a century ago and whose understanding is often framed by a clichéd image of the senseless slaughter of the trenches that has become the widely accepted description of the First World War.

The difficulties of attempting to make sense of the 'experience' of the First World War, and relating it to those who had (and have) not lived through the conflict, are all the greater because that experience and the accompanying incomprehension were neither uniform nor universal. 'Experience' is something social and cultural, and therefore specific and diverse; it relates to both the understanding of past events and the confrontation with the new and unexpected. Jay Winter has observed of 'the soldiers' tale':

> The stories soldiers relate tell us something of what they have been through; but the act of narration tells us who they are at the time of the telling. Later on, the experience changes as the narrator's life changes. Since identities are not fixed, neither is 'experience'. It is the subject's 'history', expressed at a particular moment in the language of the subject. That language is not universal; it is particular, localized, and mostly regional or national in form.[6]

Winter's comments follow from his observations of accounts left by British, French, and German soldiers of the First World War, on which a great deal of research has been done. The fluid and varied nature of 'experience' in an unprecedented conflict takes on added dimensions when we look beyond the Western Front, and cast our eyes towards the east and the south. Italian and Habsburg soldiers on the Alpine front, men in the wartime service of the Ottoman Empire, Slovenian soldiers in the forces of the Habsburg Empire, and civilians in occupied Poland or Belgium spoke different languages, in both the literal and the figurative senses, and experienced the war in many diverse ways. This poses a challenge to any attempt to make generalizations about the experiences of those who lived through the First World War.

Yet some generalization is possible. The First World War cut millions of people loose from their political and social anchors. The uprooting of huge numbers of human beings, largely but by no means exclusively along the Eastern Front, dispersed and destroyed entire communities. The deportation of tens of thousands of Belgian labourers to Germany, shocking as it was, pales when set against

---

[6] Jay Winter, *Remembering War: The Great War between Memory and History in the Twentieth Century* (New Haven, 2006), 116.

the scale of wartime forced removal in the east. It was in the east that the greatest numbers of people were uprooted, particularly with the Russian 'Great Retreat' from April to October 1915.[7] The total human displacement in the Russian Empire was staggering: over 3.3 million refugees by the end of 1915, and more than 6 million, roughly 5 per cent of the empire's total population, by the beginning of 1917.[8] In the east armies roamed over vast territories, spreading destruction and shattering social and political structures as they went, leaving in their wake masses of destitute and desperate people and a land ripe for revolution; in the west the largely stationary front in northern France left behind destruction on an unprecedented scale, creating landscapes that seemed not of this world and where the rebuilding constituted the world's largest construction project in the decade after the war.[9] The war also left behind societies bereft of millions of young men and in mourning; the postwar years were indeed 'hollow years'.[10] Nothing like this had happened in Europe within living memory.

Nothing like this had happened within living memory in another sense: the First World War was a world war, a global war. After a century during which European wars had been rather limited, national affairs, not only was most of the European Continent involved in this conflict, but its ramifications reverberated around the globe. And the global nature of the conflict in turn affected the war raging in Europe, as men from around the world—from ANZAC troops fighting in Turkey to Chinese labourers employed in service functions behind the lines of the Western Front and white European soldiers in close

[7] See Alan Kramer, *Dynamic of Destruction: Culture and Mass Killing in the First World War* (Oxford, 2007), 151; id., 'Deportationen', in Gerhard Hirschfeld, Gerd Krumeich, and Irina Renz (eds.), *Enzyklopädie Erster Weltkrieg* (Paderborn, 2009), 434–5; Peter Gatrell, 'Introduction: World Wars and Population Displacement in Europe in the Twentieth Century', *Contemporary European History*, 16, Special Issue 04 (Nov. 2007), 415–26, at 420; Richard Bessel, 'Migration und Vertreibung: Von der Massenmigration zur Zwangsabschiebung', in Michael Geyer, Helmut Lethen, and Lutz Musner (eds.), *Zeitalter der Gewalt: Zur Geopolitik und Psychopolitik des Ersten Weltkriegs* (Frankfurt a.M., 2015), 135–48.

[8] See Joshua A. Sanborn, 'Unsettling the Empire: Violent Migrations and Social Disaster in Russia during World War I', *Journal of Modern History*, 77/2 (2005), 310; Peter Gatrell, *A Whole Empire Walking: Refugees in Russia during World War I* (Bloomington, Ind., 1999), 3.

[9] See Hugh Clout, *After the Ruins: Restoring the Countryside of Northern France after the Great War* (Exeter, 1996).

[10] Eugen Weber, *The Hollow Years: France in the 1930s* (New York, 1994); Jay Winter, *Sites of Memory, Sites of Mourning: The Great War in European Cultural History* (Cambridge, 1995).

encounters with non-white people from the colonies—were drawn into a conflict whose epicentre was the European Continent.

Not only was it a global conflict, but the First World War, particularly the conflict on the Western Front, has often been regarded as 'total war' (even if the phrase was promoted after the event by Erich Ludendorff, who used the idea to criticize Germany's lack of total commitment).[11] While the idea of 'total' war is problematic—for no conflict is truly 'total', the concept of 'total war' is 'riddled with ambiguities, contradictions, and methodological confusion', and 'no one has yet produced a convincing definition of total war'[12]—it is understandable that so many people came to regard the First World War as such because of its unprecedented character. The vast numbers of people involved, killed, and injured in the conflict, its global reach and effects, the levels of violence, the harnessing of industrial economies to serve the needs of the military, invited the use of the term. The label 'total war' may have been imprecise and open to debate, but it described something that was new and shocking to those who lived through the 1914–18 conflict. The First World War may not have been 'total' in that it did not completely dominate every aspect of people's lives in countries at war, but it was on a scale that those enveloped by it had never seen before and often had difficulty comprehending.

Rather than attempting to frame our understanding of the First World War with the idea of 'total war', perhaps we should focus on what John Horne has termed its 'totalising logic': 'a set of dynamics which triggered a spiral of reciprocal violence and counter-violence that engulfed more and more of society'.[13] War is violence, and this gets to the heart of what the Great War meant to those who experienced it, a process of erosion of normative constraints and a cumulative radicalization of violence that engulfed not only the

---

[11] See Roger Chickering, 'Sore Loser: Ludendorff's Total War', in id. and Stig Förster (eds.), *The Shadows of Total War: Europe, East Asia, and the United States, 1919–1939* (Cambridge, 2003), 151–78. Generally, see Roger Chickering and Stig Förster (eds.), *Great War, Total War: Combat and Mobilization on the Western Front, 1914–1918* (New York, 2000).

[12] Roger Chickering, 'Introduction to Part II', in id., Dennis Showalter, and Hans van de Ven (eds.), *War and the Modern World*, The Cambridge History of War, 4 (Cambridge, 2012), 186.

[13] John Horne, 'A Total War? The French Experience of the First World War', lecture delivered at the Plenary Session of the 60th Annual Meeting of the Society for French Historical Studies at UQAM, 26 Apr. 2014: *H-France Salon*, 6/12 ⟨http://www.h-france.net/Salon/Volume6.html⟩ [accessed 29 July 2016].

fighting front (with the use of poison gas, the first tank warfare, massive artillery barrages with high explosives, and enormous military casualties) but also 'more and more of society'. This approach offers a way to integrate more effectively the experiences in the east and the south as well as those on the more familiar Western Front into our understandings of the conflict, to include the destruction of whole communities and the uprooting of millions of people along the Russian front, the Armenian genocide, the enormous toll of disease, and the catastrophic consequences of the conflict for the peoples of the Ottoman Empire and of the Balkans. It offers a way to integrate narratives of the more 'modern' war fought in the west, where a sophisticated infrastructure of supply and medical care could be built up on a largely stationary fighting front, with the less modern war where such infrastructure was more often absent, and where soldiers were more likely to succumb to disease—that is, on the fronts in the east and the south, from Serbia to the Isonzo front, from Galicia to Gallipoli. This 'totalising logic', unleashing violence on a colossal scale, lay at the centre of the myriad individual attempts to make sense of the experience of the First World War.

This volume is an attempt to introduce, discuss, and interrogate some of the attempts by those who lived through the conflict to make sense of their First World War. It examines ego documents, texts such as diaries, memoirs, autobiographies, travelogues, and so on, in which the personal views of the author play a central role: that is, texts which provide accounts of or testimonies to the 'self' who produced them,[14] which were generated during or after the 1914–18 conflict, and which relate in various ways the experiences of their authors during the war. Its origins lie in a conference held at the German Historical Institute London in October 2014, in which participants from across the European Continent and from North America gathered to discuss the use of ego documents to understand how the First World War was experienced by those who endured it.[15] That conference and this book are framed by the aim not only of examining the war 'from within' through the use of ego documents, but at the same time of extending the discussion beyond the more familiar war in western Europe to include the war in the east and

[14] See Mary Fulbrook and Ulinka Rublack, 'In Relation: The "Social Self" and Ego-Documents', *German History*, 28/3 (2010), 263–72, at 263.

[15] See Dorothee Wierling and Richard Bessel, 'Inside World War One? International Workshop on Ego Documents and the Experience of the First World War. Conference Report', *German Historical Institute London Bulletin*, 37/1 (May 2015), 140–5.

the south. As such, it offers discussion of countries and cultures with differing levels of literacy, differing written and oral traditions, and often very different experiences of the war.

* * *

The First World War was unprecedented not only in the scale of the conflict and the vast numbers of people it affected, but also in the mass of documentation that those who experienced it left behind. In the course of the First World War, billions of letters were exchanged between the various fronts and the home fronts; millions of soldiers of all ranks, as well as doctors and nurses, wrote diaries at least over a period of their war and front activities; men and women living under occupation did the same. Afterwards, thousands of those who had lived through the war published their memories in newspaper articles, journals, and (sometimes self-published) books. What kinds of sources are these texts offering for a better understanding of the First World War?

In our introductory remarks we would like to address a number of methodological questions which were part of our discussions during the conference and are also relevant to the essays in this volume. In a first step, we will describe the range of texts that qualify as ego documents in that they reveal personal perceptions, experiences, reasoning, emotions, and ascriptions of meaning to what befell the authors in the course of the war. Second, we will address the potential of these ego documents for our understanding of the First World War on three levels: the history of everyday life under the conditions of this war; the subjective war experience of various actors; and, finally, the creation of a meaningful interpretation of these experiences, a process of 'sense-making' (Roberta Pergher). Third, we will look at ego documents and their place in public discourses, both during and after the war. Who was included in the national canon of legitimate actors and who was not? How did seemingly private documents become public and how were they used, by whom, to establish a hegemonic narrative about the war? And, finally, how did the specific conditions of postwar societies shape postwar memoirs about the war?

Ego documents, in the broadest sense of the term, are written or oral texts which, voluntarily or involuntarily, reveal personal perceptions.[16] This applies to many texts that were not necessarily

---

[16] For a good summary of the state of the art with regard to this kind of source,

meant by their authors to reveal anything about the authors' selves, such as administrative reports, travelogues, or medical files. It would be for the reader, in this case the historian, to detect and interpret the hidden and indirect personal agenda of such texts. For historians of the First World War, however, intentional ego documents are abundant. As Sophie De Schaepdrijver observes in this volume, the Great War broke out in an age already characterized by an intense preoccupation with subjectivity, and represented an extraordinary and overwhelming experience which created an enormous desire for people to express themselves with all their hearts as individuals. They did so mainly in three different genres: diaries, letters, and memoirs.[17] For all three types of text we have to ask some basic questions. Who were the authors of these ego documents? To whom were these texts addressed? What is the range of topics raised? How did the specific conditions of war shape the act of writing and the types of text that were produced?

Diaries are often seen as the most 'authentic'—that is, immediate and unmediated—written expressions of a 'now' and an 'I'. Upon closer examination, however, these assumptions have to be relativized. First, while the diary appears to be like a chronicle, written without knowledge of what comes next, many diarists, especially under the conditions of war, were not able to write down the day's events regularly on a quiet evening; instead they might take very short notes or none at all on 'busy' days, and summarize or elaborate when they had more time, often cutting their narrative into daily sections in order to pretend that these were written on the specific date. Thus, diaries, too, are written partly with hindsight and contain more reflection and interpretation than is generally expected from the genre. In addition, although they are certainly the most personal and private genre of ego documents, diaries were often written with one or more audiences in mind: family and friends, to whom sections were sometimes sent during the war; future friends and family, whom the author wanted to inform about his or her extraordinary experience in 'great' times; and perhaps the author envisaged an

which has been used and theorized especially among early modernists, see Kaspar von Greyerz, 'Ego Documents: The Last Word?', *German History*, 28/3 (2010), 273–82.

[17] For a general introduction to work with these genres see Miriam Dobson, 'Letters', pp. 57–73; Christa Hämmerle, 'Diaries', pp. 141–58; and David Carlson, 'Autobiography', pp. 175–91, in Miriam Dobson and Benjamin Ziemann (eds.), *Reading Primary Sources: The Interpretation of Texts from Nineteenth and Twentieth Century History* (New York, 2008).

even larger, anonymous audience, postwar readers of published versions of the diary, given that the author had lived through great and extraordinary times.

The relation to an addressee and his or her indirect presence in the text are more obvious in letters. They went back and forth between front and home fronts as well as inside and between countries involved in the war, but since most of the letters which have survived are those written by men and women at the front, we can only try to make plausible assumptions about the other side of the correspondence.[18] In addition, letters almost always had a wide range of addressees not mentioned in the texts themselves, since it was understood that parents or wives would share the letters with other family members, neighbours, and friends. In the most basic sense, soldiers' letters were proof that they were still alive and well, although once a family received such a letter, they could never be certain that the author was still in the same secure situation in which he had written it. Depending on the front and the writer's position on it, but also on the intensity of military action, letters could take a couple of days or several weeks to reach their addressee; they could get lost, and were often numbered to keep track of the delivery. To what degree censorship was an important issue and shaped what soldiers or nurses would write is an open question. The frankness of the communication suggests that most correspondents did not feel they were under the total control of the authorities.[19] What seems more important when interpreting war letters is the social function they fulfilled: as self-descriptions for loved ones, attempts to reassure addressees about possible dangers, while also providing evidence of the author's brave, manly qualities.

Memoirs of the war experience were also abundant. While they

---

[18] One of the exceptions is Christa Hämmerle, '". . . wirf ihnen alles hin und schau, daß du fortkommst": Die Feldpost eines Paares in der Geschlechter(un)ordnung des Ersten Weltkrieges', *Historische Anthroplologie*, 6/3 (1998), 431–58; on the First World War and gender history see Christa Hämmerle, Oswald Überegger, and Birgitta Bader-Zaar (eds.), *Gender and the First World War* (Basingstoke, 2014).

[19] See the introductory article by Eberhard Demm, 'Censorship', in *1914–1918 online: International Encyclopedia of the First World War* ⟨http://encyclopedia.1914-1918-online.net/article/censorship⟩ [accessed 29 July 2016]. The author provides a substantial list of secondary literature. Postal censorship was only part of the broader attempt to control public communication about the war and, although thousands of army personnel were busy reading letters from the front and home front, no more than 5% of letters could be read at all. This was less about punishing soldiers (whose letters were checked more often than those of officers) than about understanding the 'mood' and intervening where there were problems.

were often based on diaries and letters, they aimed at a coherent, meaningful representation of the war as such and of the author's personality as shaped by the war. These narratives about the personal essence of the war experience were sometimes written many years after the events, when immediate impressions had settled and could be put together in a narrative that made sense. This sense, however, had much to do with the specific postwar situation in which authors found themselves. These memoirs are therefore more than a narrative construction of the war itself. They are also a comment on postwar life and how it compared to the war experience, in particular, whether it was worth the war effort.[20] The memoirs spoke to an audience for which the authors hoped to personify an authoritative voice, be it that of the hero or of the survivor who had gone through the hell of the trenches.

Not everybody who lived through the war was in a position to leave personal documents about their experiences. To begin with, there was the basic fact that in some societies involved, illiteracy was high, especially among the rural population.[21] Even if illiterate soldiers managed, with the help of comrades or superiors, to send some notes home as proof that they were still alive, these would be short and rather impersonal. Other social groups too, for whom writing was a rare activity, would not produce a lengthy correspondence. The higher their level of education, the more likely individuals were to write often, extensively, in great detail, and with a desire to reflect intensely on their experiences. As a result, there is a clear dominance of male, educated writers, most of whom held officer rank. At the same time, whole fronts populated by armies with high illiteracy rates, such as those of the Tsarist Empire, the Balkans, and the Ottoman Empire, are under-represented among the abundance of evidence, while the largest bodies of sources come from western

---

[20] Some of these memoirs gained a canonical place beyond national borders and the immediate postwar period, such as Ernst Jünger's 'Storm of Steel' ('In Stahlgewittern'). First published as his war diary, it was heavily edited by the author in 1924 and translated into English in 1929 and French in 1930. Another German version of 1961 was retranslated into English in 2003. The original diary was not published until 2010, followed by a critical edition in 2013. See Ernst Jünger, *In Stahlgewittern: Historisch-kritische Ausgabe*, ed. Helmuth Kiesell, 2 vols. (Stuttgart, 2013).

[21] According to a UNESCO study dating from the 1950s, the illiteracy rate (for those older than 6) in Italy was 37.7% by 1911; in Turkey it was 80.0% by 1935; and in Serbia it was 66.2% for males around 1900: UNESCO, *Progress of Literacy in Various Countries: Preliminary Statistical Study of Available Census Data since 1900* (Paris, 1953), 115, 137, 162.

countries (and the Western Fronts), especially since countries such as Germany, France, and Britain encouraged soldiers to write diaries and letters, and to keep them for future remembrance.

The phenomena of violence and death were what distinguished war from other extraordinary experiences. Most men who had been drafted or who had volunteered were confronted for the first time in their lives with killing and the prospect of being killed. Given the ubiquity of violence in the First World War, its relative absence in the ego documents is striking. It is true that most of a soldier's time involved waiting and activities surrounding the fighting, such as building and repairing trenches, installing telephone lines, or writing daily reports; but it is also the case that when writing home, many men would avoid descriptions of brutal battles and deadly wounds so as not to alarm their families. Diaries, however, were more likely to include such scenes and images. These differences also point to the importance of the actual act of writing. Most military activities followed a certain rhythm of roughly two weeks on the front line and then a break in the rear area. Writing in the trenches, especially while under fire, would result in short, laconic notes, often in pencil and without any details or reflections; back in the rear area there was time, soldiers were bored, and there were letters and packages waiting for them. This created a situation in which to elaborate and reflect, in both diaries and letters. The same holds true for diaries and letters written under occupation, a situation which forces otherwise active people into passivity on the one hand, or into hectically organizing a living under unusual circumstances on the other. Finally, the general, normative atmosphere encouraged a military, manly, soldierly way of expressing one's experiences—after all, comrades might find one's diary and read it—while letters to the home front might refer to a more civilian, even feminine, culture.[22]

These general observations with regard to ego documents as texts point to the basic need to contextualize a diary, a collection of letters, or a memoir as comprehensively as possible before asking the obvious question: what can we learn from them for our understanding of the First World War?

* * *

---

[22] Dorothee Wierling, 'Imagining and Communicating Violence: The Correspondence of a Berlin Family, 1914–1918', in Hämmerle, Überegger, and Bader-Zaar (eds.), *Gender and the First World War*, 36–51.

Ego documents contain a huge amount of information about what we might call the everyday of war. This concerns conditions on the ground: daily routines, life in the trenches and in mobile warfare. We learn about basic living conditions: what people eat and drink, where they sleep and rest, what they talk about, what rumours are communicated, what they read, and which songs they sing. We find out about relations between the ranks, the practices of fighting on various fronts, and the immediate impact of violence and danger. We also read directly or indirectly (through the perspective of the soldier or nurse) about conditions on the home front and the difficulties of keeping in contact with family and friends. We can reconstruct the rhythm of fighting and the conditions of medical care at the front. We hear of the material and social conditions facing civilians caught between the fronts or vis-à-vis invading troops and under occupation. We can distinguish between the conditions of men and women, and different ethnic and class segments of societies. All this is very important information which can be used to confront or even contrast the war on the ground with official military reports and often idealizing publications aimed at a larger public. Not least, as soon as we widen our perspective to include all European fronts and home fronts, as well as those beyond Europe, we not only learn about the different conditions which soldiers of various national or ethnic backgrounds faced and become aware of numerous intercultural contacts (Anna Maguire), but also discover that the war began and ended at different times in different places, such as in the Balkans (John Paul Newman) and in the Tsarist or Ottoman Empires (Mustafa Aksakal). And we might even rediscover fronts that, given the overwhelming presence in the public narrative of the Western Front, have long been neglected or even forgotten altogether.

Experience is a key term for the use of ego documents in historiography in general,[23] and for the history of the First World War in particular. After all, most participants were aware that they were witnessing a dramatic, world-changing event, and were living in 'great' times. This awareness led them to record faithfully and thoroughly not only what was happening around them but also how they experienced it personally. As a potentially life-changing event, the war

---

[23] See the still exciting discussion of 'experience' by John E. Toews, 'Intellectual History after the Linguistic Turn: The Autonomy of Meaning and the Irreducibility of Experience', *American Historical Review*, 92/4 (1987), 880–907; and Joan Scott, 'The Evidence of Experience', *Critical Inquiry*, 17/4 (1991), 773–97.

was described by many in terms of a *Bildungsroman*, a novel about the moral and psychological maturing of the protagonist. Experience is a term, however, that is used in many different ways and differently in various languages. Thus, in German there are two possible translations for the word: the first is *Erlebnis*, which refers to the immediate imprint of an event, that is, at the moment of living through it (an appropriate English translation might be 'perception'); at the same time, experience as *Erfahrung* refers to a long-term processing of an *Erlebnis*, including its adjustment to and integration into previous perceptions and experiences in the course of which the original perception might be reinterpreted in order to create coherence of meaning. Since we are dealing with written narratives of living through war, we can assume that the act of verbalizing is an important part of this mental endeavour to make sense of the most dramatic and disturbing circumstances in which people found themselves during the war, whether under occupation, on the home front, or at the fighting front. The degree of working through such impressions in order to find a verbal expression for them will vary, especially according to genre (that is, diary versus memoir) but, as mentioned above, the process is, in general, necessary for every verbalization.

Throughout this volume 'experience' refers to the subjective and implicit 'sense-making' that is linked to the attempt to create a coherent narrative of the war, be it in the form of a diary, a correspondence, or a memoir.[24] It is important to stress that it is only through those narratives that we have access, however limited, to this production of meaning. The experiences analysed in this volume vary greatly, since they were felt and expressed by individuals of all social strata and national, ethnic, or religious varieties; in addition, people were exposed to very different circumstances with regard to time, region, and branch of service. While in the eyes of the authors, a specific experience was 'theirs' as individual subjects, historians as readers will find a number of social patterns typical not only of specific fronts, but also of social groups shaped by class, gender, age, national or ethnic origin, religion, and region. The radical subjectivity of these texts thus lends itself to plausible constructions of socially based scripts so that every individual and highly personal letter or diary

---

[24] The concept of narrative is in itself multidisciplinary, and this has found expression in the emergence of a specialized field of 'narratology'. For the philosophical foundation of the concept of the narrative see Paul Ricoeur, *Time and Narrative*, 3 vols. (Chicago, 1984, 1985, 1988).

entry can also be read as the expression of identifiable social groups and communities with shared experiences or, rather, narratives. It is in this sense that each ego document is representative, not in the statistical meaning of the term, but in that it contains elements of larger social patterns of experience. Sigfried Giedion's dictum that 'even a teaspoon reflects the sun'[25] expresses our own conviction that every individual source also informs us about the society or structures in which it was possible for it to be produced. This is not an argument for 'objectifying' subjectivity. On the contrary, we acknowledge subjectivity because it matters. It matters for our understanding of why the war became possible in the first place, why people loved or hated, avoided or supported it, how they understood what was going on around them and how they acted on their understanding. Much more than war propaganda or official and 'objective' military reports, subjective sources inform us not only about the realities on the ground but also about how people coped, and why most of them continued fighting. Subjective voices also help us to understand how people changed during the war and what fears, dreams, and hopes influenced their actions beyond military discipline. Not least, it is the subjective and individual experience, embedded in social frameworks of which the authors were not always aware, that helps to explain the ways in which postwar societies functioned or failed.

Experience in the sense in which it is used here is linked closely to the production of meaning. To understand the war and to ascribe meaning to what is happening is an important function of writing in the first place. Writing about oneself during or after the war is intended to create an acceptable self-image and a perspective on the war where this self fits in. Especially at the beginning of the war and before or outside combat experience, many writers tried to become part of a national community resolved to fight. State propaganda defined meaning and language to express this collective understanding of the war. The intellectual elites of all countries involved in the war took part in this endeavour and the reading list of many a soldier or officer provides evidence of its impact, if not on the way that readers experienced the war, then on how these canonized texts shaped their explicit interpretations and the

---

[25] 'Auch in einem Kaffeelöffel spiegelt sich die Sonne': Sigfried Giedion, *Die Herrschaft der Mechanisierung: Ein Beitrag zur anonymen Geschichte* (Frankfurt a.M., 1982), 19. The book was first published in English as *Mechanization Takes Command: A Contribution to Anonymous History* (New York, 1948).

language they used to demonstrate that they belonged to the fighting nation as a community. Such texts were not necessarily written by contemporaries explicitly referring to the military conflict, but often by writers whose general philosophy lent itself to providing meaning under the conditions of war. Thus, soldiers from different nations read Nietzsche or Dostoevsky in search of a heroic or religious rationale for the war.

As demonstrated by the case of Slovenia, discussed in this volume by Pavlina Bobič, these rationales could change over the course of the war, and, especially in the context of multinational empires, be replaced by more nationalistic motivations. Basic meaning was produced by referring to the essence of war experience: the drama of life and death, the fear of dying and the euphoria of surviving, the tragedy of a hopeless fight, the emotional power of comradeship. In specific cases, such as at the Alpine front, nature itself could become an enemy, but often nature and its destruction could serve either as an image of a counter-world of continuing beauty or as an image of the enormous destruction of human nature. Thus, the search for meaning often ended in its denial, although we can see this as a mere negative meaning of war. More often, however, soldiers and civilians affected by the war sought a meaning that would explain and help them to cope with its horrors. For some, this could take the form of an explicit motivation, which in the first months of the war was often described as patriotism, based on the firm conviction that one was defending one's country against an aggressor, and loyalty to one's sovereign, religion, or culture. For others, either right from the start or after the disillusionment of their first real war experience, a sense of duty could prevail over their initial enthusiasm: the basic military duty to obey orders, or the subject's duty to obey the emperor, but also the moral duty to defend one's fatherland or empire, or a self-imposed duty to fulfil a promise or obligation, most basically, not to betray one's duty as a soldierly man or caring nurse. Endurance is another attitude that points to a sense of perseverance when no change was in sight and time seemed to come to a halt, be it in the painful waiting and boredom under the conditions of trench warfare, or in the resolve not to give in under occupation (Schaepdrijver).

The need to create meaning, however, was not just about war as killing or being killed. It was also a new experience with regard to encounters with various 'others'. At the beginning of the war, the enemy was not necessarily regarded with personal hostility but was given the respect due to a worthy adversary or someone who shared every soldier's basic misery. But as the war turned into meaningless slaughter, this could develop into hatred or utter indifference towards human suffering, a process sometimes described as dehumanization. The 'other' was not just the enemy; 'others' could be comrades, superiors, or subordinates. In this sense the relationship to these 'others' had to be defined in terms of strangeness *and* belonging, hierarchies *and* community. This concerns the definition of the simple soldier, the young officer, civilians in occupied countries, and those who were neither friend nor foe, such as the civilians in the Polish/Russian regions on the Eastern Front. Sometimes there could be utter strangeness between the ranks of officers and common soldiers, as Joshua Sanborn shows for the Russian case. It also seems, as Christa Hämmerle suggests for German-speaking Austria, that women serving as nurses at the front were not included in the concept of the 'community of trenches', a term which stood for the basic bonding experience of fighting. A most obvious cross-cultural encounter took place between the British military and colonial troops, and we find complex considerations on the nature of these people and the appropriate relationship to develop towards them. A language of infantilizing is common, as well as exoticization—friendly ways of keeping a social distance despite the shared experience of life and death.

To give meaning to the war and define the enemy is closely linked to building up a self-image or self-ideal adequate to the military world, the challenge of killing and the possibility of being killed, and the total break with a civilian life defined by peaceful work, family life, and education. For the young soldiers and volunteers, war was a rite of passage into a man's world. The assumption of the 'war as educator' was quite common among the educated European youth who made up the majority of volunteers.[26] However, it was a very different education from the one they had enjoyed in schools and universities: this one was about life and death, sacrifice and bravery.

[26] Volunteers, both military and civilian, were also central to the emotional mobilization and the initial war effort. For Germany see Jeffrey Verhey, *The Spirit of 1914: Militarism, Myth and Mobilisation in Germany* (Cambridge, 2000). In Britain, as in many other countries fighting against the Central Powers, to the present day volunteers are seen as representing the best of the national commitment, while in German popular discourses they appear more as a group of naive and nationalist enthusiasts, seduced into war by the reactionary elites. See e.g. Ulrich Herrmann, 'Erziehung für Verdun', *Zeit-online*, 30 Jan. 2014 ⟨http://la-loupe.over-blog.net/2014/02/erziehung-fur-verdun.html⟩ [accessed 29 July 2016].

Accordingly, the figure of a heroic warrior dominated the self-ideal of most of these men, heavily supported by the propaganda of the countries involved in the fighting. The attitude of a hero, closely linked to motives of patriotism and duty, could break down suddenly under the shock of the real war, or dissolve under the demoralizing experience of being in constant fear for one's life. Sometimes, and mostly among officers, the heroic self-ideal could be complemented or even replaced by the idea of the professional, a cold-blooded, rational, and efficient strategist and survivor.

To the present day, however, we generally know very little about the common soldiers drafted, often against their wishes, into a war they had been unable to imagine. In most western countries we have ego documents that can inform us about their attempts to make sense of the war, the enemy, and themselves, although sometimes in the less refined and laconic language of men for whom writing was not a common activity. But since these texts have not yet been thoroughly examined, a systematic analysis concerning the meaning they ascribed to the war remains a task for the future.[27] We can assume, however, that they, who so far we know mostly through the distanced eyes of their superiors, shared the latter's ideals, but became disillusioned much earlier and more radically, especially as they lacked the means of sublimation in the realms of art, literature, and philosophy which so many of the educated constantly used to renew their idealism. While the case of Russia shows the revolutionary power of this disillusionment of the powerless (Sanborn), the relatively close relationship between common soldiers and officers in small units could forge an intimate community of efficient fighters. In this connection, the breakdowns suffered by soldiers (and officers) faced with the unexpected horrors of this new kind of war, referred to as shell-shock in Britain and *Kriegszittern* in Germany, presented not only a professional challenge for doctors, but also a broader problem of individual self and social community ideals for meeting the challenges of war in a manly fashion (Andrea von Hohenthal).

The same holds true for people living under regimes of occupation. The enforced passivity on the one hand and the need to co-operate with the enemy-occupier on the other presented an enormous challenge mostly for the occupied, as in the case of Belgium, and to some extent also for the occupiers, as in Russian Poland, where there was

---

[27] See the pioneering study by Benjamin Ziemann, *War Experiences in Rural Germany, 1914–1923* (Oxford, 2007).

a need to control but also to win over various population groups who were not easy to define as friend or foe.

* * *

While diaries and letters were understood by their authors primarily as personal and private expressions of their subjective experience, even if they did not exclude a wider audience or indeed publication as a model testimony of what war was about, this larger public was eager to share the impressions and appraisal of those who were at the centre of war. Military and national governments in particular not only encouraged their soldiers' writing but offered immediate publication of exemplary letters, poems, or descriptions in their own brochures, as well as in literary journals and local daily newspapers. These texts both testified to the aesthetics of war and served as guides for other writers, thus developing war letters as a specific text genre that writers took as a model for expressing their own experiences. Early on, the private and public overlapped and even merged in a mutual attempt to achieve compatibility. As Gerd Krumeich shows, Philipp Witkop's 1915 edition of *Kriegsbriefe deutscher Studenten* presents an example of the experience and meaning of war being shaped publicly by a group of educated young volunteers who, in all European countries involved in the war, were the epitome of heroic purity.[28] In rare cases, such as the atrocities of Russian troops in East Prussia, the state directly intervened and supported eyewitness reports in a clear attempt to fend off and dilute reports of German atrocities in Belgium. Nevertheless, as shown by Alexander Watson in this volume, these texts can be gainfully analysed as ego documents of civilians' experiences of invasion. While these are examples of the immediate use of ego documents to shape public opinion and strengthen support for the war, the more important impact of ego documents was that which was felt in European postwar societies.

Of the huge number of diaries written and letters going back and forth during the years between 1914 and 1918, as well as memoirs published or self-published after the war, only a small percentage is available today in private or public archives, libraries, or online.[29]

---

[28] Sonja Levsen, 'Constructing Elite Identities: University Students, Military Masculinity and the Consequences of the Great War in Britain and Germany', *Past and Present*, 198 (2008), 147–83.

[29] In addition to several national online sites, the *Europeana* platform represents a pan-European online databank of all kinds of sources from all nations involved, including ego documents. It comprises 400,000 digitized items which are accessible to

The composition of these collections points to multiple asymmetries with regard to the significance of writing about one's war experience in one form or another, on both the personal and the societal level. First, there is the already-mentioned phenomenon of illiteracy in many countries involved in the war, especially in the rural areas of less industrialized and less urbanized regions of the Russian Empire, the Ottoman Empire, and Italy. Second, the habit of writing was more developed among the middle classes, including the petite bourgeoisie, and white-collar workers. However, it was more on the level of social and political institutions that the production of ego documents was encouraged and supported, and the results acknowledged as worthy testimonies of each and every participant in the war. In general, the written testimony of those directly involved in the war as soldiers, nurses, or doctors was regarded as more significant than that of their family and friends at home. Accordingly, collections of letters including both correspondents—husband and wife or son and mother—are rare. This is because not only the production but perhaps even more so the systematic collection of ego documents reveals a significant asymmetry among the various postwar nation-states.

While in the west, particularly in the United Kingdom, France, Germany, Austria, and (perhaps to a lesser degree) Italy, the war experience was an important point of reference for the postwar national narrative, this was by no means the case in most of the central and east European countries. A number of new states emerged as a result of the breakdown of the multi-ethnic empires of the Habsburg monarchy and Ottoman rule: these included Yugoslavia and Turkey. Poland regained statehood but immediately found itself involved in a revolutionary and civil war with the former Tsarist Empire. Although many citizens of these countries had fought in the First World War, they had often done so without a clear national affiliation, sometimes fighting on opposite sides of the same front. For Russia and many of the former parts of the Tsarist Empire, the First World War gained its significance as a mere prehistory for the establishment of the Soviet Union. As a consequence, in all these countries there was a lack of interest in granting the First World War itself a prominent place in the national master narrative, and in granting the respective sources a secure place in the national archives, as Robert Blobaum can show

everyone. Libraries from Germany, France, Italy, Belgium, Britain, Denmark, Austria, and Serbia are official partners of the project. See ⟨europeana-collections-1914-1918.eu⟩ [accessed 29 July 2016].

for Poland. Although we cannot be sure, it is likely that this public indifference also had an impact on the way individuals and families regarded the private ego documents that survived the war.

In looking at the body of ego documents of the First World War published after 1918, we see a clear bias that reinforces the factors already at work during the time of writing. Apart from public war heroes such as successful military leaders, the social figure of the young, educated, male volunteer (often a middle-ranking officer close to the actual fighting) featured prominently in most publications, as Marco Mondini can show for Italy. They were the embodiment not only of heroism but also of an active search for a positive meaning of the war and were at the same time advocates for values which were desperately needed and asked for in many postwar societies. The focus on the voices of this social group went hand in hand with the deliberate exclusion of others. Thus, the home front generally did not appear in public discourse; as Hämmerle has shown for Austria, nor did the experiences of women who took part in the war, often at the front, mostly as nurses.[30] In so far as the texts, such as diaries and letters, were originally written during the war, it would be interesting to explore to what degree and how these texts were edited (in the sense both of selecting and of rewriting) either by the authors themselves or by the publishers. Unfortunately, this is rarely possible even in the most influential cases, such as the German collection of student letters by Philipp Witkop. Here, we can at least compare the many subsequent editions, including the one that appeared after the establishment of the National Socialist regime in Germany, when not only were Jewish authors excluded but a new introduction adjusted the meaning of the letters to the needs of the new ideological demands.

This very homogeneous publishing policy points to the important function of war memoirs for those countries that had to recover from the many open wounds the First World War had left, in the sense both of millions of fallen men and of even more men left with permanent physical and psychological damage. To replace and reintegrate these fighters was not just a financial burden and a political challenge, but also a matter of dramatically changing cultures, involving class structure, gender roles, and demography.[31] It was, therefore, a central

---

[30] Alison S. Fell and Christine E. Hallett (eds.), *First World War Nursing: New Perspectives* (New York, 2013).

[31] Richard Bessel, 'The Great War in German Memory: The Soldiers of the First

concern to give positive meaning to a war which was seen by many as the cause of the new problems. The general challenges of postwar societies were aggravated in nation-states that had lost the war, not only because of the burden of reparations but also as a result of the humiliation of defeat. Others faced the problem of making a new nation-state carved out of old empires economically and socially viable. For yet others, the hope of nationhood was disappointed, and some found themselves in bloody, continuous warfare with their neighbours.[32] In this situation, ongoing violence or a happy outcome could be superimposed on the experience of the First World War; that experience could also be deliberately suppressed, being too painful to face and cope with. Nevertheless, in most postwar societies the war was acknowledged as a powerful, albeit difficult experience, and public narratives, in writing or in memorials, tended to give these experiences a meaning that aimed to honour the dead, comfort their families, and acknowledge the contribution of the soldiers to victory.

In the defeated countries, as in Germany, the dead were seen not only as a personal but also as a political loss. Again and again their memory was conjured up as ghosts of the past who, had they survived, would have rescued the nation from the miserable and humiliating state in which it found itself.[33] At the same time the living, those who published their memoirs in and for the postwar nations, saw themselves as a close community 'of the trenches' or *Frontgemeinschaft*, whose existential experience provided them with an aura and with the authority to demand that their society prove itself worthy of their sacrifices. They decided what mattered: unity and strength, in particular, the strength of masculinity. There were other images and voices, however, and new ideals: there were the disabled and the 'new' women, the pacifist interpretations of war, and the enjoyments of new forms of entertainment. The legacy of the veterans was powerful, but not uncontested.

World War, Demobilization and Weimar Political Culture', *German History*, 6/1 (1988), 20–34.

[32] Robert Gerwarth and John Horne (eds.), *War in Peace: Paramilitary Violence in Europe after the Great War* (Oxford, 2012); Jochen Böhler, 'Enduring Violence: The Postwar Struggles in East-Central Europe 1917–1921', *Journal of Contemporary History*, 50/1 (2015), 58–77.

[33] This kind of memorialization could take quite personal forms, as in the case of the young officer Otto Braun, who fell in April 1918 and whose friends would meet for years afterwards on the date of his death to honour him by reciting his or their own poems, playing music, and giving speeches about his legacy: Dorothee Wierling, *Eine Familie im Krieg: Leben, Sterben und Schreiben 1914–1918* (Göttingen, 2013), 398.

Our introductory remarks so far have shown, we hope, that ego documents are complicated, distinctive, and altogether not easy to interpret. This is in stark contrast to the oft-claimed promise of authenticity.[34] Authenticity is a tricky concept that can be understood on different levels. As historians, we sometimes use the term in the sense of a document's genuineness, the security of having a source that really was written by this author at this time and never forged or falsified. This concerns printed editions of handwritten letters. However, with ego documents, authenticity refers to much more: the desire for direct access to what the author really experienced and felt at the time of writing. In this sense, ego documents would fulfil the fantasy of travelling in a time machine not only 'inside World War One', but inside the intellectual and emotional selves of its participants. While the desire for such a journey is understandable, legitimate, and probably shared by many historians themselves, it can never happen. Instead, we face numerous obstacles and filters which mediate between the authors of these documents and today's readers: the very act of writing is already the first step taken in order to integrate what authors experience as their most genuine and subjective perceptions into the social world around them, a world to which they want to belong. Thus, authenticity is always a false promise we should neither expect, nor make, nor believe.

That said, ego documents still present a unique source for understanding better what happened to people during the war, why people volunteered to join the fight or tried to avoid it, how they reacted to social pressures one way or another, how they verbalized and thereby processed what happened to them, how an acceptable language about the war was developed, and how meanings of war were negotiated socially. The knowledge we gain from these sources is less of what happened than of how events became a subjective experience and gained a personal as well as social meaning. This knowledge about subjectivity matters if we want to understand the huge and long-lasting impact that the First World War had, not only on individuals and societies, but also on postwar politics in the countries involved.

To recognize the value of ego documents as a source for our understanding of the war is not to aim at privileging this type of source over other historical evidence about the war. Ego documents are not

---

[34] For the more general debate about the concept of authenticity for the humanities see Charles Lindholm, *Culture and Authenticity* (Malden, Mass., 2008).

necessarily suitable for answering questions of international politics or military strategies; we must acknowledge that these decisions did not depend on individuals alone but have to be dealt with on the level of technological standards, economic structures, and national interests, to name just a few factors. That said, however, it is only by integrating insights into objective circumstances and subjective practices, and by exploring the factor of 'rational' knowledge together with its emotional and subjective aspects, that we might indeed get deeper inside World War One—or at least as deep as historians can hope to go.

PART I
Invasion and Occupation

2

Registers of Everyday Life in Warsaw during the First World War: The Uses and Limitations of Ego Documents

Robert Blobaum

By the winter of 1916–17 Warsaw, the 'capital city' of a 'Polish kingdom' reinvented and occupied by the Central Powers, was being visited by rapidly escalating incidences of starvation, disease, death, and conflict over increasingly scarce resources necessary to sustain human life. In Warsaw today, however, one is hard-pressed to find any sign or site of public memory that might recall or reflect on the suffering of its citizens during the Great War. Overshadowed initially by the war's political outcome—the restoration of an independent Polish state—and then by the devastation and destruction that characterized Warsaw's amply documented experience of the Second World War, the deprivation and desperation marking the existential crisis of Varsovians during the Great War has been largely forgotten.

When examining the daily lives of the inhabitants of one of central Europe's great cities, it is a challenge to reconstruct the experiences and recover the voices of those most affected by the wartime collapse of basic living standards, the poor and marginalized in both the Polish and the Jewish communities. Widespread illiteracy and semi-literacy among Warsaw's lower classes before the Great War made it difficult if not impossible for its members to express themselves in writing, and thus it is necessary to seek out and find other evidence of their concerns and frustrations, which may have been given voice by others but were often politicized in the process. Additional problems are posed by the patchy and incomplete nature of archival sources caused by the twentieth century's misfortunes, as many valuable materials contained in interwar Warsaw's repositories and private collections literally went up in flames in 1944–5, including those of the German occupation authorities of the city during the Great War that had been shipped off to Berlin. These factors have naturally affected the availability of ego documents and their ability to capture the experience of the Great War in Warsaw from the perspective of those whose main concern was their next meal rather than the politics of nation- and state-building.

At the same time, there has not been a concerted effort at the Polish national or state level—as has occurred in Germany, France, the United Kingdom, and elsewhere—to solicit, recover, and collect ego documents related to that experience. This is in stark contrast to the public campaign that accompanied the launching of the Museum of the Warsaw Uprising in 2004 to retrieve ego documents and other personal and family memorabilia. The Uprising Museum thus became the major shrine in a cityscape of innumerable commemorative plaques, memorials, and monuments devoted to the Second World War which dominate Warsaw's memory culture, whereas exhibitions about the Great War, even during its centenary, have been confined to much smaller venues.

However, the problem with remembering the First World War in Warsaw as it was lived by the city's ordinary citizens may extend much deeper than a preoccupation with what came after it, to how its 'history' was recorded in the first place, in its very sources. According to Michel-Rolph Trouillot, sources 'privilege some events over others, not always the ones privileged by the actors . . . Silences are inherent in the creation of sources, the first moment of historical production.'[1] If, as Trouillot argues, 'History is the fruit of power' and 'in history, power begins at the source',[2] what can be said of the written sources, including memoirs, personal testimonies, diaries, and letters available for an examination of the everyday lives of Varsovians during the First World War?

Elsewhere I have dealt with the limitations of various types of sources: administrative and police files from the periods of both Russian rule and German occupation; documents from the quasi-state and municipal 'self-governing' institutions established during the German occupation; the minutes of meetings of NGOs such as the Warsaw Citizens' Committee, which essentially acted as home front organizations; and both the legally censored and the clandestine, uncensored Warsaw press. All of these sources, I have

---

[1] Michel-Rolph Trouillot, *Silencing the Past: Power and the Production of History* (Boston, 1995), 48, 51.   [2] Ibid., pp. xix, 29.

argued, afford us only fleeting, fragmentary, or mediated glimpses into the lives of ordinary Varsovians during the First World War, and these through lenses trained on other objects. For the rest of this essay, I will focus on the question of whether written ego documents, or at least those that are currently accessible to the historian, provide a greater, more authentic voice to the majority of Warsaw's actors during the Great War.[3]

* * *

Let us begin with personal papers and correspondence before we move on to other kinds of texts that can be regarded as ego documents for this analysis. Thanks to the research of Jesse Kauffman, we know something of the value of the private correspondence of General Hans von Beseler (1850–1921), the governor-general of the German occupation zone with its headquarters in Warsaw following the Russian army's evacuation of the city in August 1915. Though Beseler comes across in Kauffman's study as somewhat oblivious to the sufferings of those who did not enjoy access to his residence at the Royal Castle, his papers are crucial to understanding the conceptualization of and challenges confronting the efforts of the German occupation authorities to enlist the support of Polish elites in abortive state-building projects under their tutelage.[4] The personal papers of Stanisław Dzierzbicki (1854–1919) and Piotr Drzewiecki (1865–1943) housed in Warsaw's Archiwum Akt Nowych unfortunately give little indication of the Polish response, despite the key positions that brought these two men into constant contact with the occupation authorities. Moreover, one is hard-pressed to find anything in these collections that can be classified as ego documents.[5]

A civil engineer by training, Stanisław Dzierzbicki was a dedicated public servant who during the war years became involved in the provision of relief and assistance to non-combatants, most significantly as the president of the Supervisory Council of the Main Welfare Organization, or Rada Główna Opiekuńcza (RGO), after which he became a member of the Provisional State Council (Tymczasowa

---

[3] For a longer discussion of these and other issues connected to memory of the First World War in Warsaw see Robert Blobaum, 'Warsaw's Forgotten War', *Remembrance and Solidarity: Studies in Twentieth Century European History*, 2 (Mar. 2014), 185–207.
[4] Jesse Kauffman, *Elusive Alliance: The German Occupation of Poland in World War I* (Cambridge, Mass., 2015).
[5] Archiwum Akt Nowych (AAN), Akta Stanisława Dzierzbickiego (ASD), and Akta [Piotra, Ludwika, i Wiesława] Drzewieckich (AD).

Rada Stanu) sponsored by the Central Powers in January 1917. Later that year, he became the minister of agriculture under the Regency Council, which succeeded the Provisional State Council as a quasi-state institution under Central Power auspices. Those of his papers related to our purposes consist mainly of clippings from the legal and clandestine Polish press, a few official documents of the Central Citizens' Committee (formed under the Russians in September 1914 and dissolved a year later by the Germans) and the RGO that partially replaced it, correspondence related to transfers of funds to Warsaw from Stockholm and London, and copies of the correspondence between others, all of which is official rather than private. From these papers, it seems that Dzierzbicki was concerned primarily with issues related to the funding and distribution of assistance before 1917 and, as his functions changed in that year, with outbursts of unrest in Warsaw's streets and institutions of higher education.

The principal document in the Dzierzbicki collection that sheds direct light on the relationship between the German occupation authorities and those agencies attempting to feed the population of occupied Warsaw comes not from the hand of Dzierzbicki himself, but from that of Adam Count Ronikier (1881–1952), the titular chair of the RGO Directorate, in his letter of 15 July 1916 to Wolfgang von Kries (1868–1945), chief of the civil administration in the Warsaw General Government. In it Ronikier pleads for the raising of ration norms in the light of the coming harvest, 'even at unprecedented prices, to feed the starving and physically weakened population of the cities'.[6]

The Drzewiecki papers comprise family documents connected to the public activities of the brothers Ludwik and Piotr Stanisław Drzewiecki, as well as Ludwik's son, Wiesław. Of primary interest here is Piotr Drzewiecki, who presided over a number of industrial and commercial boards before the war and was one of the founding members and secretary of the Warsaw Citizens' Committee formed with imperial Russian approval in August 1914 in order to deal with the war's economic and social side effects on the Warsaw home front. As the war continued and the needs of Warsaw's inhabitants mounted, the Citizens' Committee became the main welfare agency in the city. Following the Russian evacuation in August 1915, the committee's executive branch was transformed into

[6] AAN ASD 61.

the Warsaw city administration, which Drzewiecki served as vice-president and its day-to-day chief. Following city council elections in July 1916, Drzewiecki occupied the position of 'first mayor' and, once the German occupation authorities persuaded a reluctant Prince Zdzisław Lubomirski (1865–1943) to join the Regency Council in October 1917, Drzewiecki succeeded him in the position of city president. Drzewiecki's papers for this period consist of official correspondence from the German authorities with their demands for the city administration's co-operation in registering the able-bodied unemployed for potential labour conscription, press releases revealing tensions between the Warsaw Citizens' Committee and the Germans over control of local courts and schools at the beginning of the occupation, a successful appeal of the Warsaw University Faculty Senate to students to avoid a strike in February 1916, and documents of groups opposed to Drzewiecki's political orientation during the drafting of a municipal electoral ordinance and subsequent elections in the spring and summer of 1916. A document that Drzewiecki would have had a direct hand in drafting was the memorandum of the city administration in the matter of the city budget, signed by Lubomirski and addressed to Kries on 6 April 1916. After revealing the growing gap between the city's revenues and expenditures, fuelled by a more than tenfold increase in food assistance to the population, the memorandum requested financial assistance from the occupation authorities, an end to requisitioning, and compensation for and relief from the costs of occupation. Regarding growing German failure to recruit labour in the city, the memorandum asserted: 'Our worker prefers, a hundred times over, poverty and starvation in the country to leaving for another land.'[7]

Conspicuously absent from the Drzewiecki papers, like those of Stanisław Dzierzbicki, is any private correspondence or other materials that would reveal the social selves of these individuals, both of whom were both so intimately involved in non-governmental and governmental organizations, and in the administration and distribution of public assistance during the war. We have no idea from these papers how Dzierzbicki processed the rising social tensions recorded in the press clippings he collected, or what Drzewiecki thought of Germans such as Kries, who were unmoved by the dire condition of the city's inhabitants. Instead, both the Dzierzbicki and Drzewiecki papers, with their focus on the administrative and political,

[7] AAN AD 15.

offer only side glances towards the day-to-day struggles of those they presumably served. The same could be said of Dzierzbicki's wartime diary, published in 1983, which focuses almost exclusively on the political manœuvrings of Polish elites.[8] For a far better view of the everyday struggles of ordinary Varsovians, we need to look elsewhere.

* * *

Memoirs and other personal accounts are often taken by historians as more suspect types of primary source material, even as they place too much faith in the value of archival documents and contemporary press accounts. However, despite their advantage of 'authenticity' (in the sense that they are unofficial and presumably uncensored), it is important to raise questions about which personal accounts see the light of day and to what aim. A close look at those compiled and edited by Krzysztof Dunin-Wąsowicz in his anthology of material on Warsaw during the First World War is instructive here, especially since it has remained from the time of its publication in 1971 the first place students and scholars turn to for an initiation into these kinds of ego documents. As Dunin-Wąsowicz himself admitted in his introduction to the volume, 'Warsaw memoir- and diary-writing of the period of the First World War is not as rich and varied' as for other important historical periods, particularly the Second World War.[9] From a total of 132 diaries and memoirs then located in Warsaw's archives and libraries, three-quarters of which had already been previously published, the editor selected twenty to excerpt for his anthology, only three from previously unpublished manuscripts.

Despite its claim to represent a cross-section of perspectives, Dunin-Wąsowicz's selection of twenty authors displays a clear bias in favour of political activists and journalists from the male Polish intelligentsia. Bogdan Hutten-Czapski (1851–1937), a Prussian Polish aristocrat close to the Kaiser who arrived in Warsaw in the entourage of Governor-General Beseler and became curator of Warsaw's institutions of higher education upon their reopening, is the sole voice of the German occupation authorities in the anthology.

---

[8] Stanisław Dzierzbicki, *Pamiętnik z lat wojny 1915–1918*, ed. Jerzy Pajewski (Warsaw, 1983).
[9] Krzysztof Dunin-Wąsowicz (ed.), *Warszawa w pamiętnikach pierwszej wojny światowej* (Warsaw, 1971), 35.

Meanwhile, the perspective of the imperial Russian regime still in power during the first year of the war lacks a single representative.

According to Dunin-Wąsowicz, of the then known published and unpublished diaries and memoirs from which he made his selections, only twenty were written by women, or 14 per cent of the total. By taking excerpts from only two women for his anthology, Dunin-Wąsowicz further reduced their proportion to 10 per cent, this despite Warsaw's pronounced increase in the proportion of female inhabitants during the war. Even here, however, the editor appears to have been begging rather than choosing to include women, represented by Maria Kamińska (1897–1983) and Władysława Głodowska-Sampolska (1893–?), authors with ties to the radical left ancestors of the Communist regime which ruled Poland at the time of the anthology's publication in 1971. Kamińska, then one of the first female students enrolled at Warsaw University, penned her memoirs more than forty years after the fact,[10] with only a small fraction dedicated to her university experiences during the war years. These, however, do shed some light on gender discrimination in housing and student organizations at the university:

Girls had a multitude of difficulties with their living conditions in the dormitory. And not a single representative in 'Bratniak' [the student fraternity]! It made me angry. The cause of women's equality was for me a canon. Raised among boys, I considered it a point of honour from childhood not to be outdone by them . . . I decided to go to the meeting [of 'Bratniak'] and demand the inclusion of women on the list of candidates.

Kamińska failed to convince her male colleagues, who interrupted her and claimed that 'they themselves could look after the needs of female students'.[11]

Dunin-Wąsowicz could easily have employed a portion of Kamińska's memoirs in the section of his anthology devoted to November 1918 and the end of the German occupation. Kamińska's description of these days offers an interesting perspective on the radicalization of both German soldiers and the local population and on the stillborn revolution:

Today I still have before my eyes the young boys wearing legionnaire caps running up to German soldiers on the street and, just like that, disarming them. I see officers with large red ribbons tied to German uniforms. I see the rank and file with red armbands. Red is everywhere: in the windows of homes,

[10] Maria Kamińska, *Ścieżkami wspomnień* (Warsaw, 1960).   [11] Ibid. 128–31.

in the lapels of shirts. A large red banner is hanging at the Radziwiłł palace on Krakowskie Przedmieście. This is the seat of the 'Soldatenrat'. Its main concern is the quickest possible departure to Germany of troops stationed in the kingdom. Trains with troops withdrawing from Ukraine pass through Warsaw constantly. In Warsaw, they give up their arms at the demand of Polish soldiers . . . There is unbelievable motion, the mood is unusually joyful—we are getting rid of the occupier, the partitioning power has accepted defeat. Everyone is feverish. Everyone is wearing red armbands and ribbons. It looks as if the revolution has been victorious . . . Maybe it really is revolution? These illusions soon evaporated.[12]

Głodowska-Sampolska, one of the anthology's two contributors assigned by the editor to a section entitled 'Social and Self-Governing Organizations in Warsaw', was allotted a mere seven pages, taken from her memoir published in 1965, to depict the poverty of the city's newspaper boys, with whom she worked as a volunteer teacher.[13] Despite the decades-long separation of the author from the events she describes, Głodowska-Sampolska's few pages vividly portray the effects of hunger among the boys whom she helped to establish a 'club', and more broadly in the city's streets in the spring of 1917:

People were exhausted from the unbelievable hunger. The children suffered most. The group which studied at the club in the morning, despite the compassionate and repeated efforts of its leadership to acquire money for its nourishment, looked miserable. [The boys'] complexions were pale and they fell asleep during lessons. Hunger demonstrations spread throughout the city at this time. When the German police dispersed them on one street, the demonstrators rapidly created a new procession on another street. Such spontaneous demonstrations created a major impression. I remember one of them. The crowd proceeded down Marszałkowska Street, beating on the windows of cafés and sweetshops filled with German officers . . . During this explosion of strikes and demonstrations, people demanded increased food rations, above all bread. The bread at that time was very bad; people became sick from eating it. It contained a bare amount of flour and a multitude of other ingredients such as potato peels, field peas, and milled chestnuts. This bread fell apart a day after baking and had a terrible stench.[14]

Even more removed in time from the Great War was the autobiography of Irena Krzywicka (1899–1994), 'Confessions of Scandalous Woman', which appeared shortly before her death and well after pub-

[12] Ibid. 145–6.
[13] Władysława Głodowska-Sampolska, *Czerwone zorze: wspomnienia* (Warsaw, 1965).
[14] Ead., '[Kluby gazeciarzy]', in Dunin-Wąsowicz (ed.), *Warszawa w pamiętnikach*, 340–1.

lication of the Dunin-Wąsowicz volume.[15] Fifteen years of age when the war began, Krzywicka (née Goldberg) is best known for her open challenging of conventional sexual morality and support for abortion rights during the interwar years. She admits that the Great War did not penetrate her teenage consciousness until it was awakened from the 'fog' by the blasts of German artillery fire in October 1914. Even then, she did not pay much attention to the war, which she describes as 'colourless, hungry, and boring'. In fact, far more than Kamińska and Głodowska-Sampolska, she struggles to summon up wartime memories: 'There was severe, palpable poverty—this I remember—there could be no talk of any diversions, there were only school and home, and strolls to Łazienki (the grounds of the eighteenth-century royal palace). That's it.'[16] More memorable was her confrontation with the antisemitism of Countess Wielopolska, the organizer of adult literacy courses in Warsaw, which caused her to resign from her short-lived instruction of reading and writing to seamstresses—that, and rapid changes in fashion, especially among women, 'in the way of Mademoiselle Chanel'.[17] Finally, her awareness of the enormous cultural differences between workers and the intelligentsia resulted from her contact with actual workers through her brief involvement in a small socialist cell in Warsaw's Ochota district in 1917, after which she entered Warsaw University, where she again encountered antisemitism from nationalist Polish students.

In fact, had Krzywicka's autobiography been available in the late 1960s and early 1970s, it is most unlikely that Dunin-Wąsowicz would have selected excerpts from it for his anthology, not because of its feminist perspective but because of its Jewish one. It is important to recall that the anthology appeared a mere three years after the Polish Communist regime's 1968 'anti-Zionist' campaign, a purging of Jews from the state bureaucracy, party apparatus, and white-collar professions, which ended in the last large-scale Jewish emigration from the country. Excerpts from the memoirs of two assimilated Jews, those of Kamińska (whose real name was Maria Eiger) and the journalist Aleksander Kraushar (1843–1931), do make an appearance, but their authors' ancestry remains unacknowledged by the editor. Even if it had been, however, the perspective of representatives of the actual Jewish community, whose first language was Yiddish rather than Polish, would have been missing. Wartime Warsaw thus

---

[15] Irena Krzywicka, *Wyznania gorszycielki*, ed. Agata Tuszyńska (Warsaw, 1992).
[16] Ibid. 52–3.   [17] Ibid. 72.

appears in the 1971 anthology as ethno-religiously homogeneous and without a single mention of Polish–Jewish relations. That said, Kraushar's 'eyewitness' account of the German occupation published shortly after the war is valuable for reasons unrelated to the author's ethnicity.[18]

For those like Hutten-Czapski, determined to portray the German conquest of Warsaw as liberation from oppressive Russian rule, or historians inclined to interpret the German occupation as a well-intentioned failure, Kraushar provides the most effective antidote. To be sure, Kraushar credits Beseler with being 'the only occupant among all of the satraps residing in the Royal Castle from 1815 to the present who distinguished himself by virtue of his professional and general education . . . and his erudition in the discipline of history, even Polish military history'. If, indeed, Beseler kept an eye out for certain museum pieces and archival collections as potential 'war booty for the *Vaterland* . . . one nevertheless has to admit', Kraushar maintained, 'that in contrast to his predecessors in positions of power, Beseler did not abuse his authority for personal gain. If he fleeced our country, it was in the name of an idea, of providing material resources to his own fatherland as the cost of "Poland liberated from the Russian yoke", and not for himself.'[19]

Otherwise, in Kraushar's account the Germans occupying Warsaw come off far worse than the Russians who preceded them. For example: 'In one hundred years following the Russian invasion and their living among us, they never managed to post as many Muscovite specimens of an exotic eastern character in stores and on signboards, in as many commercial establishments of different kinds, as the Germans did in barely the first few months of their economy', as the 'the new arrivals strove to give the capital city of Poland the character of a Berlin branch'.[20] About the sexual morality of the occupying forces Kraushar had this to say: 'Their cynically lascivious groups insulted all notions of propriety. The representatives of this "God-fearing nation of good customs" spread the infection of depravity, a hundred times more harmful than anything that was

---

[18] Aleksander Kraushar, *Warszawa podczas okupacji niemieckiej 1915–1918: notatki naocznego świadka* (Lwów, 1921). Kraushar's published account is a much-abbreviated version of an unpublished diary which he kept during the German occupation. It consisted of several volumes, all of which were consumed in the flames of the Second World War.

[19] Ibid. 59–61.

[20] Ibid. 22.

done in Russian times.'[21] Kraushar's final verdict on the German occupation reads thus:

> Despite the superficial order in administration, the final result of the occupation was catastrophic. The German completely destroyed the country's industry; he made us dependent on the import of his own products; he impoverished the population through currency devaluation; he took all of the wealth from the country, everything that came from the Polish land and its soil (the occupants even carted off innumerable wagonloads of black soil); he instilled the rot of corruption on a scale larger than anything that had been known in Russian times; above all he stimulated unprecedented profiteering among local merchants and craftsmen.[22]

Kraushar's harsh portrait of the German occupation is shared by those authors featured in the Dunin-Wąsowicz anthology whose excerpts were selected to address it. As in Kraushar's account, the Russians come off relatively well by comparison, which is not surprising since Warsaw's elites and public opinion strongly supported the cause of Russian arms at the outbreak of the war. This complicity deeply bothered the journalist Stanisław Dzikowski (1884–1921), a relative newcomer to Warsaw from Lwów (Lemberg) and an obvious supporter of an 'Austrian solution' to the Polish question and the Polish legions that originally fought for its realization.[23] Dzikowski was particularly critical of 'the liquidation of all hopes of free national development' among Warsaw's elites, to whom he attributed the city's 'passivity and impotence' at the outbreak of the war: 'While the rest of the world was riveted to the unfolding of the Austro-Serbian conflict, carefree Varsovians went on summer vacations.' Later, during the October fighting just beyond the city's gates, Dzikowski was incredulous that *Kurjer Warszawski*, the city's largest mass-circulation daily, 'continued to publish bulletins about Lucyna Messal, the prima donna of the Warsaw operetta'.[24]

If Dzikowski's biases produced imagined hostility towards Russia in the city, even he was forced to admit that during the Russian evacuation in the summer of 1915 Warsaw had 'remained loyal, loyal to the end'.[25] Much more reliable are Dzikowski's observations of the reactions in October 1914 of people in the streets who watched, seldom behind the shelter of a wall, the dropping of bombs

---

[21] Ibid. 23–4. [22] Ibid. 45–6.
[23] Stanisław Dzikowski, *Rok wojny w Warszawie: notatki* (Kraków, 1916). Dunin-Wąsowicz excerpted six pages from Dzikowski's account for his anthology.
[24] Ibid. 9, 11–12, 16, 20. [25] Ibid. 21–2, 44.

from German aircraft above the city and the anti-aircraft fire from machine-guns, as if it were spectator sport. 'If it were not for the sounds of artillery fire, these days in October would remind one of any autumn day, as streets quickly returned to normal, without a care in the world.' Hearing the blasts of shelling just beyond the city's gates, Warsaw's residents would wager with each other: 'Is it closer today, or further away?'[26]

As the Germans retreated from Warsaw's outskirts in late October and early November, Dzikowski followed in their footsteps, having volunteered for ambulance service to bring the wounded from the front back to Warsaw. In that capacity, he offered eyewitness testimony to the impact of the fighting on the small towns near Warsaw, which he described as 'living corpses in which the spirit of life barely circulated'.[27] As such, his is one of the few ego documents from a Polish rather than a Jewish source that addresses the plight of the Jewish population of these towns, forcibly evacuated or expelled by the Russian army. 'It looked as if the line of battle crossed the Jewish districts in all of these towns', Dzikowski noted, as he personally witnessed the violent removal of Jews from their homes on two occasions.[28] These were only the beginning of co-ordinated mass expulsions of Jews, which brought as many as 80,000 refugees to Warsaw in the spring of 1915. They were then pushed further on, thousands sent daily to the east. Dzikowski observed many of them 'living like wild animals' and fighting with the local population in and around the Jabłonna and Łochów forests to the north and east of Warsaw in order to obtain means for survival.[29]

The most important ego document to appear in the Dunin-Wąsowicz anthology was a manuscript, unpublished to this day and located in the Warsaw city archives, from the pen of Franciszek Herbst (1887–1959). Herbst's account, excerpted from memoirs about his work in the city administration covering the period 1914 to 1935, was allotted the most space for a single contribution to the volume. In his later book on Warsaw during the First World War, Dunin-Wąsowicz paid a great deal of attention to material conditions and their deterioration, clearly deriving some of his information from Herbst.[30] A journalist employed by the liberal daily

---

[26] Ibid. 24.
[27] Ibid. 31.
[28] Ibid. 33.
[29] Ibid. 46.
[30] Krzysztof Dunin-Wąsowicz, *Warszawa w czasie pierwszej wojny światowej* (Warsaw, 1974).

Nowa Gazeta before the war, Herbst served as secretary of the Labour Section of the Warsaw Citizens' Committee and continued to serve in different capacities in the city administration following the committee's dissolution in 1916.

Herbst's account is exceptional for a number of reasons. First, unlike Kraushar's account of the German occupation or that of Dzikowski concerning the first year of the war in Warsaw, Herbst's memoir covers the entire war. Second, unlike Kraushar and Dzikowski, whose anti-German and anti-Russian positions are particularly pronounced, Herbst was a politically unaffiliated and dedicated civil servant who did not have any visible axes to grind, despite being arrested by the Germans in April 1918 and spending a few months incarcerated in the Warsaw Citadel. Third, Herbst is refreshingly honest about his own role in events. For example, he makes no claims to being a principled opponent of the German occupation. In addressing the subject of his arrest and imprisonment, he attributes it solely to his association with an acquaintance under police investigation. The reasons for his release were never explained to him but he was allowed to return to employment in the Warsaw city administration.

Most importantly, Herbst was able to view social conditions in Warsaw from a number of different vantage points: from the Citizens' Committee's Labour Section, which sought work for Warsaw's unemployed, as tax commissioner for Warsaw's Fifth Police Precinct, where typhus struck its impoverished Jewish residents, and as an auditor of various income streams for an increasingly financially strapped city administration. These reporting and accounting functions performed by Herbst, and his contacts with counterparts in other sections and departments of the Warsaw Citizens' Committee and city administration, are evidenced in the quantitative particulars contained in his manuscript, whether about the numbers of refugees and refugee shelters, the placement of job candidates among unemployed workers, the level of food rations, or the budgetary woes of a city unable to pay its own employees. Herbst's eye for detail left little room for embellishment. What follows is a characteristic example of Herbst's writing about his time as a tax officer in the Jewish district, one that does not involve numbers:

I have to admit that only once as a consequence of a taxpayer's resistance was I forced to resort to the final means of executing my duties, i.e. the sale of confiscated property. This occurred in the apartment of a fairly wealthy Jewish merchant who lived on Marszałkowska Street, more or less opposite Litewska Street. This was not for collecting the city tax, but a contribution to the Jewish community, which was able to employ municipal agencies to force payment based on an agreement between the community and the magistracy. This merchant, Kenigstein by name, was unwilling to pay well over a thousand marks in dues. However, after the sale by auction of his mahogany dining room set he paid several thousands of złoty to the so-called hyenas who appeared whenever an auction was announced, so that they would leave his things alone.[31]

* * *

Such is the stuff of daily life, and in Herbst the devil is always in the details, even if they are not the most quotable. Herbst's account is also one of the few of those written by males that specifically recognizes the significant role of women in the provision of wartime assistance to the ever growing numbers of Warsaw's destitute population. For example, Herbst emphasizes that the work of the Distribution Commission of the Warsaw Citizens' Committee in supplying free or low-cost meals to the destitute in the city's public kitchens was 'entirely in the hands of women who treated their work as voluntary'.[32] Others worked to help shelter refugees or, especially in the war's first months when Warsaw was essentially a front line city, care for wounded soldiers from the Russian army. These women came mainly from Warsaw's aristocratic and bourgeois upper classes, whose wartime activities can be seen as an extension of their prewar involvement in public philanthropy. They included Princess Maria Lubomirska, devoted wife of Zdzisław Lubomirski, the founding chairman of the Warsaw Citizens' Committee under the Russians and ultimately the leading member of the ill-fated Regency Council, which the Germans hoped would implement their vision of Polish statehood. The diary of the princess is arguably the most significant ego document related to Warsaw's experiences in the Great War published over the last thirty years.[33]

Janusz Pajewski, who had also edited the published version of Dzierzbicki's diary, accepted uncritically the princess's claim that she recorded her thoughts and experiences 'for her children, not thinking about publication'.[34] Such attestations are dubious, given

[31] Dunin-Wąsowicz (ed.), *Warszawa w pamiętnikach*, 327–8. [32] Ibid. 306.
[33] Maria Lubomirska, *Pamiętnik księżnej Marii Zdzisławowej Lubomirskiej, 1914–1918*, ed. Jerzy Pajewski (Poznań, 1997). [34] Ibid. 7.

the highly stylized language of parts of the diary, the princess's vanity, which seeps through its pages, her repetition of information about wartime developments which she clearly took from the daily press, her forced efforts to display her erudition and knowledge of foreign languages (French, but also English and German), and clear signs of later editing and amendment based on information not available at the time. The princess considered her husband the country's most important statesman, and at one point in the diary, following the joint proclamation by the German and Austro-Hungarian emperors in early November 1916 of their intention to re-establish a Polish state, she even imagined herself as the future queen of this 'Polish kingdom'. The princess therefore felt that what she had to say was important and she expected it to be read, as she herself admitted in her entry of 3 August 1915.[35]

There is no question that Lubomirska's diary makes for fascinating and at times exasperating reading, with its recording of rumours, its repetition of stereotypes, its reports from a Red Cross hospital, and its empathy for the travails of her husband, who began the war as the respected head of the Citizens' Committee and ended it as a perceived and compromised collaborator of the occupying Central Powers. It begins with her genuine surprise at the popular enthusiasm in Warsaw for the Russian cause at the outbreak of the war and the voluntary enlistment of Poles into the Russian army:

> The Russian authorities have been received with model behaviour in Warsaw—there is general calm etc. The rush of recruits to the colours is completely unexpected. But will we be repaid for our sacrifice? . . .
>
> In the evening a long line of troops marches below our window accompanied by a large enthusiastic crowd, crying 'Hurrah! Long live the Army!' The whole street was in fervour. This was a shocking sight on this starlit night—a new sight, completely unexpected. Where are the ghosts of the past? Is Kościuszko [hero of the 1794 anti-Russian insurrection] turning in his grave?[36]

Such scenes were repeated following the Russian decision to defend the city from German assault in the middle of October 1914:

> The sympathy for the soldiers here is unbelievable. Groups of women gather in the streets and give them what they can: a cup of hot tea, cigarettes, fruit. The soldiers stop for a moment, they collect these items, sometimes taking a loaf of bread on their bayonets, and then they move on, a grey anonymous mass.[37]

[35] Ibid. 223.   [36] Ibid. 14–15.
[37] Ibid. 67.

The princess, who, like her husband, considered herself a loyal subject of the tsar, may have been surprised by the extent of such sympathy and support for the Russian army, but she generally shared those sentiments, however patronizing, particularly following her visit to a large Red Cross hospital in early November:

> The Russian soldier is generally amazing—his martyrdom on the battlefield, his persistence, his simple, childlike behaviour, and his resignation to fate. The nurses prefer the Russians to the Poles—they are more grateful, they will gladly share their bread or cigarettes with their brothers, and are less calculating than our countrymen.[38]

She also shared the antisemitism of her era along with the view, widespread within the Russian military establishment, of Jewish collusion with the Germans. For example, she attributes the appearance of 'revolutionary sparks'—that is, the demands of workers for representation on the Warsaw Citizens' Committee at the beginning of 1915—to 'German or Jewish money'.[39] The shortage of coin in the summer of 1915 as the Russians began their evacuation of the city is blamed on 'the same Jewish trick as at the beginning of the war, when the Germans were expected'.[40] Then once the Germans did take control of Warsaw, she 'read in the newspaper that Warsaw is the greatest Jewish community of Europe—it has 39 per cent Jews and is a metropolis of Jewish culture. The commonality of culture and language of German and eastern Jews opens up excellent perspectives for Germandom in Poland. Poor Warsaw.'[41]

The princess herself left the city with her children during the Russian evacuation and went into 'exile', first to Ukraine, then Petrograd, and finally to Stockholm, based on a decision reached with her husband that her continued presence in Warsaw following a German takeover 'would be badly viewed by the Russian government'.[42] The prince, 'even though he has been seriously compromised' by his support of the Russian side, decided to remain in the city out of a sense of duty and to prevent Warsaw from falling into the hands of 'the worst elements'. To maintain order in the rear of their advancing armies, the incoming Germans recognized the provisional authority embodied in the Warsaw Citizens' Committee and appointed Lubomirski, from his wife's perspective 'the most popular person, not

---

[38] Ibid. 83. [39] Ibid. 114.
[40] Ibid. 200. [41] Ibid. 247.
[42] Ibid. 198–9.

only in this Vistula community, but practically the entire country',[43] the acting president of the city. The consolidation of this marriage of convenience between the German occupation authorities and a Polish aristocrat who still considered himself a Russian subject enabled the princess to return at the end of November 1915 to 'this poor, empty Warsaw, as if to a city of the dead . . . to poverty, greyness, growing inflation, the spectre of hunger, the impression that nobody knows anything about what's going on, because it's not worth reading any of the newspapers here'.[44]

During the first year of the war Lubomirska's perspective literally came from above, as she observed soldiers, refugees, and crowds (or, as she was apt to put it, 'waves', 'hordes', and 'wild people') on the street below the window of the couple's urban residence. Following her return, as the princess encountered 'on the streets so many sad, lean faces next to full, even fat German soldiers',[45] the reader of her diary is sometimes afforded a less condescending view. On the eve of the second Christmas of the war, Lubomirska notes that 'the freezing weather continues, 7 degrees below zero—so much hopeless, freezing poverty around the city, that making modest holiday purchases brings tears to my eyes'.[46] By early February 1916 'our dreams at night are being disrupted by visions of potatoes', which had largely disappeared from the market while daily bread rations had been reduced to 115 grams. 'People are dying like flies', she reported shortly thereafter.[47] Ever declining rations, however, did not affect those who could afford to purchase food, even delicacies, of much better quality at much higher prices, causing the princess a moment of guilt in September 1917: 'I have all of the comforts, enough to eat, and peace and quiet: I think frequently about the desperate fate of the sick and the poor. The crazy inequality between the privileged classes and those who are not strikes me now like a blow to the head.'[48] Yet five weeks later, in her imperfect French she proudly displays her menu for the dinner which she hosted to celebrate the Regency Council, attended by Beseler and other German, Austrian, and Polish dignitaries:

Potage à la Reine
Petits patés
Selle de lièvre

[43] Ibid. 279. [44] Ibid. 276.
[45] Ibid. 290. [46] Ibid. 298.
[47] Ibid. 321, 327. [48] Ibid. 530.

Salada assortie
Choux-fleurs polonaise
Bombe au chocolat
Petits gateaux
Modest as befits wartime.
Dessert
Salted Italian walnuts
White and Red wine—ending with a sweet old Hungarian.[49]

Of such stuff are revolutions made, which became Lubomirska's constant fear, beginning in 1915 while Warsaw was still under Russian rule. In March 1916 the princess believed that revolution was at hand: 'Already in front of the Ratusz [city hall] there have been gatherings of soldiers' wives which had to be dispersed. The enraged women fell upon Zdziś and tore off the button on his fur coat. So it begins . . .'[50] 'Revolution threatens the city' yet again a month later, when potato rations are reduced. When actual revolution does overthrow the Russian autocracy in March 1917, the princess records: 'CONSTERNATION in the city.' A few weeks later, that consternation has taken the form of 'cruel outrage, hatred is growing . . . growing', as is Lubomirska's obsession with a nightmare causing her 'sleepless nights': 'We are heading for revolution . . . Hunger is the backdrop of revolution; saving our harvests will decide our "to be or not to be"', by which she means the privileged advantages and lifestyles of the Polish landed and urban elites.[51] A strike of hospital staff in Warsaw in January 1918 is being financed by 'Bolshevik money', while revolutionary Russia itself 'has today become ruled by . . . a band of international Israelites'. Following the Treaty of Brest-Litovsk in March 1918, it was the return migration of workers from the east that was 'threatening us with the Bolshevik contagion'.[52] By the autumn of 1918, she lives in fear for her life:

How times have changed. Zdziś's popularity used to accompany us like a halo. When the president's car stopped on the street, unknown people with friendly smiles would rush to open or close the doors, etc. Today, driving on the street, I think that more than one of these people would gladly launch a bomb against 'the traitors who have cut a deal with the Germans'.[53]

As the Great War nears its end, the princess is afraid to leave the

[49] Ibid. 550.
[50] Ibid. 328.
[51] Ibid. 481, 493, 503, 505.
[52] Ibid. 580, 589, 629.
[53] Ibid. 673.

family's palace on Frascati, which she also believes could come under attack at any moment, leading her to support the idea of a government formed by the right-wing populist and antisemitic Polish National Democrats, 'which can save us from the coming revolution'.[54]

* * *

Finally, there are the travellers' accounts, three of which appeared in Dunin-Wąsowicz's anthology, all of them from Kraków. Of these, the keenest eyes and ears belonged to the historian Stanisław Kutrzeba (1876–1946), the future rector of Jagiellonian University and president of the Polish Academy of Science. Kutrzeba came to Warsaw to participate in the celebration of the 125th anniversary of Poland's constitution on 3 May in 1916, an early German attempt to cultivate Polish national sentiment in the midst of increasingly acute food shortages. Dunin-Wąsowicz excerpted all seventeen pages from a brief section of Kutrzeba's 1917 account entitled 'Impressions from Warsaw' (the account is otherwise devoted to the war in Austrian Galicia).[55] While Kutrzeba proved sensitive to political divisions within Warsaw during his two-week visit, he also carefully noted the difficulties of and restrictions on travel to and from the city, which required possession of a 'red card', or permit issued by the Warsaw General Government: 'Only a few who want to enter Warsaw can get one. This is not the time to travel for pleasure or minor interests; whoever wants to receive a "red card" must have justification [showing] that real need requires it.'[56]

The reader of Kutrzeba's account is particularly drawn to its author's comparisons of prewar and wartime Warsaw. The only thing that has changed about Marszałkowska Street, he writes, is that there are no longer any Russian signs: 'They have all been replaced by new, exclusively Polish ones.' He also notes how quiet Krakowskie Przedmieście has become in comparison with the street's loud prewar rumble created by horses' hoofs, carriages, wagons, and trolleys:

This commotion began in the early morning, continual, unbroken, monotonous, it interrupted dreams and didn't allow one to sleep until 2 in the morning. It's possible to say that here Warsaw was able to get a bit of rest for

[54] Ibid. 690.
[55] Stanisław Kutrzeba, *Królestwo i Galicya: uwagi z czasu wojny* (Warsaw, 1917).
[56] Ibid. 45.

a bare two or three hours in the middle of the night. . . . The silence struck me already at the hotel and on the street even more so.[57]

Admittedly, Kutrzeba's visit coincided with a strike of trolley workers, 'but where are the carriages?' Before the war, carriages were cheap and plentiful, enabling rides of thirty minutes for twenty kopecks: 'The affordability of carriages explains why no self-respecting Varsovian could get used to taking the trolley' and why 'only recently did the electric trolley make its appearance on [Warsaw's] streets, later than in Kraków'. Kutrzeba finally finds a carriage, but the horse is too exhausted to take him because the driver cannot afford to feed it oats.[58]

Kutrzeba is also struck by the ubiquity of begging: 'It was possible to see beggars in Warsaw in the past but now they are everywhere', many of whom were unemployed adult males. More generally, 'One doesn't see here the absence of adult males, as it is with us [in Kraków].'[59] This observation needs to be treated with caution. Indeed, military conscription in Warsaw had ended with the Russian evacuation but male labour out-migration, mainly voluntary but also involuntary, to Russia and then to Germany was the principal factor in the preponderance (by 32 per cent) of women over men in Warsaw's resident population by the beginning of 1917.[60] More telling are Kutrzeba's comments on the discrepancy between what he has heard about 'the difficult conditions in our capital' and what he sees: store and sweetshop displays of white bread, 'cakes, even with cream . . . and fruits, there is no lack of tea or coffee, which doesn't require queuing, the stores are full of tobacco and it's sold on the streets'. He quickly learns that the 'difficult conditions' stem from the high prices of unrationed goods and the quality and availability of rationed items. The queues he sees, which form at dawn, are for ration coupons, and he is told that half of rationed potatoes are frequently rotten and have to be discarded. 'Beyond the coupons, practically everything is available, as much as one wants. Only it's necessary to have money, lots and lots of money.'[61]

A different traveller's account altogether is that of S. Ansky, the pen-name of the Russian Jewish writer, politician, and folklorist Solomon Zanvel Rappoport (1863–1920). Best known for his classic

[57] Ibid. 47.
[58] Ibid. 47–8.
[59] Ibid. 48.
[60] Dunin-Wąsowicz, *Warszawa*, 83.
[61] Kutrzeba, *Królestwo i Galicya*, 50.

play *The Dybbuk*, Ansky spent a month at the end of 1914 in Warsaw en route to Russian-occupied territory in Austrian Galicia to organize relief for Jews caught between the warring armies. Ansky's account of his experiences in Galicia and throughout the Russian Empire's Pale of Settlement during the war years, published in Yiddish shortly after his death, offers a wide-ranging view of the devastation of Jewish communities on the Eastern Front.[62] Though Ansky's time in Warsaw was limited, he was an acute and vividly articulate observer of the city's 'feverish state, still reeling from the furious German assault in October'.[63] He arrived as thousands of wounded soldiers and predominantly Jewish refugees, forcibly deported from their homes, poured into the city.

Awaiting a means to reach his ultimate destination, Ansky was temporarily thrust into the role of assisting in the organization of emergency medical and food distribution centres. Not only does he give us a portrait of a city 'on the move', whose 'roads were jammed, claustrophobic, choked by masses of people', but of makeshift Jewish refugee shelters, such as the one at the Hazomir literary club, 'packed wall to wall with cots, benches, and crates' where 'three to four children were sitting or lying on each cot . . . The place looked like a devastated anthill.' 'More than any other place', Ansky asserted, 'Warsaw bore the evidence of the calamity that had struck the Jews of Poland' as he repeats the refugees' 'dreadful accounts of blood and terror' as victims of 'vicious Cossack atrocities'.[64] Ansky also spent some time in the present-day Warsaw suburb of Błonie, before the war a 'rich and elegant Jewish town', which, like other Jewish shtetls surrounding the city, had been devastated by the fighting, their populations dramatically reduced by expulsions orchestrated by the Russian army:

[Błonie] was totally destroyed. At its centre, the town hall, with its roof torn off and its wall riddled and shattered, looked like an ancient ruin. It symbolized the annihilation of [Błonie]. Most of the houses and buildings had burned down. The rest were empty and desolate, their doors and windows ripped out; whole houses, especially Polish ones, had survived only in the side streets. Not a single large store had endured; they were all deserted and their doors gone.

The large synagogue was unscathed. But all of its contents were looted or smashed; the Torah scrolls were tattered and sullied. Now the building was

---

[62] S. Ansky, *The Enemy at his Pleasure: A Journey through the Jewish Pale of Settlement During World War I*, ed. and trans. Joachim Neugroschel (New York, 2002).
[63] Ibid. 12.
[64] Ibid. 12–13.

used as a military hospital for cholera patients since the local city council had informed the army authorities that this would be the most appropriate site.[65]

The other source of Jewish misery in Warsaw Ansky discovers in the 'Polish libel campaign', which he 'had heard about'. But now he 'got to see it with my own eyes':

> It was a thoroughly organized, methodical attack. The slander had poisoned every corner of Polish life, down into the most remote cracks. No matter where I went, I kept hearing rumours about Jewish espionage.
>
> I was staying at the Hotel Europa, which was filled mostly with high-level Russian officers. When I entered my room, it was being straightened by an elderly Polish maid with a simple yet respectable appearance. As soon as I arrived, she began: 'Oh, Excellency, you can't imagine what's going on here. You can't imagine what we've had to put up with. The Germans come flying with their diabolical machines, dropping bombs and killing dozens of innocent people! . . . The disasters we've seen, all because of the Germans and the Jews.'
>
> 'How have the Jews harmed you?', I asked.
>
> 'The telephones', she said vaguely. 'They tell the Germans everything. On Sunday when the flying machines came over, the Jews sent them all sorts of signals—they told them where the biggest generals were in the church. They started bombing it. Luckily they missed.'
>
> The elderly maid went on, delivering a recitation that she apparently replayed for every guest she met. The bombs had killed or wounded a dozen people, she said, all of them Poles, and all because the 'Jews have an ointment, which they smear on their bodies so the bombs won't hurt them'.[66]

For all of the light it throws on a metropolis that was breathing 'with the hot gasping of a man with a deadly disease', Ansky's record of his brief encounter with wartime Warsaw suffers from some of the same problems as those of other travellers in that it offers a snapshot rather than a panorama, from a particular moment in time, and from the perspective of a man with little knowledge of local conditions and whose most trusted contacts are from the Jewish community's secularly educated elite and its Yiddish-promoting literati. Though Ansky had also taken up the cause of Yiddish as a national Jewish language, he seems to have spent little time with representatives of the Orthodox and Hasidic religious communities, who constituted the majority of Yiddish-speaking Jews in Warsaw. And as much light as Ansky sheds on antisemitism among Poles, he also tends to embellish and generalize it to the point of stereotype.

[65] Ibid. 34–5. [66] Ibid. 14–15.

A far better perspective on the sufferings of Warsaw's Jewish community during the war comes from the published speeches of Noah Prylucki (1882–1941) delivered to the city council, of which he was a member.[67] Like Ansky-Rappaport, Prylucki became a champion of Yiddish as the national language of the Russian Empire's Jewish diaspora, first as editor of the Yiddish-language daily newspaper *Der Moment* and, following the Russian evacuation in 1915, as founder and leader of the 'Folkist' party, whose platform was to build a modern, secular Jewish nation within the borders of a Poland in which Jews would enjoy equal civil rights.[68] An experienced and talented attorney, Prylucki published his speeches in the Polish language of their delivery, as well as in Yiddish. They contain depositions and personal testimonies of discrimination and persecution suffered by Jews at the hands of municipal authorities and agencies dominated by Poles, which Prylucki read verbatim at city council sessions. Many focus on the persecution and brutality of the city militia (a Polish force), for example, in enforcing German-imposed sanitary regulations during the city's typhus epidemic. Below is Mordechai Wejnberg's unanswered complaint, sent to the chief of the militia, Prince Franciszek Radziwiłł, which was included in Prylucki's speech of 28 February 1917 during the debate over the city budget:

On Friday, the 19th of this month at 11:00 a.m. I was stopped by three patrolmen of the 11th precinct who asked where I was going. I said that I was going to buy potatoes. This occurred on Wilcza Street. Requests or persuasion didn't help me [and] I was led to the station and put behind bars.

The captain of the 11th precinct appeared [and] I spoke to him in precise terms about my arrest. The captain stated that I was clean and, after returning my passport to me, released me from the jail. At the same time two acquaintances of mine were sitting there, also arrested on the street and placed behind bars. Having heard that they needed their passports and not having them on their persons, they asked me if I would retrieve them from their homes. I agreed to carry out their request. I brought them their passports. When I was returning home, the patrolman Zakrzewski detained me. I stated that I had been certified as completely clean by the captain and had been released. For my declaration I received a strong beating from Zakrzewski and the following words: 'You will go home when you no longer have a beard and

---

[67] Nojach Pryłucki, *Mowy wygłoszone w pierwszej Radzie Miejskiej st. m. Warszawy, w b. Radzie Stanu Król. Polsk., w Sejmie Ustawodawczym Rzeczypospolitej Polskiej*, vol. i (Warsaw, 1920).

[68] For more on Pryłucki see Kalman (Keith) Weiser, *Noah Pryłucki and the Folkists in Poland* (Toronto, 2011).

only after I shave it off, so that you'll never come back to this precinct. Go to Nalewki, Krochmalna.'

I was [then] taken to the disinfection facility for shaving my beard and cutting my hair. . . .

Prylucki then added that he had many other formal complaints about sanitary regulations being used to cleanse 'Christian districts' of Jews.[69]

A few months later, on 12 July 1917 during council debates over the budget of the city militia, Prylucki read eight of the 'most characteristic' formal complaints delivered to Radziwiłł about police mistreatment and malfeasance inside the 'Jewish district' from a 'whole briefcase' in his possession, beginning with that of Jankiel Sroka from 21 December 1916:

On the 15th of this month I went to the city store no. 117 of the Food Section [a department within the city administration] at 24 Muranowska Street to purchase a few food items. I was standing in line when the doors opened and several of us waiting on the street entered the store. When the militiaman no. 437 noticed me, he ordered me to leave. I asked him to leave me alone because there was enough room in the store, but instead of answering me he grabbed me by the beard, tore off a handful of hair, and pushed me against the door, which led to the breaking of one of the store windows . . .

I complained to [four witnesses] that the militiaman had no right to tear off my beard, but he could arrest me if I was guilty of anything. Hearing this, the militiaman arrested me and took me to the commissariat. The person writing up the protocol kept me there from 9:30 a.m. to 1:00 p.m., after which he ordered me to leave. When I said that I wanted to file a complaint against the militiaman, he ordered my arrest and placed me in jail in the company of criminals until 6:00 p.m.

Finally, after the protocol had been signed a young man appeared and demanded a rouble to pay for the damaged glass in the city store . . .[70]

Such testimonies, to be sure, provide considerable evidence of civil rights violations but do not record the larger frustrations shared by Jews and Poles alike about food distribution and corruption in its administration, not to mention the quality of rationed food and its high cost. Similarly, the incidence of infectious and contagious disease and rapidly rising mortality rates crossed ethnic boundaries. These frustrations were voiced in anonymous complaints sent to the Warsaw governor-general, Beseler, one of which from May 1917 targeted both the city administration and the city council, among other

[69] Ibid. 69–70.   [70] Ibid. 149.

things for 'prices that are ten times higher than under the Russians'. Regarding the former, the writer called upon the German authorities to take over food distribution from the 'Polish bloodsuckers', a misguided demand that even Prylucki would have rejected, knowing full well that the source of the city's food crisis lay with those very German authorities. As for the city council, the anonymous writer accused it of 'doing more for the dead than the living' and 'wasting time and money' on 'various stupidities', including 'debates about street names', debates in which Prylucki participated in support of motions to change the Russian names.[71] For many Poles and Jews, the politics of nation-building during the war, whether Polish or Jewish, were irrelevant to far more fundamental issues of surviving the war.

* * *

This discussion has deliberately focused only on written ego documents. Visual ego documents in the form of motion pictures, photographs, drawings, paintings, and cartoons, especially those that tell stories such as József Rapacki's series of lithographs published in November 1918 by *Tygodnik Ilustrowany* 'in commemoration' of the German occupation,[72] require different tools of analysis and considerably more space for their illustration. Suffice it to say, however, that, like written ego documents, they too portray slices of the war in Warsaw from the perspective of their creators, highlighting certain aspects, in Rapacki's case German exploitation of the city at the expense of its inhabitants.

What, then, is to be said more generally of currently available ego documents as registers of everyday life in Warsaw during the First World War? Can they, more than police documents or reports in the daily press, come any closer to recording the quotidian reality of wartime as experienced by the majority of Varsovians, whether Polish or Jewish? I think that the answer to this question is a qualified yes, but only if one is prepared to read between the lines and to do so in juxtaposition with other sources. For example, the rumours circulating in elite circles as recorded in Princess Lubomirska's diary were not the same as those heard on Warsaw's streets, which were debunked at the time in the city's censored press. On the other hand,

---

[71] Archiwum Główne Akt Dawnych, Cesarsko-Niemieckie Generał-Gubernatorstwo w Warszawie (Kaiserlich Deutsches Generalgouvernement Warschau), 21.
[72] *Pro Memoria: Prusak w Polsce (1915–1918). 20 autolitografij Józefa Rapackiego* (Warsaw, 1918).

the princess's deepening fears of popular unrest came from an acute awareness of existing social divisions exacerbated by the collapse of basic living standards and growing anger over food deprivation, its manifestations and expressions recorded most vividly in the memoir penned by the social worker Władysława Głodowska-Sampolska. Indeed, because the princess believed that the worst was in store for Warsaw's aristocratic and bourgeois elites in the closing phase of the war, she proved far more conscious of wartime social conditions than the radical socialist Maria Kamińska, who hoped for, rather than feared, revolution. Finally, while the princess may not have shared in the same kinds of rumour and gossip as a chambermaid, they apparently shared—if we can trust S. Ansky's account of his conversation with a room servant at the Hotel Europa—an antisemitism that viewed Jews, among other things, as German spies and collaborators. The effects of that antisemitism, in the form of discrimination and police brutality, can be seen directly in the personal testimonies and complaints delivered by Noah Prylucki to the Warsaw city council.

Unfortunately, most ordinary Varsovians, like Ansky's chambermaid, did not leave behind ego documents that are accessible to scholars and from which we can hear their voices directly. They did not spend the war in a palatial residence, in a room at the Hotel Europa, in a newspaper editor's office, in a lecture hall at Warsaw University, in an underground political cell, as a department head in the city administration, or as a member of the Warsaw city council. However, ego documents generally have tended to privilege educated male middle classes and elites, and not just those pertaining to the First World War. In the case of Warsaw during the Great War, the authors of the ego documents that do exist, just like other source materials, at best may offer themselves as mediators of those voices unless they are presented directly, as Prylucki did for those Jewish merchants who had most likely sought him out for legal advice. Such testimonies, however, are a rare exception. In the case of the vast majority of ordinary Varsovians, their actions speak louder than their words, which largely remain silent, but those actions also come down to us through mediated channels, interpreted, misinterpreted, and reinterpreted. The challenge for historians in dealing with ego documents, as with all documents, is to take them for what they are: sources that are useful but inevitably limited, and in the case of the Dunin-Wąsowicz anthology, that have contributed to a narrative and memorialization of the Great War in Warsaw as backdrop to Polish independence.

One way to complicate this narrative is to make public more ego documents, especially from those whose voices have yet to be heard, and which may yet be retrieved from boxes hidden away in attics or cellars and perhaps even archives. For example, Prylucki, a notorious collector and the first director of the YIVO Institute for Jewish Research, claimed to have 'entire briefcases' of legal depositions whose fate is unknown but which could reveal a great deal about the Jewish experience during the war. The location and discovery of these and other kinds of ego documents in turn would require the same kind of concerted public campaign and financing that accompanied the Museum of the Warsaw Uprising or, more recently, the Museum for the History of Polish Jews. At this centennial moment of Warsaw's experience of the Great War, it is high time that historians, archivists, preservationists, and the educated public take up this charge, before the opportunity disappears once and for all.

3
Measuring Lost Time: Civilians' Diaries in Occupied Belgium

SOPHIE DE SCHAEPDRIJVER

Introduction: Claiming Subjectivity

One of the central paradoxes of the Great War was that it ushered in colossal claims on individual lives precisely at a time when concepts of the self had intensified. Increasing literacy, notions of national citizenship, mass politics, labour migration, and even military service had spread a sense of the individual trajectory. This shift was not, obviously, uniform across the belligerent world. There were vast differences even within north-western Europe: for instance, France's war generation was fully literate, but Belgium's was not. Yet for all the differences in articulateness (or, to be more precise, differences in access to standard modes of expression), the Great War brought a flowering of subjectivities. More and more people— soldiers, civilians, men, women—laid claim to the irreducibility of their very own war experience. Dilettante writings proliferated: ditties, cartoons, novels, poetry, plays, local chronicles, and didactic texts such as sermons and speeches. And life writing exploded: memoirs, private diaries, and, of course, letters (including postcards), tens of millions of which circulated weekly to and from the fronts.[1] Professional authors, too, charted their war. Some, like the French war novelist Roland Dorgelès, strenuously claimed that only literary men possessed the vision to go beyond the subjective and to write not *their* war but *the* war.[2] But he, too, left subjective writing—his

---

[1] For France see Martha Hanna, 'A Republic of Letters: The Epistolary Tradition in France during World War One', *American Historical Review*, 108/5 (Dec. 2003), 1338–61; ead., *Your Death Would Be Mine: Paul and Marie Pireaud in the Great War* (Cambridge, Mass., 2004).

[2] Leonard V. Smith, *The Embattled Self: French Soldiers' Testimony of the Great War* (Ithaca, NY, 2008), 196; id., 'Masculinity, Memory, and the French World War I Novel: Henri Barbusse and Roland Dorgelès', in Frans Coetzee and Marilyn Shevin-Coetzee

correspondence.[3] In other words, Dorgelès, too, wrote *his* war, as did so many of his contemporaries, who, to a man, to a woman, laid claim to their own experience, perspective, and conclusions.[4] Even those writings that pretended only to chronicle events implicitly claimed the uniqueness of the individual experience.[5] As one contemporary put it in October 1914: 'Although in this war our individuality is lost in the greatness of that which goes on we still have a good share of egotism which cannot be so easily got rid of.'[6] Here, precisely, lies the value of wartime life writings: not so much in what they tell us about events as in what they tell us about contemporaries' experiences of events. As Dorothee Wierling has observed, letters and diaries, for all the tantalizing aura of intimacy they carry, do not deliver authenticity—an undefinable quality to begin with. But they offer a sense of the writer's interpretation of her or his experience, both in what is written and in how it is written. And wartime life writings offer a glimpse into the ongoing creation of the self, in that they aim to demonstrate to oneself and to others 'who one wants to be and how one holds one's own in the war'.[7]

(eds.), *Authority, Identity and the Social History of the Great War* (Oxford, 1995), 251–74, esp. 264–6.

[3] Roland Dorgelès, *Je t'écris de la tranchée: correspondance de guerre 1914–1917*, ed. Micheline Dupray and Frédéric Rousseau (Paris, 2003).

[4] See the pertinent remarks in Jean Hébrard and Rebecca J. Scott, 'The Writings of Moïse (1898–1985): Birth, Life, and Death of a Narrative of the Great War', *Comparative Studies in Society and History*, 44/2 (2002), 263–92. See also Fabio Caffarena, *Lettere dalla Grande Guerra: scritture del quotidiano, monumenti della memoria, fonti per la storia. Il caso italiano* (Milan, 2005); Santanu Das, 'Sepoys, Sahibs and Babus: India, the Great War and Two Colonial Journals', in Mary Hammond and Shafquat Towheed (eds.), *Publishing in the First World War: Essays in Book History* (London, 2007); Antonio Gibelli, *L'officina della guerra: la Grande Guerra e le trasformazioni del mondo mentale*, 2nd edn. (Turin, 2003), ch. 1; Margaret Hall, *Letters and Photographs from the Battle Country: The World War I Memoir of Margaret Hall*, ed. Margaret Higonnet (Charlottesville, Va., 2014); Aribert Reimann, *Der Grosse Krieg der Sprachen: Untersuchungen zur historischen Semantik in Deutschland und England zur Zeit des Ersten Weltkrieges* (Essen, 2000); Salīm Tamārī, *Year of the Locust: A Soldier's Diary and the Erasure of Palestine's Ottoman Past* (Berkeley, 2011).

[5] This is a point made by Christophe Prochasson, 'La littérature de guerre', in Stéphane Audoin-Rouzeau and Jean-Jacques Becker (eds.), *Encyclopédie de la Grande Guerre 1914–1918: histoire et culture* (Paris, 2004), 1189–201, at 1189.

[6] The 40-year-old English–French–German–Belgian housewife Constance Graeffe, writing in occupied Brussels. See Sophie De Schaepdrijver, *'We who are so cosmopolitan': The War Diary of Constance Graeffe, 1914–1915* (Brussels, 2008).

[7] Dorothee Wierling, *Eine Familie im Krieg: Leben, Sterben und Schreiben 1914–1918* (Göttingen, 2013). On the interpretation of experience in life writings see also John Horne, 'Entre l'expérience et la mémoire: les soldats français de la grande guerre', *Annales-ESC*, 60/5 (Sept.–Oct. 2005), 903–19; Suzanne zur Nieden, *Alltag im Ausnahmezustand: Frauentagebücher im zerstörten Deutschland 1943–1945* (Berlin, 1993).

In what follows I chart one particular war experience: that of military occupation, or, to be more precise, that of civilians living under military occupation. Specifically, I look at the German occupation of Belgium; the analysis can be extended to other regions, although *mutatis mutandis*, as I explain below. This essay will, so to speak, chart the charting of the occupation experience via one particular type of ego writing: private diaries. It will analyse these from the angle of the question of endurance. The 'war effort' of occupied civilians, as I explain below, was widely defined as consisting of endurance. How did private diaries express this particular type of war effort, and how did they express it over time?

Defining Civilian Duty as Endurance

'Occupied provinces are not conquered provinces. Belgium is no more a German province than Galicia is a Russian one.' This statement was made at the close of the year 1914, as the war of movement raged in the east, while in the west the front had hardened and the German imperial armies' conquest of parts of northern France and most of Belgium (altogether, one of the world's most densely populated and highly industrialized regions) was fast consolidating. It was made by Cardinal Désiré-Joseph Mercier, head of the Catholic Church in Belgium, in *Patriotism and Endurance*, his pastoral letter for the New Year 1915.[8] This pastoral letter has received ample commentary. In 1949 the medievalist Ernst Kantorowicz referred to it in his study of the thirteenth-century genesis of the concept of the fatherland as a 'mystical body'.[9] Kantorowicz pointed out that Mercier's pastoral letter was part and parcel of a very long development in that it sacralized the idea of dying for one's fatherland, and on a theologically shaky basis at that. Kantorowicz's brilliant analysis has remained justly famous. But it carries one silence, telling, perhaps, on the part of an author who in his youth had been fiercely committed to imperial Germany's

---

[8] Text in Fernand Mayence, *La Correspondance de S.E. le Cardinal Mercier avec le gouvernement-général allemand pendant l'occupation 1914–1918* (Brussels, 1919), 448–67, quotation at 463. For the Dutch (Flemish) version see Désiré-Joseph Mercier, *Vaderlandsliefde en standvastige lijdzaamheid* (Amsterdam, 1915).

[9] Ernst Kantorowicz, '*Pro Patria Mori* in Medieval Political Thought', *American Historical Review*, 56/3 (Apr. 1951), 472–92. Kantorowicz first presented his text at a conference in Oakland in Dec. 1949.

war:[10] it barely acknowledges that the pastoral letter was written under military occupation. Kantorowicz claimed, for instance, that Mercier 'distributed' his letter, when in fact it was seized by the occupation authorities and made the rounds as an underground text. Moreover, Kantorowicz disregarded the fact that *Patriotism and Endurance* was, first and foremost, a statement about military occupation (*all* military occupation, including by Entente powers, hence the pointed reference to Galicia).

Specifically, the pastoral letter was a statement about civilians' duties under military occupation. Mercier defined these as twofold: first, patriotism, namely, the stolid denial of legitimacy to the occupation regime. 'The Power which has invaded our soil and temporarily occupies most of it . . . is not a legitimate authority. In your heart of hearts you owe it neither respect, nor loyalty, nor obedience.' And second, endurance: civilians had to stick together and stick it out. 'Compared with the brave ones [at the front], tell me, what have you endured? . . . Let us stop complaining. Let us be worthy of our liberation.' Mercier exhorted civilians stoically to accept the hardships of the occupation. Those hardships might bring wear and tear to lives, such as depleted savings, paralysed businesses, postponed investments, educational careers, and marriages, and dashed prospects. (Mercier was addressing the Belgian bourgeoisie, which was facing adversity but not starvation; he urged it to share its resources with those in immediate need.) Yet those depredations were only apparent, for time was on the side of those who endured, and the rewards were eternal both for the individual soul and for the collective, namely, the nation.[11]

Patriotism and Endurance, then, presented civilians under occupation with a horizon of expectation, to use Reinhart Koselleck's term, that fitted attritional warfare. Living under military occupation was no longer an ordeal to be passively undergone; it became a *project*. 'Endurance' as Mercier defined it was not passive but active; it was a type of war effort, a specifically civilian one. Mercier went out of his way to exhort civilians to refrain from armed actions that would inevitably endanger their fellow citizens.

---

[10] John B. Freed, 'Ernst Kantorowicz: An Accounting', *Central European History*, 32/2 (1999), 221–7; Jerzy Strzelczyk (ed.), *Ernst Kantorowicz (1895–1963): Soziales Milieu und wissenschaftliche Relevanz. Vorträge des Symposiums am Institut für Geschichte der Adam-Mickiewicz-Universität Poznań, 23.–24. November 1995*, 2nd rev. edn. (Poznań, 2000).

[11] Mayence, *La Correspondance de S.E. le Cardinal Mercier*, quotations at 462–3.

The occupation regime's ban on the pastoral letter vastly increased its impact among the occupied civilians. Having become a persecuted text, its form now underscored its message.[12] It was widely acclaimed, including by non-Catholics. Two novelists' diaries (among other sources) testify to this. Both belonged to the Liberal, even anti-clerical, end of the confessional spectrum. In Ghent the elderly writer Virginie Loveling (1836–1923) wrote that the pastoral letter, for all that it had the convoluted style of all ecclesiastical texts, 'bravely and devastatingly [denounces] the barbarian violations of human rights. It is an act of heroic daring in these times of harsh repression.' (She was referring to Mercier's open mention of the taboo subject of the massacres of civilians during the invasion.)[13] In Brussels the middle-aged novelist Georges Eekhoud (1854–1927) called the letter 'decidedly very bold'.[14]

The question is: how did the exhortation to 'endurance', to solidarity, confidence, and the delegitimization of the occupation regime, fare over fifty months of occupation? What impact did attrition and time have on the occupied civilians' sense of this particular war effort? Private diaries, I argue, are a privileged source through which to address these questions, not because they are socially representative, which they are not (I will return to this), but because private diaries not only speak of endurance but are an act of endurance, an ongoing effort, in and of themselves (I will return to this point as well).

The Case of Occupied Belgium

In what follows I confine the analysis to occupied Belgium in order to attain a certain degree of precision. But the scope could be extended to all of the war's occupied territories. Annette Becker, for one, has studied diaries written in northern France during the invasion and occupation, and Jovana Knežević has fruitfully studied two Serbian

---

[12] The pastoral text launched the Belgian underground press, which became the most active in occupied Europe. See Sophie De Schaepdrijver and Emmanuel Debruyne, 'Sursum Corda: The Underground Press in Occupied Belgium, 1914–1918', *First World War Studies*, 4/1 (Mar. 2013), 23–38.

[13] Bert Van Raemdonck (ed.), *In Oorlogsnood*: *Virginie Lovelings dagboek 1914–1918*. *Tekstkritische editie*, available online at ⟨http://www.kantl.be/ctb/pub/loveling/html/index.htm⟩, entry of 21 Jan. 1915.

[14] Archives et Musée de la Littérature (AML), Brussels, Georges Eekhoud, Journal, M.L. 2954/12, on 6, 7, 14 Jan. 1915.

civilians' diaries, by the officer's wife Natalija Arandjelović, and by the female physician Slavka Mihajlović.[15] That being said, an extended analysis should be alert to different circumstances: the occupied civilians' 'war effort' was not defined in a similar manner across Europe.[16] In the tsarist lands invaded by the German and Austro-Hungarian armies, prewar imperial rule hardly possessed the same legitimacy vis-à-vis the new occupying regimes that prewar national governments enjoyed in invaded northern France, Belgium, or Serbia; and the violence perpetrated by invading or retreating Russian armies in 1914–15 made them, and not the new rulers, take on the guise of aggressors, especially among the most vulnerable ethnic groups, above all the Jews.[17] Another example is Montenegro, where ambivalence towards national authority (and, for that matter, about the concept of the state's monopoly on legitimate violence) was such that the idea of a division of labour between civilians and 'their' army, with the former abstaining from bearing arms, hardly commanded the same consensus as in the occupied lands behind the Western Front.[18]

This is not to say that occupied Belgium was *sui generis*. But the question of the occupied population's war effort took on a specific form in Belgium for a number of converging reasons.

[15] Annette Becker (ed.), *Journaux de combattants et civils de la France du Nord dans la Grande Guerre* (Lille, 1998); ead., *Les Cicatrices rouges 14–18: France et Belgique occupées* (Paris, 2010); Jovana Knežević, 'The Austro-Hungarian Occupation of Belgrade during the First World War: Battles at the Home Front' (Ph.D. thesis, Yale University, 2006). See also Tammy M. Proctor's use of civilian occupation diaries in *Civilians in a World at War, 1914–1918* (New York, 2010), ch. 4: 'Caught between the Lines'.

[16] For a general view see Sophie De Schaepdrijver, 'Populations under Occupation', in Jay Winter (ed.), *Cambridge History of the First World War*, 3 vols. (Cambridge, 2013), iii. 476–504; Jay Winter (ed.), *Military Occupations in First World War Europe*, themed issue of *First World War Studies*, 4/1 (Mar. 2013).

[17] Aviel Roshwald, *Ethnic Nationalism and the Fall of Empires: Central Europe, the Middle East, and Russia, 1914–1923* (Abingdon, 2001), 122–7; Peter Gatrell, 'War, Population Displacement and State Formation in the Russian Borderlands, 1914–1923', in Nick Baron and Peter Gatrell (eds.), *Homelands: War, Population and Statehood in Eastern Europe and Russia 1918–1924* (London, 2004), 10–34; Theodore R. Weeks, 'Jews and Others in Vilna-Wino-Vilnius: Invisible Neighbors, 1831–1948', in Omer Bartov and Eric D. Weitz (eds.), *Shatterzone of Empires: Coexistence and Violence in the German, Habsburg, Russian, and Ottoman Borderlands* (Bloomington, Ind., 2013), 81–99; Alexander V. Prusin, 'A "Zone of Violence": The Anti-Jewish Pogroms in Eastern Galicia in 1914–1915 and 1941', ibid. 362–77; Jesse Kauffman, *Elusive Alliance: The German Occupation of Poland in World War I* (Cambridge, Mass., 2015).

[18] Heiko Brendel and Emmanuel Debruyne, 'Resistance and Repression in Occupied Territories behind the Western and Balkan Fronts, 1914–1918', in Wolfram Dornik, Julia Walleczek-Fritz, and Stefan Wedrac (eds.), *Frontwechsel: Österreich-Ungarns 'Grosser Krieg' im Vergleich* (Vienna, 2013), 235–58.

First, the invasion had galvanized a sense of the national (as it had in northern France and Serbia). Second, the invading army had committed violence that had highlighted the vulnerability of civilian society (again, as was the case in northern France and Serbia). However, and this is the third circumstance, civilian society had remained more or less intact in spite of the violence and mass flight: local authorities were still in place, and (quite unlike the situation in northern France and Serbia), most men of draft age were still present.

At the same time, military occupation meant a regression, in Belgium as elsewhere. If a salient feature of this war was, as Dennis Showalter has argued in a brief and thought-provoking essay, its 'semi-modern' nature—in brief, 'modern' on the Western Front, but much more beholden to traditional strains on logistics and organization elsewhere[19]—then the war experience of occupied Belgium, for all that it was situated behind the Western Front, evinces a clear pattern of 'demodernization'. The government, overwhelmed and in exile, had to leave organizational efforts (specifically relief) to the best efforts of civil society, which led to a great deal of improvisation. Nor could the Belgian state ensure communications, and so, tragically, no letters passed between the Belgian army and its now-occupied home front. Inside the occupied country, communication was scarce, rumours rampant, and mobility severely hampered by barriers, bans, and the German armies' takeover of the railway network and confiscation of vehicles, with the result that distances were measured, once again, in walking-time. Civilians felt disconnected, trapped inside their own narrow environment. A sense of purpose beyond sheer survival was hard to come by. 'It might be better to let ourselves live like brutes, without reflecting', wrote one diarist, in anguish at his own feeling of aimlessness ('one is seized by an intolerable sense of indecision'). He wrote this barely weeks into the occupation. By 1918 his despondency was complete: 'every day, we die a little more of our despair at being useless'.[20]

---

[19] Dennis Showalter, '1914–1918: The Paradox of Semi-Modern War', Oxford University Press blog post, 7 June 2014 ⟨http://blog.oup.com/2014/06/first-world-war-paradox-of-semi-modern-war/⟩ [accessed 9 Sept. 2016].

[20] The Brussels journalist Paul Max: Paul Max, *Notes d'un Bruxellois 1914–1918*, ed. Benoît Majerus and Sven Soupart (Brussels, 2006), entries of 19 Sept. 1914, 5 Oct. 1914, 28 July 1918.

Endurance, Time, and the Occupation Diary

Diaries shed light on how civilians thought through military occupation as time went on, because the keeping of a diary in and of itself was an attempt to give shape to the amorphous period of occupation. To begin with, as the literary scholar Béatrice Didier has noted, diaries in general, by charting even 'empty' time (observations, impressions, moods), are a way of ensuring that time is not passed uselessly.[21] As I have suggested above, diarists writing under military occupation were particularly and painfully aware of time passing uselessly, for under occupation the domain of normal activities shrank. Multifarious restrictions (on mobility, communication, transport, trade, public activity), material scarcity, and, in places, self-imposed inactivity hamstrung a wide swath of pursuits, such as manufacturing, business, public administration, higher education, and services. Unlike unoccupied home fronts, occupied Belgium offered no mobilization on behalf of the national war effort. What activity was available might serve the needs of the occupying regime and so was shunned and/or suspect. For many, therefore, time passed, possibly in vain. Keeping a diary was a form of discipline, at least: a regular endeavour that paralleled the general injunction sternly to 'see it through' and keep a dignified bearing.

This is not to say that private diaries are a straightforward source. For one thing, they are not socially representative: diarists had to possess at least a modicum of time and space reserved to themselves and, of course, they had to be educated. This severely circumscribed the private diary's social range, especially in Belgium, which was a considerably less literate society than Germany or France. (The corpus, as it stands so far, includes a diary written by a governess and another written by a skilled worker turned socialist politician; but the subjective experience of men and women of lesser social status must be cobbled together from postwar testimony.[22])

---

[21] Béatrice Didier, *Le Journal intime* (Paris, 1976), 52.

[22] Sophie De Schaepdrijver and Tammy M. Proctor, *An English Governess in the Great War: The Secret Brussels Diary of Mary Thorp* (Oxford, 2017); Louis Bertrand, *L'Occupation allemande en Belgique, 1914–1918*, 2 vols. (Brussels, 1919). Likewise, diaries written by urban dwellers are easier to find than diaries by rurals, including rural notables, though this may be attributable not so much to the rural bourgeoisie's lesser penchant for life writing as to the fact that the papers of urban diarists more readily found their way into major public archival collections.

As a result, the historian of occupation diaries charts aspirations to proper deportment as they were enunciated by citizens, ranging from petits bourgeois to aristocrats, whose education had been steeped in exhortations to proper deportment.[23] (These citizens were also, as I have mentioned above, the intended audience of cardinal Mercier's call to endurance.) Deportment, bearing, endurance—the occupation diaries of First World War Belgium are replete with comments on these values. And they have a great deal to say on their perceived disappearance. The Brussels novelist Georges Eekhoud, for one, in May 1917 lamented the steep rise in food prices and attributed it to 'the moral downfall of most if not all of my contemporaries'. Eekhoud observed rampant 'gluttony' among his fellow Belgians and called it a national vice typical of a people of 'moronic hedonists' (*jouisseurs abrutis*).[24] Should these observations be taken at face value? Another Brussels bourgeois, a dermatologist in his early 50s named Adrien Bayet (1863–1935), also noted the rise in prices (and therefore in war profiteering), but he tended to stress the dignity of most of the occupied civilians. 'The good citizens of Brussels do not complain,' he noted in July 1918. 'They would be ashamed to do so. They aspire not to peace [at any price] but to victory, even if it means [going hungry].'[25]

It is hard, not to say impossible, to decide one way or the other between these two visions of the occupied population (and of its attitude towards material comfort). An answer to that question would require different sources, such as relief files, or police material on black marketeering. The wider point to be made, or rather to be repeated, is that diaries bring us no nearer to *wie es eigentlich gewesen*, but they do shed light on subjectivity.[26] What made Eekhoud despair of his fellow citizens where Bayet saw mainly resilience? Was there something that predisposed one diarist to take a jaundiced view and

---

[23] See Manfred Hettling and Stefan-Ludwig Hoffmann (eds.), *Der bürgerliche Wertehimmel: Innenansichten des 19. Jahrhunderts* (Göttingen, 2000).

[24] Eekhoud, Journal, M.L. 2954/17, 7 May 1917; see also M.L. 2954/11, 10 Oct. 1914; M.L. 2954/12, 5 Jan. 1915; M.L. 2954/17, 7 June 1917; M.L. 2954/18, 5 June 1918.

[25] AML, Brussels, Adrien Bayet, Journal d'un Bruxellois pendant l'occupation allemande, M.L. 3546 notebooks 1 to 25; notebook 14, p. 4055 (21 July 1918). One notes as well that on the Yser front, the trench press concluded on the basis of what information it received from the occupied country that the occupied civilians refused a compromise peace. See F. Bertrand, *La Presse francophone dans les tranchées* (Brussels, 1971), 50.

[26] Mary Fulbrook, 'Life Writing and Writing Lives: Ego Documents in Historical Perspective', in Birgit Dahlke, Dennis Tate, and Roger Woods (eds.), *German Life Writing in the Twentieth Century* (Rochester, NY, 2010), 25–38.

the other to take an upbeat view? Did it matter that Bayet seems to have been an assertive character, secure in his status as a physician, whereas Eekhoud was an easily wounded man whose brittle sense of self hinged on his identity as an *homme de lettres*?[27] The diaries of both men, at any rate, illuminate the intersection between, on the one hand, the individual life trajectory and the individual perspective, and, on the other hand, the collective experience of war.

The corpus, such as it is, of Belgian civilian diaries of the occupation period is a collection of attempts to think through the occupation, if possible to draw a moral map of it, and to find one's bearings within it. One notes that many a diarist abandoned this effort after a while—an abdication expressed not only in the words but also in the form of the diary. To mention one striking example: six months in, the Brussels lawyer and writer Edmond Picard (1836–1924), who had started his war diary on a note of confidence, called the occupation a 'hiatus in our existences', whose end was nowhere in sight. 'If only one could sleep until deliverance!'[28] Picard never managed to give shape to the occupation, a term he only ever used in quotation marks.[29] His very journal lost form. From August 1914 to July 1915 Picard wrote his entries in two large notebooks with neatly numbered pages, and confidently gave the project a title: 'The European–German War'. But from then until the end of the war he jotted down his impressions on sundry paper of all sizes, never paginated, a total of 1,082 sheets in all.[30] Other diarists, by contrast, saw the very monotony of occupation life as a challenge, a means of getting closer to this particular war experience. 'When one writes one's daily impressions like this', wrote Picard's coeval, Virginie Loveling, the Ghent novelist, in June 1916, 'one winds up always writing the same thing and always observing the same aspects of military occupation. It is monotonous. But one only has to reread one's notes to find that in this very repetitiveness lies the essence of a great city in wartime.'[31]

Certainly, occupation diaries give the historian a keen sense of

---

[27] Information on Bayet is taken from the diary and from his prewar publications; on Eekhoud see Sophie De Schaepdrijver, 'An Outsider Inside: The Occupation Diary of Georges Eekhoud', in Serge Jaumain *et al.* (eds.), *Une guerre totale? La Belgique dans la Première Guerre mondiale* (Brussels, 2005), 79–95.

[28] AML, Brussels, Edmond Picard, La Guerre Européo-allemande, M.L. 2229/1 and 2, entry of 3 Feb. 1915.   [29] e.g. 15 Nov. 1914, 25 Jan. 1915, 3 Feb. 1915.

[30] Royal Library, Brussels, Manuscripts Department, Edmond Picard, Journal, 1915–1918, Mss III 224, folders 1–4.   [31] Loveling, entry of 26 June 1916.

time passing and energies wilting—or, conversely, of endurance. In Brussels Adrien Bayet purposefully put pen to paper on 1 August 1914; by war's end, his diary ran to 6,352 pages over twenty-five notebooks. At first, he filled his notebooks with press clippings documenting military events taken from German-censored newspapers which he annotated copiously, critically, and in a spirit of confidence in the victory of the Entente. (His annotations, of course, were his own way of giving himself heart.) But by and by, he ceased commenting on dispatches from the front. He wrote that many people around him thought likewise. 'At the start of the war, all we thought about was the war; we went through periods of exaggerated optimism and pessimism . . . we still imagined that the war hinged on single events . . . and we would feverishly discuss the taking or the relinquishing of the smallest stretch of trench', he wrote in December 1915, and noted that, for a year now, he and his fellow *bruxellois* had gradually paid less and less attention to 'particularities', privileging instead what he, Bayet, grandiloquently referred to as 'the inexorable line of fatality'.[32] Military events might fall where they may; Bayet's 'inexorable line' led straight to an Entente victory and to liberation. 'We *will* pick up the course of our lives again, if not this year then the next', he wrote on 1 January 1916, 'and it does not matter if the Allies suffered a setback in Mesopotamia or in the Argonne. One has to look at the whole.'[33] Yet even Bayet could not keep up this imperturbable come-what-may confidence; in the months to come he occasionally felt the need to bolster it with the odd encouraging, or at least encouragingly annotated, newspaper clipping. He charted his misgivings and his hopes, and, around him, observed both endurance and increasing material misery.

The view of time passing afforded by occupation diaries includes the time of the human body. Ever observant, Virginie Loveling in January 1915 saw a young man hop onto a tram in Ghent. 'Suddenly I realize he has only one leg. He is 20 years old, fit as a fiddle, and his mutilation has not got to him yet! He looks about him with an air of proud vigilance. Knowing he has done his patriotic duty has so far consoled him for his misfortune. But what will he do past this first intoxication?'[34] Diaries also express, usually in discreet terms, the neediness of the diarist's own body. From Easter 1916, for example,

[32] Bayet, Journal, M.L. 3546/6, 28–30 Dec. 1915.
[33] Bayet, Journal, M.L. 3546/7, 1 Jan. 1916.
[34] Loveling, entry of 25 Jan. 1915.

Georges Eekhoud got into the habit of recording good meals in great detail, something that he had never once done until then. In the countryside near Antwerp the writer Marie Gevers (1883–1975) documented sexual longing. She wrote her diary in the form of a series of letters to her husband. The couple had fled to Holland at the start of the war, but had voluntarily separated in August 1916, she to return to the occupied country with the children to look after their property, he to volunteer for army service. If the stern dutifulness of this choice consoled her at first, she increasingly missed her husband. She described erotic dreams, including interrupted ones: in one dream, the couple was kissing in the garden when a stranger came to disturb them. 'I started singing the *Marseillaise* and that scared him off . . . but I woke up too soon, alas.'[35]

Endurance and Patriotism?

How did diaries express the 'duties' of occupied civilians (defined as patriotism and endurance)? And how did this expression fare over time? Before addressing this question, it is important to point out that occupation diaries were by no means an exclusively patriotic medium. Those who acquiesced in the occupation, or even actively collaborated with the occupation regime, were no less likely to 'write their war' than were the more patriotically minded.[36] In Ghent, for instance, the journalist Alida Wynanda Sanders Van Loo (1860–1939) made fun in her diary of 'those daft defeated Belgians' and their, as she saw it, pathetic gestures of defiance vis-à-vis the occupation armies.[37] Admittedly, as a Dutch citizen Sanders Van Loo may have been at some remove from the patriotic feelings

[35] AML, Brussels, Fonds Marie Gevers, Cahier d'Exil I et II (FSLV 17/8 et 17/9); Troisième Cahier (15 Aug. 1916–1 Jan. 1917) (FSLV 17/10); Quatrième Cahier (23 Jan. 1917–15 Sept. 1917) (FSLV 17/11); Cinquième Cahier (19 Sept. 1917–15 Dec. 1918) (FSLV 17/12). Quotations: 19 Sept. 1917; 26 Dec. 1916. In the event, Marie Gevers's husband did not join the army. For her ambivalence on that score and her occupation diary in general see the fine article by Agnese Silvestri, 'Une écrivaine dans la Belgique occupée: les "Cahiers" de 1915–1918 de Marie Gevers', in Annamaria Laserra and Marc Quaghebeur (eds.), *Histoire, mémoire, identité dans la littérature non fictionnelle: l'exemple belge* (Brussels, 2005), 136–50.

[36] I thank Robert Gerwarth for his suggestion in discussion (at the German Historical Institute London, Oct. 2014) that such a pattern might have obtained, thus offering an opportunity to clarify this matter.

[37] Entry of 10 May 1915. See Sylvia Van Peteghem, 'Alida Wynanda Sanders Van Loo (1860–1939): biografie van een vergeten schrijfster, journaliste en vertaalster. Met een gannoteerde editie van haar reisdagboek en met haar oorlogsdagboek in bijlage'

of the occupied. But less than patriotic Belgians, too, chronicled 'their' war. The diary of the Brussels journalist and playwright Paul Max (1886–1944) shows him casting about for purchase on a frightening situation, demanding nothing more than to take the military authorities at their word. Having observed a civilian being mistreated by a German military policeman, he reassured himself that the Militärpolizei's commanding officers would not have condoned such brutality if they had known of it.[38] Max's main diary entry concerning Mercier's pastoral letter was a clipping from a newspaper containing the text of the relevant German communiqué.[39] This informed civilians that the occupying forces had not reacted to the cardinal's 'hurtful words towards Germany' with undue force. This statement was both true and disingenuous. The occupation regime's reaction to Mercier's statement did express a resolve to step back from the extreme violence that had marked the invasion in parts of Belgium.[40] But it escaped no one's attention that the very recent memory of the invasion still hovered as an unspoken threat of which Paul Max, for one, was keenly aware. The fact that he pasted the German communiqué into his diary without any comment may indicate his overriding desire for reassurance.[41]

The main point to be made here is that the diarists of the occupation ranged from the fiercely patriotic to those who rejected patriotic discourse (or adopted a patriotic counter-discourse, about which more below), with many gradations in between. And some

(Ph.D. thesis, University of Ghent, 1994), Annex, p. 43. With sincere thanks to Dr Van Peteghem for granting me access to her work.

[38] Max, *Notes d'un Bruxellois*, 56 (4 Jan. 1915).

[39] Ibid. 57–8 (11 Jan. 1915).

[40] I elaborate this point in 'No Country for Young Men: Patriotism and its Paradoxes in German-Occupied Belgium, 1914–1918', in Richard Butterwick-Pawlikowski, Quincy Cloet, and Alex Dowdall (eds.), *Breaking Empires, Making Nations: The First World War and the Reforging of Europe* (forthcoming Warsaw, 2017).

[41] A more explicit example of an ego document (albeit, in this case, a retrospective one) by a less than patriotic chronicler is provided by another Brussels journalist, Ray Nyst (1864–1943), who ran a very popular column in a Pressestelle-launched daily newspaper. On trial for journalistic collaboration after the war, he defended himself in a 500-page memoir, apparently based on wartime notes, entitled, defiantly, *Malgré Tout!* [*And Yet . . .!*], in which he defined himself as having stood above the fray throughout the war. See Ray Nyst, *Malgré tout! Complément et examen des débats du procès du journal 'La Belgique'* (Brussels, self-published, n.d. [1920]). A similar example is the occupation memoir by Leopold Wartel (c.1890–c.1971), a young man who had worked as an informant for the German secret police. He wrote it while awaiting trial. See Sophie De Schaepdrijver, *Gabrielle Petit: The Death and Life of a Female Spy in the First World War* (London, 2015).

diarists switched stances, as I will show. There is, indeed, no reason why only the patriotic would have thought through 'their' occupation. The diary offered a locus for all civilians, regardless of their take on the nation-at-war, to get a grip on what was happening, and define for themselves what they thought and where they stood.

Diaries also offered a broad register in which to do so, ranging from uncommented clippings over terse observations to hopes or fears for the future, ruminations, and flights of rhetoric. Register, as it turns out, is a particularly useful dimension for analysing occupation diaries. When it came to patriotism, especially, the differences in emphasis are striking. Some diarists concentrated intensely, even vehemently, on the fatherland-at-war, as did Picard and Eekhoud, who exulted over the 'live epic' of 'the sublime Belgians'.[42] Adrien Bayet, too, dwelt on patriotism, if occasionally examining his own feelings from a distance. In October 1914, for instance, he reminisced about his feelings during the first days of the invasion: 'even today, I can't analyse it—that deep, intense sorrow at seeing my fatherland trampled'. Even though patriotism was nothing but 'parochialism writ large', impossible to justify rationally, one had to know, Bayet concluded, when to surrender to 'its bitter grip'.[43] As for Marie Gevers, the diary she wrote during her time in the Netherlands adopted an elevated tone, though her register became more matter-of-fact after her return to occupied Belgium.[44]

Other diarists expressed their take on the imagined national community in the interstices of workaday prose. One example was the Brussels housewife Henriette Bovy (1858–1945). At the start of the war she was 54 years old, and her two youngest sons joined the army. The Bovys and their extended family belonged to the industrial, Catholic *bonne bourgeoisie*; some of them worked for the resistance press at considerable risk. Yet Henriette Bovy's journal does not dwell on patriotic ideas. She noted on 6 January 1918 that Cardinal Mercier had sent the family a photograph of himself with handwritten good wishes for her youngest son Daniel. She merely registered it, before briskly noting: 'and then the magic vanishes: lots of work'. That day, she had received a message from her son Élie. She did not know that he had died at the front in August

---

[42] Eekhoud, Journal, M.L. 2954/12, 15 Nov. 1914 (he wrote this after a soirée at Edmond Picard's). [43] Bayet, Journal, M.L. 3546/1, 11 Oct. 1914.
[44] Silvestri, 'Une écrivaine dans la Belgique occupée', 4–5.

1917. (As mentioned earlier, communications between the occupied country and the Belgian army on the other side of the lines were extremely rare.) Daniel would be killed too, in June 1918; his mother heard only in August of that year. Even at this point she did not dwell on matters in general terms; instead, she tersely noted the funeral arrangements and masses, with catafalques standing in for the absent bodies.[45]

By contrast, another prosperous Brussels housewife, Constance Graeffe (1874–1950), who had turned 40 at the beginning of the war and whose two oldest sons reached draft age in 1916 and 1918 respectively, turned her diary into one long discussion of national engagement in wartime. She had ample reason to do so. She was of English and French origin, while her husband's family was of German descent. All had Belgian citizenship. The extended Graeffe family shared the general indignation at the invasion of Belgium, and the draft-age cousins volunteered for the Belgian army. By May 1915 two were dead. Constance Graeffe's oldest son had also volunteered in August 1914, but had been rejected because of his age. His parents subsequently sent him to a Swiss boarding school. His letters home and his parents' replies are all transcribed in Constance Graeffe's diary (in a mixture of English, German, and French). The correspondence paints a family drama, for Constance Graeffe's own household, in contrast to the extended Graeffe family, gravitated ever more towards the German orbit, which eventually caused a family rift. In June 1917 Constance, her husband, and their children all took German citizenship, and the two older sons both joined the German army. The journal, which runs from August 1914 to December 1915, sheds light on what had predated this momentous decision. It was Constance's husband Otto who had decided on this course, and her journal shows her by and large adhering to his choice. But it is telling that she took to keeping a diary to think through her stance, and that she wrote it in the form of letters to an old school friend, a Scotswoman now living in Australia, who stood in as a symbolic witness to Constance's moral dilemmas. Her diary reflected on the invasion; on the massacres of civilians by the invading armies (which, she decided, were justified retaliations against civilian snipers); on the sinking of the *Lusitania*; on the execution of the English nurse Edith Cavell in Brussels in

[45] Henriette Bovy, Journal, private collection, with sincere thanks to Odile le Jeune d'Allegeershecque and Jean-François Tackoen.

October 1915; and other events crucial to the moral mapping out of the war. In the diary, Constance Graeffe's moral judgements mingled with seemingly anodyne (but in fact ethically weighty) details about daily life. She reflected, for instance, on the rising price of potatoes and blamed Belgian hoarders, ignoring the fact that the occupation armies had seized most of the harvest, just as she passed over the military occupation more generally. In her view, she and her household were citizens of the world, standing above the fray, ideally suited to appeasing Belgians' feelings of hostility towards Germany, but misunderstood.[46] If she had an inkling that the issue might not have been national (Belgians against Germans) so much as situational (occupied against occupiers), her diary does not show it.

In other diaries, too, an emphasis on the national seems to have made for an inability to detect what was at stake under occupation. Georges Eekhoud, who at the start of the war had exulted over what he saw as a national apotheosis that elevated literary men to their proper place ('our soldiers have hallowed our poets!'), soon chafed at the long silence that was occupation, and longingly imagined the literary prestige that would be his in a German cultural realm. In March 1915 he compared the status of academics in Germany favourably with their situation in Belgium and France: Germany's 'hierarchical spirit' created a healthy respect for 'intellectual superiorities', he wrote, whereas in Belgium and France 'the democratic spirit has become basely egalitarian, with contempt for all things superior, especially all things intellectual!'[47] In July 1918 he bitterly reflected on the 'careful reviews' his work would have garnered in the *Frankfurter Zeitung*, the *Berliner Tageblatt*, or the *Neue Freie Presse*, while in Belgium, even before the war, 'there was nothing, or next to nothing'.[48] By then, Eekhoud had taken a serious step: he had signed a lucrative contract with a German publisher. This broke with an unwritten patriotic directive. Belgian writers had enjoined each other not to publish their work, to protest against censorship, to express solidarity with their confrères at the front, and, importantly, to demonstrate that regular cultural life in occupied Belgium had not resumed, in spite

---

[46] De Schaepdrijver, '*We who are so cosmopolitan*'.
[47] Eekhoud, Journal, M.L. 2954/12, 16 Nov. 1914 ('our soldiers') and M.L. 2954/13, 11 Mar. 1915 ('hierarchical spirit').
[48] Eekhoud, Journal, M.L. 2954/18, 19 July 1918. See also 10 June 1918.

of claims in the German press. More generally, patriots were at pains to deny the occupation armies any opportunity to assert that life in Belgium was normal. The governess Mary Thorp (1864–1945) noted in the winter of 1917–18 that locals broke the ice on the frozen lake in a Brussels park so that German army photographers could not take snaps of people skating happily.[49] Eekhoud's choice, then, flew in the face of patriotism-and-endurance principles. In his diary he justified it obliquely: 'at least the Germans appreciate [cultural] worth!'.[50]

A parallel example is that of Edmond Picard, the jurist. Before the war Picard had coined the term 'the Belgian soul'; as war broke out, he passionately praised the Belgian government's position on national defence ('we have acted, in all simplicity, to uphold the honour of Right and the cult of Liberty'); in the first winter of the war he lambasted Belgian refugees—in other words, those who were not experiencing the war under occupation—as shirkers from sacrifice.[51] Yet Picard found himself eventually supporting the occupation regime, although in a roundabout way. In 1917 he published an 'open letter' to the Belgian government, accusing it of wanting to pursue war at all costs and of distorting the situation of the civilians under German occupation.[52] He also issued statements on the laws of war that highlighted 'the precarious character of international treaties', seemingly neutral scholarly comments that de facto justified Germany's violation of Belgian neutrality.[53]

Those diarists less prone to flights of rhetoric, by contrast, seemed better equipped to assess the military occupation. One example is provided by the novelist Stijn Streuvels (1871–1969), who lived

[49] De Schaepdrijver and Proctor, *An English Governess in the Great War*.

[50] Eekhoud, Journal, M.L. 2954/16, 3 Mar. 1916. On Eekhoud's occupation diary, his wartime choices, and postwar fate see De Schaepdrijver, 'An Outsider Inside'.

[51] AML, Brussels, Edmond Picard, La Guerre Européo-allemande, vol. 1, 2 Sept. 1914. Picard expressed his contempt for refugees in the satirical poem 'Les francs-filés en Angleterre' ('The Cowardly Scarperers to England'), which did the rounds in Brussels. See Louis Gille, Alphonse Ooms, and Paul Delandsheere, *Cinquante mois d'occupation allemande* (Brussels, 1919), vol. i. 243 (30 Jan. 1915).

[52] Edmond Picard, *Lettre-pétition au gouvernement belge* (Brussels, 1917). The occupation administration was delighted: Oscar von der Lancken Wakenitz, Head of the Political Department of the Brussels Government-General, praised it in a report. See Michaël Amara and Hubert Roland (eds.), *Gouverner en Belgique occupée: Oscar von der Lancken-Wakenitz, rapports d'activité 1915–1918. Édition critique* (Brussels, 2004), report of 31 Jan. 1917. The resistance press lambasted Picard as a cynic: e.g. Théophraste [=Oscar Grosjean], 'Profils Défaitistes I: M. Bourguignon', *Le Flambeau*, 14 July 1918.

[53] Picard, Journal, Mss III 224, folder 4, unpaginated page, n.d. [but Aug. 1917].

in and wrote about the West Flemish countryside. Streuvels, as it happened, had run foul of patriotic directives early in the war. At the beginning of 1915 he had published excerpts from his invasion diary; they had appeared in the Netherlands, and the German press had gladly referred to them, because they painted the invasion in terms refuting the 'German atrocities' discourse. Streuvels gave an ironic account of farmers fleeing in groundless panic before returning, shamefaced, to villages resounding with relieved fraternization. His publication of those vignettes had garnered much opprobrium from Belgian patriots; Marie Gevers, still in the Netherlands, had called him a cynic. In his diary Streuvels protested that he had only depicted what he had seen. He failed to acknowledge that if his diary had borne witness to violence, he would have been at great risk. During the invasion weeks, a Jesuit priest had been shot for taking notes about a massacre, a fact widely known among the occupied. And Streuvels would certainly not have been able to publish such a testimony. Whether or not the experience chastened him, Streuvels never published another excerpt, but kept up his war diary, which offered close observations of rural occupation. Shortly after the publication fracas, he noted a conversation between two farmhands watching a horse and carriage drive past carrying a fur-clad German officer complacently viewing the scenery: ' "Doesn't it make you see red that you have to watch this in your own country and there's nothing you can do about it?"—"You said it mate, and here we are looking on like idiots, afraid even to lift our heads".' The brief conversation made Streuvels reflect on rural patriotism ('and I had always thought they had no inkling that a country could possibly be theirs'). His diary, then, for all that it repudiated patriotic rhetoric, was alert to the widely felt unacceptability of the occupation.[54]

Similarly, the down-to-earth Loveling was not given to patriotic statements or gestures. Disregarding the unspoken ban on socializing with Germans, she sought them out: 'if one refuses to talk to the enemy, one blinds oneself'. She had lengthy talks with a nephew (Loveling's father was of German descent) now serving with a medical unit. It is true that those talks dismayed her: '[he tells me that] Belgian women plucked out the eyes of German wounded men. . . .

[54] Stijn Streuvels, *In Oorlogstijd: het uitgegeven en het onuitgegeven oorlogsdagboek 1914–1918*, ed. Luc Schepens (Bruges, 1979), 420 (entry of 27 Jan. 1915). See Sophie De Schaepdrijver, 'Drie Vlaamse schrijvers en de *Groote Oorlog*: over de oorlogsaantekeningen van Virginie Loveling, Stijn Streuvels en Cyriel Verschaeve', *Handelingen der Maatschappij voor Geschiedenis en Oudheidkunde te Gent*, NS, 56 (2002), 283–98.

So Germany's vengeance was justified. . . . How can an educated man be so ignorant and stupid?'[55] But she did continue to receive the young man's visits. Loveling's cousin, the medieval historian Paul Fredericq (1850–1920), exhibited similar insight in his diary. Noting that the German military police in Ghent cracked down on patriotic protesters, he could not resist drawing a parallel with the prewar brutality of Belgian gendarmes beating down socialists.[56]

The contrast between Streuvels, Loveling, and Fredericq on the one hand, and Eekhoud and Picard on the other, might suggest that receptivity to patriotic exaltation had something to do with linguistic affiliation or, to be more precise, linguistic *choice*—it was less about *being* Flemish than about *choosing* Flemish. Streuvels, Loveling, and Fredericq had made a deliberate choice to write in Flemish rather than in the more prestigious language, although they knew French to perfection—even Streuvels, who, unlike the other two, was not a member of the bourgeoisie. By contrast, Eekhoud, who was Flemish, had chosen to write in French, as had Gevers. The question, then, is whether a choice not to write in French could have predisposed a war diarist to adopt a certain distance vis-à-vis patriotic rhetoric. It might well have done. Belgian patriotic discourse was more often couched in French; most of the clandestine press, for instance, was francophone (with Flanders playing a larger role than Wallonia).[57] Not that this discourse was meant for francophone Belgians only. Much of it, such as King Albert's speeches and Mercier's pastoral letter, for example, was available in both languages. Yet to the extent that most purveyors of patriotic content targeted the educated bourgeoisie, which was called upon to interpret the patriotic message for the benefit of the wider citizenry, they assumed (correctly) that their addressees knew French; they also assumed (not always correctly) that their use of French as a lingua franca did not matter.

Another question is whether French, as a language, lent itself more easily to flights of rhetoric. It certainly did compared with the Flemish spoken at the time by most Flemings—namely, not standard high Dutch, but an array of dialects, unreceptive to the exalted register. (At the Belgian front, observers noted how officers'

---

[55] Loveling, entries of 30 July 1915 and 12 Mar. 1915.
[56] Bibliotheek Universiteit Gent, Handschriftenafdeling, Dagboek Paul Fredericq, HS 3702, vols. 5–9 (1914–16).
[57] De Schaepdrijver and Debruyne, 'Sursum corda'.

attempts at oratory foundered on the uncomprehending ranks' vernacular mutterings.[58]) Where this left observers such as Loveling, who wrote impeccable standard Dutch, is not easy to determine. Certainly it was possible to express Belgian patriotic exaltation in standard Dutch. One example, admittedly from unoccupied Belgium on the other side of the front, is that of the Flemish priest Cyriel Verschaeve (1874–1949), who waxed lyrical at seeing Ypres burn, symbolically detecting the Belgian tricolour in the blaze. It did not stop him from taking an anti-Belgian stance later on. Still using the same high-flown register, Verschaeve encouraged Flemish soldiers to go over to the German lines; in his private writings, he commented on what he defined as his mission.[59]

The example of Verschaeve shows how the war generated yet another discourse: that of Flemish counter-nationalism, as stimulated (though not generated) by the occupation regime.[60] The Flemish Movement, which supported equal cultural rights and a measure of administrative autonomy, long predated the war. But the specific circumstances of the occupation had stimulated a specific kind of Flemish militancy. The occupation regime's divide-and-conquer policies had found a receptive audience not among the prewar champions of the Flemish Movement—members of parliament, authors, organizers—but among less-known militants and educated young men marooned in the occupied country. This separatist Flemish nationalism, which defined Belgium as an empire instead of a nation and considered Germany a liberator, called itself 'activism' and generated its own exalted register, as is evident, for instance, in student diaries.[61]

Given that this 'activism' profited from an occupation regime that exploited the population it claimed to represent—for Flemish civilians, too, suffered from exploitation and were deported as forced labourers—and that it failed to acknowledge the regime's untenability, Loveling and Fredericq condemned it, though both

[58] Sophie De Schaepdrijver, 'Death is Elsewhere: The Shifting Locus of Tragedy in Belgian First World War Literature', *Yale French Studies*, 102 (2002), 94–114.

[59] De Schaepdrijver, 'Drie Vlaamse schrijvers'.

[60] On this counter-discourse see Sophie De Schaepdrijver, 'Occupation, Propaganda, and the Idea of Belgium', in Aviel Roshwald and Richard Stites (eds.), *European Culture in the Great War: The Arts, Entertainment, and Propaganda, 1914–1918* (Cambridge, 1999), 267–94.

[61] Examples are the brothers Herman and Walter Bossier in occupied Bruges, and the history student Leo Picard (no relation to Edmond Picard) in Ghent.

were Flemish militants.[62] Fredericq paid for this. In 1916 his stance against the Flemish University of Ghent under occupation brought him deportation to German prisons for the remainder of the war. Loveling escaped such a fate, but her criticism of regime-friendly Flemish militancy was no less sharp. Describing a procession of university students in occupied Ghent, she wrote that 'almost all of those who see them parade past, smoking and singing, curse them as traitors . . . and secretly clench their fists . . . murmuring death threats'.[63]

Linguistic affiliation, then, did not create a pattern. The pattern lies elsewhere: inflated expectations of national cohesion (and, importantly, about one's own place in a national apotheosis of togetherness) formed a confusing lens through which to observe military occupation. Loveling did not paint an idyllic picture of the occupied citizenry, and that was precisely why she was able to train a lucid eye on the occupation. Gevers (who, unlike Loveling, wrote in French), too, entertained few fond illusions about her compatriots, but she expressed indulgence towards those who were forced to work for the German army, while at the same time calling permanent occupation 'insupportable'. In other words, her vision of occupation was understated but clear.[64]

By contrast, 'over-investment' in the conceit of the nation seems to have predisposed diarists, or at least some of them, to reject completely all notions of a community-at-war from the moment this community showed the slightest flaw. Both Edmond Picard and Georges Eekhoud, as we have seen, celebrated the idea of the fatherland as war broke out. But the actual occupied society, with its rifts and flaws, could not possibly live up to their exalted idea of national valour and unity. And so both men soon abandoned it altogether. On close reading, their diaries reveal how hard it was for them to let go of the idyll of the united nation. Eekhoud's diary, for instance, contains one very telling detail. At the start of the war he made a point of rereading Guy de Maupassant's cruel short stories of the Prussian occupation of France in 1870–1, misanthropic vignettes on mistrust and exploitation among the occupied French. Eekhoud rejected them as having nothing to do with what invaded

---

[62] As did other Flemish intellectuals, some of whom left ego documents. Examples are the writers Karel Van de Woestijne, August Vermeylen, Alfred Hegenscheidt, and Herman Teirlinck.   [63] Loveling, entry of 4 Nov. 1917.
[64] Gevers, 27 September 1917.

Belgium was experiencing. 'It is ingenious stuff, [but] cynical . . . and cold, cold, cold.' So wrote Eekhoud in early September 1914. But later on (presumably in 1918) he noted in the margins of this diary entry that he had changed his mind about Maupassant's stories and their relevance to the Belgian experience.[65] In other words, Eekhoud now subscribed to Maupassant's 'cold', 'cynical' view of civilians under occupation. This change of perspective caused Eekhoud to withdraw from the occupied citizenry altogether. There was no option in between: either occupied Belgium was a valiant community, united against the invader, or it was a cut-throat universe in which only the German occupation officials represented the principle of justice.

A similar pattern obtains for the virtue of endurance. All diaries dwelt on the leitmotiv of ill-shared sacrifice. All spoke of a great rush of solidarity in 1914 that was soon replaced by the harsh logic of every man for himself.[66] Yet here, too, the perspective on this shift was influenced by a priori assumptions. Those diarists who, as the war started, harboured the most fervent dreams of a united community were subsequently the least able to withstand any flaw in this picture, and they were the first to relinquish all hope and to wax cynical. 'We are not at the Germans' mercy at all', lamented Eekhoud; 'alas, no, we are terrorized and menaced by our own compatriots, our dear, our very dear Belgians!'[67] Picard, in the summer of 1917, ranted against the lack of solidarity among occupied civilians: 'people steal from each other, people rob each other . . . with alacrity. . . . Oh, what a scoundrel at heart man is.'[68] Other diarists, by contrast, were better able to countenance the complexity of their fellow civilians' choices.

Conclusion: Endurance versus Patriotism?

The above reflections are based on a corpus of one dozen occupation diaries, written by middle-class men and women with a median age of 50: in other words, people with an established trajectory

[65] Eekhoud, Journal, M.L. 2954/11, 9 Sept. 1914.

[66] This perspective also suffuses narrative prose on the occupation. See Sophie De Schaepdrijver, 'Vile Times: Belgian Interwar Literature and the German Occupation of 1914–1918', in Pierre-Alain Tallier and Patrick Nefors (eds.), *When the Guns Fall Silent: Proceedings of the International Colloquium, Brussels, November 2008* (Brussels, 2010), 535–54.

[67] Eekhoud, Journal, M.L. 2954/16, 31 Mar. 1916.

[68] Picard, Journal, Mss III 224, folder 4, unpaginated page, n.d. [but summer 1917].

now intersecting with the war.[69] This, of course, is but a fraction of the overall corpus of available diaries written during the German occupation of Belgium in the First World War. This corpus keeps expanding, as local historical societies and private collections open up their holdings to scholarship and to interested audiences, a process intensified by the centenary commemorations of 2014, which were marked by great public interest in the ego document. Moreover, the study of military occupation diaries should be complemented by scrutiny of private chronicles kept by Germans in occupied Belgium—that is, officials, members of the military, and private citizens. The above survey, then, by no means claims exhaustiveness. Nor has it exhausted the possible avenues of study even of this small corpus. Gender, age, faith, rural–urban differences, and other dimensions remain, for now, unexplored. Likewise, this investigation, for lack of space, has offered no systematic analysis of how major aspects of the occupation, such as the deportation of forced labourers or the Allied bombings, are refracted in diaries. That being said, such an expanded view of how diarists charted different episodes of the occupation would only strengthen two of the conclusions that even this small study allows: the essential subjectivity of diaries; and their function as ever renewed attempts to gain a grip on events and on the passing of time.

The passing of time, as we have seen, was particularly anxiogenic under the specific circumstances of occupation, namely, forced immobility and inactivity, and lack of communication. It was all the more anxiogenic for citizens of a culture which, like all early twentieth-century Western cultures, passionately valued energetic endeavour, however defined, and feared 'slackness' in all its (presumed) manifestations. In chronicling daily events, observations, and thoughts, diarists attempted to define a project for themselves (or to situate themselves in a common project); their very diaries were a project, as well as a tangible repository of endeavour. Some

[69] To repeat: this essay is based on the diaries of Adrien Bayet (50 when the war broke out), Henriette Bovy (54), Georges Eekhoud (60), Paul Fredericq (64), Marie Gevers (33), Constance Graeffe (40), Virginie Loveling (78), Paul Max (28), Edmond Picard (78), Alida Sanders Van Loo (54), Stijn Streuvels (43), and Mary Thorp (50). I classify Streuvels, a baker turned professional author, and Thorp, a governess from a middle-class background working for a wealthy family, as middle class. One further notes that all but three (the housewives Henriette Bovy and Constance Graeffe, and the governess Mary Thorp) were published authors, though only two (Georges Eekhoud and Paul Fredericq) were lifelong diarists: in other words, they kept a diary outside of the war years.

diarists, as we have seen, succeeded better than others in investing their occupation experience with meaning. The paradox here is that an initial over-investment in the conceit of the national—in other words, precisely in that conceit which, to the modern European bourgeoisie, represented the essence of collective endeavour and of bundled energies—seems to have predisposed diarists rather early in the war to pull away from the collective under occupation, indeed, from the very idea of a collective under occupation: initial over-investment leading to early disinvestment. Patriotism, in other words, may have stood in the way of endurance. It would not do to state this point too peremptorily on the basis of such a modest corpus; but one does detect a pattern. This pattern is not, as I have argued, coterminous with ethnicity, or rather with linguistic choice: writing in French did not automatically predispose one to embrace the national idea with fervour, although, as we have seen, the register of expression mattered.

More importantly, perhaps, this pattern brings out what was specific about the experience of occupation. Across the belligerent world, the highly ritualized entry of citizens into the conflict—military mobilization, public declarations, parades, outbursts of xenophobia—made for a widespread, if worried, acceptance of war as necessary and of its attendant death and harm as 'sacrifice'. This sudden entry, as it were, into the self-evidence of war, called 'war culture' by some historians, can be traced in several Belgian diaries. Georges Eekhoud, for one, on the morning of 3 August 1914, expressed horror at the coming of war ('it's the end of civilization and Progress!'). But late that evening a fellow writer, 'quivering with indignation and enthusiasm', came to inform Eekhoud that the Belgian government had chosen to reject the German ultimatum; and by the next morning Eekhoud exulted at 'the patriotic élan of all Belgians, regardless of caste or party'.[70] Such an ardent vision of a national community was bound to be disappointed before long. And 'war culture', with its emphasis on voluntary sacrifice, was but a blunt conceptual instrument with which to approach the complexities of the occupation experience. Some Belgians, for example, considered forced labourers suspect because they had, ultimately, worked for the enemy. Moreover, the notion of sacrifice could and did serve those who actively collaborated with the occupation regime. In the face of opprobrium (clandestinely

[70] Eekhoud, Journal, M.L. 2954/11, 3 Aug. 1914.

expressed) from the patriotic, they defined themselves as martyrs for a greater cause.

Conversely, and to return to this modest corpus of occupation diaries, other chroniclers refrained from portraying civilian sufferings as so many 'sacrifices' making military occupation into a school of virtue. They defined endurance not as a kind of sublime test meant to solder a nation, but as a base consensus around the fundamental unacceptability of an occupation regime. For all that occupation diaries shed light first and foremost on diarists' subjectivity, then, it does look as if a close reading of the meaning of endurance in these diaries reveals differences in range and lucidity. The less occupation diarists embraced the culture of war, the keener was their vision of what was at stake under military occupation.

4

Ego Documents from the Invasion of East Prussia, 1914–1915

ALEXANDER WATSON

Introduction

The historiography of ego documents has, from its inception, been bound up with the human experience of war, murder, and destruction. Jacob Presser, the Dutch historian who coined the term in 1958, acquired his understanding of the complexity of accounts of personal experience through his use of Jewish Holocaust survivor interviews. Since his writings, the rise of 'discourse analysis' has cast doubt on how much ego documents can convey about individuals' inner lives, yet even hardened postmodernist critics have been prepared to accept that the haze of socially rooted discourse can be broken, if only occasionally, by cries of individual anguish.[1] This essay thus situates itself in a long tradition of drawing on ego documents to expose and understand experiences of extreme violence. It uses these sources to illuminate the travails and suffering of the victims of Russian military atrocities in the German province of East Prussia in 1914–15. It also seeks to underline these sources' complexity by showing how these apparently individualist, personal documents could be co-opted, utilized, or, indeed, written for the purposes of wider groups, be it to strengthen regional community identities or mobilize still wider circles for national war efforts.

The Russian army's invasions of Germany during the First World War, the context of the sources under investigation in this paper, are today barely remembered. They comprised two major incursions and a bloody raid. The first attack began in mid August 1914, when

[1] For accounts of the origins of the term 'ego documents' and a survey of their use by historians see Rudolf Dekker, 'Introduction', in id. (ed.), *Egodocuments and History: Autobiographical Writing in its Social Context since the Middle Ages* (Hilversum, 2002), 7–20, esp. 7–13; and Kaspar von Greyerz, 'Ego-Documents: The Last Word', *German History*, 28/3 (Sept. 2010), 273–82.

two armies invaded from the east and south-east and briefly overran two-thirds of East Prussia. One army, the Second Army under General Aleksandr Samsonov, was encircled and destroyed by the Germans at the Battle of Tannenberg in the last days of August. The Russian First Army, led by General Pavel Rennenkampf, was then beaten eastwards and hurriedly retreated from German soil in the first half of September. At the start of November a second invasion was launched by a new tsarist army, General Sievers's Tenth Army. This force conquered less land, taking only one-fifth of the province, but it held the ground for much longer. Not until mid February 1915 was the occupied territory liberated by a German counter-attack. The tsarist army's final incursion onto German soil was a raid by 4,000 troops on the northerly city of Memel (today Klaipėda in Lithuania) in March 1915. The strategic rationale for the operation is difficult to divine, and it lasted only five days thanks to a rapidly dispatched German relief force. Although brief, it was bloody: the invaders murdered more than seventy civilians and forcibly deported another 472, three-fifths of whom were women and children, into the tsarist Empire.[2]

The tsarist army behaved brutally in East Prussia, and as its violence is the backdrop to our sources, it is necessary briefly to explain the reasons. Ethnic-related preconceptions were central. In the decade before 1914, the Russian officer corps had embraced ethnic profiling, and the tsar's General Staff had commissioned ethnographic studies of the territories over which it might have to fight. These sought to assess how their inhabitants would behave in the event of invasion. Germans were regarded as highly dangerous.[3] When the first invasion of East Prussia began in August 1914, Russian commanders therefore advanced with the expectation of meeting civilian hostility. Among General Rennenkampf's first actions on crossing the German border was to issue a chilling warning to the enemy populace:

[2] The military history of the first invasion is best recounted in Dennis E. Showalter, *Tannenberg: Clash of Empires* (Hamden, Conn., 1991). For the other invasion and raid see Reichsarchiv, *Der Weltkrieg 1914 bis 1918: Der Herbst-Feldzug 1914. Im Westen bis zum Stellungskrieg. Im Osten bis zum Rückzug*, 14 vols. (Berlin, 1929), v. 542–8; id., *Der Weltkrieg 1914 bis 1918: Der Herbst-Feldzug 1914. Der Abschluß der Operationen im Westen und Osten*, 14 vols. (Berlin, 1929), vi. 324–40; and id., *Der Weltkrieg 1914 bis 1918: Die Operationen des Jahres 1915. Die Ereignisse im Winter und Frühjahr*, 14 vols. (Berlin, 1931), vii. 282–3.

[3] For this military ethnic profiling see Peter Holquist, 'Les violences de l'armée russe à l'encontre des Juifs en 1915: causes et limites', in John Horne (ed.), *Vers la guerre totale: le tournant de 1914–15* (Paris, 2010), 191–219.

Announcement
To All Inhabitants of East Prussia

Yesterday, the 4th/17th August, the imperial Russian Army crossed the border of Prussia and, in combat with the German Army, continues its advance.

The will of the Emperor of all Russians is to spare peaceful inhabitants.

According to the authority invested in me from on high, I let the following be known:

1. Any resistance carried out by the inhabitants against the imperial Russian army will be ruthlessly punished, regardless of gender or age.
2. Places in which even the smallest attack on the Russian army is perpetrated will be immediately burnt to the ground.

. . . Signed: von Rennenkampf.[4]

The fast-paced, disorienting, and fluid combat fought by troops who were difficult to see because of their camouflage uniforms and smokeless weapons appeared to Russian officers to confirm their presumption that German civilians would resist, either by shooting or—the primary paranoia of the tsar's army—by spying. Punishments and reprisals were ordered. Moreover, further endangering East Prussians' lives was the patchy discipline of the invading forces. Under officer supervision, large bodies of infantry generally behaved well. However, rear-line units and small cavalry patrols were venal and brutal. The latter were singled out by East Prussia's clergy as having 'stolen, robbed, murdered to their heart's content'.[5]

Civilians in East Prussia thus experienced a level of violence during the Russian invasions which was comparable to that of the better-known, contemporaneous German military 'atrocities' in Belgium and France.[6] Worse still, this violence radicalized in ways not seen in the west. The overwhelming majority, up to 90 per cent, of the approximately 1,500 civilians killed by the invaders were murdered in the course of looting, executed, or massacred during the first campaign in August and September 1914. During the second invasion, the tsarist army relied more on forced deportation to secure the

---

[4] 'Bekanntmachung allen Einwohneren Ost.Preussens [*sic*]', signed by Rennenkampf, 18 Aug. 1914, in Hessisches Hauptstaatsarchiv: Plakate und Kriegsdocumente, Nr. 3012/3472.

[5] Report of Königliches Konsistorium der Provinz Ostpreußen to Evangelischer Ober-Kirchenrat in Berlin-Charlottenburg, 23 Oct. 1914, Geheimes Staatsarchiv (hereafter GStA), Berlin: I. HA Rep. 90A, 1059, page 3 of report.

[6] This and the following paragraph are based on the full analysis of the violence in Alexander Watson, '"Unheard-of Brutality": Russian Atrocities against Civilians in East Prussia, 1914–1915', *Journal of Modern History*, 86/4 (Dec. 2014), 780–825.

territory it had occupied. The Russians had already arrested and removed military-aged men in the summer operation, but over the winter of 1914–15 they deported whole communities. By one official estimate, around 30 per cent of inhabitants who stayed under occupation were ripped from their homes and taken deep into Russia. Among the more than 13,000 civilians forced out were 4,000 women and 2,500 children. Lethal winter journeys and hard conditions in exile resulted in the deaths of nearly a third of those deported, over 4,000 people. These deportations should be understood in the context of much wider forced removals inflicted broadly simultaneously by the tsarist army on hundreds of thousands of German, Jewish, and Muslim Russian-subject minorities living in the Russian Empire's western borderlands and the Caucasus.[7]

Alongside the official 'atrocities' of executions and deportations were ill-disciplined acts of violence such as looting or rape. Sexual assaults by Russian soldiers in East Prussia numbered a minimum of 338. There was plenty of robbery, often accompanied by beatings. Moreover, even if their bodies escaped harm, civilians frequently saw their property reduced to ash. Mostly through fighting, but also as the result of deliberate Russian military reprisals, more than 100,000 buildings were damaged or destroyed. By the spring of 1915, after the last tsarist troops had been repelled from German soil, three-fifths of East Prussia's small towns and over a quarter of its farms and villages lay in ruins. The population was also displaced. More than 800,000 people, nearly half of the province's population, had either briefly or for longer periods abandoned their homes for the safety of nearby forests, for the provincial capital, Königsberg, or for the interior of Germany.

Ego Documents

The Russian invasions generated a diverse and very large quantity of documentation, a fact which makes it surprising that historians for so long have dismissed or doubted the violence perpetrated there against civilians.[8] The major repositories today are the Geheimes

---

[7] For the wider context of the Russian army's deportations, see Eric Lohr, *Nationalizing the Russian Empire: The Campaign against Enemy Aliens during World War I* (Cambridge, Mass., 2003), 121–65; and Michael A. Reynolds, *Shattering Empires: The Clash and Collapse of the Ottoman and Russian Empires 1908–1918* (Cambridge, 2011), 144.

[8] See Imanuel Geiss, 'Die Kosaken kommen! Ostpreußen im August 1914', in id.,

Staatsarchiv Preußischer Kulturbesitz in Berlin and the Archiwum Państwowe in Olsztyn, Poland. These archives contain official records of the invasion and its impact, such as government minutes, police and military reports, and statistics and returns on the damage compiled by the provincial administration. Among these files are also very many sources that would fall into the category of ego documents, above all, eyewitness accounts of the invading Russian army's actions, and witness and victim testimony submitted to local officials and law courts. The primary reason for their abundance is that in the immediate aftermath of the invasion, great efforts were made to encourage and collect personal accounts of the invasion and atrocities from East Prussians.

Two related but distinct drives were made to collect East Prussians' personal accounts. The first was centrally inspired and began early, already during the summer invasion. Determined to establish whether the reports and rumours of Russian military violence were true, the Prussian interior minister in Berlin ordered at the end of August the heads of East Prussia's three counties, Allenstein, Gumbinnen, and (a little later, in mid September) Königsberg, to organize investigative commissions. Initially, these relied principally on the accounts of local state and church officials, but in November 1914 the Prussian state's court system was ordered to assist.[9] For two years, until the autumn of 1916, judicial officials roved the liberated countryside, taking sworn testimonies from all who had suffered at Russian hands. Appeals were also quickly issued in newspapers across Germany for 'reliable accounts' of 'atrocities and depredations by Russian troops in East Prussia'.[10] This testimony-taking was motivated by two considerations. First, there was a financial motive. Article 3 of the Hague Convention of 1907, which laid down the laws of war, including military forces' treatment of enemy civilians, obligated belligerents whose soldiers violated its provisions to pay compensation. Victim and witness accounts would help Reich authorities to identify such cases. The second motivation was

Das Deutsche Reich und der Erste Weltkrieg (Munich, 1978), 58–66. John Horne and Alan Kramer in *German Atrocities 1914: A History of Denial* (New Haven, 2001), 78–81, do accept that some violence took place, but underestimate its extent and brutality.

[9] See letters of Minister des Innern to Regierungspräsidenten, 28 Aug., 12 Sept. and 18 Nov. 1914, Archiwum Państwowe (hereafter AP) Olsztyn: Oberpräsident (hereafter OP) Ostpreußen: 3/528, fos. 5–6 and 86–7.

[10] See e.g. the appeal in the *Frankfurter Zeitung und Handelsblatt*, vol. 59, no. 244, Zweites Morgenblatt, 3 Sept. 1914, p. 2.

diplomatic and propagandistic. By late August, accounts of the German army's own violence against Belgian civilians were circulating in Entente and neutral lands. The German government wished to counter the negative international publicity produced by these reports and attract sympathy by issuing a painstakingly researched, incontrovertible diplomatic document describing its own people's suffering at the hands of barbaric eastern invaders. In March 1915 an official 'White Book' appeared, entitled *Atrocities of Russian Troops against German Civilians and German Prisoners of War*. Among the documentation it reproduced was a small selection of the mass of collected sworn testimonies.[11]

The second collection of personal testimony from the invasion was run at the provincial level. Behind it stood the East Prussian senior president (the province's chief civil servant), Adolf von Batocki, and a new organization, the Provincial Commission for East Prussian War History, established in September 1915. The purpose was to gather material for a history of the province's war experience. Even by today's standards, the project was visionary and carried out with impressive systematism. Teachers, the upstanding representatives of the state in East Prussia's many small villages, had already since the beginning of 1915 been collecting, at Batocki's behest, the accounts of refugees. This practice was widened, so that across the province over the winter of 1915–16 hundreds of teachers interviewed their neighbours, noted down their war stories, and then, following a set schema, used them to write war chronicles of their localities. These chronicles were scrutinized and given additions by both parish and district committees before being deposited with the Provincial Commission.[12] Almost all of what must have been a fascinating archive appears to have been destroyed in the Second World War, although fortunately not before the high-school teacher and later professor and director of the Königsberg City Archive, Fritz Gause, had used it to write a superb study of the invasions.[13] Moreover, extracts from the accounts were published in the five-

[11] Auswärtiges Amt, *Greueltaten russischer Truppen gegen deutsche Zivilpersonen und deutsche Kriegsgefangene* (Berlin, 1915). A copy is held in the Bundesarchiv-Militärarchiv Freiburg: RM5/2514. For the county commissions and process of collecting testimony see Fritz Gause, 'Die Quellen zur Geschichte des Russeneinfalls in Ostpreußen im Jahre 1914', *Altpreußische Forschungen*, 7/1 (1930), 82–106, at 86–7.

[12] Gause, 'Die Quellen zur Geschichte des Russeneinfalls', 89–6.

[13] Fritz Gause, *Die Russen in Ostpreußen 1914/15: Im Auftrage des Landeshauptmanns der Provinz Ostpreußen* (Königsberg, 1931).

volume pamphlet series *Ostpreußische Kriegshefte* between 1915 and 1917 and fragments survive, stored in Berlin, from the districts of Johannisburg and Insterburg.[14]

Neither the state investigation nor the Provincial Commission was conceived as a means to incite German citizens to anger or hatred against the Russian enemy. Officials' personal accounts of Russian violence were published in newspapers and during the war a few wrote books about their experiences in the invasion.[15] However, the authorities refused to release ordinary citizens' testimonies of atrocities for fear that they might be exploited for crude sensationalism. This did not stop private accounts of invasion from having a profound impact on the German public. The press printed letters from East Prussians detailing their ordeals, and the hundreds of thousands of refugees housed across northern, western, and central Germany also widely disseminated tales, some true and others exaggerated, of horrendous violence and suffering. These moved many people: more than 12 million marks were raised by public donations in order to alleviate suffering in the invaded province. The best-known expression of Germans' shock and anger appeared in the infamous appeal issued by ninety-three intellectuals in October 1914 on Germany's behalf 'To the Civilized World', which contained an anguished warning of 'earth . . . saturated with the blood of women and children unmercifully butchered by the wild Russian troops'.[16]

A few surviving examples from the archives can give a taste of the type of source material collected by the provincial teachers, administration, and state courts. They also illustrate the ordeals through which East Prussians passed in the years 1914–15.

---

[14] See August Brackmann (ed.), *Ostpreußische Kriegshefte*, 5 vols. (Berlin, 1915–17). The surviving material from Johannisburg and Insterburg districts is held in GStA, Berlin: XX. HA, Rep. 235.

[15] See e.g. the account by Amtsvorsteher Graap of the massacre in the village of Abschwangen, the bloodiest atrocity of the invasion, in which sixty-one people were killed, in the *Frankfurter Zeitung und Handelsblatt*, vol. 59, no. 249, Zweites Morgenblatt, 8 Sept. 1914, p. 2; also, for a mayor's autobiographical account of the invasion, A. Kuhn, *Die Schreckenstage von Neidenburg: Kriegserinnerungen aus dem Jahre 1914* (Minden, n.d.).

[16] J. von Ungern-Sternberg and W. von Ungern-Sternberg, *Der Aufruf 'An die Kulturwelt!' Das Manifest der 93 und die Anfänge der Kriegspropaganda im Ersten Weltkrieg: Mit einer Dokumentation* (Stuttgart, 1996), 162. For the public donations see Watson, 'Unheard-of Brutality', 818.

(1) A refugee interview collected under the president of East Prussia's historical programme.[17]

Recorded
by H. Klaber,
I. Teacher

Home District: Johannisburg
Parish: Arys
District of Residence: Mohrungen
Place: Himmelforth, 18 February 1915.

The farmer's wife Anna Salamon from Schlagekrug states the following:

We had to flee from the Russians several times. The first time, we fled on 3rd August. The Cossacks had set alight houses and killed people in the area, e.g. in Klanßen and in Drygallen. Our soldiers withdrew and urged us to withdraw. We travelled as far as Kokosken. After a few days we could return again, as our soldiers marched towards the border. After a few weeks, the Russians broke in again and burnt. We headed to the nearby forest. There we stayed, day and night, one week long. Late in the evenings we crept home, in order to feed the domestic animals. There, late one evening, Russian infantry marched through our village. As we noticed that they were marching towards Johannisburg, we went home from the forest and stayed there three weeks. . . . After three weeks they were beaten and marched back through our village. We hid ourselves again in the forest. The Russians searched for us. It's said that in the village of Drygallen they killed people.[18] After a few weeks the Russians broke in again. We didn't manage to evacuate and had to stay at home. Many hid themselves again in the forest. The Russians took several men from us with them, including the farmer Johann Lidwin. His wife and his children remained. Two men escaped from them in Poland. In our house, a Russian officer came and demanded roast goose. I went outside with a burning lantern, in order to fetch a goose. Outside I encountered Cossacks. As these saw me, they opined that I was signalling to [German] troops to come over, and one shot at me, but without hitting. The Russians retreated again. However, they came for a fourth time and we had again to evacuate. We travelled on the cart to Arys and then from one village to another, until we came to Rastenburg. On the journey we often had to sleep with the small children in barns. In Rastenburg we gave up the horses and travelled with the railway to Mohrungen und are now lodged in the village of Him[m]elforth.

[signed] Anna Salamon

(2) Anna S. (a different woman from above) was the wife of a wealthy farmer in the district of Rössel, in the south of East Prussia. This

[17] Refugee interview, GStA, Berlin: XX. HA, Rep. 235, 16 (Kreis Johannisburg), fos. 1–2.   [18] This was true. See Gause, *Die Russen in Ostpreußen*, 216.

story was taken down in mid September 1914 by an official at the Allenstein County offices, where she had gone to plead for help. Her account was corroborated and confirmed by a witness and by the local Catholic church.[19]

Heard
Allenstein, 11 September 1914.

The farmer's wife Anna S. (maiden name B.) from Lokau near Seeburg appears uninvited and gives the following statement:

On 31 August a Cossack patrol rode by our farm, which lies around 100 metres from the railway line. They shot at our German [military] patrol and it returned the fire, but had to withdraw in the face of [the enemy's] superior numbers. The horse of one Cossack was shot, and was left lying in our farmyard. Immediately afterwards came what appeared to be Russian infantry, who asked everyone where the German soldiers were hidden. All residents were threatened with bayonets and they were told to state our soldiers' hiding place.

My husband had hidden himself in the haystacks. These were set alight by the Russian soldiers. When my husband rushed out, he was asked by the soldiers to hand over all his cash. My husband gave them 200 marks and pleaded for his life, for the sake of his eight children. The Russians said to him, after they had the money, he need not worry and could go; they wouldn't do anything to him. Scarcely had my husband taken a few steps, when he was shot down by them.

My 14-year-old son Paul was likewise shot by Russian soldiers. He has several bullet splinters in arm and foot.

My husband died from his wound—a serious stomach shot—on the next day.

After that all buildings apart from the labourer's cottage were totally burnt to the ground. Contents and all cattle were victims of the flames. My 6-year-old son Joseph burnt with them, as did the nurse and a female labourer. I fled barefoot without any possessions with my seven remaining children. The day labourer Kalski, employed by us, was likewise shot by the Russians. As I am totally without means, without accommodation and beds for the children, I beseech you, give me whatever is necessary in my hand to enable me to have the remaining labourer's cottage furnished basically for our habitation and, for the coming period, to purchase food.

read out, approved, signed
Anna S. (maiden name B.)

[19] Anna S., testimony (and supporting statements by others, including the local Catholic church), 11 Sept. 1914, AP Olsztyn: Königlicher Regierungs-President zu Allenstein (Rejencja Olsztyńskie) (hereafter RP Allenstein): 178, fos. 3–4.

(3) Reproduced in full below are the sworn testimonies of two women raped by Russian soldiers, given at the court of Bialla, in East Prussia's south-eastern corner, on 19 July 1915. Gottliebe P.'s testimony, which was read out in Polish and unsigned, offers a reminder of East Prussia's 340,000-strong Polish-speaking Masurian minority and of the importance of these legalistic ego documents in providing a voice for the illiterate.[20]

Labourer's wife Gottliebe P., born J., from Bialla, 48 years old, Protestant.

Around the middle of August last year three Russians forced their way by night into my home. My husband and I were already asleep. The Russians dragged me violently out of the bed in front of the house door of our farmstead, threw me to the ground, and, while one Russian raped me, both of the other Russians positioned themselves on either side and prodded my legs and left hip with their bayonets. They inflicted 6 wounds on me, so that I had to place myself in medical care. My husband could give me no help, because he feared the Russians, as the Russians threatened to stab him.

>Read out in Polish and approved and due to illiteracy not signed.
>Witness was sworn to truth.

Bricklayer's wife Heinriette P., born R., from Bialla, 51 years old, Protestant.

At the beginning of September [1914], I stayed with my husband in Bialla in a lodging that was not my own because I believed that I would be safer there than in my own. Nonetheless, in the night Russian soldiers broke into the house and one among them—a Cossack—dragged me into the back room and raped me. The Russian abused me in many ways and held my mouth shut and since that time I have been sickly.

>read out, approved, signed
>signed Heinriette P.
>Witness was sworn to truth.

(4) A letter written by a small landowner, Bernhard F., in Bischofstein, to the chief civil servant of Allenstein County, 29 September 1914. His son, Josef, was one of the several thousand unfortunate young German men arrested and deported by the invader during the summer invasion. The Russians may have suspected that the youth was a soldier in disguise. He had volunteered for the army on the first day of mobilization, and although he had been sent home after a week, he was wearing a blue military tunic with

---

[20] Gottliebe P. and Heinriette P., sworn statements to the court in Bialla, 19 July 1915, AP Olsztyn: RP Allenstein: 180, fos. 220–1.

civilian trousers at the time of his capture. This case was also noted by the local police.[21]

To
the President of Allenstein County

According to newspaper reports, atrocities by the Russians should be brought to the attention of the high County.

On 29 August forty or more Cossacks stormed onto my land, which lies by the town. Bullets whistled, the main yard was suddenly full of Russians. My wife, my only child, my 17-year-old sturdy son Josef, and I fled from one room to the other, and finally in the furthermost chamber fell together on our knees and jointly prayed. The savages fell upon us as a cat or a wild beast falls on a bird family in its nest. We were mercilessly punched, pushed, thrown about. My wife screamed, was punched half to death, and body-searched. They pushed me to and fro with their rifles and mercilessly carried away my only son. The boy cried . . . 'Father, save me, father, save me'. I pleaded, implored, cried as only a father can for his only child. Nothing helped. I would have gladly given everything, my farmstead and cattle and stocks and everything gladly [*sic*], if only it could have rescued my child. . . . My child was stolen. It was in broad daylight. My God, my God! I ask you to assist me to get back my child, dead or alive. . . .

Yours respectfully,
Bernhard F.

(5) This account of a soldier given on oath to a military court of investigation differs from the above sources in a number of ways. The soldier is not a victim, but purports to be a witness. Unlike the above, his account is also a clear fabrication. Fritz Gause's history of the invasions looked closely into stories of mutilation and torture, and found them to be untrue. Whether the soldier believed his own tale and what his motives were in relating it must remain open questions.[22]

Heard Schwerin, 24 January 1915
[List of officers and court functionaries present]
Summoned: Wehrmann [Private in the Landwehr] Aug. Schult, at this time

---

[21] Bernhard F. to Regeriungspräsident Allenstein, 29 Sept. 1914, AP Olsztyn: RP Allenstein: 179, fos. 85-7. The police report, 'Bericht des Fußgendarmerie-Wachtmeisters Sahm I aus Bischofstein vom 11. September 1914', mentioning the case is in the same file, fo. 20.

[22] Military court record, AP Olsztyn: RP Allenstein: 179, fo. 465. For Gause's discussion and rejection of the verity of atrocity stories see Gause, *Die Russen in Ostpreußen*, 229-30. James Morgan Read reached the same conclusion in his *Atrocity Propaganda, 1914-1919* (New York, 1941; repr. 1972), 48-9.

of E Company, Landwehr [Infantry Regiment] 76, born 13.5.1880, Protestant, labourer by occupation[,] resident in Lehsten.

The Private Aug. Schult . . . belonged on active service to the 8th Company, Landwehr Infantry Regiment 76, and testifies the following:

To the Matter: In a village near Hohenstein, whose name I do not know, when I withdrew with a comrade into a house in order to escape machine-gun fire, I saw lying in the rooms a dead woman. She was clothed, with disembowelled abdomen, and children who had been cut into pieces were hung on hooks on the wall.

read out, approved, signed.
signed August Schult.

Private Schult swore to the truth of his statement after the interrogation, according to §§ 191 ff. of the Military Criminal Law Regulations, after he was advised by me of the significance and sacredness of the oath.

signed Entholt, Lieutenant
and Court Officer

signed Bokranz, Corporal
as Military Court Clerk

Analysis

These accounts of the experience of Russian invasion and violence in East Prussia in 1914–15 have a strong claim to be classed as ego documents. The court testimonies, provincial interviews, and appeals to local authorities provide insight into how events usually recounted only in narrow military terms swept up civilians and changed their lives. Many were people belonging to groups such as peasantry with only quite basic literacy, who rarely leave private narratives to the historical record. The documents' content could scarcely be more personal. All powerfully reflect the horror of war. These sources recount experiences of abandoning home in fear, of watching helpless as loved ones were taken away or witnessing their violent deaths, and of suffering the violation of one's own body. They break customary silences on taboo subjects, and leave a rare record of lives broken and personal anguish.

Nonetheless, these sources, gathered by the courts investigating Russian atrocities, the East Prussian administration, and the Provincial Commission for East Prussian War History, are both more and less than ego documents. To an unusual degree, most of the accounts belong not solely to their narrator. The person who recorded the oral account had an important influence over both how the story was related and what remains of it in the written document. More than that, these tales belong to the state and provincial authorities, without whose actions most would never have been recorded. The will to preserve them came from and had motives beyond the individual who experienced and related the events. Once taken down as statements they became possessions of a collective. The testimonies helped a national community to wage its war effort: they were mobilized as material proof of enemy barbarity and German suffering in order to sway international opinion. For provincial authorities they were never primarily private documents but rather the building blocks for a communal war narrative which during and after the conflict would succeed in reshaping and strengthening East Prussian identity.[23]

The state or provincial involvement in the creation of these sources places limitations on how much light they can shed on individuals' perceptions and interpretations of their experiences. The mediation by a second party (the interviewer, judge, or clerk) in the transmission of these accounts is especially important. The questions asked (of which we have no record) in the course of the interview or cross-examination surely influenced the shape and structure of the narrative. Moreover, local officials, such as the county administrator who took down Anna S.'s terrible and well-attested story, tended to filter out emotion. Interviewees relating their traumatic or humiliating experiences to teachers or before court officers may also not have wished to display their feelings. It is significant that the most unequivocal expression of emotion in the sources above appears in the one narrative that was written by the subject himself, rather than by an intermediary: the letter of Bernhard F. recounting the arrest of his son. The letter begins formally, justifying itself with reference to the official appeal for reliable accounts of Russian atrocities published in newspapers. However, raw emotion quickly spills into the text, as the farmer breathlessly recounts his family's panic as the Russians arrived, the brutality of the encounter, and his powerlessness to prevent his son being led away. The incongruity between the two styles of writing in the document—the initial static, formal language of address to authority and the sudden rush of personal narrative and broken syntax—accentuates the account's drama and the impression of deeply felt desperation, despair, and bereavement.

The court testimony and interviews conducted by the provincial

[23] See Robert Traba, *Ostpreußen — die Konstruktion einer deutschen Provinz: Eine Studie zur regionalen und nationalen Identität 1914–1933*, trans. P. O. Loew (Osnabrück, 2010).

war history commission lack such clear and unambiguous marks of emotion, but they can still offer suggestive insight into the subjects' inner states. Anna Salamon's sequential narrative of flight and encounters with Russian troops focuses on the events themselves, with few explicit reflections on how it felt to pass through them. Yet the choice of vocabulary in her interview—'flee' (*flüchten*), 'crept' (*schlichen*), 'hid' (*versteckten*)—as well as the circumstances she described speak clearly of extreme anxiety. The same is true of the stylistically similar interview extracts reproduced in the *Ostpreußische Kriegshefte*. Thus, for example, the exclamation of a labourer's wife and daughter to their interviewer that 'the 9th of August will remain unforgettable for us and all inhabitants of Dluggen' surely indicates feelings of deep shock. On this day, Cossacks had clashed with German cycle troops in their village, and then callously murdered a wounded soldier.[24] In Anna S.'s account of the murder of her husband and burning of her farm there are similar clues. Her testimony is presented as pragmatic and does not dwell on how she felt at losing her partner and her 6-year-old son. It provides no information on how she looked or whether she wept. Nonetheless, her mention of fleeing barefoot and her plea at the end of her account for money to provide at least the barest essentials for her seven remaining children testify to her desperation.

In victims' court testimony, an apparent lack of emotion might have been not solely because an official or interviewer had filtered it out in his report. It could also signal a distancing strategy for coping psychologically. This is particularly notable in cases of rape. The brief, matter-of-fact way in which both Heinriette P. and Gottliebe P. recounted their rapes was a style frequently used by other female victims of sexual assault. French women sexually attacked by Germans in August 1914 commonly adopted a similar tone, and the official German 'White Book', *Atrocities of Russian Troops*, published similarly styled testimonies by rape victims.[25] Even if the court clerks charged with transcribing these traumatic accounts were responsible for imposing a distanced, factual tone, the notable brevity of some narratives may indicate that the women recounted

[24] See Albert Brackmann (ed.), *Ostpreußische Kriegshefte: Auf Grund amtlicher und privater Berichte*, i. *Die August- und Septembertage 1914* (Berlin, 1915), esp. 34.
[25] Auswärtiges Amt, *Greueltaten russischer Truppen*: see esp. Anlagen 47, 48, 49. Archived rape testimony can be found within files entitled 'Völkerrechtswidrige Handlungen der Russen' in AP Olsztyn: RP Allenstein, 181–200. For the rape of French women by German soldiers see Horne and Kramer, *German Atrocities*, 196–200.

only the bare essentials of their experiences out of shame or to protect themselves from emotional pain. The lasting psychological suffering inflicted by these attacks is alluded to in Heinriette P.'s final admission after recounting her rape that 'since that time I have been sickly'.

Close reading of interviews and court testimony also offers deeper insight into East Prussians' understanding of their experiences. The historian Robert Traba has examined memoirs from the 1914–15 invasions and identified three core themes: defence, flight from the invader, and the material and psychological suffering inflicted on the inhabitants. In the crucial question of the invaded population's perception of the enemy he notes a pronounced distinction between 'Russians' and 'Cossacks'. Russians appeared in memoirs frequently as 'good', humane', and 'normal people'. Cossacks, by contrast, were always 'evil', 'wild', 'cruel', and perpetrators of atrocity.[26] Ego documents gathered by the courts, by contrast, reveal a far more universally threatening environment. Anna S.'s husband and 6-year-old son were murdered by Russian infantry, not roving Cossack cavalry. Russian soldiers also raped Gottliebe P. For Heinriette P. and Bernhard F., Russians and Cossacks appear to have been interchangeable. The official German 'White Book' broadly supports these impressions. Among its civilian victims' and witnesses' sworn testimonies, 'Russians' predominated as perpetrators, although twelve identified Cossacks. If Cossacks were therefore overrepresented among troops who committed violence against German civilians, this court testimony evidence nonetheless implies strongly that for the latter all enemy troops were highly dangerous. Lastly, suffering, not flight or a heroic defence, is understandably the central theme of these legal documents. They remind us of the intense vulnerability of civilians in the war zone.[27]

That vulnerability brought particular problems for German men. Military-aged males were most likely to become victims of atrocities: the Russian army executed only men, although some women, such as Anna S.'s nurse and female labourer, were killed through arson or in massacres, or died in the mass deportations of the winter

---

[26] Traba, *Ostpreußen*, 288–304.
[27] Auswärtiges Amt, *Greueltaten russischer Truppen*, Anlagen 3, 9, 12, 17, 18 (2 testimonies), 19, 23, 25, 26, 42, and 51 refer to Cossack atrocities perpetrated against East Prussian civilians.

occupation.[28] Moreover, beyond its physical danger, invasion posed a stark challenge to male inhabitants' masculine pride. Male identity in Germany had been heavily shaped by the experience of peacetime military service during the second half of the nineteenth century, and was defined by the image of the man as defender and protector of family and fatherland.[29] The intrusion of enemy troops onto one's own soil was thus a humiliation for civilian men, exacerbated by the distinctly unheroic and even perceivedly feminine behaviour—passivity, flight, or the concealment and then begging for one's life that Anna S.'s husband unsuccessfully tried—to which it reduced them. Sexual anxieties were triggered by invasion. Some diarists betrayed paranoia about the possible attraction of the Russian troops ('for the most part strong, stalwart men') for local women.[30] Distressingly, invasion also brought brutal demonstrations of men's powerlessness to protect their womenfolk. Bernhard F. faced this when his wife was violated and beaten. Emasculation was at its most explicit and traumatic in the ordeal of Gottliebe P.'s husband, cowed at the point of a bayonet and impotent while a Russian soldier raped his wife. Heinriette P. was also clearly with her spouse on the night she was attacked, but he receives no mention once she begins to recount her rape. His presence is an irrelevance; he may as well have ceased to exist.

The male anxieties unleashed by invasion were shared by German soldiers fighting in defence of East Prussia. Private August Schult's horror fantasy of stumbling across a disembowelled woman and dismembered children hanging off hooks was far from unique. Stories of Russian barbarity, also taken up by some newspapers, proliferated within the German army's ranks in the summer of 1914. Other troops claimed to have seen women with breasts cut off and vagina sliced open or nailed through the tongue to a table.[31]

---

[28] Gause, *Russen in Ostpreußen*, 168–9 and 175–6. See also 'Auszüge aus den Akten der Kriegskommission Allenstein zur Untersuchung Völkerrechtswidriger russischer Grausamkeiten', 29 Oct. 1914, AP Olsztyn: OP Ostpreußen: 3/528, fos. 43–63.

[29] Ute Frevert, *A Nation in Barracks: Modern Germany, Military Conscription and Civil Society* (Oxford, 2004).

[30] See Rittel, 'Aus meinem Tagebuch während der Russenzeit', AP Olsztyn: Akta Miasta Olsztyn 259/169.

[31] Auswärtiges Amt, *Greueltaten russischer Truppen*: see Anlagen 41 and 74. Newspapers discussed Russian atrocities but mostly avoided such brutal examples or graphic details. For a typical example see the German officer's letter first published in the *Berliner Tageblatt* and republished in the *Frankfurter Zeitung und Handelsblatt*, vol. 58, no. 228, Erstes Morgenblatt, 18 Aug. 1914, p. 2.

There was cross-fertilization of rumours between terrified East Prussian civilians and German soldiers: Schult's Landwehr Infantry Regiment 76 had encountered refugees even before it arrived at the front, who told exaggerated stories of Russians cutting off women's breasts and nailing down infants.[32] Investigating eerily similar tales circulating contemporaneously in the French army on the Western Front, the historian Ruth Harris has argued convincingly that they reflected male subliminal fears. The imaginary mutilated women may have embodied men's anxiety about the dismemberment of their invaded nation, typically represented in female form. The consistent choice of young women and children, figures instantly and emotively recognizable as 'innocents', as the victims in these atrocity fantasies emphasized Russian barbarity and probably reflected great apprehension for the safety of one's own family in defeat. Tales of the vicious mutilation of civilians may well also have been projections of troops' dread at the prospect of their own wounding and maiming.[33]

The disturbing atrocity fantasies of August Schult and other German soldiers offer a shocking reminder that ego documents, whether transmitted at first hand or through an interviewer or court official, should never be treated in Rankean terms as wholly authentic accounts of the past, history *wie es eigentlich gewesen*. They are warnings of the malleability of memory. Perhaps Schult and all other men who recounted these brutal stories to the courts deliberately lied, but the solemn admonitions to truth, the oath they swore, the lack of profit in deceiving, and the criminal consequences if one were exposed make it improbable. Psychiatric research has revealed how easily false memories can be constructed.[34] Suggestion—from frightened civilians in the battle zone, comrades or officers spreading rumours, and press accounts of Russian brutality—amplified in effect by the confusion of combat and genuine memories of seeing soldiers' bodies mutilated by shot or shellfire, provides a more convincing explanation for these convinced atrocity testimonies. Today, too, veterans' statements can be highly unreliable. A 2005 study of Vietnam veterans in treatment for post-traumatic stress disorder found that many who had served in non-combatant roles

---

[32] H. Holsten (ed.), *Landwehr-Infanterie-Regiment 76 im Weltkriege* (Stade, 1938), 17–18.
[33] Ruth Harris, 'The "Child of the Barbarian": Rape, Race and Nationalism in France during the First World War', *Past and Present*, 141/1 (1993), 170–206, esp. 188–91.
[34] E. F. Loftus and J. E. Pickrell, 'The Formation of False Memories', *Psychiatric Annals*, 25/12 (Dec. 1995), 720–5.

nonetheless reported first-hand memories of atrocities and other traumatic battle phenomena.[35]

Conclusion

The ego documents from the invasion of East Prussia in 1914–15 are testaments to a new type of warfare. Ethnic stereotyping—the idea implanted in Russian officers through their training that not just German soldiers but all Germans, even women and children, would behave with implacable hostility and posed a threat—lay behind many of the killings and deportations that they describe. The approximately 5,500 East Prussians who died on the battlefield or in the harsh conditions of internment were but a tiny fraction of the civilians who were persecuted and killed because of similar prejudices in the First World War, and in their millions throughout the twentieth century. Highly significant, too, is the way in which the stories of civilians in the invasion zone were co-opted by the German state and propagandists. The conflict of 1914–18 demanded not just unprecedented economic resources but also the direction of public opinion, both domestic and international. As the history of these East Prussian ego documents reveals, even human suffering could be usefully mobilized in the pursuit of victory. This really was a 'total war'.

These sources from East Prussia also illustrate the complexity of ego documents. Analysis of individuals' interpretations of and emotions during their experiences from these documents requires close and careful reading, and the conclusions cannot be definitive. As is attested by the readiness of people to swear under oath to having witnessed the most ghastly atrocity fantasies, memory is fickle, capable of confusing, conflating, or even fabricating past experiences. Interpretation is further complicated where the narrative is transmitted by a second party, such as an interviewer or court official. Yet ego documents are never wholly owned by their narrator. Their content is shaped by the audience at whom they are directed, the environment in which they are recounted, and manifold external

[35] See B. Christopher Frueh, Jon D. Elhai, Anouk L. Grubaugh, Jeannine Monnier, Todd B. Kashdan, Julie A. Sauvageot, Mark B. Hamner, B. G. Burkett, and George W. Arana, 'Documented Combat Exposure of US Veterans Seeking Treatment for Combat-Related Post-Traumatic Stress Disorder', *British Journal of Psychiatry*, 186/6 (June 2005), 467–72, and Simon Wessely's discussion of this paper in the same issue, 473–5.

influences that might prompt or intervene between the experience and its narration. The testimony on Russian war crimes collected by the German state and the interviews gathered by the Provincial Commission for East Prussian War History demonstrate with unusual clarity how apparently intensely personal narratives could, in fact, also be the possessions of local or national collectives, who sponsored, preserved, and utilized them for their own ends. In this sense, these sources from wartime East Prussia are not simply ego documents; to retain the Latin qualifier, they are 'nos documents'.

PART II
Soldiers, Doctors, and Nurses

5

'It was more than madness . . .': Perceptions of War among Slovenian Soldiers, 1914–1918

Pavlina Bobič

A young officer cadet and aspiring artist, Jože Cvelbar,[1] tried to unveil the perplexity of his combat experience in one of his letters to his childhood friend Frida Dinsacher:

> You can kill neither the memory nor the heart; neither the present nor the consciousness that rushes into your soul and makes you feel all alone; alone without the smallest sweetness and comfort, like a stone thrown in the depths of a river, and you don't know why or what for; [and] you do not know whether this misery is going to bring you blessings or damnation.[2]

Problems of war and the quest for meaning are interwoven in people's everyday experience of anxiety and grief and can never be dissociated from dread of physical destruction. Peter Naglič, a highly talented and devoted amateur photographer,[3] wrote in his reminiscences of the war that the seriousness of military life became apparent to him only after he had taken a solemn oath to the Habsburg emperor Franz Joseph, which in the omnipresent (and state-promoted) Catholic imagery was synonymous with taking up 'the arms of fear of God, the arms of obedience to the emperor, and

---

[1] Jože Cvelbar (1895–1916) was a Slovenian painter and poet. He graduated from grammar school in Novo Mesto in 1915, when he began his training at the officers' school. A year later he was badly wounded while fighting in the South Tyrolean mountains. Cvelbar died shortly afterwards at the field hospital in Monte Cucca.

[2] Narodna in univerzitetna knjižnica, Ljubljana (hereafter NUK), MS 1774: J. Cvelbar to F. Dinsacher, 22 Apr. 1916.

[3] Peter Naglič (1883–1959) was an ardent mountaineer and a devoted pilgrim who amassed an impressive petrographic collection. His greatest passion, however, was amateur photography. His photographic collection consisted of 10,000 glass and polyester negatives that, along with positives, were taken between 1899 and 1959. He produced a large series of photographs during the First World War, which he spent mostly away from the firing line. Quite possibly with the approval of the commanding officer Karl Ritter von Kern, Naglič documented everyday life in Ljubljana and of the Italian POWs confined in the castle above the city.

of love for the Austrian emperor'.[4] This oath was regarded as holy and the conscripts were expected to follow it 'loyally' in order, just as in the old days, to win the crown of victory.[5] However, Naglič added, '[m]y fantastic dreams [about being the emperor's soldier] were very different from what came afterwards'.[6]

What was the predominant perspective on the Great War among the Slovenian soldiers in the Austro-Hungarian army, and how deeply did the notion of sacrifice (for the Habsburg Empire or another higher goal) permeate their understanding of the conflict? Did it constitute their determination to fight and, if so, what tools were they to employ when identifying the meaning of their suffering in the field? Did they associate sacrifice with patriotism and the Catholic faith?

Religious symbols proved to be essential in producing a medium capable of channelling and enhancing the Habsburg Empire's (political) interests, in that they possessed that eternal trait which bestowed upon the Empire the appearance of an immutable force associated with stability and endurance. During the war both characteristics served as imperial ideals, but the reality gradually exposed the frailty of the patriotic principle upon which the old dictum 'All for faith, homeland, emperor' was based, and ultimately failed to fulfil the expectations and demands of the imperial subjects.

Slovenian men, called to arms in 1914, were to see service to the country as their sacrifice to God and, consequently, as an act of martyrdom. In other words, blood that was shed in a war (interpreted by the Catholic Church in the Habsburg monarchy as defensive and therefore righteous) was the blood of martyrs, an explanation that concurred with the attempt to make the war—that begets heroes— appear holy and honourable.[7]

Did the soldiers' experiences at the front, which they most often and powerfully expressed in terms of 'horror' and 'hell', subtly echoing the biblical scourge of God, underline the decline of traditional values and the advent of nihilism as a new creed? After all, according to theologian Karl Barth, the First World War raised the questions of the relation of God to history and of his existence in perhaps the

---

[4] Anonymous, 'Slovesna zaprisega naših vojakov', *Glasnik najsvetejših src*, 13 (1914), 144.
[5] Cf. ibid.
[6] Peter Naglič, *Moje življenje v svetovni vojni: fotodnevnik vojaka 1914–1918* (Ljubljana, 2007), 48.
[7] See Hugolin Sattner, 'Vojska', *Duhovni pastir*, 31 (1914), 17–20.

most intense and transparent way.[8] How, then, were the realities of suffering and (ultimate) sacrifice understood and expounded by the soldiers?

Personal accounts from the early months of the war reveal that among religiously minded men the idea persisted that they were indeed part of a mission to fight for the emperor and the 'venerable Empire'. These notions were congruent with the ideas that Slovenian Catholic priests faithfully disseminated through the sermons that they delivered before the departure of the mobilized men, and in the contents of religious publications that the conscripts read as members of various Catholic associations. It needs to be stressed that the majority of draftees were of rural origin, which traditionally represented the backbone of Catholicism in the Slovenian lands. By contrast, liberal-minded men, who comprised only a small minority of the educated elite, invariably supported the Yugoslav idea and were thus marked as politically unreliable by the (semi-)absolutist Habsburg regime; they were equally critical of the Catholic Establishment, in particular with regard to the Church's political connections with the Habsburg state. As for all those caught up in the flames of war, existential dilemmas were reflected in outspoken faith as well as in shattering doubts about moral righteousness; in this respect both responses powerfully revealed the ways in which people tried to identify the meaningfulness or absurdity of their being. The majority of the personal narratives (regardless of the author's political inclinations) reveal not only a distinct desire for peace but also a firm trust in God's will, which seemed the men's only hope in view of their broken lives. There is no notion of war as a liberating experience which could release them from the chains of social constraints; nor were there any signs of eagerness to display manly heroism, which may have been convincing enough for the young conscripts of Western nations at some point. This phenomenon is significant in that it raises the question of what cause the Slovenian men believed they were fighting for. Would they confirm that they were, above all, victims of the war and thus ultimately compelled to renounce the ideals embodied in the multinational Empire?

For the conscripts, leaving for the front was the first step towards a radical transformation in their lives. Born at a time of relative stability, the men had no personal points of reference in their memory to which they could relate the war. In their attempts to describe the

[8] See Karl Barth, *The Epistle to the Romans* (Oxford, 1933).

(often) inexplicable, the conscripts most commonly spoke of their experience of horrifying bloodshed as 'hell': as a painful darkness that constantly threatened to absorb them. A young Slovenian soldier and (future) writer, Juš Kozak,[9] wrote in a letter to his brother Ferdo[10] that for him, ever since he had seen that 'powerful, limitless death, the humiliation of man is so terrible that I cannot trust humanity any longer'.[11]

Despite the horror, initially the war could exercise a certain appeal, reflected in the enthusiasm of the members of the Catholic sports association Orel: 'We are convinced that Austria will win with the help of Slovenian heroism and deep faith in God, which inspires us.'[12] While stressing steel-like character and a sense of duty, which were the hallmarks of the good education received by the Catholic youth, they asserted: 'Deep faith gives us hope even in the hardest times, and our goal is eternal happiness!'[13] The spirit of heroism was combined with faith that God would not abandon those who followed him; these men were willing to accept that the war could reveal to them the glory of God—for why would the Lord send suffering if not for the benefit of his chosen ones? Experiencing the effects of shelling, where they could watch, smell, and anticipate death at almost any moment, they saw suffering as the medium through which despair and evil became no less powerful, but more graspable and apparent.

Reality, however, seemed to be exposing all the sickness of the age; Stanko Majcen[14] described the war as a 'valve, pouring out the stench

---

[9] Juš Kozak (1892–1964) was a Slovenian writer, playwright, and editor. In 1914 the Habsburg authorities arrested and imprisoned him for his alleged links with the radical pro-Yugoslav organization Preporod. While in prison, he was able to exercise his literary ambitions and wrote to his brother Ferdo asking him to send some of the books he wanted to study: Dostoevsky's *Crime and Punishment* and *Brothers Karamazov*, Tolstoy's *War and Peace* and *Anna Karenina*; he was especially keen to get hold of the *Brothers Karamazov*. Juš likewise wanted to read Ivan Cankar's essay 'Bela Krizantema', his novel *Aleš iz Razora*, and his play *Lepa Vida*. Several months later he asked to be sent a historical atlas. See NUK/R, Juš Kozak to Ferdo Kozak, 24 July 1914; 7 Sept. 1914, 1/61. On his release from prison, Kozak was drafted into the Austro-Hungarian army and sent to the Eastern Front, from where he was deployed to the Italian front.

[10] Ferdo Kozak (1894–1957) was an author, playwright, editor and politician. During the First World War he served in the Austro-Hungarian army and fought on the Eastern Front.   [11] NUK/R, Juš Kozak to Ferdo Kozak, 7 Dec. 1916.

[12] Josip Mulec, 'Samo tedaj si zaslužimo nebesa, ako voljno prenašamo križe in težave', *Mladost*, 10 (1915), 75–6, at 75.

[13] Ivan Birsa, 'Orel-značaj', *Mladost*, 9 (1914), 107–8, at 107.

[14] Stanko Majcen (1886–1970) was a playwright, poet, lawyer, and politician. He was conscripted during the First World War, by the end of which he was working in the Habsburg military administrative service in occupied Belgrade.

and rot of the century', referring not only to the extreme violence but also, at the same time, to its purifying, cathartic effect.[15] Regardless of the difficult and dehumanizing conditions on the front, however, soldiers were astonished to realize in their diaries that they were able to adapt even to that form of life. 'It seemed as if the end of the world was nigh', reminisced a Slovenian survivor of the extremely fierce battles at Doberdò plateau that broke out after Italy entered the war against Austria-Hungary in May 1915.[16] Metamorphosis looms behind the men's writings, subtly disclosing the mental traumas that could not be entirely comprehended by anyone other than those who had endured them.

The ongoing horror created a feeling that people were being initiated into a secret, that they were allowed a glimpse of eternity, identified with unrest and absence of meaning. All-pervading sadness had become a 'disease', wrote Stanko Majcen, 'digging through cells of the body and injecting poison into the bloodstream' of men whose dismay gradually became their vocation. Yet hope was sustained on the front despite even the worst fears—of an 'eternal separation from loved ones'[17]—by believing that all this would be over one day and that 'a new, much happier time than ever before will start again'.[18]

The anguish was combined with a sense that the war marked the advent of a new era which would be radically different from anything experienced hitherto. Invariably, people felt that they were standing on the threshold between a vanishing age of security and the great unknown. At a time of transition, suffering was thought to be essential to psychological transformation, because, as was clear from the Catholic standpoint, it was hoped that its flames would 'disinfect' the wounds of sin.[19] Yet the healing flames could easily turn into a destructive fire.

Following the first Austro-Hungarian defeats on the Russian and Serbian fronts, it became obvious that the war would end neither

[15] This was certainly a common trope in Germany, where cultural pessimism sometimes turned into euphoria vis-à-vis the dramatic experience of the war, at least in the summer of 1914. See e.g. the correspondence of a Berlin family in Dorothee Wierling, *Eine Familie im Krieg: Leben, Sterben und Schreiben 1914–1918* (Göttingen, 2013).
[16] Amandus Pepernik, *Doberdob, slovenskih fantov grob* (Ljubljana, 2005), 82. According to Marko Simič's estimates, the first two battles on the Isonzo claimed the lives of 46,640 men: see Marko Simič, *Po sledeh soške fronte* (Ljubljana, 1996), 46, 53.
[17] See Tomaž Košar, 'V pismih iz prve svetovne vojne', *Borec*, 44 (1992), 61–3, at 61.
[18] Ibid.
[19] Izidor Cankar, 'Drobiž: odlomki iz pisem', *Dom in svet*, 29 (1916), 110–11, at 111.

quickly nor chivalrously. Moreover, the desire for peace grew stronger over time and was expressed in the majority of soldiers' letters, which blatantly reveal human misery. It was therefore impossible to endure it without an attempt at rationalizion. This may have been the point at which, to each individual, suffering emerged as damning or redeeming, paradoxically exposing either the agony or 'purity of heart' of a man's quest for ethical integrity that ultimately led to a richer form of being.

Jože Cvelbar described his time at the front in the Tyrolean mountains as the climax of agony, which appeared even more depressing because of the realization that there was no life ahead of him. He wrote to his friend on 7 February 1916 of how extremely tired he was of the monotony, of the 'never-ending waiting and uncertainty'. In his imagery thoughts of the future and death became one, because nothing could be present more powerfully in the soldier's mind than the thought of impermanence. In Cvelbar's words, the only thing that he could still perceive as stimulating was 'beauty, but devoid of happiness'.[20]

Yet the example of this young officer cadet shows a man constantly seeking to overcome the obstacles to personal fulfilment: the heavier the melancholy, the greater was the will to supplant the omnipresent misery with his artistic talent. He ardently employed it as a tool of irony to mediate his objections to the ugliness and inhumanity of war. Influenced by the works of Friedrich Nietzsche, Leo Tolstoy, and Maxim Gorky,[21] he began to see his suffering as a necessary path to joy; the very tragedy of the young soldier's idealism lay in the fact that Cvelbar had recognized the proximity of death as the preserving force of spirit. 'Everything is full of deep, deaf pain and loneliness. A heavy consciousness that I am not needed in this world is descending upon me—together with a thirst for life.'[22]

For other soldiers, war could confirm them in their religious philosophy. Ivan Podlesnik thus saw suffering as a means of achieving a closer union with God, which helped him to rationalize the situation to which he was being subjected. In Catholic imagery, faith was an instrument for alleviating pain, and pain theoretically was honourable, even saintly, when the soldier's soul was offered to God

---

[20] NUK/R, MS 1774, J. Cvelbar to F. Dinsacher, 20 June 1916.
[21] Quoting Maxim Gorky, he exclaimed in his diary: 'To be a citizen—is nothing; to be human—is everything!': NUK/R, MS 1053, J. Cvelbar, 'Diary', 16 Jan. 1915.
[22] Ibid., 10 Aug. 1915.

and the soldier's body to the emperor, who, in Franz Grillparzer's poetic words, 'never dies'.[23]

The nearness of death, the agonizing realization that their very existence and survival were at stake, triggered in the soldiers an immense yearning for life and connection with the world outside their reality of dirt and stench, and the almost constant rumble of gunfire that many of them believed would never stop. 'For us, peace meant the time when the thunder went quiet for a while', Amandus Pepernik observed on the Isonzo front. Although the hardships at the front could not be entirely disclosed in what soldiers wrote to those at home, men expressed more about their state than intended (or allowed) through their simple (yet perhaps formulaic) greeting to their loved ones, which in slight variations appeared again and again in numerous postcards: 'I greet you all with a sad heart.'[24]

Behind the soldiers' psychic dramas that evolved during the fierce battles on the Isonzo also stands the bizarre fear that men were being stripped of their human qualities, such as a sense of guilt and compassion. One can note the overwhelming suffering of the men on the Doberdò plateau between the summer and early winter of 1915, a feeling that lived on in the memory of the man who recollected in his memoirs: 'There were moments when we forgot we were human', leaving open what was meant by 'being human'.[25]

Suspending the ethical in order to place heavy emphasis on the otherness of the enemy seems to be at the core of all warfare. This exposes the reciprocal process by which the soldier 'eliminates' the humaneness of the enemy; only when enemies are regarded as things is it possible to employ force against them. But what turns a man into a sheer thing is force, which is necessarily twofold. As the philosopher Simone Weil perceptively asserted during her own experience of combat in the Spanish Civil War: 'to define force is that x that turns anybody who is subjected to it into a thing.'[26] The

---

[23] Egon Schwarz and Hannelore M. Spence (eds.), *Nineteenth Century German Plays: Franz Grillparzer, Johann Nepomuk Nestroy, Friedrich Hebbel. King Ottocar's Rise and Fall, The Talisman, Agnes Bernauer* (New York, 1990), 67. In the German original: 'Ich bin nicht der, den Ihr voreinst gekannt! Nicht Habsburg bin ich, selber Rudolf nicht. In diesen Adern rollet Deutschlands Blut. Und Deutschlands Pulsschlag klopft in diesem Herzen. Was sterblich war, ich hab es ausgezogen, *Und bin der Kaiser nur, der niemals stirbt.*'

[24] Pokrajinski Arhiv Maribor (PAM), Okrajno sodišče Maribor, 635, T 149/20.

[25] Pepernik, *Doberdob*, 100.

[26] Simone Weil, *The Iliad or Poem of Force* (Wallingford, Pa., 1956), 1.

dehumanizing effects of force are applied to the perpetrator as well as to the recipient.

The men subjected to this kind of violence were certainly distressed because they felt trapped in a situation with so little prospect of survival. This is most vividly reflected in Cvelbar's recognition that

> at the beginning and the end of every thought are the anticipations of freedom, return, limit, hope, despair, denunciation; remembering in all its bitter sweetness; looking forward in all its bitter hopelessness. . . . what kills souls is neither bullets nor shells, but the feeling of subjugation . . . and the [acute] lack of everything that is dear to you, of all that you live on; and which turns your life into pure negation.[27]

Soldiers therefore often looked for a refuge to enable them to endure the monstrosity of war in the ties that bound them to a normal life outside the hell of combat. As Ferdo Kozak recorded in his sketch about experiences at the front, a man was always 'halfway turned towards the direction that he came from',[28] and, when necessary, derived strength from the 'memories of the past', which resounded in the present through 'sweetness of yearning, as well as in rare glimpses of existing beauty'.[29] The thought of life as it used to be brought forth caring emotions along with the sad recognition that the men were wasting their lives when they could have been of help at home. Anton Ažman, a man from the countryside, mentioned in one of his letters to his wife that his heart had hardened in the face of the destruction that he had witnessed, and that the bodily wounds would soon be cured, but not the wounds he had suffered 'within'. The recurring thought in his writings was his request for prayers and his belief that these had protected him through 'fire', while he hoped wholeheartedly that there would soon be a better future without hostilities, since time could be 'better used at home'.[30] Anton Okoren similarly wrote to his mother from the Carpathians that all she could do for him was 'pray'. Thoughts of the family alone persuaded him to remain an Austrian soldier, since he had twice escaped from Russian captivity; he asserted that 'in

---

[27] NUK/R, MS 1774, J. Cvelbar, 'Diary', 19 Mar. 1916.
[28] Ferdo Kozak, 'Dialog v zaledju', *Ljubljanski zvon*, 37 (1917), 35–9, at 36.
[29] NUK/R, MS 1774, J. Cvelbar, 'Diary', 27 Mar. 1916.
[30] Anton Ažman in a letter to his wife, 24 April 1916: The First World War Museum, Kobarid.

spirit' he was always 'at home, although so far away from home'.[31] Yet there were days, asserted Ferdo Kozak, when it was impossible to think about anyone except oneself, and when the soldier was bound into a world that was absolutely alien to the 'previous' one, for the gulf between the two appeared unbridgeable.[32] However, even the feeling of alienation could not have come about without the soldiers' sharpened ability to reason, which was (at least for some individuals) synonymous with the will to live. In addition, pious devotions on the front proved to have an indispensable function, in that they were able to bind the two seemingly incompatible realities, and to soothe the sufferers' anguish.

The soldiers' letters and postcards sent home from different theatres of war display a remarkable level of depth prompted by realization of the frailty and brevity of human lives. Faith in God's help, or a hope that there was a God who would save the fighting men at moments of extreme fatigue and pressure during the onslaught, permeated many of the writings that the families received from their loved ones on the front. In numerous last letters that the soldiers sent home they wrote that in battle they readily submitted themselves to God; in the middle of 'inexplicable suffering' they thought that only Christ and the Virgin Mary could deliver them from death. Ivan Tratnjek, a landowner from Lipovci, who in 1914 had departed with the 15th Honved infantry regiment, wrote to his family, for the last time, from the Russian front: 'The blessed Virgin will help us, you at home, and me in this great trial!'[33] The recruits also disclosed that they felt safe through prayers said for them at home, and hoped that the guardian angels and saints would not abandon those in need of comfort. 'I have hope to see you and our children again, because your prayer will help', recorded Anton Ažman in a letter to his wife.[34] In home parishes clergymen attempted to sustain the ardour of faith by tirelessly organizing prayers of the rosary, Stations of the Cross, and processions to the sanctuaries closest to home, dedicated to the men's safe return home.

One of the few things that the soldiers could be certain of was that after the unbearable moments had passed, only dreariness remained. 'There has not been a day of happiness for me ever since I left home,

---
[31] See Janez Jereb, *Odmevi prve svetovne vojne v župniji Škocjan pri Turaki* (Župnijski urad, 2006), 40. The letter is dated 23 Dec. 1914.   [32] Kozak, 'Dialog v zaledju', 36.
[33] PAM, Okrajno sodišče Maribor, 643, T 115/22. The card is dated 5 Apr. 1915.
[34] Anton Ažman, letter of 16 June 1916: The First World War Museum, Kobarid.

only much fear and suffering',[35] is merely one of the many lines epitomizing the feeling of disillusionment as well as the desire for peace which was the men's greatest hope in the darkest hours of their existence. The sombre mood provided the setting in which the war could be perceived as a profound Good Friday. In the second year of the war, the Catholic daily *Slovenec* unambiguously asserted: 'Also for us in Austria Easter Sunday has to come. In God we trust. In the firm union with our Christian faith, may God seal faith in the victory of our arms, honourable peace, and resurrection of our—at present still suffering and crucified—homeland.'[36] Suffering and the death of love on the cross could easily be allegorically identified with the crucifixion of men's souls to sanctify their lives. In this vein Franc Rueh drew the association between the sufferings of Christ and his three years of service in the army as a reserve lieutenant in the 17th regiment, wondering whether he would ever experience the light of Easter, which would come only after the horrible punishment that was befalling mankind.[37]

A study of literature read at the front is equally revealing of the ways in which soldiers tried to grasp their own selves, along with their emotions and suffering. Authors whom the soldiers—obviously the educated ones, who were therefore more likely to be officers than ordinary privates—regularly put on their reading list included Fyodor Dostoevsky, Leo Tolstoy, Arthur Schopenhauer, Henrik Ibsen, and a number of renowned Slovenian authors, such as Josip Jurčič, Simon Gregorčič, Ivan Cankar, Oton Župančič, and Vladimir Levstik. The men in the field regarded reading as a necessary mental exercise to help them release their extreme tension by (momentarily) distancing themselves from the reality of warfare, and not always relying on Catholic authors, as the reading list shows. Shortly before he was mobilized in September 1914, Juš Kozak wrote to his brother that upon immersing himself in the works of Tolstoy and Dostoevsky he finally understood the greatness of Christianity, which was revealed to him through Dostoevsky's philosophy of suffering—that, despite the agony, it was possible to retain an ability to love the entire world as it was.[38]

* * *

[35] Ibid.
[36] *Slovenec*, 4 Apr. 1915.
[37] See Franc Rueh, *Moj dnevnik 1915–1918* (Ljubljana, 1999), 115.
[38] NUK/R, MS 1/62, J. Kozak, letter dated 7 Sept. 1914.

Although Catholic authors tried to boost the men's morale by publishing articles such as those entitled 'comforting letters to wounded soldiers', thus assisting the efforts of the military chaplains in the field, the Habsburg Empire ultimately failed to inspire the army with a sense of higher purpose, a failure that became irreversible when national patriotism came to be regarded as an absolute moral imperative in the latter half of the war. Eventually, nationalism trumped religious faith when looking for a source of inspiration to give the war an acceptable meaning.

The words of young Cvelbar appear very significant in this context. He recorded in his diary: 'Life without suffering is no life. But the worst thing is having to beat your eyes and heart against your conviction.'[39] Similarly, Franc Arnejc, who in 1914 was drafted in his native Carinthia, wrote thoughtfully on receiving news of Franz Joseph's death in November 1916 that he had almost entirely lost his love for the Austro-Hungarian homeland: 'I see myself as a forced soldier, as I am not for the emperor and Austria, given that everywhere they treat us [Slovenians] with injustice.'[40] These statements are particularly meaningful because they reveal fermenting national frictions in the Danube monarchy that later (in conjunction with war-weariness and starvation in the interior) would prove sufficiently strong to bring the Empire to an end.

The Catholic Church in the Slovenian lands asserted its support for the Habsburg throne by taking a decisive role in igniting the people's patriotic fervour and readiness to fight for the 'peace-loving emperor', while interpreting the war against the Entente as essentially just. The enlisted men were to go to war gladly—with unwavering faith in victory under heavenly protection—for the Empire, which was being 'viciously' attacked by the unspecified but ungodly enemy with the intention of destroying the Danube monarchy (because it was Catholic). From the perspective of the Church, the combatants' physical strength depended on their moral qualities, which were an essential requirement if they were to fight boldly and virtuously. Moreover, death in the field was shown as honourable in that it opened the gates to heaven to all who, through their military service, had been awarded the 'crown of

[39] NUK/R, MS 1774, 'Diary', 10 Apr. 1916.
[40] Franc Arnejc, *Od Dnestra do Piave: spomini iz prve svetovne vojne* (Klagenfurt, 1970), 63.

martyrdom' and so had taken their place mong the ranks of soldier saints.[41]

Slovenian soldiers saw themselves as sacrificial victims—a view that was perhaps best reflected in their constant reference to the 'resurrection' that would proceed from their perception of physical (and mental) destruction—but spoke of the war as a repugnant event and an index of the monarchy's weakness rather than its ardently supported vigour. A simple, yet succinct, remark made by one of the soldiers—'if the state cannot feed its army, it should not wage war'[42]—highlights the monarchy's growing internal dilemma, exposing it as a decaying structure ready to collapse rather than showing it as a vigorous organism. On the existential level, their faith helped to sustain them in the face of the horrors they witnessed on the front—at least those who, in the records they left behind, expressed a hope for God's protection—because at the front there was no other shield to protect them from the deadly splinters of stone and steel. The central thought in the soldiers' records was an incessant longing for peace and life that most radically brought forth the feelings of national patriotism (rather than patriotism for the state), once Italy entered the war on the side of the Entente in May 1915. Only with reference to this sentiment was Lieutenant Albin Mlakar able to remark in his war diary how sweet the awareness of defending his own country had become.[43] The meaning of sacrifice undoubtedly gained significance in campaigns against the 'hideous and faith-breaking' Italian enemy, an allusion to the treason of Catholic Italy encroaching upon Slovenia, a fellow Catholic land.

As the war continued, the rhetoric of the 'sweetness of death for country' lost its meaning and gave way to the increasingly powerful currents of nationalism sweeping across Austria-Hungary, thus paving the way for the inevitable. The Danube monarchy failed to produce an alternative political vision for a brighter future, or convincing (and durable) content for the empty concepts of emperor and multinational 'fatherland'. This became manifest when the Austrian

---

[41] The quoted expressions in this paragraph are phrases typical of Catholic war propaganda.

[42] I. Lučić, 'Na soški fronti: spomini iz let 1915–18', in *Glasnik slovenske matice 1–2* (Ljubljana, 1998), 49.

[43] Albin Mlakar, *Dnevnik 1914–1918* (Kobarid, 1995), 149. Mlakar was one of the most renowned Slovenian officers in the Habsburg army and fought first on the Eastern Front and then on the Isonzo front. He was awarded the Imperial Order of the Iron Crown and gold medal for bravery.

parliament reconvened in 1917, only to echo the nationalist 'malady' of the century and the ensuing (fatal) political fragmentation of the state. By that point the Yugoslav idea had won the hearts and minds of the Slovenian soldiers and had turned into a radical new creed. The leading Slovenian politicians who, in their ardent belief in Yugoslavia, were prepared to break with the old dynastic past while securing for themselves the crucial support of the Catholic Church fanned popular enthusiasm for the formation of a Yugoslav state under the Habsburg sceptre. The military and social collapse of the Habsburg Empire in 1918 ultimately prompted the rise of the State of Slovenes, Serbs, and Croats, the making of which was accompanied by irrational expectations. At least at first glance it seemed that the 'endless suffering of mankind' had earned for the people 'rebirth and resurrection'.

The high hopes of the Slovenian people, who found themselves politically and existentially divided between the newly redrawn borders of Austria in the north and Italy in the west, were soon to be shattered in the immediate postwar era. In 1929 the Kingdom of Yugoslavia yielded to the dictatorial power of the (Serbian) king that led to the dissolution of all political parties in the country. Extreme nationalist and racist ideologies swept across the Old Continent. The much-desired, and yet deceptive, post-Versailles peace ironically ushered in decades of fresh totalitarian terror and brought about an unprecedented transformation of European lives.

In the Austro-Hungarian war, religion had a double function: on the one hand, it was a propaganda tool in that Catholicism was equated with the Empire and the emperor; at the personal level, on the other, it gave hope for survival and meaning to death through transcendence. While this worked for certain groups and for the first half of the war, eventually the political and religious authorities failed to preserve Catholic loyalty to the state and thus created a void which could be filled with nationalism.

6

The Thin White Line: Experience and Memory of the Alpine Front in the First World War

ROBERTA PERGHER

I

On 23 May 1915 Italy declared war on its allies, Germany and Austria-Hungary. After the two Central Powers had deliberately started military action against Serbia and the Entente powers in the preceding summer, Italy initially maintained a state of neutrality, claiming that through their aggressive stance, its associates had forfeited the alliance's obligation of mutual military support. Italy, however, was not going to stand on the sidelines of what had quickly turned into a world conflict. In a war that promised to redraw the map of the world, Italy saw an opportunity to gain 'irredentist' territories in the north and north-east as well as colonies in Africa. Negotiations with both belligerent sides ensued, and lured by the more substantial promises of the Allied powers, Italy joined them in a war that had already claimed lives in the millions. Austria, having sustained great losses against Russia and embattled in a difficult war against Serbia, saw itself forced to open a third front, one that stretched over 600 kilometres from the Italian–Swiss border to the Adriatic Sea north of Trieste, mostly through inaccessible, mountainous regions. The 'thin white line' in my title refers to the thinly stretched Austrian forces arrayed along snow- and ice-covered peaks and the white karst mountains of the eastern Alps, a force hastily dispatched to keep their 'turncoat' ally at bay.[1]

In spite of the massive loss of life and material, the war between Italy and Austria was a sideshow in the Great War, and has remained one in the war's overall narrative. For the Austrians, it was in the

---

[1] The expression 'thin white line' borrows and modifies the terminology of a 'thin red line', which denotes any thinly spread military unit holding firm against attack. I will come back to this figure of speech later in the essay.

battles against Russia and Serbia that the conflict was decided and the end of the Empire sealed. In Italy's case, it is true, this was no sideshow, and there is a massive national historiography on the war—as the first major and victorious conflict of the recently unified country and as a war that both united and divided the country, leading to near-revolution and the rise of Fascism. But elsewhere, this front line is perhaps most famously immortalized in Ernest Hemingway's *A Farewell to Arms*, rather than the work of historians. The love story between the American ambulance driver Frederic and the British nurse Catherine includes a famous scene in which Frederic witnesses the staggering defeat and precipitous retreat of the Italian army at Caporetto, a defeat still today etched in Italian public memory as a moment of utter national dissolution. But the front between Italy and Austria-Hungary was not restricted to the famous battles along the Isonzo and Piave rivers. The most challenging and probably the most scenic sector was further west, cutting through the Austrian crownland of Tyrol. It was certainly here that the demands placed on the participants by terrain, altitude, and weather were at their most intense.

This essay focuses on that sideshow of a sideshow: the Tyrolean front line, the western sector of the Alpine front, which stretched from the Ortler massif in the east, near the Swiss border, to the Sexten peaks in the west. It ran through some extraordinarily challenging terrain, with soldiers perched on cliffs 10,000 feet above sea level and hiding in tunnels dug into glaciers. The spectacular but taxing mountain setting and the use of modern artillery raise a series of compelling questions about the modern battlefield 'experience'. This essay draws on research for a larger project on nationalism, nature, and technology on the Tyrolean front in the First World War, which explores how mechanized trench warfare was planned, fought, endured, and remembered in the high mountains of the Alps, on both the Italian and the Austrian side. While the overall project aims at a parallel, integrated analysis of the Austro-Italian war, this essay will focus on the Austrian side of the story, exploring specifically the tensions between the experience of the front as recorded in war diaries and the way in which the war has been subsequently commemorated. The 'Italian' side, however, will not be entirely absent, as several of the diaries consulted were written by Italian-speaking soldiers who fought for the Austrian monarchy. After some methodological reflections about soldiers' 'experience' on the battlefront, I will present some initial findings from Austrian war diaries from the Tyrolean front. These findings were so at odds with the prevailing regional accounts of the war on this front that they led me to analyse the memory politics of the conflict over the course of the last century. The essay concludes with a discussion of the tension between front experience on the one hand, and the meanings and narratives that emerge from public commemoration on the other.

II

If the front between Italy and Austria has been eclipsed by other fronts and confrontations, then this is all the more true of the mountainous western sector. In part, this is a legitimate reflection of the Tyrolean front's relatively limited strategic significance.[2] Yet given the many facets of the First World War that have garnered attention, it is still surprising how slow historians have been to address the particularities of the front line amidst cliffs and glaciers, even within the nations most directly involved. The histories of the war, and the principal historiographical questions and interpretations all revolve around interpretations of what happened on the eastern sector of the front for Italy and on the Russian and Serbian fronts for Austria.[3] No doubt because of this, the accounts written about the Ortler and Dolomites campaigns have remained largely untouched by the main currents of historiographical debate about the war.[4] They tend to be written for a popular regional readership, and typically

---

[2] With the exception of one major offensive on either side, both Austria and Italy treated the conflict in the western sector mainly as a defensive campaign. In May 1916 the Austrians launched an offensive, nicknamed 'Strafexpedition' ('punitive operation'), near Asiago. The Italians responded the following year, in June 1917, with the Battle of Ortigara. Neither operation brought about major gains.

[3] Austrian public memory has, however, continuously afforded this front particular significance, as it allowed a narrative of heroic and successful military defence. See Werner Suppanz, 'Die italienische Front im österreichischen kollektiven Gedächtnis', in Nicola Labanca und Oswald Überegger (eds.), *Krieg in den Alpen: Österreich-Ungarn und Italien im Ersten Weltkrieg (1914–1918)* (Vienna, 2015), 307–30.

[4] Great strides have been made in the last decade, spearheaded in particular by the research and co-ordination of Oswald Überegger. See Labanca und Überegger (eds.), *Krieg in den Alpen*; Hermann Kuprian and Oswald Überegger (eds.), *Katastrophenjahre: Der Erste Weltkrieg und Tirol* (Innsbruck, 2014); and Hermann Kuprian and Oswald Überegger (eds.), *Der Erste Weltkrieg im Alpenraum: Erfahrung, Deutung, Erinnerung* (Innsbruck, 2006). See also the collection of primary sources in Oswald Überegger, *Heimatfronten: Dokumente zur Erfahrungsgeschichte der Tiroler Kriegsgesellschaft im Ersten Weltkrieg*, 2 vols. (Innsbruck, 2006).

combine beautiful illustrations with a rather old-fashioned patriotic, impressionistic, and anecdotal narrative.[5] The centennial has seen a resurgence of such works, celebrating military endeavours and feats of individual heroism, and uncritically reproducing the same few testimonies by high-ranking officers, often without commentary or broader contextualization. To be fair, however, even the most assiduous local historian will not find many ego documents to work with. In comparison with other theatres of battle there is a striking lack of either published or archival testimony, especially when it comes to the Austrian side.[6] And yet this remarkable front raises so many intriguing questions about the experience of war.

Begun after millions had already lost their lives in the killing fields of the Western and Eastern Fronts, the Alpine war reproduced the trappings of modern warfare—trenches and technology—but its natural environment presented its own challenges and, at times, provided the backdrop for feats of individual heroism. This prompts us to ask how the combatants on this front understood the relationships between technology and nature, and between ingenuity and endurance. The terrain called for particular strategies, not only in attack and defence, but also in perseverance. Armies had come through those valleys over the centuries, forts had historically been constructed to cut off valleys and control plateaux, but never before had fighting taken place on peaks and glaciers, or continued in the same place for years.

Apart from the spectacular topography, what makes the Tyrolean front particularly intriguing is the regional population's social and ethnic composition. Austria's crownland Tyrol was inhabited by

[5] See e.g. Michael Wachtler and Andrea De Bernardin, *Die Stadt im Eis: Der Erste Weltkrieg im Innern der Gletscher* (Bolzano, 2009); Sebastian Marseiler, Udo Bernhart, and Franz Josef Haller, *Zeit im Eis* (Bolzano, 1996); Gunther Langes, *Die Front in Fels und Eis: Der Weltkrieg 1915–1918 im Hochgebirge* (1932), 4th rev. edn. (Bolzano, 1972).

[6] During the last decade a few new and genuine diaries have appeared in print: Josef Wegl, *Das Kriegstagebuch des Josef Wegl: Ein Niederösterreicher an der Dolomitenfront 1915/18* (Salzburg, 2015); Isabelle Brandauer, '*Der Krieg kennt kein Erbarmen': Die Tagebücher des Kaiserschützen Erich Mayr (1913–1920)* (Innsbruck, 2013); Carla Cordin, *Ettore Cordin: Das Tagebuch eines k. u. k. Soldaten im Ersten Weltkrieg. Edition und Analyse* (Frankfurt a.M., 2012); Johann Mittermaier, *Der Schrecken des Krieges: Die Erinnerungen eines Südtiroler Kaiserjägers aus dem 1. Weltkrieg* (Vahrn, 2005); Fridolin Tschugmell, '*Während der Messe sangen die Granaten': Kriegstagebuch 1915–1918 Dolomiten/Südtirol* (Schaan, 2004); Matthias Ladurner-Parthanes, *Kriegstagebuch eines Kaiserjägers: Nach dem Originalmanuskript bearbeitet von Josef Rampold* (Bolzano, 1996). The efforts of the Museo Storico Italiano della Guerra in Rovereto, which has published several soldier diaries as well as ego documents of civilians, have been commendable.

German, Ladin, and Italian speakers, the latter populating Tyrol's southernmost part, the Trentino. Some of the Italian-speaking Tyroleans defected and fought for Italy, but most fought loyally for the Kaiser, though they were often mistrusted and mistreated by their commanding officers and comrades.[7] There were, moreover, troops from all corners of the Empire employed on this front, and a good number of prisoners of war as well. And even though many locations were remote, there were people living there who had to be evacuated, not only because of the danger of artillery fire, but also because they were deemed untrustworthy by either side.[8] Despite the various regional accounts that have been written, or rather in part because they have so narrowly targeted particular regional and language publics, we have as yet little idea of the degree to which the ethnic and linguistic fault lines that criss-crossed this front are reflected in the ego documents of the combatants.

As already mentioned, the main confrontation between the two former allies unfolded further east, along the Isonzo river. The marginal status of the Tyrolean front was clear to the soldiers themselves, who knew that more deadly assignments were to be had on either the Eastern Fronts against Serbia and Russia or against the Italians in one of the notorious battles of the Isonzo. They must also have known of the carnage on the Western Front. How, then, did they assess their specific assignment on the Tyrolean front, and also more broadly their role in a worldwide conflict? And how might their sense-making have differed from that of contemporaries on the Western or the Eastern Fronts? The ego documents of the Tyrolean front offer an opportunity to ask how distinctive soldiers' perceptions were here, or whether the shared fate of a mechanized, industrialized war in which soldiers were stripped of agency, possibly

---

[7] See Quinto Antonelli, *I dimenticati della Grande Guerra: la memoria dei combattenti trentini (1914–1920)* (Trento, 2008); and Gianluigi Fait (ed.), *Sui Campi di Galizia (1914–1917): gli italiani d'Austria e il fronte orientale. Uomini, popoli, culture, nella guerra europea* (Rovereto, 1998).

[8] Claudio Ambrosi, *Vite internate: Katzenau, 1915–1917* (Trento, 2008); Matteo Ermacora, 'Le donne internate in Italia durante la Grande Guerra: esperienze, scritture e memorie', *Deportate, esuli, profughe*, 7 (2007), 1–32; Giovanna Procacci, 'L'internamento di civili in Italia durante la prima guerra mondiale: normativa e conflitti di competenza', *Deportate, esuli, profughe*, 5/6 (2006), 33–66; and Mario Eichta, *Braunau-Katzenau-Mitterndorf 1915–1918/Il ricordo dei profughi e degli internati del Trentino. Braunau-Katzenau-Mitterndorf 1915–1918: Erinnerung an die Flüchtlinge und Internierten des Trentino* (Cremona, 1999).

to a greater extent than in any previous or subsequent conflict, led the troops in different theatres to experience the war in similar ways.[9]

Beyond its physical, technical, and demographic characteristics, the front has one other claim on our attention, namely, that after the war it ceased to mark the boundary between two powers. Thanks to postwar territorial grants in Paris, Italy after 1918 would extend well north beyond the former front line, with the result that former combatants on both sides were now living side by side. This in turn raises intriguing questions about the relationship between wartime experience and postwar memory, one of the core issues in my enquiry.

Experience itself, particularly as revealed through ego documents and testimony, is a complex and contested category for historians. As the discursive framework of the cultural turn has begun to lose its appeal, 'experience' is again being treated as a category that captures something beyond the text. At the same time, experience is now widely understood to involve much more than momentary perceptions of a particular event. Instead, it is seen as encompassing a person's past knowledge, his contemporary stance, but also his view of the future, and his relation to the potential reader, be it only his imagined self.[10] The use of experience as an analytical category hinges on the understanding that once we 'experience' something, our articulated or narrated experience necessarily contains contextualization, abstraction, interpretation. In other words, what we perceive or undergo becomes 'experience' only through thinking, telling, sharing, writing, reading, and remembering.[11]

Built into this understanding of experience is thus the dimension of memory. There is, however, a certain ambiguity in the way in which we conceptualize the relationship. On the one hand, the discussion above suggests that 'experience' is always, in fact, remembered experience. There is no experience without memory. On the other hand, a staple theme of recent writing about the experience of war is the sharp contrast between the contemporary

---

[9] On the fault lines and new mentalities in the context of the Austro-Italian war see the classic work by Antonio Gibelli, *L'officina della guerra: la Grande Guerra e le trasformazioni del mondo mentale* (Turin, 1991).

[10] For an early attempt at rescuing the concept of 'experience' from the straitjacket of 'discourse' see Kathleen Canning, 'Feminist History after the Linguistic Turn: Historicizing Discourse and Experience', *Signs: Journal of Women in Culture and Society*, 19/2 (1994), 368–404.

[11] Leonard V. Smith, 'Introduction', in id., *The Embattled Self: French Soldiers' Testimony of the Great War* (Ithaca, NY, 2007), 1–19.

experience of war and its later remembering and commemoration. This ambiguity—does experience incorporate memory or does it stand in opposition to it?—provides the starting point for the present piece. Even a cursory glance at First World War diaries makes it clear that of the verbs that provide the mechanisms by which experience takes shape and becomes communicable (thinking, telling, sharing, writing, reading, and remembering), it is the last one, 'remembering', that is particularly significant here. Even allowing for the fact that diaries are never written in the 'now', diaries of the First World War rarely have the immediacy we associate with personal diaries written under 'normal' circumstances.[12] When intended for publication, they were always reworked. Even when they were not meant to be published, but were kept for family use, their authors often revised them after the war. In that sense we can talk of these diaries as containing 'experience fit for memory'. And yet, the diaries found so far for this project are strikingly at odds with the public narrative of the war that has been enshrined in the region.

The general proposition that changing national and international constellations cause past conflicts to be remembered in new ways is perhaps not remarkable. And yet the production of narratives surrounding Tyrol's involvement in the war raises an important aspect of this process that has not yet received the attention it deserves. While we are, of course, aware that the First World War was a war between empires, one, indeed, that saw the collapse of four venerable imperial monarchies, we have not tended to reflect so much on the relationship between the imperial contexts in which world war ensued, and the post-imperial ones in which it was remembered. In the case of Tyrol this relationship is complex and intriguing, evolving over several decades.

III

With these considerations in mind, this section offers a foray into First World War diaries from the Tyrolean front. As expected, diaries and memoirs provide invaluable insights into Austrian soldiers' perceptions of nature, mountaineering, and technological warfare in this extremely harsh environment. For the men it was a struggle as much against nature as against the enemy. Officers wrote of the

[12] Robert A. Fothergill, *Private Chronicles: A Study of English Diaries* (Oxford, 1974).

face-off with nature—storms, avalanches, rock falls, bitter cold—as a glorious, ennobling fight. Often, in fact, the fight against the forces of nature stood in for a non-existent fight against the enemy. Posted at 3860 m on the peak of the Königspitze, Landeschützen Lieutenant Hannes Schindler, in charge of a special mountaineering unit, recorded in his diary a lightning strike on the soldiers' quarters.[13] 'Have we been blown up? . . . Shouting everywhere, a seething mass of people. . . . The enemy—nowhere.' Schindler noted that the injured were quickly taken care of, the fire extinguished, the men returned to their posts, 'and life, which seemed interrupted, went on'.[14] Particularly remarkable are the juxtapositions between magnificent natural spectacle and merciless battle in memoirs published in the 1930s. Here is an excerpt from Lieutenant Josef Pölzleitner, who served with the Landsturm reserves: 'The Italian fusillade grows ever weaker. Finally it is completely extinguished. The enemy is annihilated. The landscape shines wondrously in the rising sun, which radiates over a chaos of motionless corpses. Those still alive are left to the mercy of their inescapable fate.'[15]

The officers' valiant and exalted tone, however, is not the only voice left behind by the conflict; a different mood pervades the few surviving narratives from common soldiers, men who had toiled in farms and workplaces at the feet of those very mountains. In their accounts, too, the struggle against the forces of nature was keenly felt, but it was nothing but a burden, a calamity. Approximating Pölzleitner's juxtaposition, yet striking an entirely different tone and suggesting a more menacing relationship between nature and death, Landesschützen reservist Erich Mayr wrote: 'The mountains today stood and blazed in the red evening light; now the pale full moon shines over them. Behind them lurk a thousand deaths.'[16] And Kaiserjäger recruit Johann Mittermaier, who was hastily trained as a reserve officer, reminisced: 'To be sure, in winter I had often looked up to the snow-covered mountains. But never could I have dreamt that holding out in these most violent winter storms would be so unbearable.'[17] We thus have a first hint of differences in perception between the Alpine enthusiasts, often bourgeois or

[13] The various Austrian military units will be briefly introduced in the next section.
[14] Cited in Langes, *Die Front in Fels und Eis*, 172.
[15] Josef Pölzleitner, *Berge wurden Burgen: Erzählungen eines Frontkämpfers* (Salzburg, 1934), 80.
[16] Brandauer, 'Der Krieg kennt kein Erbarmen', 371, entry for 20 Aug. 1918.
[17] Mittermaier, *Der Schrecken des Krieges*, 32.

upper class, and those, often the poorer foot soldiers, who did not revel in the challenge of conquering raw nature—a discrepancy that undoubtedly calls for more research.

Officers, moreover, wrote of the individual feats of courage and ingenuity that could trick the enemy and bring about a small victory, such as the occupation of a mountain top or pass, which carried disproportionate meaning on either side. Perhaps more than similar accounts from the Western Front, which are so often entrenched in horror, pity, and folly (though there are significant national as well as temporal differences), we find here a surviving memory that hinged on notions of individual bravery and sacrifice. In a memoir allegedly based on his lost diary, Major-General Freiherr von Lempruch wrote: 'Sangfroid and the ability to make quick, independent decisions under every circumstance are attributes of particular importance in the Alpine war. The Alpine war is thus a battle of individualities, not of masses!'[18] In a 1917 publication Lieutenant Walter Schmidkunz commented: 'The mountain soldier is a mixture of American Indian, mercenary, highwayman, hunter, and pirate, with a drop of ultra-modern sportsman's and engineer's blood thrown in. The mountains inhibit almost any deployment of mass troops; here guerrilla warfare, the tournament between man and man, celebrates its triumphs; here all personal manly virtues come to the fore.'[19]

Again, this kind of narrative tends to differ from the accounts of common soldiers, who did not seem interested in participating in or recording acts of bravery. The dominant notes in their diaries are the confusion of battle, the courage to charge ahead because everyone else did, the writers' sense of duty, and their trust in god and family. Here is the authentic tone of the grunt from Johann Mittermaier: 'Gufler, eight men, and I were supposed to take the peak in broad daylight, without rifles and without a preparatory artillery bombardment. The obedience ingrained in us during training forced us to take on this utterly hopeless endeavour.'[20] 'In the early morning the most terrible thing awaited us: the attack. . . .

---

[18] From the diary of Major-General Freiherr von Lempruch, published in Helmut Golowitsch (ed.), *Ortlerkämpfe 1915 1918: Der König der Deutschen Alpen und seine Helden. Von Generalmajor Freiherrn von Lempruch ergänzt durch historische Beiträge* (Nuremberg, 2005), 114.

[19] Walter Schmidkunz, *Der Kampf über den Gletschern: Ein Buch von der Alpenfront* (Munich, 1917; repr. Erfurt, 1934), 126–7.

[20] Mittermaier, *Der Schrecken des Krieges*, 38.

The grey fog weighed heavily on our souls.'[21] As he pondered death in what seemed like another suicide mission, he wrote: 'If I have to die, then all the same as a soldier staunchly faithful to the Kaiser. So that my father can proclaim: My son Johann was killed in action, on the front line, for God, Kaiser, and fatherland.' Though he also added: 'But this is not what my father wanted.'[22]

This is not to say that the distinctions of tone always followed those of class or rank. Combatants from different walks of life expressed pride in fulfilling their duty and holding on to their faith, and officers' accounts were not always characterized by the same heroic, martial tone. In fact, many espoused good old bourgeois values.[23] It was those values of family and Tyrolean and imperial loyalty that inspired them to acts of valour, at least if their written accounts are to be believed; it is harder to say whether these were their actual motivations.

As important as nature and individual heroism in colouring war narratives was the power of technology. This was mechanized warfare, with huge artillery being hauled up onto mountain tops. Soldiers wrote about the barrage of fire, the technology of cableways, and the use of aeroplanes—but also about the limitations of their resources. Many complained about not being given enough ammunition, for example. Helmets, too, were in short supply; and soldiers also complained about not having the latest firearms. 'The Italian artillery pounded us without respite, while I saw little and heard even less from ours. We were generally short of artillery all the time', wrote one paramedic.[24]

What is striking in these accounts is that the soldiers did not write about the nature of the war as if they were taken by surprise, unaware of the realities of mechanized warfare. There are, true enough, signs that they were traumatized by the ongoing artillery barrage, shrapnel fire, and so on. Standschützen volunteer Karl Mayr wrote

---

[21] Ibid. 43.
[22] Ibid. 40.
[23] For a similar observation on the Italian side see Marco Mondini, 'The Construction of a Masculine Warrior Ideal in the Italian Narratives of the First World War, 1915–68', *Contemporary European History*, 23/3 (Aug. 2014), 307–27; and, in particular, Lorenzo Benadusi, '*Borghesi* in Uniform: Masculinity, Militarism, and the Brutalization of Politics from the First World War to the Rise of Fascism', in Giulia Albanese and Roberta Pergher (eds.), *In the Society of Fascists: Acclamation, Acquiescence and Agency* (New York, 2012), 29–48.
[24] Mittermaier, *Der Schrecken des Krieges*, 28.

of 'fits of madness' among his fellow soldiers.[25] Sometimes soldiers did some explaining, as if they wanted to introduce the weapons used to someone entirely unfamiliar with them: 'Close by stands the mortar. "Nikita" is the name of the beast. This is no ordinary piece of artillery. It is an artful machine. . . . Every shot costs a little fortune and is precisely recorded.'[26] And some diarists expressed their interest in the weaponry: 'The artillery fires diligently the entire day. It was deafening. I went over there and had the gunners explain all sorts of things to me about these cannons.'[27] The same diarist later on pondered: 'Maybe afterwards tourists will visit this front and see what can still be seen from the war. One contemplates all sorts of things when the day is long and the front is quiet in the current deep, deep snow.'[28] But at the same time, soldiers did not express bewilderment about the face of mechanized war. On the contrary, they gave every appearance of having expected that this is what war would be like. Of course, it might be that they were just describing in a matter-of-fact way what they saw, but still, it is a question that invites further investigation, and a comparative perspective in regard to soldiers on other fronts and their perceptions of military technology.

These remarks are offered here as examples of the kinds of questions that can be posed to the diaries, and the sorts of answers they yield. The diaries certainly revealed soldiers' 'Eigen-Sinn' in the classic meaning of the term, in that we see the writers trying to make sense of the war around them and asking what it meant for their own lives to be in the thick of it.[29] But as I was exploring the combatants' war experience and their narratives of duty, faith, heroism, tragedy, and so forth, what struck me was what the diarists did not say. What was missing was what I had come to expect as the core of soldiers' shared self-understanding on the Tyrolean front. The search for their 'experience' thus led me to tangle with the politics of memory.

---

[25] Michael Wachtler, *Wir schließen Frieden: Der achtzehnjährige Standschütze Karl Mayr und sein Tagebuch des guten Herzens* (Bolzano, 2004), 43.
[26] Wegl, *Das Kriegstagebuch*, 39.
[27] Tschugmell, '*Während der Messe sangen die Granaten*', 73.
[28] Ibid. 117.
[29] For a discussion of 'Eigen-Sinn' see Alf Lüdtke, *Eigen-Sinn: Fabrikalltag, Arbeitererfahrungen und Politik vom Kaiserreich bis in den Faschismus* (Hamburg, 1993). See also Oskar Negt and Alexander Kluge, *Geschichte und Eigensinn* (Frankfurt a.M., 1981), 766.

IV

On the Austrian side, including the German-speaking Tyrol annexed by Italy after the war and also in parts of the annexed Italian-speaking Tyrol, the key image in popular memory of this war was that of a 'letztes Aufgebot', a 'last reserve' called up to defend the homeland against the Italian invader. This regional narrative, which I first absorbed as a schoolgirl growing up in the region in the 1980s and which is still propagated in print and public discourse today, presents the civilian Tyrolean male population as the last line of defence, and as the only resource with the necessary qualities to endure the harsh mountain environment of the Alpine front. In particular, it alludes to the fact that at the time of Italy's declaration of war in May 1915, Tyrol had been deprived of its mainline troops, dispatched to fight on the Eastern Front a year earlier, and had instead to fall back on reservists, volunteers, and civilians to hold the line.

In order to understand this narrative, it is necessary to review, in the broadest brushstrokes, the dual monarchy's military formations and their deployment on the Italian front.[30] Tyrolean men fulfilled their regular military service either in the Landesschützen, which were part of the Austrian Landwehr (which had its equivalent in the Hungarian Honvéd), or the Kaiserjäger, which belonged to the overarching imperial army of Austria-Hungary. Landesschützen and Kaiserjäger were dispatched in 1914 to the Eastern Front, where they sustained heavy losses against Russia and Serbia.

But the monarchy could count on another unit in case more men were needed in the war effort: the Standschützen, which comprised the members of local shooting clubs. Some Standschützen were already called up in 1914 as part of the Landsturm, the reserves that complemented the Landesschützen and Kaiserjäger regiments in wartime. But since 1887 the Standschützen themselves were considered integral to the defence of the crownland.[31] Those who had not been enlisted in 1914 because of their age or other reasons that had rendered them unfit for service were called to arms in spring 1915,

---

[30] See Christa Hämmerle, 'Opferhelden? Zur Geschichte der k. u. k. Soldaten an der Südwestfront', in Labanca und Überegger (eds.), *Krieg in den Alpen*, 155–80.

[31] Wolfgang Joly, *Standschützen: Die Tiroler und Vorarlberger k. k. Standschützen-Formationen im Ersten Weltkrieg. Organisation und Einsatz* (Innsbruck, 1998).

when an Italian attack was imminent. Before the Landesschützen and Kaiserjäger on the Eastern Front were sent back to shore up the defence of the Tyrolean homeland in the autumn of 1915, the Standschützen defended the front. They certainly played an essential role in the first few months after Italy's declaration of war, though the Italian delay in launching any major attack on the Tyrolean front rendered their task much more manageable. They continued their service in the war for the next three years, but their significance in direct military action became less critical. They served under a commander of their own choosing, with men of the same village or town grouped into companies; and their relationship to the regular troops was not always easy, as they were considered rough and unprepared.

The extraordinary circumstances of the region under attack, and with its men decimated on other battlefields, engendered a narrative of Tyrolean men rising themselves, of their own initiative, to defend their homeland. This image of a 'last reserve' was not new; on the contrary, it already had a powerful hold on popular memory in the form of the tragic story of the Tyrol in the Napoleonic Wars. The Tyrolean troops' heroic stand in 1809 had been immortalized by the renowned regional artist Franz Defregger in a couple of paintings from the 1870s and 1880s entitled *Das letzte Aufgebot*. In the case of the First World War, the image conveyed not just a heroic commitment to make the ultimate sacrifice for the homeland, but also a whiff of betrayal by a modernizing Empire whose interests lay elsewhere. In fact, the deployment of Tyrolean soldiers in distant lands was a novelty in the long history of Tyrolean military service for the Empire. Since 1511, the County of Tyrol had held a privileged position within the Empire whereby its men were called to arms only to defend the county itself. This agreement was revised in the second half of nineteenth century, with the introduction of standardized military service across the Empire and a broader institutional and administrative reorganization of the monarchy.

The narrative of a hastily assembled army whose men held the line against all odds is familiar from other wars. For Britain, the equivalent of the 'letztes Aufgebot' was the 'thin red line' of the red-coated 93rd regiment of the British Sutherland Highlanders in the 1854 Battle of Balaklava in the Crimean War. In this battle, Highlanders in red uniforms set up a line two men deep, forming a 'thin red line' against the advancing enemy, and, although hopelessly outnumbered, were able to beat the charging Russian cavalry. This image, too, found artistic expression in a painting, this time Robert Gibb's 1881 canvas *The Thin Red Line*, and Rudyard Kipling further memorialized the image in his 1890 poem 'Tommy'. The 'thin red line' of the Battle of Balaklava became a figure of speech used for victory against all odds because of exceptional bravery, and it fits the bill of the Tyrolean case in the First World War, though there we had a 'thin white line' of brave men suspended on the white cliffs of the Dolomites and hovering in the snow and ice of the long winter months. Like the 93rd Highlanders, the Austrian troops successfully held the line in a war that was otherwise disastrous for the Austrian forces—mismanaged and increasingly unpopular. And as the 93rd had galvanized the British public, so the Alpine war lent itself to heroic depictions for an increasingly disillusioned Austrian population.

Not that I believed that such heroic depictions really reflected how things were. As a historian, I long suspected that this 'letztes Aufgebot' or 'last reserve' did not capture the essence, or even mark the contours, of the three-year conflict. The situation was dire, no doubt, but in reality the defence along the Tyrolean border did not depend on a spontaneous mobilization from below, but rested on Austria-Hungary's ability to marshal both its regional strengths and its imperial military resources. Rather than being caught off guard by Italy's war declaration, Austria had suspected for months that its former ally would enter the war against it. Moreover, the 'last reserve' did not have the significance later claimed for it. As already mentioned, Italy was slow to attack, and the Standschützen saw little fighting. Regular army troops soon arrived at the Southern Front; and even before that, the German Alpenkorps was deployed, though it did not participate in military operations initially, as Italy declared war on Germany only a few months later, on 28 August 1915. However, even if the mythic quality of the trope of the 'last reserve' was obvious, I had assumed that it was 'real' in the sense that it had resonated with people at the time. It therefore came as a surprise that soldiers in their diaries, letters, and early postwar memoirs made no reference to the notion of a last reserve, and did not in any way make use of it to encapsulate their experiences on these peaks. I like to think that my perplexity must have been similar to Leonard Smith's realization that during the war French soldiers were not telling the obvious story of victimization and tragedy that has become so thoroughly ingrained in our view of the Western Front. As Smith shows, soldiers at war did not see their experience inevitably in those terms and only came to employ the tropes of victimization and tragedy over time.[32] In my case, the analogous revelation was that soldiers in general, but even the Standschützen themselves, did not rely on the 'last reserve' narrative, although it would have greatly enhanced their contribution in the war.

Arguably the most famous Standschütze was Sepp Innerkofler, a mountain guide from Sexten who fell early in the war. After reporting for duty on 19 May 1915, he began patrolling the mountains above Sexten the next day and continued to do reconnaissance until he was killed by enemy fire on 4 July 1915. He left almost daily, albeit very brief, notes.[33] During his two months of service, he expressed neither a sense of precariousness nor one of special responsibility, as part of an army of reservists called up to defend the homeland. Then there is the example of Karl Mayr, a 17-year-old volunteer in 1915, whom we have already encountered recording fellow soldiers' 'fits of madness'.[34] Students in the Gymnasium were promised that they would be deemed to have graduated from secondary school if they signed up for service. Mayr joined a Standschützen regiment in Hall, far off the front line, and was then sent to Sexten. He initially worked on fortifications and saw his first combat in July 1915. Mayr clearly rewrote his 'diary' from hindsight, but even so, it contains no sense of belonging to a last reserve or making a last stand.[35] He did, however, mention that his unit was considered 'irregular' and 'undisciplined' (a charge he did not deny) and thus sometimes treated harshly by the regular troops and their commanders.

Innerkofler and Mayr were German speakers, but Italian speakers too were involved in the defence of the homeland.[36] As with their

[32] Smith, *The Embattled Self*.

[33] The diary 'Innerkofler, Sepp: Mein Tagebuch während des Krieges mit Italien' is published in Oswald Ebner, *Kampf um die Sextner Rotwand* (Bregenz, 1937). The diary was published in a version revised by Otto Langl, president of the Austrian Alpine Club, and the extent of his revisions is unclear. I return to the politicization of war diaries in the next section.

[34] Michael Wachtler, *Wir schließen Frieden: Der achtzehnjährige Standschütze Karl Mayr und sein Tagebuch des guten Herzens* (Bolzano, 2004).

[35] Mayr tried to publish his diary but did not succeed. It is not clear whether he revised notes from the war or directly transcribed what he had written down during the war.

[36] Federico Mazzini, 'Patriotismo condizionato: identità e patrie dei soldati trentini, 1914–1920', *Contemporanea: Rivista di Storia dell'800 e del'900*, 13/3 (2010), 457–86.

German-language counterparts, it is evident that either they or someone else often revised their personal notes in the postwar years. Standschütze Simone Morandini from Predazzo kept a diary for the first seven months of the war.[37] He served near his home, and on one occasion his wife and daughter even visited him at the front. He did not see much fighting, but worked mainly behind the lines. He wrote that he felt 'unease' about the war, but was used to following orders. Nowhere do his notes indicate that he may have seen his service as a glorious stand taken against all odds. Luigi Michielli from Cortina was already 58 when he was sent to defend the front line with his fellow Standschützen.[38] A peasant and the village vet, Michielli, a married man with four children, worked mainly on fortifications, but also saw some fighting above Cortina and on the Col di Lana before he asked to be excused from service. After some difficulties, he succeeded. He did not hold back when he confided in his diary and criticized his superiors and the politicians who had unleashed the war, but he did not present himself or his comrades as a 'last reserve'. Ettore Cordin was born in Switzerland after his father had moved there in the 1860s to find work.[39] The German-speaking Cordin from an Italian-speaking emigrant family was, however, liable for service in Tyrol. Initially deemed unfit, he was placed in the reserves and then called up in 1915. He clearly did not want to go to war; but at the same time, he did not want to shirk his duty either. He presented himself as a brave soldier, one who, armed with a sense of humour, was able to withstand the privations of war. Because he was deemed to come from the Italian-speaking southern Tyrol, he was considered untrustworthy and was later sent to work in the hinterland. Like the others mentioned here, he too never conveys the idea of a fragile last reserve.

Curious about the absence of a 'last reserve' in soldiers' accounts, I started to look for it in other places. When Italy declared war on Austria in May 1915, this distant, imperial war—albeit one that had already engaged Tyrolean men—literally hit home. The contemporary published Tyrolean sources do not make much of the fact that so many of the region's young men had already been deployed, and many of them killed, on distant fronts. Rather,

[37] Simone Morandini, *Feldtagebuch: la prima difesa dei Lagorai nel diario di uno Standschütze di Predazzo* (Rozzano, 1996).
[38] Luigi Michielli, *Dio fulmini i tiranni . . . 'che vogliono distruggere l'Europa': diario di guerra e d'esilio di Luigi Michielli, 19 maggio 1915–28 ottobre 1917*, ed. Paolo Giacomel (Cortina d'Ampezzo, 2000). [39] Cordin, *Ettore Cordin*.

they foregrounded a strong sense of betrayal and of the 'moral perfidy' of the former ally. This was the tenor of the Kaiser's communication to the peoples of the Empire after Italy's war declaration, a communication published in all Tyrolean newspapers. The same tone recurs repeatedly in later reports. The insistence on Italy's betrayal must have made life difficult for the Italian speakers in the region, in terms of how they were viewed and treated by German speakers, and in particular by the Austrian army. The situation was tense enough to compel even the Germanophile mayor of Bozen/Bolzano, Julius Perathoner, to publish a call to his citizenry on 26 May 1915 in the *Bozner Nachrichten*. The mayor voiced outrage over Italy's disloyalty, but called on the citizens not to harm speakers of Italian in their midst, who were loyal citizens and not to blame.[40] He added that the front was in the good hands of Austria's soldiers, without even the slightest hint of worry or concern that the front was undermanned, or that everything hinged on an army of reservists and volunteers.

Based on 'British newspapers', in late May 1915 local news outlets reported that the Austrian troops were in place and the Italians were fleeing, not attacking. It seems that apart from the occasional reference to the 'usual gun fights', July and August saw very little reporting (and, in fact, very little battle) on the Tyrolean front. When the *Bozner Zeitung* of 9 September mentioned Italian attacks on the Kreuzbergsattel, where 'at least 1000' Italian soldiers were killed, there was no word on how many Austrians were killed, or which battalions were fighting. For the Tyrol front, as for the other fronts, generally the local press conveyed the official announcements on the war's progress, rather than engaging in any direct reporting. Because of the centralized system of official communication, and no doubt reflecting the weight of the actual fighting, the local press devoted many more column inches to fighting in Russia, Serbia, and on the Isonzo than to the local front. For those first few months, no news reports could be found that specifically referred to the Standschützen or their particular role in a military emergency. Nor was there, indeed, any coverage that conveyed a sense of alarm, even allowing for the fact that the press was, of course, enjoined to maintain public morale in wartime.

The situation was different from the vantage point of Tyrol's leadership. As Italy's entry into the war became ever more likely,

[40] *Bozner Nachrichten*, 26 May 1915.

various Standschützen commanders conveyed their concerns over the defence of the homeland in their internal correspondence. The head of Innsbruck's Standschützen wrote to Tyrol's commander-in-chief as early as February 1915 that the population was ready to defend Tyrol against the 'arch-enemy', but he also stated that the Standschützen's firearms were 'completely inadequate' and that his men did not have enough ammunition. Given that this 'last reserve may be called up any day', he demanded the same weapons as regular troops for the Standschützen, '*or else they should not be put in the firing line!*'.[41] With deployment imminent, District Sergeant Galli from Meran wrote to Governor Toggenburg that the population understood that every man had to serve, but that with the arrival of regular troops, the Standschützen should be disbanded quickly.[42] Galli, moreover, criticized the seemingly indiscriminate recruitment of men without concern for 'their fitness or their ability to fight'. The result was villages entirely devoid of men between the ages of 17 and 50. Galli described the population as 'depressed and disheartened'.[43]

It is thus perhaps even more noteworthy that the Standschützen themselves did not betray any sense of emergency, urgency, or distinctiveness. The notion of a last stand or last reserve was not even hinted at. There was certainly an awareness that the Standschützen were different from the regular army; the men to some extent even acknowledged that they were not really fit for service. But they did their duty. Or at least this is how they tended to present their participation in the war. Incidentally, although Austria-Hungary lost the war, its defensive campaign on the Tyrolean front was successful, with hardly any territory lost to the enemy.[44] It was only later, in the changing national and international constellations of the postwar period, that the conflict came to be remembered in new ways.[45]

[41] Document no. 20, Oberschützenmeister Gotthard Freiherr An der Lan, k. k. Landeshauptschießstand Kaiser Franz Joseph I., Innsbruck, to Theodor Freiherr von Kathrein, Landesoberstschützenmeister, Innsbruck, 13 Feb. 1915 (no. 19/12) (emphasis original), in Überegger, *Heimatfronten*, i. 39.

[42] Document no. 327, Bezirkshauptmann Franz Galli, Meran, to Statthalter Toggenburg, Innsbruck, 29 May 1915, in Überegger, *Heimatfronten*, ii. 570.

[43] Document no. 328, Bezirkshauptmann Franz Galli, Meran, to Statthalterei Innsbruck [1915], in Überegger, *Heimatfronten*, ii. 571.

[44] For its entire duration, the war in the Tyrolean Alps was a relatively stationary conflict, with small movements.

[45] On the postwar memorialization of the Tyrolean front see Laurence Cole,

V

Before entering the war, Italy had been promised Tyrol up to the Brenner Pass by the Entente, and this promise was kept at the peace negotiations.[46] As a result Tyrol's entire Italian-speaking part (the Trentino) as well as a large chunk of the German-speaking part (the South Tyrol) and all Ladin-speaking areas became Italian. It was in this particular context, the division of Tyrol and the secession of half of its territory to Italy, that the notion of a last reserve, and a last stand, emerged, though with connotations that evolved over time.

The notion of a last reserve and last stand, one would imagine, made a lot of sense as a final endeavour to save the Habsburg Empire. The trope worked well for those wanting to emphasize Tyrol's unique bond with the monarchy. Even after the Second World War authors such as Bernhard Zallinger-Thurn continued to paint the Tyroleans as some sort of Habsburg vanguard that had defended the state and its Catholicism.[47] But with the Empire gone for ever, the narrative had no political traction, even if it enjoyed an elegiac appeal.

For *großdeutsch* nationalists, by contrast, the Empire's demise was what gave their narrative plausibility and power. While some Tyroleans had supported the idea of all-German unity before the war, it was only after 1918 that German nationalism became a powerful force in the region, and in particular in the German-speaking part attached to Italy, the so-called South Tyrol. Quite

'Geteiltes Land und getrennte Erzählungen: Erinnerungskulturen des Ersten Welkrieges in den Nachfolgeregionen des Kronlandes Tirol', in Hannes Obermair, Stephanie Risse, and Carlo Romeo (eds.), *Regionale Zivilgesellschaft in Bewegung: cittadini innazi tutto. Festschrift für/scritti in onore di Hans Heiss* (Vienna, 2012); Oswald Überegger, 'Die Tiroler Historiographie und der Erste Weltkrieg: Tabuisierung—Instrumentalisierung—verspätete Historisierung', *Geschichte and Region/Storia e Regione*, 11/1 (2002), 127–47; Christoph Hartungen and Leopold Steurer, 'La memoria dei vinti: la Grande Guerra nella letteratura e nell'opinione pubblica sudtirolese (1918–1945)', in Diego Leoni and Camillo Zadra (eds.), *La Grande Guerra: esperienza, memoria, immagini* (Bologna, 1986).

[46] In Article 4 of the secret Treaty of London, April 1915, Britain, France, and Russia granted that 'Italy shall obtain the Trentino, Cisalpine Tyrol with its geographical and natural frontier, as well as Trieste' among other territories, 'under the treaty of peace'. See ⟨http://www.firstworldwar.com/source/london1915.htm⟩ [accessed 11 Mar. 2016].

[47] Bernhard Zallinger-Thurn, *Die Grundlagen der Südtiroler Politik* (Bolzano, 1949). Among the clerical Catholic and imperial Austrian accounts see also the diary of Johann Schwingshackl, *Gefangen in Sibirien*, published in weekly instalments in the *Katholisches Sonntagsblatt* of Bolzano between January and December 1985. See Hartungen and Steurer, 'La memoria dei vinti', 479.

apart from the real threat of Italianization that the German speakers faced under Fascism, it was the collapse of the Habsburg Empire, the creation of a little-rump Austria that many believed unviable, the general growth of nationalism in postwar Europe, and in particular the growth of Nazism that encouraged identification with a greater Germany. In this context, the war was rethought—no longer as a war for the survival of the Empire, but rather as a war for a greater Germany. Tyrol was here reconceived as both an outpost territory on the cultural and linguistic frontier and a reservoir of pure and deep-rooted Germanness.

Local politician Eduard Reut-Nicolussi presented a *großdeutsch* version of Tyrol's history as early as 1919.[48] But it was the *völkisch* publications of the 1930s—memoirs, novels, as well as historical accounts of the war—that most strongly reinterpreted the narrative of the last stand in a German nationalist key. When Otto Langl, president of the Austrian Alpine Club, wrote the foreword in 1934 for the publication of Sepp Innerkofler's revised diary, he used the word 'deutsch' seven times on one single page, extolling Innerkofler's heroism, toughness, and sacrifice for the German cause.[49] Innerkofler himself had never mentioned German concerns in his notes.

In the *völkisch* publications of the 1930s, the notion of a 'last reserve' revolved above all around the local individual who belonged to a lineage of sturdy, self-possessed peasants. They had come together to defend their homesteads, their mountains, their way of being, which was presented as unabashedly German.[50] It was, in other words, the autochthonous Germanness of these men that distinguished them. And it was their local knowledge of territory and climate that could outsmart the Italian invader. Consequently,

---

[48] Eduard Reut-Nicolussi, writing in Karl von Grabmayr (ed.), *Süd-Tirol: Land und Leute vom Brenner bis zur Salurner Klause* (Berlin, 1919), cited in Hartungen and Steurer, 'La memoria dei vinti', 470–1.

[49] Langl, 'Vorwort', in Ebner, *Kampf um die Sextner Rotwand*.

[50] See Pölzleitner, *Berge wurden Burgen*, and Schmidkunz, *Der Kampf über den Gletschern*; but also many other memoirs and novels published at the time, e.g. Christian Röck, *Die Festung im Gletscher: Vom Heldentum im Alpenkrieg* (Berlin, 1935), and Luis Trenker, *Berge in Flammen* (Berlin, 1931). I would also include the work of Fritz Weber in this category, even though he has often been read as a pacifist. On this controversy see Christa Hämmerle, '"Es ist immer der Mann, der den Krieg entscheidet und nicht die Waffe . . .": Die Männlichkeit des k. u. k. Gebirgskrieges in der soldatischen Erinnerungskultur', in Kuprian and Überegger (eds)., *Der Erste Weltkrieg im Alpenraum*, 35–60.

the non-German Austro-Hungarian troops—Czechs, Romanians, Slovaks—were criticized for their unpreparedness, unfamiliarity, and lack of commitment.[51] In his ode to the Standschützen, Anton von Mörl repeatedly ridiculed and scorned the 36th Landwehr regiment from Kolomea, which included mainly Ruthenian and Polish soldiers. 'We had to literally drag the men of the 36th, who do not know the mountains, up the steep slopes. All the while they whined terribly. These were the people with whom we were supposed to storm a mountain top!'[52] When a directive to weed out anti-state propaganda reached the Alpine front, the Czechs were immediately suspected.[53] And some Czech officers were later accused of having played a double game with the Italians.[54] At the same time, we find great admiration in these accounts for the German troops that came to help secure the front.[55]

The representation of the Italian enemy is more mixed. Some accounts continued to stress Italy's 'betrayal', but others presented the Italians as a worthy enemy, one who knew mountain warfare and was well equipped and inventive in the use of technology, above all, the digging of mines to blow up enemy positions.[56] When Hans Schneeberger published a memoir in 1940, he also wanted to memorialize 'the adversary' as 'courageous, tough, and resolute', and asked an Italian 'comrade' to write the foreword.[57] This representation of the former Italian enemy had the advantage of placing the Tyrolean achievement in even higher relief. It also, of course, made sense in the light of the Nazi alliance with Fascist Italy.

In spite of this alliance, Italo-German relations in South Tyrol were tense, and we can observe the emergence of a broader South Tyrolean victimization narrative beneath the surface of Fascist censorship, and propagated abroad in Austria and Germany. This narrative recast the 'last reserve' as yet another moment of victimization and abuse in Tyrol's history, followed by Tyrol's division

---

[51] See the assessment of Anton von Mörl in *Die Standschützen im Weltkrieg* (Innsbruck, 1934), commenting on the Eastern Galicians in his regiment; cited in Hartungen and Steurer, 'La memoria dei vinti', 451.

[52] Anton von Mörl, *Standschuetzen verteidigen Tirol, 1915–1918* (Innsbruck, 1933; rev. edn. 1958), 136.   [53] Ibid. 276.

[54] Ibid. 328–9.

[55] Ibid. 112 and 202.   [56] See e.g. Trenker, *Berge in Flammen*.

[57] Hans Schneeberger, *Der berstende Berg: Vom Heldenkampf der Kaiserjäger und Alpini* (Berlin, 1940).

and the Italianization drive of the Fascist regime in South Tyrol. But it was only after the Second World War, when South Tyrol remained Italian in spite of concerted efforts to bring about the unification of South, North, and East Tyrol inside Austria, that the victimization narrative could be more openly embraced and came to suffuse public discourse. Because the Tyroleans had fought a purely defensive war against all odds, they did not deserve to be the subject of postwar deliberations in which they had no part, be it at the Paris peace conference in 1919, or again in Paris in 1947. Publishing in 1985, Helmut Golowitsch could exalt the Tyroleans' willingness to sacrifice their lives in the name of 'democracy and liberty', and bemoan how 'Tyrol, though undefeated in battle, had to bend to political caprice'.[58] Painting the Tyroleans as victims in war, victims of Fascism, victims of Nazism, victims of postwar deliberations twice over—such a narrative could not bring about South Tyrol's annexation to Austria, but it certainly played a role in securing regional autonomous status within Italy.

Golowitsch's account engaged in a celebration of Tyroleanness that became ever more accentuated in the age of Euro-regionalism.[59] Still central in this version were the generations of Tyrolean fighters lined up against the Italians, as was their German character, though their Germanness was now presented as part and parcel of their regional distinctiveness and identity rather than marking their membership in a *Volksgemeinschaft*. The fact that before the First World War Tyrol had been a multi-ethnic crownland was conveniently passed over. The martial tone was softened, and Tyrol's 'last reserve' presented as fighting in defence of peace and their ancestral family homesteads. It was the Tyroleans' love and respect for the natural environment, their local knowledge, perseverance, and sense of community that enabled them to withstand three long years of warfare in the high mountains.

In fact, in this 'Euro-regional' iteration, the narratives often seek to embed their sympathetic descriptions of warfare within a celebration of war as a thing of the past. They thus waver between celebration of heroism and post-national celebration of international peace. A typical account of this sort might begin with the homily that it is good to tell the stories of yesterday's heroes so

[58] Back cover of Helmut Golowitsch, '*Und komme der Feind ins Land herein . . .*': *Schützen verteidigen Tirol und Kärnten. Standschützen und Freiwillige Schützen 1915–1918* (Nuremberg, 1985). [59] See also Golowitsch (ed.), *Ortlerkämpfe 1915–1918*.

that today's youth can appreciate living in peace.[60] In his foreword to a 1990s reissue of a classic study of the war by Heinz Lichem, mountaineer Hannes Gasser could wax lyrically: 'Mountaineering today: that is peace, freedom, and a life together, for each other.'[61] While attentive to the suffering and sacrifice of soldiers, regional popular histories of camaraderie and *Heimatliebe* from the 1980s and beyond celebrate the Standschützen's commitment to duty as much as the beauty and majesty of the mountains. They tend to remain stuck in descriptive and impressionistic detail, clouding over the wider international context of the war and obscuring even the experience on the Alpine front itself.

VI

In lieu of a conclusion, I would like to close with a couple of observations about the discrepancy between experience and commemoration and the question of authenticity. First, I do not mean to suggest a simple contrast between the authenticity of soldiers' recorded 'experience' and its manipulation or refraction in the postwar histories of the region. It certainly is the case that evolving postwar contexts created new logics for narratives of war. While we are, of course, aware that the First World War was a war between empires, one, indeed, that saw the collapse of four venerable imperial monarchies, we have not tended to reflect so much on the relationship between the imperial contexts in which world war ensued and the post-imperial ones in which it was remembered. In the case of Tyrol this relationship is complex and intriguing, evolving over several decades. Most iterations of post-imperial memory wrote some of the combatants—notably the Italian speakers who had fought for Austria-Hungary—out of the story altogether, both on the Italian and on the Austrian/German side. To that extent, the diaries are vital in reminding us of their battlefront experience. At the same time, it is clear that historical scholarship has moved beyond operating with any naïve notion of authenticity. In addition to acknowledging the constructed nature of each and every written narrative of experience, we need to recognize that many of the diaries were rewritten after the war, and in that sense were

---

[60] A good example is the publication of Karl Mayr's diary by Wachtler.
[61] Heinz von Lichem, *Der einsame Krieg: Erste Gesamtdokumentation des Gebirgskrieges 1915–1918 von den Julischen Alpen bis zum Stilfser Joch* (1974; repr. Bolzano, 1996).

themselves also refracted through postwar experience. Some of the logics of writing and rewriting, as in the case of the Italian-speaking Austrian soldiers, were clearly different from the public histories, but some elements of the soldiers' narratives, in particular about their sturdiness and resilience, clearly cut across the public accounts of the war.

The other question about authenticity is whether the public postwar narratives might be in some ways more 'authentic' than the diaries: that is, whether they convey relevant experience from the war years that is somehow occluded in the soldiers' ego documents. It is easy to see why concerns about public morale might have kept the story of a regional community under siege out of the newspapers at the time—it could have made the region's defence seem too vulnerable—but what about the front diaries? I wonder whether there might be something that is palpable enough to be part of the collective mood, but not acute enough to make it into individual accounts from the battlefront. As this research project unfolds, a key area of enquiry will therefore be whether there is some other kind of source, perhaps from the home front, that might provide the missing link between soldiers' sense-making and postwar commemoration.

7
Counter-Narratives of the Great War? War Accounts of Nurses in Austro-Hungarian Service

CHRISTA HÄMMERLE

In 1934 Maria Pöll-Naepflin, a former Swiss nurse who had served on the side of Austria-Hungary during the First World War, self-published her war memoirs. The subtitle of her book—its second edition appeared in the same year—stated that it was the 'only work by a Swiss nurse of the First World War!'[1] Pöll-Naepflin therefore dedicated her publication to this group of women in the following words of commemoration:

Caring and encouraging we stepped up to stand by the soldiers' side! Who can comprehend the agony of the inner fighting which the nurses had to endure because of misery and sorrow, wounds and suffering in the face of the increasing cruelty and bloodiness of the fury of war? And for whom? And the thanks? . . . No heroes' memorial and no honour roll lists the names of the Swiss nurses whose hearts were crushed by the weight of superhuman strain or who were carried off by a malicious disease.[2]

Despite this drama, and despite the waters of forgetfulness, this appeal by a former war nurse appears at first glance to have been more or less successful. The library catalogues show that Pöll-Naepflin self-published a third edition in 1935. In 1938 she found a publisher for the fourth edition, which was released in Meiringen in the canton of Bern by the Leopthien-Verlag.[3] Further editions followed, probably until 1962, when the ninth edition was published by Splügen-Verlag

---

[1] Maria Pöll-Naepflin, *Fortgerungen, durchgedrungen: Ein erschütterndes Lebensbild einer Krankenschwester aus der Zeit des großen Krieges, der Revolution und der Arbeitslosigkeit. Einziges Werk einer Schweizer Krankenschwester aus dem Weltkrieg!* (Constance, 1934 [self-published]). The first edition comprised 156 pages, and the second, which was supplemented by an appendix ('Nachtrag') on the author's 'political flight', 191 pages.

[2] Pöll-Naepflin, *Fortgerungen*, 3 (cited from the third edition of 1935).

[3] The book was released under the author's maiden name Maria Naepflin and was entitled *Fortgerungen, durchgedrungen bis zum Kleinod hin: Schicksalswege einer Schweizer Krankenschwester im Weltkriege*, 4th edn. (Meiringen, 1938).

in Zurich.[4] In total, the print run is estimated at 20,000 copies,[5] a substantial number of which were also distributed in Germany, where Pöll-Naepflin moved in 1933 with her child and her Austrian husband, an illegal National Socialist. (She had previously lived in Innsbruck, where she married after 1918.) Initially her book was highly praised by the National Socialists, but according to her own postwar account, fell out of favour with the Third Reich in November 1934 because of its pacifist and religious tendencies. It was first confiscated, and then allowed to be sold only in religious bookshops, hospitals, and asylums.[6] Later Pöll-Naepflin was divorced and returned to Switzerland, where she continued to publish books,[7] despite many personal difficulties and a rather bad reputation, which has even been echoed in subsequent research.[8]

What can this story, so full of ambivalences, incoherence, and ruptures, tell us about experiences of First World War nurses? And what can historians who are interested in ego documents or in the commemoration of the First World War learn from Pöll-Naepflin's view of the lack of postwar recognition? To what extent can the bitter statement about the hegemonic culture of war remembrance after 1918 cited above be generalized? How should we evaluate the success of a single book in such a context, and was it really a success which significantly changed public remembrances or attitudes? Did the nurses try to contribute to this aim, and in what forms did they

---

[4] This edition had the same title as the one issued in 1938; the book now comprised 259 pages (including 53 pages of illustrations). Maria Pöll-Naepflin also published three other books: *Eine Schweizerin kämpft um ihre Heimat* (Zurich, 1936); *Deutsche Städte und Baudenkmäler vor der Bombardierung* (Zurich, 1947); *Heimatlos, Staatenlos: Die Abenteuer einer Rotkreuz-Schwester in Österreich, Hitler-Deutschland und in der Schweiz* (Zurich, 1946).

[5] ⟨https://de.wikipedia.org/wiki/Maria_Naepflin⟩ [accessed 2 Jan. 2015] presumably refers to the introduction of Maria Pöll-Naepflin's later book *Heimatlos, Staatenlos*, 8, where this figure is mentioned.   [6] Pöll-Naepflin, *Heimatlos, Staatenlos*, 37.

[7] See n. 4.

[8] This may also be a consequence of her frankly admitted morphine addiction, which she did not overcome until the 1920s. Maria Pöll-Naepflin's life was very difficult after the First World War. She first lost her Swiss citizenship because of her marriage to an Austrian, and later lost her Austrian one because of her and her husband's illegal National Socialist activities and their 'flight' to Germany in 1933. Back in Switzerland by 1935, after she had—dangerously—abjured National Socialism, she was *persona non grata* in her home country and had to endure many difficulties (for example, she was maliciously accused of being mentally ill), until she finally regained Swiss citizenship through a marriage of convenience. In 1938 her daughter died. For the perpetuation of a primarily critical view of Pöll-Naepflin and other Swiss nurses who served for foreign belligerent countries see esp. Alfred Fritschi, *Schwesterntum: Zur Sozialgeschichte weiblicher Berufskrankenpflege in der Schweiz 1850–1930* (Zurich, 1990; repr. 2006), 147–51, where her problematic or deficient 'psycho-structure' is underlined.

communicate their efforts during the war and all the hardship they had to endure? Is the example of Pöll-Naepflin representative of the situation of war nurses? What happened to them and their 'voices' in postwar society, after the Austro-Hungarian Empire had lost the war and fallen apart?

In this essay I will try to answer these questions for texts written in German and originating from the western half of Austria-Hungary or from the newly established First Austrian Republic after 1918. I will argue that Pöll-Naepflin, who remained in the service of Austria-Hungary until the end of the war,[9] was, to some extent, part of the war history of the Austrian Empire, as were many other nurses originally mainly from Switzerland and Germany.[10] They came in the initial period of the war, as Austria-Hungary was experiencing a serious shortage of trained nurses at that time, not least because of the inadequate professionalization of female nursing.[11] Fully trained domestic and foreign nurses were clearly in an absolute minority there at the beginning of the war, probably (much) more so than in other countries such as Britain or Germany.[12] They worked with

[9] Apart from two spells of home leave and breaks due to illness and exhaustion (not least because of her morphine addiction), Maria Pöll-Naepflin was deployed at several places in Galicia, in the Balkans, and in the Czech Pardubitz; at the end of the war she worked in a barracks hospital for blind soldiers, amputees, and so on at Plan/Planá.

[10] She was one of over 200 nurses from German-speaking Switzerland who served on the side of warring Austria-Hungary until 1916. See Sabine Braunschweig, '"Ohne Unterschied jedem verwundeten Krieger helfen": Schweizer Krankenpflegerinnen in ausländischen Militärspitälern im Ersten Weltkrieg', in ead. (ed.), *'Als habe es die Frauen nicht gegeben': Beiträge zur Frauen- und Geschlechtergeschichte* (Zurich, 2014), 145–60, at 151. An even larger number of Swiss nurses from western regions, known as the Romandie, served on the side of the Entente. Neutral Switzerland was therefore divided during the First World War, and the nurses were heavily criticized for their decision to go to war on whatever side. For German nurses in the service of Austria-Hungary see the references in Astrid Stölzle, *Kriegskrankenpflege im Ersten Weltkrieg: Das Pflegepersonal der freiwilligen Krankenpflege in den Etappen des Deutschen Kaiserreichs* (Stuttgart, 2013), 199, where a figure of around 2,000 is mentioned.

[11] A first nursing school (Krankenpflegeschule) was founded in 1882 as part of the Viennese Rudolfinerhaus, a private hospital with religious affiliation. It was not until 1913 that the main public hospital in Vienna (AKH) and the Red Cross also opened nursing schools, not least in response to the dramatic shortage of nursing staff during the Balkan Wars. See Birgit Bolognese-Leuchtenmüller, 'Imagination "Schwester": Zur Entwicklung des Berufsbildes der Krankenschwester in Österreich seit dem 19. Jahrhundert', *L'Homme: Zeitschrift für feministische Geschichtswissenschaft*, 8/1 (1997), 155–77.

[12] In these and some other European countries, the institutionalization and professionalization of female (military) nursing had begun more intensively soon after the Crimean War and Florence Nightingale's engagement there. See e.g., for Britain, Anne Summers, *Angels and Citizens: British Women as Military Nurses 1854–1914* (London,

large numbers of untrained or semi-trained assistant nurses from various backgrounds, served in the hinterland, and—this is the main focus of this essay—very close to the front lines in different kinds of field hospitals and medical units. Here nurses and auxiliary nurses from Austria-Hungary, whose overall number is unknown,[13] worked mainly for the Red Cross, the Order of Malta (Malteserorden), and the Knights Hospitallers (Deutscher Ritterorden). The three organizations were the main pillars supporting the Habsburg military medical service and were joined by similar voluntary healthcare associations such as the German deaconesses and Catholic women's congregations.[14] This also indicates that the women engaged in war nursing came from different religious, social, and, especially in Austria-Hungary, ethnic backgrounds. Some were paid or partly paid, others were unpaid volunteers; some could leave their positions and apply for another one, others could not. These women worked wherever the brutal consequences of 'modern' and industrialized warfare occurred. Like male soldiers, many of them travelled a great deal during their war service, visiting areas where they had never been before. As a result, female mobility rose as sharply as the presence of women in the male-dominated military field, numbering thousands upon thousands, in these years.

Against this background Pöll-Naepflin's war memoirs and the narratives she unfolds in her book appear to be characteristic of the main currents of the Austrian culture of war remembrance after 1918, regardless of all the differences between a defeated and a

1988); and for Germany, Stölzle, *Kriegskrankenpflege*, 28–32; and Annett Büttner, *Die konfessionelle Kriegskrankenpflege im 19. Jahrhundert* (Stuttgart, 2013).

[13] All in all, there must have been tens of thousands of women, as, for example, in Germany, for which Stölzle, *Kriegskrankenpflege*, 19, states that a total of 112,000 nurses and auxiliaries were on duty during the whole war; or in Britain, where the Voluntary Aid Detachment (VAD) alone was able to provide 47,196 nurses in August 1914, a figure that grew to 82,857 by April 1920 and was complemented by more than 23,500 trained, partly trained, or untrained nurses of the Queen Alexandra's Imperial Military Nursing Service and Territorial Force Nursing Services. See Santanu Das, *Touch and Intimacy in First World War Literature* (Cambridge, 2005), 185; Susan R. Grayzel, *Women and the First World War* (London, 2002), 39. In France, the three branches of the French Red Cross reached their peak level with 63,000 fully qualified nurses, and, from 1916 onwards, their workforce grew with a new category of around 30,000 lower-class salaried women; see Margaret H. Darrow, *French Women and the First World War: War Stories of the Home Front* (Oxford, 2000), 140–1, 163.

[14] See Daniela Claudia Angetter, *Dem Tod geweiht und doch gerettet: Die Sanitätsversorgung am Isonzo und in den Dolomiten 1915–18* (Frankfurt a.M., 1995), 190–213; Brigitte Biwald, *Von Helden und Krüppeln: Das österreichisch-ungarische Militär-Sanitätswesen im Ersten Weltkrieg*, 2 vols. (Vienna, 2002).

neutral state, and despite the fact that the women who had left their neutral homeland to serve one of the warring countries were likely to be severely criticized or even denounced at home. A closer look at ego documents by First World War nurses will reveal the tense relationship between the hegemonic culture of remembrance on the one hand and antagonistic or marginalized war accounts on the other. We will see that self-published (and probably self-financed) war memoirs such as Pöll-Naepflin's were not at all uncommon. On the contrary, it seems that nurses, and especially those who were in front-line nursing for long periods of the war and were thus confronted with the brutality of modern warfare,[15] believed that writing and self-publishing their war accounts was the only way of being heard at all. Their books testified to their difficult and important work and to their suffering and endurance, which was intended to pave the way for their acceptance into the community of male war veterans.[16]

In what follows the significance of these female war memoirs will be illustrated first by evaluating the source material and exploring what war accounts by nurses and assistant nurses can be found for the Austrian context. This will be discussed against the backdrop of the Austrian market for publishing First World War ego documents. In this context, shifts from the war itself to the postwar period, and again from the postwar period to the years of Fascist commemoration, have to be considered. Second, a sample of ego documents written by 'front-line' nurses and auxiliaries who served Austria-Hungary will be analysed in the light of the ambivalent reputation that they already had during the war, which apparently impacted on their war memoirs. When reading and analysing these ego documents we have to bear in mind the circumstances under which they were (self-)published, or perhaps could not be published at all for years. Existing difficulties and ambivalences clearly had an impact on the nurses and their writings.

[15] See, among others, Margaret R. Higonnet (ed.), *Nurses at the Front: Writing the Wounds of the Great War* (Boston, 2001); Darrow, *French Women*, 133–69; Christine E. Hallett, *Containing Trauma: Nursing Work in the First World War* (Manchester, 2009); Alison S. Fell and Christine E. Hallett (eds.), *First World War Nursing: New Perspectives* (New York, 2013); Das, *Touch and Intimacy*, 175–228.

[16] For an earlier analysis, which mainly concentrates on front-line nursing and the related experience of war violence, see Christa Hämmerle, '"Mentally broken, physically a wreck . . .": Violence in War Accounts of Nurses in Austro-Hungarian Service', in ead., Oswald Überegger, and Birgitta Bader-Zaar (eds.), *Gender and the First World War* (Basingstoke, 2014), 89–107.

In other words, by attempting to make their war experiences public and incorporating them into the prevailing hegemonic culture of remembrance, these women, among other things, were indeed torn between two 'images' of the war nurse circulating at that time. For France, Margaret Darrow has described this phenomenon as the Janus-faced dichotomy between the idealized, motherly, caring, self-sacrificing, religious, and even nun-like 'white angel' on the one hand, and the notorious, sexualized 'nurse *mondaine*' or 'false nurse' on the other.[17] In the German-speaking countries after the war, such polarized and highly gendered depictions of female nurses can also be traced back to wartime, when they resulted in many visual representations.[18] Concerning the second dimension mentioned above, this was based on underlying allegations, such as a supposed thirst for adventure and immoral attitudes, and could even culminate in the accusation that war nurses or assistant nurses were prostitutes. The German sexologist Magnus Hirschfeld collected these sexualized, pejorative prejudices and commented on them in his *Sittengeschichte des Ersten Weltkriegs*, published in 1930.[19] It was decades before research finally addressed this topic, first and most famously in Klaus Theweleit's study *Männerphantasien*. Theweleit also explored perceptions circulating about the 'red nurse', which again exhibited strong tendencies to stigmatize and sexualize these women in contrast to the idealized image of nurses.[20] As women's and gender history of both world wars has shown, this applied above all to those women who left their homes to work at the front and shared the male soldiers' war experiences there. As a result they stood between the two gendered spheres of war society, in a kind of a 'no man's land', as Regina Schulte has defined it.[21]

[17] Darrow, *French Women*, 142–51, esp. 146, 151.
[18] See the examples in Rudolf Jaworski, *Mütter — Liebchen — Heroinen: Propagandapostkarten aus dem Ersten Weltkrieg* (Vienna, 2015), 119–30; Heidrun Zettelbauer, 'Krankenschwestern im Ersten Weltkrieg: Zwischen gesellschaftlichen Normvorstellungen und Gewalterfahrungen', in Diethard Leopold, Stephan Pumberger, and Birgit Summerauer (eds.), *Wally Neuzil: Ihr Leben mit Egon Schiele* (Vienna, 2015), 131–51.
[19] Magnus Hirschfeld and Andreas Gaspar, *Sittengeschichte des Ersten Weltkriegs*, 2 vols. (Leipzig, 1930). An abridged English translation was published in 1934 in New York by Panurge Press.
[20] Klaus Theweleit, *Männerphantasien*, 2 vols. (Frankfurt a.M., 1978); esp. vol. i: *Frauen, Fluten, Körper, Geschichte*, ch. 1, 121–77.
[21] Regina Schulte, 'The Sick Warrior's Sister: Nursing during the First World War', in Lynn Abrams and Elizabeth Harvey (eds.), *Gender Relations in German History: Power, Agency and Experience from the Sixteenth to the Twentieth Century* (Durham, NC, 1997), 121–41, at 122. Similarly, this was the case with Etappenhelferinnen or, as they were

From Patriotism to the Myth of Comradeship:
The Publication Market and its Gaps

Before we consider the implications of such ambivalent and contradictory perceptions for the writings of nurses, let us take a closer look at the Austrian publication market for ego documents of the Great War. It is no surprise that the war accounts of nurses and assistant nurses which were published during the war had a primarily patriotic, heroic, and idealizing orientation, and often shared the characteristics of travel and adventure fiction. They were published as short texts in newspapers and magazines or, surprisingly, less frequently in the women's press and women's anthologies.[22] This is all the more astonishing as voluntary nursing was defined as a genuinely female task and as the most appropriate equivalent to male soldiering. But the current state of research does not permit us to be certain whether this discourse was as intense in former Austria as it was in France,[23] where the women's movement strongly propagandized this view of nursing, and 'personal accounts of war nurses found a wide and appreciative audience'.[24]

In Austria, the ideological promotion of war nursing triggered at least one remarkable publication, a larger collection of texts in a book entitled *Wahre Soldatengeschichten: Erzählt von Roten Kreuz-Schwestern und freiwilligen Pflegerinnen 1914–1916*, containing thirty short or very short stories by various nurses from different areas. Although these texts differed significantly in structure and tone, they all focused on the soldiers' fate, to which the nurses' hard work was devoted, as conveyed in the title of the book. The fact that it

called in Austria-Hungary, the Weibliche Hilfskräfte der Armee im Felde (Women's Auxiliary Labour Force).

[22] See e.g. Olly Schwarz, 'Skizzen aus dem Leben einer Krankenschwester', *Neues Frauenleben*, 17/1 (1915), 8–13; and, for nursing in the Styrian hinterland, Lina Kreuter-Gallé, 'Kriegserinnerungen einer freiwilligen Pflegerin', *Mitteilungen des Vereines Südmark*, 1/2 (Jan.–Feb. 1915), analysed by Heidrun Zettelbauer, 'Ideelle und materielle Kriegsfürsorge als Ort der Aushandlung geschlechtsspezifischer Handlungsräume vor und im Ersten Weltkrieg', in Werner Suppanz and Nicole-Melanie Goll (eds.), *Heimatfront: Graz und das Kronland Steiermark im Ersten Weltkrieg* (forthcoming, Essen, 2018). In contrast, but also adopting a quite patriotic tone, a short account in the form of a letter from a nurse deployed near the Eastern Front, which was published in the *Arbeiter-Zeitung* on 19 Sept. 1914, p. 6, underlines the dangers of front-line nursing.

[23] See Darrow, *French Women*, 134, who describes voluntary nursing as 'the most popular representation of French women's patriotism'.

[24] Ibid. 135.

was published by the Kriegshilfsbüro (War Assistance Office) of the Ministry of the Interior reveals its official character.[25] The preface claims that future historians

> will also have to commemorate the large contribution of women and girls to the unprecedented, immense struggle for existence . . . Above all, they will have to highlight the extraordinary merits of our Red Cross nurses and female voluntary attendants, who during this war proved themselves as social fighters, as heroic soldiers in the service of science and philanthropy. In the darkest hours they stood by the side of our brave soldiers in the field; they sat at the bedside of the seriously wounded in military hospitals, conjuring up a bit of sunshine and optimism in despairing hearts; and in difficult struggles they fought for and won over many victims of the war.[26]

Although uncommon, there was also a written commemoration practice that derived from more private contexts. For Italy, the German historian Oliver Janz has examined the publication of commemorative books that remembered fallen soldiers as part of an intense individual or familial 'cult of mourning' among the bourgeoisie.[27] It seems that women, too, could be remembered in this way, if they had died as a result of their war commitment.[28] This applies to Maria Sonnenthal-Scherer, born in 1884, who in 1905 had married a Styrian country doctor, Horaz Sonnenthal. Soon after the outbreak of the war, he worked on the Serbian border as a senior physician. In November 1914 his wife, having been his assistant for years, left their child in the care of her mother-in-law and followed him. She first worked as a voluntary assistant nurse with her husband and from March 1915 independently as a surgical nurse at several theatres of war in Upper Hungary and Kolomyia, Ukraine. In spring 1916, after a period of home leave, Sonnenthal-Scherer decided to join a medical service expedition to Syria as an official army nurse, a status

---

[25] Kriegshilfsbüro des k. k. Ministeriums des Innern. Zu Gunsten der offiziellen Kriegsfürsorge (ed.), *Wahre Soldatengeschichten: Erzählt von Roten Kreuz-Schwestern und freiwilligen Pflegerinnen 1914–1916* (Vienna, n.d.). [26] Ibid. 3.

[27] Unsurprisingly, this happened only in the case of officers. See Oliver Janz, 'Das symbolische Kapital der Trauer: Nation, Religion und Familie im italienischen Gefallenenkult des Ersten Weltkriegs', *Quellen und Forschungen aus italienischen Archiven und Bibliotheken*, 84 (2004), 386–405, at 387; id., 'Zwischen privater Trauer und öffentlichem Gedenken: Der bürgerliche Gefallenenkult in Italien während des Ersten Weltkriegs', *Geschichte und Gesellschaft*, 28/4 (2002), 554–73.

[28] Autobiographical sources as analysed in this essay refer to such cases. We do not have a figure for these war casualties, however, as statistics did not include them. For Germany, Stölzle, *Kriegskrankenpflege*, 120, mentions that during the third year of the war statistics listed 90 female nurses as having died by then.

she now accepted for the duration of the war. After Syria she went to Jerusalem and Beersheba, where a new field hospital for epidemic diseases had been established, and died there of cholera in September 1916. As early as 1918, her husband's cousin published a selection of her letters and diary notes with the obvious intention of memorializing her 'complete self-sacrifice', her 'boundless *joie de vivre*', her 'pure womanhood', and so on, as shown in the long introduction by the editor.[29] The family made every effort to distribute and promote the publication.[30] Its overall tone is patriotic and completely omits any references to the horrors of war or traumatic experiences that Maria Sonnenthal-Scherer was likely to have had. Instead, the underlying objective of the publication seems to be to describe and legitimize the hard, selfless, and adventurous work of this war nurse.

But was all this truly remembered after the war, when tens of thousands of female nurses and female assistant nurses who had worked for Austria-Hungary were demobilized? Many of them were unable to find adequate work, even if they had wanted to. Only those who had worked for a religious order could go back to their old jobs, while the majority, and above all the masses of auxiliary nurses who lacked full training,[31] faced great difficulties in finding an appropriate occupation, despite the efforts of the authorities (including the Red Cross) to integrate former war nurses into the nursing profession, which, in the meantime, had been almost completely feminized.[32] Many, however, simply 'disappeared' and worked in other occupations that were often badly paid; some even became domestic servants or factory workers.[33]

---

[29] Hermine von Sonnenthal (ed.), *Ein Frauenschicksal im Kriege: Briefe und Tagebuch-Aufzeichnungen von Schwester Maria Sonnenthal-Scherer* (Berlin, 1918), 9–25, at 17, 19. Maria Sonnenthal-Scherer was the daughter of Wilhelm Scherer, the literary historian and scholar of German language and literature, and the singer Marie Scherer (née Leeder).

[30] Staatsbibliothek Berlin, Wilhelm and Marie Scherer Papers, based on Sabrina Payrhuber's investigation.

[31] In the Habsburg monarchy, the professionalization of nursing lagged behind other countries such as Britain and Germany.

[32] See Ilsemarie Walter, Elisabeth Seidl, and Vlastimil Kozon, *Wider die Geschichtslosigkeit der Pflege* (Vienna, 2004); Ilsemarie Walter, 'Zur Entstehung der beruflichen Krankenpflege in Österreich', *Historicum* (Spring 2003), 22–9; Bolognese-Leuchtenmüller, 'Imagination "Schwester"'. Again, it has to be noted that for former Austria we still lack basic research on the demobilization of nurses and assistant nurses and all those women who worked in a war-related occupation during the war, such as female armaments workers or those women who, from 1917 onwards, were recruited as Weibliche Hilfskräfte der Armee im Felde.

[33] Although there has been some research on this, we still do not have a complete

These women also disappeared in another respect, contrary to the assumption quoted above that future war historiography would have to integrate the nurses' war efforts. Neither historical accounts nor the culture of war remembrance included these women. Historians such as Oswald Überegger and Ernst Hanisch have examined the public discourses of the First Austrian Republic, which were soon dominated almost entirely by the upper classes and a cult of masculinity or, in other words, by the 'official' war remembrance, which was monopolized by former officers and their perceptions of the war.[34] Yet this research has also shown that initially, in the immediate postwar period, there were, in fact, opposing interpretations of the war and different forms of mourning in the public sphere. There was even a strong pacifist current, Nie wieder Krieg (Never Again War), which was promoted mainly but not solely by the Socialist Party, and considered itself the voice of the victimized common soldiers. Soon, however, the former elites won the public 'memory wars' (*Erinnerungskriege*), and war historians from the Austrian War Archive propagated the myth that Austria had been 'undefeated in the field' ('Im Felde unbesiegt'). This, along with the comprehensive remilitarization of Austrian society, which was divided into two political camps, dictated the publication market for war memoirs. As a consequence, only very few war memoirs by common soldiers were published; their remembrance was thus limited to the private sphere.[35]

picture of the demobilization process of war-related female work after 1918. For a short summary of the recent state of research see Christa Hämmerle, 'Krank, feige, mutlhos . . .: Eine "Krise der Männlichkeit" nach dem Ersten Weltkrieg?', in ead., *Heimat/Front: Geschlechtergeschichte/n des Ersten Weltkriegs in Österreich-Ungarn* (Vienna, 2014), 183–201, 268–76, at 186–91 (first published 2008). For Germany see Susanne Rouette, *Sozialpolitik als Geschlechterpolitik: Die Regulierung der Frauenarbeit nach dem Ersten Weltkrieg* (Frankfurt a.M., 1993).

[34] Oswald Überegger, 'Vom militärischen Paradigma zur "Kulturgeschichte des Krieges"? Entwicklungslinien der österreichischen Weltkriegsgeschichtsschreibung im Spannungsfeld militärisch-politischer Instrumentalisierung und universitärer Verwissenschaftlichung', in id. (ed.), *Zwischen Nation und Region: Weltkriegsforschung im interregionalen Vergleich. Ergebnisse und Perspektiven* (Innsbruck, 2004), 64–122, at 70–97; id., *Erinnerungskriege: Der Erste Weltkrieg, Österreich und die Tiroler Kriegserinnerung in der Zwischenkriegszeit* (Innsbruck, 2011); Ernst Hanisch, 'Die Rückkehr des Kriegers', *Transit: Europäische Revue*, 16 (1999), 108–24; id., *Männlichkeiten: Eine andere Geschichte des 20. Jahrhunderts* (Vienna, 2005), 48–69.

[35] Cf., as an early exception, Alois Öller, *Kriegserlebnisse eines Vierzehners* (Rohrbach, n.d. [*c*.1920, self-published]). Later, in the context of riots between left-wing and right-wing groups which also arose when Erich Maria Remarque's film *All Quiet on*

Unsurprisingly, this public atmosphere hardly allowed 'authentic' female voices to be heard and female war remembrances to be recognized. For the former war nurses, this meant that during the First Republic no memorials to them were erected, and that their war memoirs did not attract the interest of publishing houses. Instead, and along with some fictionalized testimonies to female war nursing,[36] there are, according to my research, at least two further remarkable examples of self-published war memoirs written by former Austrian nurses. Like the first editions of Pöll-Naepflin's book, they must therefore be situated between the public and the private, in a semi-public sphere. This seems to have been the best possible position that female war commemoration could achieve at that time, if it could gain any at all.

The first memoir was written by Agathe Fessler, born in 1870 in Bregenz near Lake Constance. Fessler had founded an institution for unmarried female servants and factory workers (the Marienheim) in her home town in 1905. As a single woman, she had invested all her energy and money in this project, which became the starting point of 'modern' social work in Bregenz.[37] Here the Patriotic Women's Benevolent Societies of the Red Cross offered nursing courses for women—for example, in 1907, 1909, and 1913, when Agathe Fessler herself attended the course.[38] She was called up after war broke out, and went to Galicia in October 1914, where she witnessed heavy battles and extensive population movements. Fessler later worked

the *Western Front* (1930) was initially banned in Vienna, a remarkable and unique collection of short war remembrances 'from below' was published by the Social Democratic newspaper *Volksblatt*: *Ein Volk klagt an! 50 Briefe über den Krieg* (Vienna, 1931). See Christa Hämmerle, 'Fritz Weber: Ein österreichischer Remarque? Soldatische Erinnerungskulturen', in ead., *Heimat/Front*, 161–81, 257–68, esp. 179–80 (first published 2006); ead., 'Opferhelden? Zur Geschichte der k. u. k. Soldaten an der Südwestfront', in Nicola Labanca and Oswald Überegger (eds.), *Krieg in den Alpen: Österreich-Ungarn und Italien im Ersten Weltkrieg 1914–1918* (Vienna, 2015), 156–80.

[36] See e.g. Paula Schlier, *Petras Aufzeichnungen oder Konzept einer Jugend nach dem Diktat der Zeit* (Innsbruck, 1926); for Germany see Henriette Riemann, *Wie Schwester Emma den Krieg erlebte* (Leipzig, 1930), which was later included in the Nazi list of 'damaging and undesirable writing' ('Liste des schädlichen und unerwünschten Schrifttums'). These texts are excluded from what follows.

[37] Meinrad Pichler, 'Selbstverwirklichung im Dienst an Anderen: Leben und Werk der Bregenzer Sozialarbeiterin Agathe Fessler (1870–1941)', in id., *Quergänge: Vorarlberger Geschichte in Lebensläufen* (Hohenems, 2007), 160–87.

[38] She gives an account of these events in her unpublished diary of 1913, p. 16: 'Again, a well-attended medical course was held. I myself participated in everything, and enrolled with the Red Cross in the event of war', in Diary, Agathe Fessler Papers, Stadtarchiv Bregenz.

in other theatres of war, including a hospital for infectious diseases in Caracal, Romania. In 1918 she was deployed close to the Italian front. Soon after her demobilization, she returned to her home town, where in 1916 she had sold her Marienheim to a female congregation (Barmherzige Schwestern), and self-published a booklet of 64 pages, entitled *Aus der Mappe einer ehemaligen Armeeschwester*.[39] The booklet is structured chronologically and contains sketches and short stories based on notes, photographs, postcards, and letters written or collected during the war, which she had 'combed through', as Fessler wrote in her preface.[40]

The second autobiographical book was written by R. M. Konrad. We do not know much about her and her background. Konrad was a former Red Cross nurse and served throughout the entire war. She self-published her war memoirs in diary form in two volumes, the first being released in 1922, the second probably in 1929.[41] The first volume starts with an entry from early December 1915, shortly after Konrad had moved from a hospital in the hinterland to the front lines because she 'wanted to participate directly in caring for the wounded', to 'search' for them immediately 'after the battle', and to 'apply the first emergency dressings, and accompany those in need of help under a protective roof'.[42] When she received her 'marching orders' to the 'much-embattled town of Gorizia' on the Isonzo front, she bought paper on her way to the deployment in order to keep a war diary and to write down 'little war episodes' concerning her patients to be,[43] which again illustrates the close relationship between front-line nursing and writing. In this case, Konrad took her diary to several field hospitals. We do not know exactly where she was deployed because she anonymized many locations and the names of the medical staff. However, it becomes clear that she worked somewhere near the Italian front, in Hungary, and in Bohemia.[44] During this time, she came to 'love' her 'so-called diary like a true friend',[45] and often employed a second-person point of view as a narrative voice: that is, she addressed this 'friend' in dialogue form

---

[39] Agathe Fessler, *Aus der Mappe einer ehemaligen Armeeschwester 1914–1918* (Bregenz, n.d. [1919]); today held by the Stadtarchiv Bregenz as part of her papers.

[40] Fessler, *Aus der Mappe*, 3.

[41] R. M. Konrad, *Schwestern als Menschen: Aus den Aufzeichnungen einer Armeeschwester*, 2 vols. (Innsbruck, n.d. [1922, 1929 (?), self-published]). Taken together, these two volumes run to 568 pages.

[42] Ibid. i. 4.

[43] Ibid. i. 5.

[44] Ibid. ii. 2.

[45] Ibid. ii. 1.

by using the pronoun 'you'. And she imagined this 'friend' as 'of the third sex', a characterization that was, according to Konrad, 'also used for nurses'.[46]

Before discussing this remarkable statement, let us continue to explore the possibilities, or lack thereof, for publishing nurses' war accounts in Austria. It is reasonable to assume that there are still an unknown number of unpublished autobiographical texts hidden either in archives or in private homes, awaiting further research, such as the memoirs of Marianne Jarka, born in 1889, a Red Cross surgical nurse who served in two mobile military hospitals close to the Isonzo front from early 1916 until the end of the war. After the war she worked as an unskilled factory labourer to provide for her two illegitimate children because she could not find a job commensurate with her training. In the early 1930s Jarka emigrated to the United States, where she penned her memoirs thirty years later at the request of her son, who typed up her manuscript and sent it to an archive in Vienna. Descriptions of her war commitment form a substantial part of this text.[47]

Equally intriguing are the autobiographical notes by Louise Valentini, in the form of a one-volume, lockable diary with a leather cover, which was only recently discovered at a flea market in Vienna. In April 1915 Valentini (born in 1888) left Wels in Upper Austria via Vienna for Wadowice in the former Habsburg Kingdom of Galicia and Lodomeria as a Red Cross assistant nurse. This was when she started the diary, writing down her war experiences until mid July 1915, when her notes abruptly end. At that time Valentini was still deployed on the Eastern Front, but had already resigned since she felt 'completely exhausted', as she noted in her last entry, of 17 July 1915.[48]

It is striking that the history of Austrian nurses' commercially published war accounts started only at the beginning of Austro-Fascism and National Socialism (and then picked up again, long after the war, from the 1970s). This means that the war experiences of ex-service nurses effectively disappeared from the public sphere

[46] Ibid. i. 239.
[47] Marianne Jarka, 'Erinnerungen 1889–1934', undated typescript, part of 'Dokumentation lebensgeschichtlicher Aufzeichnungen', Department of Economic and Social History, University of Vienna, 111 pp.; partially analysed in Hämmerle, '"Mentally broken, physically a wreck . . ."'.
[48] I am grateful to Mathias Markl, who lent me this unpublished diary. It is stored in his private archive and is now being explored by Sonja Gasser in her master's thesis in progress at the University of Vienna under my supervision.

in the immediate postwar period (which is also true for France and other belligerent countries),[49] and that this situation changed only slightly in the revisionist and warmongering atmosphere of the years from 1933–4 on. At this very time, the Nazis in Germany were initially very interested in Maria Naepflin's war memoirs, although, as mentioned above, only briefly. But in both Nazi Germany and Fascist Austria, other veteran nurses were now portrayed in a highly idealized light. They were even included in the Heldendenkmal (Heroes' Monument), the large First World War memorial on the Äußeres Burgtor, a triumphal arch on Vienna's Ringstraße that was erected in 1934 to commemorate the fallen soldiers of the First World War, although this remained an exception. The murals in its Hall of Fame (Ruhmeshalle) show not only a range of famous generals and other male figures from the glorified past of the Habsburg Empire, but also, among them, a First World War nurse, granting her a seat in the Austrian Valhalla.[50] Only two years later, in 1936, the prominent former major general Hugo Kerchnawe explicitly praised these women as 'brave, courageous sisters, *our* sisters, our female comrades'. In the same text that he had, allegedly, already written during the war, Kerchnawe contrasted these 'genuine and true angels of mercy' with those who had volunteered 'out of snobbery' and 'because it was fashionable to show off a coquettish nurse's cap and a Red Cross armband in a hospital or on a railway station platform'. He idealized the first group of women as 'female soldiers. It goes without saying that we soldiers cannot grant a higher honour than the proud word: "soldier". This is all the more true in times of war.'[51]

Closely related to these 'militarized' definitions of war nursing, some extracts from diaries, letters, or memoirs of First World War nurses were published, in whole or in part, in the 1930s. For Germany, Regina Schulte has stated that these publications were intended 'to serve propagandistic ends of, respectively, supporting one war and preparing for the next'.[52] This can also be assumed for Austria,

[49] For France see Darrow, *French Women*, 135.
[50] The monument was closed in 2012 because of its Fascist orientation and the discovery of an avowal of National Socialism by its architect, Wilhelm Frass.
[51] Hugo Kerchnawe, 'Die Schwester', in Rudolf Rauch (ed.), *Ärzte und ihre Helfer im Weltkriege 1914–1918: Herausgegeben über Anregung von Univ. Prof. Dr. Burghard Breitner, Innsbruck, unter Mitarbeit einer Reihe prominenter, im Kriege erprobter Wissenschaftler* (Klagenfurt, 1936), 244–6.
[52] Schulte, 'The Sick Warrior's Sister', 123. See Helene Mierisch, *Kamerad Schwester 1914–1919* (Leipzig, 1934); Elfriede von Pflugk-Harttung (ed.), *Frontschwestern: Ein*

where such, at least in part, highly ideological and apologetic autobiographical texts were not uncommon as well. This includes the 'multi-layered and rich' war memoirs of Eveline Hrouda (born 1892 near Lososice in Moravia),[53] printed by a well-known publishing house in 1935, during the Austrian Fascist period but before the *Anschluß* to the Third Reich in 1938. The book, entitled *Barmherzigkeit* ('Compassion'), is highly informative about the meaning given to front-line nursing and related experiences, first regarding the Red Cross and later the Maltese Order, in Galicia and behind the Isonzo, where many bloody battles were fought between the Italian and Austro-Hungarian armies.[54]

It was a very long way from this edition (or Margarete von Rohrer's voluminous book, published in 1942[55]) to publications released long after the Second World War. Individual books were still extremely rare: the only examples are the *Russisches Tagebuch 1916–1918* of 1976 by Countess Nora Kinsky, born in 1888, who travelled to Russian prisoner camps for the Red Cross and nursed Austro-Hungarian prisoners of war,[56] and the short war account by Mary Gasch, born in 1894 in Austrian Silesia, who in the summer of 1914 volunteered with her sister. Later she worked as a member of a surgical team of the Order of Malta and at the end of the war was deployed to the Western Front. She was not able to self-publish her narratives of these years until 1978.[57] The only other text of this kind was not released until 2015, when an edition of letters and autobiographical texts written by two Maltese Order nurses of aristocratic background appeared under the striking title *Zwei Schwestern an der Front*.[58] Its uniqueness

---

deutsches Ehrenbuch (Berlin, 1932; 2nd edn. 1936), containing 52 fragments from diaries and memoirs of German First World War nurses. In this period, literary texts were also published, such as Countess Edith Salburg, *Kamerad Susanne: Ein Erleben* (Dresden, 1936).

[53] Schulte, 'The Sick Warrior's Sister', 123.

[54] Eveline Hrouda, *Barmherzigkeit: Als freiwillige Malteserschwester im Weltkrieg* (Graz, 1935); partially analysed in Hämmerle, '"Mentally broken, physically a wreck . . ."'.

[55] Margarete von Rohrer, *Im Krieg gegen Wunden und Krankheit* (Brünn, n.d. [1942]).

[56] Nora Gräfin Kinsky, *Russisches Tagebuch 1916–1918*, with a preface by Fürstin Gina von Liechtenstein, ed. Hans Graf Huyn (Stuttgart, 1976).

[57] Mary Gasch, *Im Dienste des Nächsten: Oberschwester Mary Gasch berichtet über ihre Tätigkeit an allen Fronten des 1. Weltkriegs* (Vienna, 1978 [self-published]), 20 pp. The preface is written by Hedda Vogl, who helped to release the memoirs as a self-publication.

[58] *Zwei Schwestern an der Front: Edina Gräfin Clam-Gallas und Therese Gräfin Buquoy als Malteserschwestern im Ersten Weltkrieg (1915–1918)*, ed. Sudetendeutsches Institut e. V. (Munich, 2015).

demonstrates the persistence of a blind spot that seems to hinder the acquisition of comprehensive knowledge of the circumstances and experiences of First World War nurses in former Austria, and goes hand in hand with a continuing lack of fundamental research.[59] All these women were generally ignored in public commemorations and in the historical literature. If they did appear on the public stage, either they had to face the ambivalent reputation of war nurses, or their stories were politically instrumentalized and incorporated into hegemonic war narratives which only partially corresponded to their own interpretations.

Tensions and Contradictions: The Complexity of the Nurses' War Accounts

These interpretations, which are naturally quite heterogeneous, can be analysed from two perspectives: first, by focusing on how they were inscribed into the dominant cultures of war remembrance and established gender-based hierarchies, which shaped nurses' war accounts given the time of their origin (and publication); and second, by looking at ambivalences, intertwined contradictory passages, or war interpretations that do not fit into such patterns, and therefore undermined hegemonic discourses in many ways by offering counter-narratives. The character of these accounts depended strongly on the level of experience. In war accounts of nurses who had served at the front and, in so doing and unlike other women, had left the traditional 'private sphere' or the strongly feminized spaces that were ascribed to nursing before the Great War, the second perspective is quite strong. This is true even though their texts were at the same time (gender-)ideologizing and patriotic or even tendentious and apologetic,[60] not least because women were attempting to achieve agency in the public domain and in the dominant culture of war remembrance.

But let us return to Regina Schulte's statement, quoted above, that all these documents represent 'a many-layered and rich corpus of texts'.[61] Margaret Darrow has underlined this view by analysing the memoirs of French nurses, which she defines as a 'mixed genre,

[59] See Hämmerle, '"Mentally broken, physically a wreck . . ."', 93–5.

[60] See Schulte, 'The Sick Warrior's Sister'; or, for another context with regard to colonialism and appropriate rhetoric, the micro-study by Alison Fell, 'Nursing the Other: The Representation of Colonial Troops in French and British First World War Nursing Memoirs', in Santanu Das (ed.), *Race, Empire and First World War Writing* (Cambridge, 2011), 158–74.   [61] Schulte, 'The Sick Warrior's Sister', 123.

including obvious propaganda . . . as well as documentary chronicles of women's war experience'.[62] The last part of this essay will focus on this aspect, and ask why former war nurses came to write in a more or less strongly antagonistic or ambivalent, not to say contradictory fashion, which relates, in the words of Alison Fell, to the fact that '[c]ultural constructions of nursing . . . failed to account for the diverse realities of women's experiences'.[63] This will be illustrated, albeit only in a quite fragmentary manner, by some war accounts dating from the 1920s, the early 1930s, and the period after 1945.[64]

It is obvious that they all presented various 'stories' and interpretations which can hardly be reduced to homogeneous discursive patterns. This might be why Pöll-Naepflin's war memoirs were read in so many different and sometimes disparaging ways: they were initially praised by the Nazis because of an inherent heroization of front-line nursing and of the soldiers of the First World War, but fell out of favour shortly afterwards because of their realistic war descriptions, pacifist statements, harsh war criticism, and accusations.[65] Such a variety of interpretations corresponds with the position of these women who, initially, were supposed to be deployed behind the lines only, a policy that proved to be unfeasible soon after the outbreak of the war and had to be reversed.[66] Evoking the famous figure of Florence Nightingale, Duchess Therese von Buquoy remembered in the 1960s that '[w]e, too, had to fight against traditional and conventional opinions and prejudices, and to break down many barriers'.[67] This is to say that in many ways nurses had to transgress the conventional ascription of feminine roles and virtues.

We can therefore ask how these women should be categorized in terms of gender. Obviously, they were often not acting in a

[62] Darrow, *French Women*, 153.

[63] Alison Fell, 'Witness or Participant? British and French First World War Nursing Memoirs', *Knjiženstvo*, 5/5 (2015), online at ⟨http://www.knjizenstvo.rs/magazine.php?text=150⟩ [accessed 20 Oct. 2016].

[64] Excluded, therefore, are war accounts by nurses which were published during the First or the Second World War, or in the context of the National Socialist regime.

[65] Religiosity in a positive sense is not, as such, a topic of these war memoirs. On the contrary, they are characterized by harsh criticism of representatives of the Catholic Church and a loss of religiosity as a result of the drama of war. However, Pöll-Naepflin turned towards religiosity again in the early 1930s, describing her experience in her last chapter, which was later integrated into her account, as a very spiritual conversion.

[66] This happened in the Habsburg monarchy as it did in other warring countries. For Germany see Schulte, 'The Sick Warrior's Sister', 106.

[67] *Zwei Schwestern an der Front*, 507.

way that society defined as appropriate to women, although they fulfilled a genuinely female task. But were they really 'comrades' or even female 'soldiers', as the senior officer Kerchnawe put it? Why were some so keen to be integrated into the postwar construct of the traditional purely male-gendered 'front community'? These questions acquire all the more importance when we remember what Konrad said about her diary and the 'third sex' of nurses. Their war accounts show a collective tendency which seems, at first glance, to be odd, and on closer inspection rather original in terms of gender: the connection between female front-line nursing—that is, working in places or spheres where women were not, in fact, supposed to be—and writing about war was historically new.[68] To 'go to the front', and thus to enter the field of military action and combat, was above all what caused them to keep a diary or take notes during their deployment and, subsequently, to write their memoirs based on this material or on 'hundreds of . . . photographs' taken during the war, as mentioned by Pöll-Naepflin in her text.[69] In this, nurses of the First World War clearly resembled male combatants. More generally, the 'immense need for self-expression that warfare has always aroused, from the Napoleonic Wars to more recent conflicts' also applied to these women. They, too, tried to 'recount their experiences of war, describe its violence, or at least try to say something about it', although, as Stéphane Audoin-Rouzeau and Annette Becker point out as well, perhaps without success.[70] However, it seems to me that postwar society did not appreciate this effort, still less because it came from women.

Recent research has suggested that such texts, like those of male soldiers, should be read as 'trauma narratives', which were often written in a fragmentary, elliptical, incoherent, impressionistic, or modernist style.[71] This seems to correspond to the nurses'

[68] Naturally, women had also written many diaries, letters, and memoirs before that, but not in response to this sort of a relationship with the war and the military. For an early exception dating from the Napoleonic Wars, see Regula Engel, *Frau Oberst Engel: Memoiren einer Amazone aus Napoleonischer Zeit* (1821; repr. Zurich, 2009).

[69] Pöll-Naepflin, *Fortgerungen*, 139.

[70] Stéphane Audoin-Rouzeau, *Annette Becker, 14–18: Understanding the Great War* (New York, 2002), 16.

[71] M. R. Higonnet, 'Authenticity and Art in Trauma Narratives of World War I', *Modernism/Modernity*, 9/1(2002), 91–107; Das, *Touch and Intimacy*, 177–228; Santanu Das, 'The Impotence of Sympathy: Touch and Trauma in the Memoirs of First World War Nurses', *Textual Practice*, 19/2 (2005), 239–62; Christine E. Hallett, 'Portrayals of Suffering: Perceptions of Trauma in the Writings of First World War Nurses and

often shocking, exhausting, and challenging, if not overwhelming, experiences on the 'second battlefield'—that is, in the surgery units or mobile hospitals and casualty-clearing stations near the front, where the medical staff fought a constant battle, often in vain, against the 'real' enemies of the wounded soldiers, namely death and pain.[72] This is also a topic of the nurses' war accounts, although they differ significantly in how often these events are described. Nevertheless, it can be found in all the texts under consideration here, including the short account by Mary Gasch, who also writes about 'low-flying aeroplanes' in Kalusz in Galicia that 'dropped twenty bombs onto our hospital during the night',[73] or about her work at Camporosota 'directly at the front line' in Italy, where her group of Maltese Order nurses consisted 'almost completely' of volunteers after the chief physician's appeal for staff. The situation there was 'simply horrible': 'In one night, we had to amputate ten legs with Dr Hofer. They were all very serious cases of gas phlegmon.'[74]

Other former nurses told many more such stories and elaborated them in detail, mostly in the context of describing the consequences of various battles. In so doing, they left no doubt about the destructiveness of modern weaponry and industrialized warfare, which they sometimes experienced at first hand, as it was not uncommon for casualty-clearing stations to be targeted by artillery or air raids. These scenes of war also accompanied the women travelling to and from their deployment sites. The descriptions of such events in nurses' accounts are similar and even use expressions such as 'baptism of fire' to describe the first time they were confronted with battle.[75] They depicted the sound of grenades and the exploding of mortars and how the local population and animals fled and retreated together with the soldiers, and so on. I can give only brief examples

Volunteers', *Canadian Bulletin of Medical History/Bulletin canadien d'histoire de la médecine*, 27/1 (2010), 65–84.

[72] The term 'second battlefield' for the place of deployment of medical staff in war hospitals was coined by the American novelist Mary Borden, who was herself a war nurse on the Western Front. See Angela K. Smith, *The Second Battlefield: Women, Modernism and the First World War* (Manchester, 2000); Higonnet (ed.), *Nurses at the Front*.

[73] Gasch (ed.), *Im Dienste des Nächsten*, 9.

[74] Ibid. 13.

[75] This could mark the beginning of the nurses' disillusionment, starting shortly after they had described their departure as filled with war enthusiasm, or even determination. See Schulte, 'The Sick Warrior's Sister', 103–4; Hämmerle, '"Mentally broken, physically a wreck . . .'", 95–6.

here,[76] such as the narrative by R. M. Konrad, in which she described the events of December 1915 at the hospital in Ljubljana. She 'heard a muffled bang, followed by people scurrying about'. Then a nurse, 'looking completely frightened', approached her 'and said that the surgery had been bombed, two men were dead', and the surgery was 'a heap of rubble'. This was followed by 'another bang', which again made her 'knees go weak and quiver'.[77] There are similar descriptions by Marianne Jarka, whose memoirs are still unpublished, and by Eveline Hrouda, whose book, as we have seen, was released in 1935 during the period of Austro-Fascism. Nevertheless, it contains passages describing in detail the consequences of the bloody battles at the Isonzo front in August and September 1917, which allows us to understand why Hrouda was completely exhausted and collapsed:

But they weren't corpses; arms and legs were scattered about, heads without eyes, torsos without heads and without limbs, half rotted, completely black relics of men as well as pieces of bodies full of worms . . . The sight was horrible. But we live in the age of humanity.[78]

And then the wagons with injured soldiers arrived. . . . What a sad burden that was. . . . And then there was the stitching up, amputations. Skull and abdominal operations during the whole night, one after another, throughout the day and again at night, until all of them had been cared for or poorly and hastily buried under debris.[79]

It is perhaps unnecessary to mention again that Pöll-Naepflin's book, the starting point of this essay, contains many such passages, which could also culminate in rather war-critical, accusatory, or even pacifist statements. In some but not all of the cases discussed here, such remarks were intertwined with descriptions of the brutal consequences of war, mass murder, the pain of the soldiers, and so on. Sometimes they consisted of only one sentence or a sarcastic phrase, such as the critical reference to the 'age of humanity'; at other times a more elaborate paragraph was included assigning blame for the catastrophe, as in this passage by Agathe Fessler using arguments probably drawn from her previous social work:

---

[76] For more examples and further analysis see Hämmerle, '"Mentally broken, physically a wreck . . ."', 95–101.
[77] Konrad, *Schwestern als Menschen*, 15.
[78] Hrouda, *Barmherzigkeit*, 147–8.
[79] Jarka, 'Erinnerungen 1889–1934', 71–2.

The four years of service for the fatherland passed by over many a night. Was it possible? In the twentieth century? To force so many millions to take up weapons and to set them at each other like mindless animals? To force them to kill? And what was the driving force behind the horrible world war? It was the stock exchange; the bloodthirsty greed for money: the currency trade with its fabulous, effortless profits, benefiting from the confusion of different European languages with which people can easily be divided, but most of all it was the alcohol, capitalism's right hand.[80]

An abundance of similar remarks can be found again in Pöll-Naepflin's autobiographical text, corresponding to the statement in her preface, where she wrote that 'as a woman', she 'condemns war'. The National Socialists, as we know, did not appreciate this at all. It is also doubtful whether they, or the remilitarized Austrian society of the 1930s, would have agreed with Jarka. According to her unpublished account, her war experiences were permanently traumatizing:

How many dressings encrusted with blood have I cut! Among them those who had injured themselves in order to be returned home. They had to be reported, and were liable to be court-martialled. The physician was obliged to do so. But nobody had told me anything like that. When I detected one of them, I brutally treated the wound with iodine, and the black of the gunpowder with a sharp spoon. They clenched their teeth, und I did not feel guilty. If he managed to be returned home, I had saved a mother's son, a father of children, at least for the time being. Who knows, for how long?[81]

Naturally, this attitude was not what the army expected from nurses. Although we do not know how often they acted like this, Jarka's story suggests that many of these women must have been torn between the expectation of treating injured soldiers for the purpose of getting them fit for action again, their empathy with the wounded men (including enemy soldiers), and their wish for the war and the suffering it caused to end.

Let us finish by turning to another aspect and looking at the tension nurses had to balance in the texts under examination here, which resulted from the sexualization of their occupation and the negative reputation of the new mass phenomenon of female nursing in the form of rumours, pictures, and fantasies pertaining to nursing.[82] It has become clear that these women, who experienced the brutal

[80] Fessler, *Aus der Mappe*, 64.   [81] Jarka, 'Erinnerungen 1889–1934', 72.
[82] This becomes clear e.g. in the voluminous diary of Bernhardine Alma, a young Viennese woman from a wealthy middle-class family, whose parents forbade her to

consequences of industrial warfare far from home, who often had to endure miserable, shocking living conditions for years, and were integrated into military structures,[83] could not be 'women' as conventionally understood. That is to say, they would have been lost had they continued to act in a 'feminine' fashion. It therefore seems plausible that, whether they belonged to a religious order or not, they might have tried to adopt the role of a 'third sex', a human being without any sexual identity who acted as a sister, a mother, or a comrade of the soldier.[84] At the same time, they had to face the allegation that many nurses or assistant nurses behaved wrongly, acting as 'false nurses' or 'nurses *mondaines*', whose 'key failing', as Margaret Darrow has put it, 'was their sexuality'.[85]

A close reading of some of the texts analysed here shows how their authors responded to these prejudices. They prove, first, that such a discourse did, in fact, exist and, second, that the sexualization mentioned above created discriminatory divisions among nurses and auxiliaries that shaped their identity in many ways. Thus, these women themselves contributed to the construction of an image of the 'false nurse' through their writings and publications. They either underlined their own respectability and (sexual) integrity, or, often at the same time, wrote about women who apparently belonged to the 'other' group. In Konrad's diary-like book, this even becomes the main narrative. Konrad, who worked as a senior nurse, repeatedly mentions that many of her subordinates serving in the rear of the Italian front line displayed inappropriate or even immoral behaviour: they smoked and drank alcohol, were identified as thieves, became obsessed with pleasure-seeking, sexual adventures, and so on.[86] 'And a nurse could fall into disrepute quite easily. Therefore, the nurses should keep to themselves,' she wrote.[87]

Let us conclude with Pöll-Naepflin. She also perpetuated the image of the 'false nurse' and therefore contributed, indirectly, to the sexualized denunciation of a large proportion of nurses and assistant

volunteer and become a Red Cross nurse after the war had broken out, although she had a strong desire to do so. The topic is frequently addressed in her diary: see Sammlung Frauennachlässe, Institut für Geschichte, Universität Wien, NL 9. Parts of this diary have now been edited and are available online: ⟨http://www.univie.ac.at/Geschichte/salon21/?p=16604⟩ [accessed 20 Oct. 2016].

[83] Indeed, these nurses were subjected to military jurisdiction and the military disciplinary code. For Germany see Stölzle, *Kriegskrankenpflege*, 37.
[84] Schulte, 'The Sick Warrior's Sister'.   [85] Darrow, *French Women*, 148.
[86] Konrad, *Schwestern als Menschen*, vol. i, e.g. 48, 53, 58.   [87] Ibid. 94.

nurses in the First World War. Pöll-Naepflin wrote about nurses in the rear area of the Serbian front, where 'many sugar babies and proper prostitutes' also worked.[88] In Czech hospitals 'nurses had rendezvous with their lovers', couples would meet 'in the dressing room for the most intimate tête-à-tête', and nurses 'did their shift in the casino instead of on the ward'.[89] More often than not 'these manmad women' had to be 'replaced after three or four months, either because of an infectious disease or because they became pregnant'.[90] She gives the following summary:

> Nurses needed great strength and inner stability to overcome everything. It was not easy to be a nurse in professional terms, but it was even more difficult to remain a respectable nurse. In my experience, I must underline that the majority of professional nurses were driven by a feeling of honest duty, and lived a modest and moral lifestyle. It is undeniable that sometimes nurses and officers or doctors developed a certain fondness for each other, but this often led to marriage . . . But the female auxiliary personnel who were often arbitrarily thrown together consisted mainly of adventurers and coquettes, who degraded our profession through their nymphomaniac behaviour, and brought ridicule on us and provided much material for sarcasm.[91]

Outlook

The last quotation points to the main functions that these texts had for their authors: the nurses were not only driven by their wish to be heard and valued after the end of the catastrophe, as they had given so much during the First World War. Their writing also had an apologetic or self-justifying aim which resulted from the fact that these women had entered the military field during the conflict, and had experienced and supported the war close to the battlefield. In gender terms their war effort had proved difficult, as it upset the hegemonic gender order and moved female non-combatants closer to male combatants; it also blurred the boundaries between these groups, at least regarding their own identity as constructed in their texts and in some public descriptions. Such constructions must be read against the backdrop of wartime and postwar societies, and all their ambivalences and contradictory tensions must be integrated into our analysis.

[88] Pöll-Naeplfin, *Durchgerungen*, 77.
[89] Ibid. 136.   [90] Ibid. 137.
[91] Ibid. 90.

In this regard, some of the arguments presented in this essay remain tentative, and much will be left to future research. It has been my intention to introduce a set of remarkable and long-forgotten ego documents of the First World War. They originated in different contexts of writing and publication (or its denial), but were all penned by women who had previously served as professional, partly trained, or volunteer front nurses for Austria-Hungary. We have seen that their voices, however much they may have been edited, were marginalized or neglected in most cases, and did not attract the wider public interest of postwar society, which to some extent contrasts with the situation in Britain.[92] This is the consequence—albeit not the only one—of a strongly gendered culture of war remembrance and historiography on the one hand, and the ambivalent reputation of war nursing in the former Austria on the other.[93] Also after 1918, the former nurses had to cope with it in their texts.

[92] According to Christine E. Hallett's analysis, at least a small number of VAD-E. writings, including the one by Vera Brittain, gained attention and readership from the beginning: Christine Hallett, '"A very valuable fusion of classes": British Professional and Volunteer Nurses of the First World War', *Endeavour*, 38/2 (2014), 101–10. For France, Darrow refers to similar waters of forgetfulness: see Darrow, *French Women*; ead., 'French Volunteer Nursing and the Myth of War Experience in World War I', *American Historical Review*, 101/1 (1996), 80–106.

[93] This had already started during the Balkan Wars, as Elisabeth Malleier argues in '"Das Débacle der Frau als Pflegerin": Sexismus und Nationalismus in österreichischen Debatten zur Kriegskrankenpflege im frühen 20. Jahrhundert', in Andrea Thiekötter, Heinrich Recken, Manuela Schoska, and Eva-Maria Ulmer (eds.), *Alltag in der Pflege: Wie machten sich Pflegende bemerkbar? Beiträge des 8. Inernationalen Kongresses zur Geschichte der Pflege 2008* (Frankfurt a.M., 2009), 231–44.

8

Front Experience and Psychological Problems: The Voices of Doctors and Patients in Case Studies and Patient Files

Andrea Gräfin von Hohenthal

Introduction

New studies in military medicine during the First World War have taken the soldier-as-patient as the subject of research, rather than focusing on the physician.[1] English-language historians in particular have attempted to explain the therapeutic setting and the relationship between the patient and the physician informing contemporary discussions and thought regarding disciplinary developments in medicine.[2] Although 'patient history' began in the historiography of medicine, there was a strong mutual influence between this and social and military history. The ordinary soldier became a focal point of research, and historians developed an interest in social demoralization, humiliation, and the devastating effects of war on

---

I am currently working on my Ph.D. in history at the University of Freiburg. My dissertation is a comparative study of the development of psychology in Britain and Germany during the First World War. While holding a scholarship from the German Historical Institute London, I conducted research at the National Archives, the Welcome Library, the Imperial War Museums, the Archives of the British Psychological Society, and the British Library.

[1] Petra Peckl, 'What the Patient Records Reveal: Reassessing the Treatment of "War Neurotics" in Germany (1914–1918)', in Hans-Georg Hofer, Cay-Rüdiger Prüll, and Wolfgang U. Eckart (eds.), *War, Trauma and Medicine in Germany and Central Europe (1914–1939)* (Freiburg, 2011), 139–59; P. Rau, 'Die militärpsychiatrischen Therapiemethoden im Ersten Weltkrieg: Diskurs und Praxis', in H.-W. Schmuhl and V. Roelcke (eds.), *'Heroische Therapien': Die deutsche Psychiatrie im internationalen Vergleich, 1918–1945* (Göttingen, 2013), 29–47.

[2] e.g. E. Jones, 'Doctors and Trauma in the First World War: The Response of British Military Psychiatrists', in Peter Gray and Kendrick Oliver (eds.), *The Memory of Catastrophe* (Manchester, 2004), 91–105; Ben Shephard, 'Psychiatry at the Front, 1917–1918', in id., *A War of Nerves: Soldiers and Psychiatrists 1914–1994* (London, 2002), 53–71.

soldiers' minds and bodies.[3] Scholars have only recently drawn on patient-related sources from doctors for their research.[4] This essay discusses how and why patient files and patient cases published by psychologically minded psychiatrists strengthened the belief in 'authentic' access to understanding the war and in their potential to inform us about the feelings, emotions, and war experiences of the patients and doctors. In this essay I will focus on the question of whether these sources can be seen as ego documents. The Dutch historian Jacob Presser, who first coined the term, defined ego documents as 'documents in which an ego intentionally or unintentionally discloses, or hides itself'.[5] Kaspar von Greyerz, however, critical of the growing interest in ego documents, concludes that the majority of these texts 'tell us more about groups than they do about individuals'.[6] The problem with patient-related sources is that they combine at least two voices: the doctor who asks, examines, and writes about the patient, and the patient who answers and talks about his experiences. Is it possible to distinguish these voices and to identify the ego of either the doctor or the patient talking about personal war experiences?

I will focus on eight psychologically minded psychiatrists, all members of their national professional societies in Britain or Germany, and will discuss whether their case studies, published in articles and books, can tell us anything about the personal experiences of these doctors or the soldiers who were the object of their treatment. Patient files kept by two of these psychiatrists will be analysed in the same way. I do not intend to discuss the problem of diagnosis and treatment of shell-shocked soldiers in general, but I want to look at the potential of sources to provide an insight into

[3] Gerd Krumeich, 'Kriegsgeschichte im Wandel', in Gerhard Hirschfeld, Gerd Krumeich, and Irina Renz (eds.), *Keiner fühlt sich hier mehr als Mensch: Erlebnis und Wirkung des Ersten Weltkrieg* (Essen, 1993), 11–24; Wencke Meteling, 'Neue Kulturgeschichte', in Gerhard Hirschfeld, Gerd Krumeich, and Irina Renz (eds.), *Enzyklopädie Erster Weltkrieg*, 2nd edn. (Paderborn, 2014), 1047–51.

[4] Maria Hermes, *Krankheit Krieg: Psychiatrische Deutungen des Ersten Weltkrieges* (Essen, 2012), 139–59; E. Jones, R. Shahina, and B. Everitt, 'Psychiatric Case Notes: Symptoms of Mental Illness and their Attribution at the Maudsley Hospital, 1924–35', *History of Psychiatry*, 23/2 (2012), 156–68; E. Jones and S.-C. Linden, 'German Battle Casualties: The Treatment of Functional Somatic Disorders during World War I', *Journal of the History of Medicine and Allied Sciences*, 68/4 (2012), 627–58.

[5] R. Dekker, 'Introduction', in *Egodocuments and History: Autobiographical Writing in its Social Context since the Middle Ages* (Hilversum, 2002).

[6] Kaspar von Greyerz, 'Ego-Documents: The Last Word?', *German History*, 28/3 (2010), 273–82.

the personal experiences of both doctors and soldiers coping with trauma.

I will proceed in three steps. First I will introduce four British and four German psychologically minded military psychiatrists who worked with patients at the front or in a hospital at home. I will then discuss general problems of using case studies and patient files in history. Finally, I will use these published case histories and some patient files to attempt to reveal the views of doctors and patients in the First World War who were confronted with the mental injuries of war.

All of the psychologically minded doctors in my case study published their articles or worked at the front around 1916. This was an important year for the psychiatry of mentally disturbed soldiers. In 1916, during the Battles of the Somme and Verdun, incidences of shell shock spiralled out of control, forcing the medical and military authorities to acknowledge mental health problems which until then had been ignored. Between April 1915 and April 1916, 1,300 officers and 10,000 men from the lower ranks had been admitted to special hospitals in Britain.[7] The year 1916 also saw an increase in shell-shocked soldiers in Germany. Both countries were concerned about possible future pensions for which these soldiers might be eligible after the war, so that it became increasingly important both to develop new psychotherapeutic methods to explain and treat soldiers' psychological problems, and to prevent such problems occurring among new recruits. This presented an excellent opportunity for doctors, especially psychologically minded ones, to promote their special knowledge and competence. Faced with multiple expectations from military authorities, public interest, and psychiatric suspicion, these psychological experts fought for their cause[8] and offered new treatments to address the mental problems linked to warfare.

In the scientific communities of both countries there was no consensus about the diagnosis or treatment of the multiple symptoms seen in mentally troubled soldiers. The very term 'shell shock', which had become common, was soon discouraged by the British Army medical services, so that even the newspapers tried to avoid it.[9]

---

[7] Fiona Reid, *Broken Men: Shell Shock Treatment and Recovery in Britain 1914–1930* (London, 2011).
[8] See e.g. the articles mentioned here, published in *The Lancet* in 1916.
[9] At the end of 1915 the Army Council tried to replace the term 'shell shock' with the

Since no one was able to provide a suitable alternative, however, it soon became commonplace even for professionals to use the term while simultaneously apologizing for it.[10] As William Brown reported of a discussion at the Royal Society of Medicine: 'Much variety of opinion on origin, symptoms and treatment came to light.'[11] Was shell shock a 'collection of different nervous affections from concussion to sheer funk, which have merely this much in common that nervous control has at last given way?'[12] Organic causes were discussed, such as scattered haemorrhages after shell explosions or inhalation of poisonous gases. It was obviously linked in many cases to a loss of memory and the occurrence of nightmares, which triggered the symptoms. Treatment was controversial. Was it sufficient to make friends with the patient or give him low-level narcotics? Electro-shock therapy, more widely used in the Habsburg Empire and in Germany, was dismissed by their British colleagues: 'Dr. Head emphasized the uselessness of treating acute dread by putting a man in bed and treating him with electricity.'[13] It was in this context of scholarly debates that the psychological psychiatrists published their articles, discussing new methods for dealing with the problem of shell-shocked soldiers.

In Germany the situation was similar, but the solution was different. Although it was soon common opinion that the psychological problems experienced by soldiers and officers were related to well-known peacetime conditions such as hysteria and neurasthenia, in September 1916 at a conference in Munich the medical community tried to arrive at a consensus about the cause and treatment of the functional and psychic symptoms of First World War combatants.[14]

category 'Not Yet Diagnosed Nervous' (NYDN). See Anthony Babington, *Shell-Shock: A History of the Changing Attitudes to War Neurosis* (London, 1997), 62. The *Journal of the RAMC* rarely used the term and *The Times* preferred to write about 'shock' or 'nerves'. See Reid, *Broken Men*, 27.

[10] 'The term "shell shock" is used unwillingly in this paper in order to avoid multiplication of names': H. Wiltshire, 'A Contribution to the Aetiology of Shell Shock', *The Lancet*, 17 June 1917, 1207–12, at 1207. 'I am fully aware of the inadequacy and inappropriateness of this term, but the plain English word is less likely to give rise to misunderstanding': G. E. Smith, 'Shock and the Soldier', *The Lancet*, 187, 15 Apr. 1916, 813–17, at 813.

[11] William Brown, 'A Discussion on Shell Shock', *The Lancet*, 187, 5 Feb. 1916, 306–7.
[12] Ibid. 306.   [13] Ibid. 307.
[14] 'Verhandlungen psychiatrischer Vereine: Kriegstagung des Deutschen Vereins für Psychiatrie am 21. und 22. September 1916', *Allgemeine Zeitschrift für Psychiatrie und psychisch-gerichtliche Medizin*, 73/2–3 (1917), 163–233.

Most of the psychiatrists, among them the psychologically minded, who took part in this meeting agreed that the soldiers' nervous problems were the result not of physical injuries to the brain but rather of psychological problems. The doctors decided, however, that this problem was caused not by the war experience itself but by an inner disposition which made the soldiers more vulnerable to stress and strain. Since this inner disposition was the cause, the affected soldiers should not be entitled to a pension. From this time on, more aggressive methods of treating the soldiers were recommended, methods that were intended to force them out of their illness by making conditions in the clinic more uncomfortable than those that obtained at the front. Nevertheless, soldiers were not sent back to the front after their treatment, but were made to work in war industries.[15]

The Psychologists

Gentlemen,—From the combatant's point of view this has been described as industrial warfare; from the medical point of view it might be well characterised as nerve warfare, for an outstanding feature has been the large number of soldiers . . . who have suffered from what are very properly called functional disorders, with or without injuries or organic disease. Of such patients 110 have come under my own notice; a study of the material will be, I hope, not only a contribution to our knowledge of the psycho-neuroses but perhaps a help to an understanding of the psychology of the soldiers.[16]

Montague David Eder opened his speech at the Malta Medical Conference on 9 April 1916 with these words. As a temporary captain of the Royal Army Medical Corps (RAMC), he was the medical officer in charge of the neurological department in Malta, and had worked there throughout the Gallipoli campaign.[17] One year later, he published his experiences during his work on the South-Eastern Front. Eder is in many respects an interesting figure. According to Freud, besides being the first to practise psychoanalysis in England, Eder also made substantial contributions to other causes, most notably

---

[15] Paul Lerner, *Hysterical Men: War, Psychiatry, and the Politics of Trauma in Germany, 1890–1930* (Ithaca, NY, 2003), 124–62.
[16] M. D. Eder, 'The Psycho-Pathology of the War Neuroses: Delivered at the Malta Medical Conference on April 9th, 1916', *The Lancet*, 188, 9 Aug. 1916, 264–8.
[17] M. D. Eder, *War-Shock: The Psycho-Neuroses in War Psychology and Treatment* (London, 1917), 1.

Zionism and socialism.[18] Those beliefs shaped the intentions with which he wrote his book, *War-Shock*, published in 1917. He wanted to stress the importance of psychotherapeutic treatment, the contributions of the working class to the war effort, and the psychology of the soldier.

In 1916 two other authors, who were working in France on the Western Front, Charles Myers[19] and William Brown,[20] also published their experiences with neurotic soldiers. All three were members of the Psychological Society, doctors, and temporary RAMC officers. They were part of a small but significant group of psychologically minded doctors who were responsible for important advances in psychiatric diagnosis, psychopathology, and treatment, and were involved in the organization of British military psychiatry.[21] Myers, born in 1873, was a doctor who had worked as a psychologist at the University of Cambridge. In 1915, in part because of his networking skills, he was made responsible for the psychological cases admitted to French hospitals, and in 1916 was appointed consultant psychologist to the British armies in France, where he organized psychological treatment centres near the front.[22]

Myers was the first to use the term 'shell shock' in an article in *The Lancet*, in which he described three cases of injured soldiers with peculiar symptoms, all of whom had been near a shell explosion. One reported that a shell exploded near him, giving him a blow 'like a punch on the head, without any pain after it'. After being dug out of the trench, he remembered: 'It was dark when they dug me out. After I got out, a chap said, "The fellow's mad," and I said "you're a liar".'[23] Myers, who repeated the soldier's words exactly, was clearly astonished by these symptoms, as his concluding remarks reveal:

---

[18] J. B. Hobman and M. D. Eder, 'Foreword', in *David Eder: Memoirs of a Modern Pioneer* (London, 1945).

[19] Charles S. Myers, 'Contributions to the Study of Shell Shock', *The Lancet*, 187, 8 Jan. 1916, 65–9; 18 Mar. 1916, 608–13; 9 Sept. 1916, 461–8.

[20] See above, n. 11.

[21] Edgar Jones and Simon Wessely, *Shell Shock to PTSD: Military Psychiatry from 1900 to the Gulf War* (Hove, 2005), 47; Jones, 'Doctors and Trauma in the First World War'.

[22] F. C. Bartlett, 'Myers, Charles Samuel', in *Oxford Dictionary of National Biography* (Oxford, 2004), 1; online at ⟨www.oxforddnb.com⟩ [accessed 26 Aug. 2015].

[23] Charles S. Myers, 'A Contribution to the Study of Shell Shock: Being an Account of Three Cases of Loss of Memory, Vision, Smell, and Taste, Admitted into the Duchess of Westminster's War Hospital, le Touquet', *The Lancet*, 188, 13 Feb. 1915, 316–20.

They [the cases] appear to constitute a definite class among others arising from the effects of shell shock. The shells in question appear to have burst with considerable noise, scattering much dust, but this was not attended by the production of odour. It is therefore difficult to understand why hearing should be unaffected, and the dissociated 'complex' be confined to the senses of sight, smell and taste (and to memory). The close relation of these cases to those of 'hysteria' appears fairly certain.[24]

Myers later developed a more sophisticated understanding of shell shock as a psychological condition,[25] but the idea that the 'wind of the explosion', the wind of the shell, could cause nervous injuries persisted.[26]

William Brown, born in 1881, was also a psychological researcher before the First World War. Having taken further degrees in medicine and surgery, he was involved in medical work during the war. He served in Egypt,[27] and then as a specialist at the 'Not Yet Diagnosed Nervous' (NYDN) Centre[28] in France between November 1916 and March 1917,[29] and published articles about his work with shell-shocked soldiers and officers at the front and at two military hospitals.[30]

Although not clinical psychiatrists, all three researchers were put in charge of the mentally troubled soldiers who began to pour in from the Western Front. They were neither experienced in psychiatry nor leading members of the RAMC, but they were appointed by the military forces to leading positions with considerable responsibility, possibly because of the lack of others available, or because the authorities expected new results from the science of psychology.

[24] Ibid.; see also Charles S. Myers, *Shell Shock in France: 1914–18* (Cambridge, 1940).

[25] Charles S. Myers, 'A Final Contribution to the Study of Shell Shock: Being a Consideration of Unsettled Points Needing Investigation', *The Lancet*, 193, 11 Jan. 1919, 51–4.

[26] In *The Lancet* this subject was often mentioned throughout 1915, e.g. Anon., 'Nervous Injuries Due to Shell Explosions', *The Lancet*, 186, 2 Oct. 1915, 766.

[27] W. Brown, 'The Treatment of Cases of Shell Shock in an Advanced Neurological Centre', *The Lancet*, 192, 17 Aug. 1918, 197–200.

[28] NYDN centres ('Not Yet Diagnosed Nervous', to avoid using the terms 'shell shock' or 'war neurosis') were established in November 1916, in the aftermath of the Somme, to guarantee special treatment near the front for mentally disturbed soldiers: Jones and Wessely, *Shell Shock to PTSD*, 26.

[29] Ibid. 29; National Archives, WO 95/414, 25 Nov. 1916: 'Captain Brown reported his arrival. He is for special duty with shell shock . . . 291 cases.'

[30] Brown, 'A Discussion on Shell Shock', 306–7; id., 'The Treatment of Cases of Shell Shock', 197–20; id., 'War Neurosis: A Comparison of Early Cases Seen in the Field with Those Seen at the Base', *The Lancet*, 193, 17 Mar. 1919, 833–6.

The psychologist and psychiatrist Richard Gundry Rows was in a different situation, working at the Maghull Red Cross Military Hospital near Liverpool. He attracted other psychologists to come and work at his hospital, which became a model for the psychotherapy of shell-shocked soldiers.[31] His work is interesting because he published some case studies and we also have some of his patient files, so the informative value of these sources can be discussed.

Since German military psychiatry was better organized and prepared at the beginning of the war, outsiders such as psychologists working at universities were not able to exert as much influence as in Britain. Nevertheless, some members of the Psychological Society (Gesellschaft für Experimentelle Psychologie) did work with shell-shocked soldiers. Military organization in Germany differed from that in Britain: in Germany there were no hospitals near the front for shell-shocked soldiers; the patients were sent back to Germany, where (after 1915) they were treated in small hospitals in the countryside.[32] In contrast to the British procedure, the soldiers were not sent back to the front even when cured, but were employed in war industries.

I would like to focus on four of these psychiatrists: Friedrich Emil Otto Schultze, a pedagogue, psychologist, and psychiatrist who worked with shell-shocked patients in a military mental hospital after 1914;[33] Willi Hellpach, born in 1877, a former psychiatrist and neurologist, who was put in charge of a hospital for shell-shocked soldiers at the end of 1915 and wrote about his experiences;[34] Walther Poppelreuter, born in 1886, who studied psychology and medicine in Berlin and from the beginning of the war worked with brain-damaged and shell-shocked soldiers (we have a description of his case studies and patient files);[35] and, finally, Willibald Sauer, who worked

---

[31] Ben Shephard, 'The Early Treatment of Mental Disorders: R. G. Rows and Maghull 1914–1918', in G. E. Berrios and Hugh Freeman (eds.), *150 years of British Psychiatry* (London, 1996), 434–64.
[32] R. A. Hoffmann, 'Über die Behandlung der Kriegshysterie in den badischen Nervenlazaretten', *Zeitschrift für die gesamte Neurologie und Psychiatrie*, 55 (1920), 114–17.
[33] F. E. O. Schultze, 'Über die Kaufmannsche Behandlung hysterischer Bewegungsstörungen', *Münchener Medizinische Wochenschrift*, 63 (1916), 1349–53.
[34] W. Hellpach, 'Lazarettdisziplin als Heilfaktor', *Medizinische Klinik*, 44 (1915), 1207–11; id., *Wirken in Wirren: Lebenserinnerungen. Eine Rechenschaft über Wert und Glück, Schuld und Sturz meiner Generation* (Hamburg, 1949).
[35] Walther Poppelreuter, *Die psychischen Schädigungen durch Kopfschuß im Kriege 1914/17: Mit besonderer Berücksichtigung der pathopsychologischen, pädagogischen, gewerblichen und sozialen Beziehungen* (Leipzig, 1917). Poppelreuter worked in a military hospital in Cologne, in

near the front and applied psychoanalytical methods.[36] Schultze, Sauer, and Hellpach published their articles in medical journals, while Walther Poppelreuter wrote about his experiences in a book in 1917.

I have chosen these psychologically minded psychiatrists because all were members of psychological societies. At the beginning of the twentieth century such societies were founded across Europe.[37] At that time psychology was neither a practical profession nor an examined subject at university, but was taught in philosophy faculties. The psychological societies assembled a group of modern thinkers who were willing to measure and solve the problems of the mind through scientific observation and experiment. Some of them were trained as doctors and were involved in the treatment of mentally troubled soldiers. I will show the differences between the British and German psychologists' methods of asking questions to get information about their patients, and argue that applied psychotherapy shaped the way in which questions were formulated and information about the patients was acquired. However, the First World War was also a time of transition, when the demands of war, with unprecedented numbers of mentally disturbed soldiers, required new diagnostic methods and treatments. Consequently, personal remarks and attempts to promote new psychological methods in the scientific community were quite common. In a situation in which there were obviously new psychological problems, military psychiatrists often cited soldiers' personal experiences to underline the practical usefulness of psychological measures.

Case Studies and Patient Files

All the authors mentioned here used case studies in their publications to substantiate their results. From the first half of the nineteenth century, rules had been developed for writing case studies. These

which patients with brain and nerve injuries were treated; some also had mental health issues. I had the opportunity to look through about 120 patient files, of which 37 were from Poppelreuter. Most were written during wartime, from 1915 until 1918, while two of them were of a later date but referred to war-related injuries.

[36] W. Sauer, 'Zur Analyse und Behandlung von Kriegsneurosen', *Zeitschrift für die gesamte Neurologie und Psychiatrie*, 36/1–2 (1917), 27–53.

[37] Britain: British Psychological Society, 1901; France: Société Psychologique, 1901; Germany: Gesellschaft für Experimentelle Psychologie, 1904. See David B. Baker, *The Oxford Handbook of the History of Psychology: Global Perspectives* (Oxford, 2012), 14–16.

rules, designed to encourage the comparability of cases, were accepted by most doctors.[38] The case studies reported here came from patient files, where personal data were collected systematically, and all of the patients were examined by the doctors themselves. The function of the narrative of these cases is threefold: first, they try to underline the theoretical and practical assumptions about the illness, which seemed to be a novelty; second, the language is mostly highly scientific and intended to impress colleagues; and third, some of the case studies are quite exotic, interesting, and seem to illustrate the author's assumptions.[39] The cases are numbered and the rank, age (sometimes also the date of admission), and symptoms are provided. The description is always given in highly medical language, possibly because many of the symptoms were not mental but functional disturbances that presented as physical symptoms.

The patient files are a different type of document: their main purpose was to document the illness and communicate with colleagues. The two sorts of file described and discussed in this paper differ in some regards. For example, the files created by Walther Poppelreuter, who worked with patients with shell shock and head injuries in a hospital in Cologne, are systematic and elaborate. As well as containing the usual clinical information, they document some psychological tests and working observations. These differ from the files normally used for psychiatric patients. The files from the British hospitals are mostly quite short, only occasionally revealing longer treatment procedures, and often they were clearly rushed. In recent years, historians have shown a growing interest in patient records as a source of information about the war experience of doctors and their patients.[40] Although they were patients of

[38] Sibylle Brändli, B. Lüthi, and Gregor Spuhler, *Zum Fall machen, zum Fall werden: Wissensproduktion und Patientenerfahrung in Medizin und Psychiatrie des 19. und 20. Jahrhunderts* (Frankfurt a.M., 2009), 103.

[39] This is clear from the examples that Montague David Eder selected for his presentation to the medical conference in Malta, in contrast to those he describes in his book.

[40] Peckl, 'What the Patient Records Reveal'; S.-C. Linden and E. Jones, 'German Battle Casualties: The Treatment of Functional Somatic Disorders during World War I', *Journal of the History of Medicine and Allied Sciences*, 68/4 (2012), 627–58; S.-C. Linden, E. Jones, and A. J. Lees, 'Shell Shock at Queen Square: Lewis Yealland 100 Years On', *Brain*, 136 (2013), 1976–88; P. Leese, *Shell Shock: Traumatic Neurosis and the British Soldiers of the First World War* (New York, 2002), 91; M. Hermes, *Krankheit: Krieg. Psychiatrische Deutungen des Ersten Weltkrieges* (Essen, 2012); ead., *Psychiatrische Krankheitsauffassungen als diskursive Strategie: Deutungen des Ersten Weltkrieges in Krankenakten des Bremer St. Jürgen-Asyls* (Berlin, 2008).

(military) psychiatrists, the shell-shocked soldiers' situation differed from that of civilians in peacetime. While the soldiers were patients in a mental hospital, they remained members of the armed forces and could be forced to undergo special treatment or diagnosed as malingerers. These psychiatric patients were unlike those seen in peacetime: they had not previously been mentally disturbed;[41] they were young, male, and often physically injured as well.

Reports about soldiers based on patient files have been used by many historians to illustrate the situation and experience of individual soldiers.[42] Other researchers have used them to explore the relationship between medical reports in journals and medical practice in local clinics.[43] Contemporary case studies published in journals or books are often based on patient files, but they have mostly been selected to underline a particular argument about the diagnosis or therapy of nervous disease. Another difficulty in working with patient-related sources is reflected in the theoretical debates[44] between Roy Porter and his followers, who claim to look from the patients' perspective and 'do medical history from below',[45] and researchers such as David Armstrong, who, like Foucault, argues that the patient can be seen only through the medical gaze, constructed through knowledge, discourse, and social demands. As the patient files and case studies are written by doctors and not patients, this question must be discussed.

The Doctors

All the doctors who dealt with shell-shocked patients were confronted with a wide variety of emotional and physical complaints, symptoms without physical wounds. The recorded symptoms varied greatly: 'The symptoms are protean—palsies, analgesia, amblyopia, mutism, deafness, afflictions of the vegetative system such as the

[41] German recruits were examined before serving as soldiers; the British soldier patients admitted to the hospital where Rows worked were asked about previous psychiatric symptoms. See Martin Lengwiler, *Zwischen Klinik und Kaserne: Die Geschichte der Militärpsychiatrie in Deutschland und der Schweiz 1870–1914* (Zurich, 2000), 199–202.
[42] e.g. Leese, *Shell Shock*, 24.
[43] Peckl, 'What the Patient Records Reveal'; Jones, Shahina, and Everitt, 'Psychiatric Case Notes'; Hermes, *Psychiatrische Krankheitsauffassungen*.
[44] F. Condrau, 'The Patient's View Meets the Clinical Gaze', *Social History of Medicine*, 20/3 (2007), 525–40.
[45] Roy Porter, 'The Patient's View: Doing History from Below', *Theory and Society*, 14 (1985), 175–98.

soldiers' heart, vomiting, diarrhoea, insomnia, loss of memory, somnambulism, phobias and obsessions of all kinds.'[46] Every doctor tried to label categories in order to distinguish different groups of symptoms, a difficulty which persisted after the war.[47] Myers tried to differentiate between groups of symptoms;[48] William Brown distinguished between cases seen in the field and those seen later in a base hospital;[49] and David Eder differentiated between patients who displayed mainly emotional problems and those with physical symptoms.[50] Shaking and tremors were described among British soldiers,[51] but not as frequently as among the soldiers of Germany and the Habsburg monarchy (*Kriegszitterer*).[52] For the Western Front, 'shell shock has been given prominence on account of its prevalence and the various hysterical symptoms that have followed high explosives'. For the Eastern Front, David Eder stated that 'exactly the same symptoms have occurred, however, after shrapnel wounds, falls, and without previous injuries at all'.[53] The view that physical wounds were the cause, as the term 'shell shock' indicated, was rejected: 'Shell shock, gas-poisoning, or other physical injuries do not cause the disease.'[54] All the psychologists identified the cause of these symptoms as a hysterical functional disturbance caused by overwhelming stress,[55] but avoided the word 'hysteria' because of its negative connotations. The same response can be seen in contemporary case files, in which most symptoms were either diagnosed

---

[46] Eder, *War-Shock*, 4.

[47] One example was 'soldier's heart', not a category under nervous illnesses in the official RAMC report.

[48] e.g. Charles S. Myers, 'Contribution to the Study of Shell Shock: Being an Account of Certain Disorders of Cutaneous Sensibility', *The Lancet*, 187, 18 Mar. 1916, 608.

[49] W. Brown, 'A Comparison of Early Cases Seen in the Field with Those Seen at the Base', *The Lancet*, 17 Mar. 1916, 833–6, at 833.

[50] Eder, *War-Shock*, 8.

[51] Case No. 5 in Charles S. Myers, 'Contribution to the Study of Shell Shock: Being an Account of Certain Cases Treated by Hypnosis', *The Lancet*, 187, 8 Jan. 1916, 65–9, at 65.

[52] As seen in the work of Stefanie C. Linden, Volker Hess, and Edgar Jones, 'The Neurological Manifestations of the Lessons from World War I', *European Archives of Psychiatry and Clinical Neuroscience*, 262 (2012), 253–64; E. Jones *et al.*, 'Post-Combat Syndromes from the Boer and Gulf Wars: A Cluster Analysis of their Nature and Attribution', *British Medical Journal*, 9 Feb. 2002, 321–4, at 324; H.-G. Hofer, *Nervenschwäche und Krieg: Modernitätskritik und Krisenbewältigung in der österreichischen Psychiatrie (1880–1920)* (Vienna, 2004), 238.

[53] Eder, *War-Shock*, 4.

[54] Ibid. 144.

[55] Ibid. 5.

as 'neurasthenia' or not diagnosed at all.[56] Often a diagnosis was written later in different handwriting and ink. The files seem to have been finished in a hurry. At this time neuroses were seen as the result of stressful external conditions acting on a mind which was more sensitive than average, implying that the symptoms of mentally ill soldiers could be the result of a vulnerable predisposition, a view shared by many German psychiatrists.[57]

Discussing 'war-shock', Montague David Eder instead stressed the influence of external factors: 'In war-shock the external psychic factor is overwhelmingly greater than the second factor—the predisposition.'[58] He distanced himself from the argument about a bad disposition:

> With regard to the common assertion that hysteria is a sign of degeneracy, and the assertion, which was made not in Germany but by writers in this country who claimed to speak with authority, that the English people are a 'degenerated race', it is worth noting that 19 out of 100 cases were Anzacs, and the majority of these 19 were men not from the cities but from the bush . . . However, one can say that the up-country Anzac is not immune, in war anyway, from hysteria.'[59]

Here he echoes racial prejudices concerning British Empire troops,[60] but also displays sympathy with the soldiers: 'Being wrenched away from their customary calling and life, the new discipline, the peculiar and terrible mental strain of the conditions of modern war acting upon this sensitive mind cause the disease among soldiers.'[61] Like some patient files from this time, these case reports by psychological researchers display no marked difference between the diagnoses of soldiers and of officers. In much of the literature on shell shock there is a categorical distinction between hysterical men and neurasthenic officers.[62] This may stem from the military practice of sending officers to special hospitals, thus reinforcing existing class boundaries.[63]

---

[56] e.g. National Archives London (hereafter NA): MH 106/2101 Mental Illness/Neurasthenia Sample Sheets.

[57] Hermes, *Psychiatrische Krankheitsauffassungen*, 18; Lerner, *Hysterical Men*, 61 ff.

[58] Eder, *War-Shock*, 2.

[59] Ibid. 17. 'Anzacs' refers to soldiers of the Australian and New Zealand Army Corps.

[60] J. Leonhard, *Die Büchse der Pandora: Geschichte des Ersten Weltkriegs* (Munich, 2014), 502–3.   [61] Eder, *War-Shock*, 144.

[62] Reid, *Broken Men*, 17.

[63] NA: MH 106/1890: Admission and Discharge for Field Service. Craiglockhart War Hospital at Slatsford. All officers were diagnosed as neurasthenic; only one was suffering from influenza.

R. G. Rows also displayed a rather sympathetic attitude towards his patients. He understood that mental and nervous disturbances occur 'among those who have experienced the strains and shocks of a shorter or longer period at the seat of war'.[64] Taking a psychoanalytical approach, he aimed to demonstrate and explain to the patient 'the relation of cause and effect in the origin and development of his illness'.[65] He assumed that 'when this relation is appreciated both the patient and the physician will begin to realize that they have some ground in common'.[66] He proposed that 'the physician should be prepared to give at least an hour for an interview'. His main aims were not only to provide 'a means of treatment for the individual' but also to 'collect a mass of evidence which will help to develop a new and enlarged view of psychological medicine'.[67] Unlike most German psychologists, Rows defined his role as a doctor rather than as a member of the military.

When treating shell-shocked soldiers, all of the psychologists stressed the importance of psychotherapy and proposed rather unusual methods: 'The treatment par excellence is hypnotic suggestion', claimed the British psychologists.[68] They had to argue against other psychiatrists, even psychologically minded doctors who recommended rest alone, pleasant surroundings,[69] or electro-shock therapy as treatment.[70] Above all, they emphasized their success in returning the soldiers to the front,[71] sometimes exaggerating their results: 'The majority of war-shocked patients so cured can return to the front in three to six weeks.'[72] At the same time, the psychologists affirmed the military character of their therapy: important

[64] R. G. Rows, 'Mental Conditions Following Strain and Nerve Shock', *British Medical Journal*, 25 Mar. 1916, 441–3, at 441.
[65] Ibid. 443. [66] Ibid.
[67] Ibid.
[68] Eder, *War-Shock*, 145.
[69] 'I do not find hypnosis or psychoanalysis necessary or even desirable; only common sense and interest in the welfare and amusement of these neurotic patients are necessary for their recovery': F. Mott, 'Lettsomian Lectures', *The Lancet*, 11 Mar. 1916, 563.
[70] Lewis Ralph Yealland and Edward Farquhar Buzzard, *Hysterical Disorders of Warfare* (London, 1918), p. vi.
[71] 'While in charge of an advanced neurological centre in France during the period November 1916–Februrary 1918 I have had to deal with between two and three thousand cases of psychoneurosis . . .The great majority of cases came under my care within 48 hours of their breakdown, and I was able to return 70 per cent of them to line after an average of a fortnight's rest and treatment in hospital': Brown, 'The Treatment of Cases of Shell Shock', 197.   [72] Eder, *War-Shock*, 145.

remarks 'must be repeated and forced upon the patient's notice',[73] and 'regularity is insisted upon all habits—alimentation, excretion, sleep, exercise. The patients are put on physical drill and sent for short route marches.'[74] The 'tone of certainty in the doctor's voice' and the 'enthusiastic expectancy of a rapid recovery' were seen as essential conditions of success.[75] The military context promoted the success of hypnotic therapy: 'The soldier is peculiarly susceptible to suggestion: the whole training and discipline make him respond to the authority of the Medical Officer.'[76] In the view of the British psychologically minded doctors, they learnt much about their patients' feelings, thoughts, and illness by interpreting their dreams or putting them into a trance. The patients seem to have appreciated this approach, which perhaps allowed them to express their emotions in safer surroundings. The use of hypnosis triggered considerable resistance among military authorities: 'Perhaps against no method of treatment has there been greater prejudice than against hypnosis. Early in the war I remember the commandant of one military hospital telling me that he would not in any circumstances countenance its employment because the reputation of his unit would suffer thereby.'[77] The psychoanalytical reports of David Eder also gave cause for alarm among the medical community: 'the sooner that psychoanalysis of this kind ceases to be practised in England, the better it will be for all concerned'.[78] At any rate, soldiers seem to have found the therapy quite helpful: 'several of the patients protested to me that they had "received no treatment"'.[79]

Not only the treatment but also the soldiers themselves had to be defended against the military authorities, as the medical community continued to link shell shock with malingering. Willpower and commitment to recovery were seen as essential attributes of a brave soldier. While the psychologists saw that 'to confuse functional diseases, war shock, with malingering is no more excusable than would be the mistaking of an innocent tumour for a malignant tumour',[80]

[73] Brown, 'The Treatment of Cases of Shell Shock', 197. [74] Ibid. 199.
[75] Ibid. 197.
[76] Eder, *War-Shock*, 130.
[77] Myers, 'A Final Contribution to the Study of Shell Shock', 54.
[78] A. F. Hurst, *Medical Diseases of the War* (London, 1918), 75.
[79] Charles S. Myers, 'Contributions to the Study of Shell Shock: Being an Account of Certain Disorders of Speech, with Special Reference to their Causation and their Relation to Malingering', *The Lancet*, 187, 9 Sept. 1916, 461–7, at 464.
[80] Eder, *War-Shock*, 123–4.

they also admitted that 'of course there are some patients who are ready to malinger with major hysterical symptoms'.[81] Myers showed a more tolerant attitude: 'From the therapeutic standpoint, the difficulty is not of great importance, as long as treatment is confined to such procedures as persuasion, isolation, or anaesthesia, by which means I have "cured" several cases of intentional malingering.'[82]

The situation of the psychological medical officers shown here was a difficult one. On the one hand, as members of the armed forces, they had to follow military rules, send as many soldiers as possible back to the front, and ensure military discipline. On the other hand, they had sympathy with the psychologically injured soldiers and tried to help them with new, exotic methods such as hypnosis or psychoanalytical psychotherapy. These methods, mirroring in some way the hierarchical structure of the armed forces, seem to have worked well but provoked some hostility among the medical and military authorities. Does this tell us something about the doctors themselves? They did not seem to be self-conscious about their work or involvement with the military but had decided to use psychoanalytical methods. They stressed the influence of war experiences as traumatic events and showed sympathy with the shell-shocked soldiers.

The situation was more difficult for the German psychologists, among whom there was no consensus about methods or diagnosis either. Their most commonly used term was 'war neurosis' (*Kriegsneurose*), and after the Munich conference of September 1916 the medical community agreed to use more aggressive methods, such as electro-shock therapy. All the German psychologists mentioned here were involved in this debate. Friedrich Schultze used painful electric shocks, a method he had learnt personally under Fritz Kaufmann, the psychiatrist who had developed this treatment. Schultze defended himself against the accusation of cruelty to his patients, comparing the pain they felt to that of women in labour.[83] He seemed to despise the mentally disturbed soldiers, comparing their reaction during electro-shock therapy to that of children or the mentally disabled. He viewed their pain and screaming without pity, describing his attitude

---

[81] Brown, 'The Treatment of Cases of Shell Shock', 199. See also Myers, 'Contributions to the Study of Shell Shock: Being an Account of Certain Cases Treated by Hypnosis', 67; id., *Shell Shock in France*, 40.

[82] Myers, 'Contributions to the Study of Shell Shock: Being an Account of Certain Disorders of Speech', 466.

[83] Schultze, 'Über die Kaufmannsche Behandlung hysterischer Bewegungsstörungen', 1349.

as that of a surgeon; he justified this by explaining that he had applied electric shocks to himself and did not feel terrible pain. He seemed to have enjoyed himself during the therapy, especially during the military exercises that followed electro-shock treatment: 'As I once had to provide treatment for three hours, I felt more refreshed than otherwise after three hours of work.'[84] He stressed the advantage of the military context, in which a soldier could not refuse treatment; treatment, although painful, would reduce the costs for the state.[85] Following his theory, which ascribed the cause of the symptoms to the soldier himself, Schultze did not ask soldiers about their war experience or special feelings; he described only physical symptoms, and referred to slight anger or irritability during the sessions.[86] Nevertheless, he talked about his success, assuming that 'between laughter and weeping some [patients] hide their happiness, which comes with a sudden recovery. One [patient] telegraphed immediately after a session: I am able to walk again.'[87]

Schultze presented his method as a psychological one, using military surroundings and suggestion to strengthen the soldier patients' will to recover. He showed no sympathy for the pain of the soldiers treated with electric shocks; instead he stressed the energy and effort required of the working doctor, admitting that he sometimes found the task difficult.[88] This article clearly shows the feelings of a psychiatrist about using electro-shock therapy and his efforts to defend this method. The view of the patients, however, is less clear-cut; one can see their pain (and their relief when the treatment ended successfully), but their feelings and their experience of the war are overlooked. Schultze asked only about events before the onset of the various symptoms, distinguishing between sudden onset (for example, following a shell explosion or gas attack) and the slow development of symptoms caused by physical overexertion.[89]

The psychologist and neurologist Willi Hellpach, working in a hospital for shell-shocked soldiers in the countryside, did not use electro-shock therapy but stressed the 'healing influence of discipline in a field hospital'.[90] The task of a military psychiatrist was to heal a soldier not only for his own sake but also for that of the nation.[91] A doctor had to strengthen the will of the soldier to fight again, and

[84] Ibid. 1350.
[85] Ibid.
[86] Ibid. 1352.
[87] Ibid. 1350.
[88] Ibid. 1353.
[89] Ibid. 1352.
[90] Hellpach, 'Lazarettdisziplin als Heilfaktor', 1207–11.
[91] Ibid. 1208.

Hellpach believed the best way to achieve this was to apply military discipline during the recovery process in hospital. For this the doctor had to adopt a harsh attitude towards his patients. Hellpach was not sympathetic towards shell-shocked patients, and was astonished when the sound of shell explosions near the hospital made a brave officer nervous.[92] He did not ask about individual war experiences, but stressed the soldiers' desire to get away from the front.

Walther Poppelreuter worked at a military mental hospital in Cologne and also used psychological methods, but with different soldier patients and different intentions. From the beginning of the war he worked with patients suffering from head injuries, initially following his scientific goals, then later developing a method of treatment and social care.[93] He stressed his intention to develop his method and treatment even in times of peace: 'There have to be institutes for the research, treatment, and care of those with head injuries. I want to stress the relation to normal pedagogic and pathological psychology and try to give it a name: Institute for Clinical Psychology!'.[94] All of his patients with head injuries needed psychological treatment.[95] However, he stressed that every neurologist should exploit the necessities of the military situation,[96] demanding that doctors should treat not only the illness but also the ill citizen.[97] In his view, the labour even of a disabled person could be useful both for the patient himself and for the war economy.[98]

Poppelreuter's patient files reveal his methods.[99] He introduced a new kind of psychological diagnosis, one which not only relied on psychological tests, but also involved the assessment and observation of specific work tasks. Unlike Rows, Poppelreuter did not follow standard psychiatric practice. He was not content with psychological and neurological diagnosis, but wanted to see how patients functioned in real work situations. His patient files were used not only to communicate with his colleagues and to document malfunctions of the brain but also to address his own research agenda. His questions underlined his theoretical concepts of psychological impact, always asking about the 'will to recover' or the patient's emotional character or personal qualities. However, he never asked patients about their

[92] Ibid. 1207.   [93] Poppelreuter, *Die psychischen Schädigungen*, p. v.
[94] Ibid. 18.   [95] Ibid. 6.
[96] Ibid.   [97] Ibid. 7.
[98] Ibid.
[99] See e.g. Leonhard B. Patient at Cöln Lindenthal, 21 Aug. 1915; patient of Walther Poppelreuter.

feelings during the war, only about their attitudes towards rehabilitation and further work. One task he set for his patients was to write an account of their life or illness, which was used mainly to assess their ability to write and to express themselves. The patient files allow a comparison between the clinical reports and the theoretical results. Poppelreuter did not make personal remarks about his own feelings or experiences with the patients. His theoretical approach meant that he did not ask about special feelings or events experienced by his patients either. Consequently, in his files and case studies it is difficult to find an ego beyond his ambitions as a researcher.

A very different way of communicating with shell-shocked soldiers appears in the case studies of Willibald Sauer, a psychoanalyst from Munich, who worked at a military hospital and wrote his article at the end of 1916. In contrast to Schultze and Poppelreuter, he was a follower of Freud, believing that an emotional reaction following a traumatic experience caused the functional symptoms. Sauer therefore asked his patients about their situation before their illness and about their feelings while they were unwell. He tried to describe the situation in the words of the patients, recording emotional and physical gestures. To reveal more unconscious experiences and to uncover underlying emotional reactions, Sauer used hypnosis to trigger an abreaction of the affect and thus reduce the functional symptoms.[100] Sauer regarded himself as an outsider for his use of psychoanalytical methods; however, far from criticizing the brutal methods used by his colleagues, he compared his work with theirs, stressing the advantages of psychoanalysis: 'The effect of the shock will be replaced through a new, experimentally induced, and intentionally graded shock.'[101] He compared his method with those of other psychiatrists who used quite painful procedures,[102] and did not criticize their way of treating soldiers, primarily because he wanted to stress the success of the psychoanalytical method.[103] Nor did he have any qualms about sending cured patients back to the front.[104] While some historians have stressed that emotions played a limited role in

---

[100] Sauer, 'Zur Analyse und Behandlung von Kriegsneurosen', 38–9, 43.

[101] Ibid. 44.

[102] Ibid.: such as, for example, Otto Muck, who threatened his patients with suffocation. See Otto Muck, 'Psychologische Betrachtungen bei Heilung funktionell stimmgestörter Soldaten', *Münchener Medizinische Wochenschrift, Feldärztliche Beilage*, 63 (1916) 26.

[103] Sauer, 'Zur Analyse und Behandlung von Kriegsneurosen', 45.

[104] Ibid. 44.

the German psychiatric-neurological debates,[105] I would argue that the theoretical approach is more important than national difference. Following Freudian thinking, both British and German psychiatrists asked for emotional reactions and thus got the answers they were seeking. Poppelreuter's patients also related their war experiences in their personal remarks, but because these experiences did not fit in with his theoretical assumptions, they were not mentioned in the case studies.

The Patients

Any given case history can be regarded only as a portrayal of the patient as a single actor in a network of other actors, the most influential of these being the doctor in charge. Unlike published case studies, patient files are private documents not intended for publication, but used for the conservation of information and communication within the medical community. They were not censored like published articles.[106] The ability of case studies or patient files to reveal any 'real war experience' is a matter of controversy among historians. On the one hand, Joachim Radkau, the first researcher to use patient files to explore the treatment of neurasthenia, is relatively optimistic that they can reveal a variety of personal stories about patients' lives and suffering.[107] On the other, Hans-Georg Hofer denies that personal experiences of the war can be accessed from patient files, and asserts that they reflect only the view of the doctors.[108] The portrait of the patients described here differs according to the concept of illness. German psychologists,

[105] e.g. S. Michl and J. Plamper, 'Soldatische Angst im Ersten Weltkrieg: Die Karriere eines Gefühls in der Kriegspsychiatrie Deutschlands, Frankreichs und Russlands', *Geschichte und Gesellschaft*, 35 (2009), 209–48, esp. 224.

[106] In Germany, published scientific articles were censored by the war ministry: Kriegsarchiv München, Bestand des stellvertretenden Generaloberkommandos I AK, San A 459, 28 Aug. 1915, gez. Von der Tann: Betreff: Literarische Veröffentlichungen durch Heeresangehörige. See J.-B. Köhne, *Kriegshysteriker: Strategische Bilder und mediale Techniken militärpsychiatrischen Wissens (1914–1920)* (Husum, 2009), 82.

[107] J. Radkau, 'Zum historischen Quellenwert von Patientenakten: Erfahrungen aus Recherchen zur Geschichte der Nervosität', in D. Meyer (ed.), *Akten betreuter Personen als archivische Aufgabe: Beratungs- und Patientenakten im Spannungsfeld von Persönlichkeitsschutz und historischer Forschung* (Neustadt an der Aisch, 1997), 1–30.

[108] H.-G. Hofer, 'Was waren Kriegsneurosen? Zur Kulturgeschichte psychischer Erkrankungen im Ersten Weltkrieg', in Hermann J. W. Kuprian and Oswald Überegger (eds.), *Der Erste Weltkrieg im Alpenraum: Erfahrung, Deutung, Erinnerung/La Grande Guerra nell'arco alpino: esperienze e memoria* (Innsbruck, 2006), 309–22, at 314. The same opinion is expressed in Guenter B. Risse and J.-H. Warner, 'Reconstructing Clinical Activities:

stressing the role of the inner disposition of the patient as the cause of the illness, did not ask about emotional reactions or war experiences. Nevertheless Poppelreuter encouraged his patients to write a short essay about their illness, and so we have some personal reports from his patients. One of them reported:

> Three comrades were with me in the trenches, we were lying on our stomachs for one and a half hours, when two metres away a shell exploded, killing two of my comrades immediately; the other lived for half an hour and his head was cut in half; and I had to watch this for three hours, because we were buried all the time and I was deaf because of the air pressure.[109]

Later he described his feelings during the campaign: 'I opted to keep watch and enjoyed shooting at the foreign "rabbits"; we are all human beings, but if we had not shot, they would have killed us.'[110] Although this report was written some time after the event, it shows what the patient was able to tell of his story as he remembered it, and that he was able to talk about it. Poppelreuter did not use these personal stories in his case studies or in his articles.

Other patient files, from the Federal Military Archives in Freiburg, show a similar procedure: the patient was asked about the situation at the onset of his symptoms and remembered a particular event in the war. Seaman B. reported,[111] from the Kiel military hospital, that his symptoms stemmed from a war experience in May 1916, when his ship was hit by a shell near Riga and he was thrown into the air. Later, as the ship sank, he had to stay in the water for many hours. Since that time he had suffered from functional symptoms. The patient was not asked about emotions and did not talk about them. However, it is possible to derive some information about the patient. Like Myers's British patient, he regarded his war experience as the cause of his illness. The same illness (hysteria) was diagnosed, although it was not caused by a specific incident on the Western Front. The German doctor was not interested in any inner conflict, dreams, personal experiences, or emotions, but he sounded quite sympathetic. Instead of recommending electro-shock therapy, he sent the patient to a convalescent hospital.[112] The psychologist Otto

Patient Records in Medical History', *Society for the Social History of Medicine* (1992), 183–205.

[109] Leonhard B., patient at Cöln Lindenthal, 21 Aug. 1915; patient of Walther Poppelreuter.   [110] Ibid.
[111] Military Archive Freiburg Pers. 9/10429, Seaman B.
[112] This is in line with the results of Petra Peckl, who looked through about 300

Schultze, similarly, did not ask about his patients' personal emotions or war experience in his case studies. He referred only to disturbing reactions during the treatment: one patient was described as short-tempered, but more obedient after the treatment;[113] many patients would scream and cry during the treatment, but afterwards some of them were happy to have been cured.[114]

The case studies by Willibald Sauer are different because, as a psychiatrist using psychoanalytical methods, he asked about emotional reactions and experiences before the onset of the symptoms. Both patients he described in case studies related their symptoms to war experiences, but they could talk about emotions and exact memories only under hypnosis or in a similar state of mind.[115] Both patients referred to accidents following heavy artillery fire, a situation in which, according to Sauer, it was impossible to react, mentally or physically, in a way that would have allowed the patient to cope with his experience.[116] Although the patient does not mention them himself, emotions such as anxiety and excitement are recorded by Sauer. Under hypnosis, the patient described the triggering event and the associated experiences even more vividly. In this situation it was possible, and even expected by the attending physician, for the patient to express fear and anxiety. Sauer reported that most functional symptoms vanished after the patient recalled his war experiences.[117] It is impossible to tell whether these were 'real war experiences', but they were stories that could be told and memories that resolved the patients' stressful experiences. Although Sauer always referred to childhood experiences as well, he never underestimated the importance of the traumas left by war experiences.

Montague David Eder viewed his patients differently, always referring to his patients' dreams.[118] Other psychologists described the patients making typical gestures expressing strong feelings: 'they made a sorry show with their hanging heads and furtive looks'.[119] Often the horror could be expressed only through body language: 'This patient also lies on his back oblivious to his surroundings . . .

patient files in the Military Archive Freiburg and found that only about 25 per cent of the patients were treated with aggressive therapies: Peckl, 'What the Patient Records Reveal', 158.

[113] Schultze, 'Über die Kaufmannsche Behandlung hysterischer Bewegungsstörungen', 1352. [114] Ibid. 1350.
[115] Sauer, 'Zur Analyse und Behandlung von Kriegsneurosen', 37.
[116] Ibid. 34. [117] Ibid. 40.
[118] Eder, *War Shock*, 114–17. [119] Brown, 'War Neurosis', 833.

His whole body is in a state of continual tremor and his face wears a fixed stare of horror . . . This is the veritable petrifaction of fright.'[120] Nearly all of the patients from the Western Front recalled the onset of their symptoms and related it to a shell explosion: 'A shell burst about two yards away; it lifted me into the air. I don't know what happened afterwards. [When I came to myself] I was watching the trench mortars coming over and killing my mates, and I could not tell them [what was the matter] because I could not speak.'[121] Most patients recalled having no special feelings during the event: 'My feelings during the shelling are hard to define, as I was too fully occupied to allow for much thought on the subject.'[122] The emotions resurfaced only under hypnosis or in dreams. Under hypnosis '[the patient] immediately begins to twist and turn on the couch and shouts out in a terror-stricken voice. He talks as he talked at the time when the shock happened to him. He really does relive the experience of that awful time.'[123] The revival of these emotions was, according to William Brown, 'the essential process in dealing with the majority of war neuroses'.[124] Richard Rows also stresses the revival of unconscious emotions, assuming that 'physical expression of a special emotion, such as fear or terror, persists for a long time without much change'.[125] For example, he described a soldier who

> after a charge, was placed on outpost duty. It was dark and he was in a state of considerable tension. He heard a noise . . . Suddenly the area around him was illumined by a flare light and he saw a man crawling over a bank. Without challenging, he fired and killed the man. Next morning he found to his horror that he had killed a wounded Englishman who had advanced beyond his comrades and was crawling back. The physical expression of horror, together with an intense sweating and a very marked stammer, persisted for months. At the same time he was tormented with a fearful nightmare, and in his sleep he was heard to say, 'It was an accidental shot, sir. Yes, major, it was not my fault.' In the daytime also his attention was concentrated on the memory of the incident, so that 'I cannot forget it no matter how I skylark'.[126]

Rows thus presented a personal experience of wartime, albeit one shaped by the therapeutic situation, which allowed the soldier to talk

[120] Ibid.
[121] Myers, 'Contributions to the Study of Shell Shock: Being an Account of Certain Disorders of Speech', 462.
[122] Brown, 'The Treatment of Cases of Shell Shock', 198.   [123] Ibid.
[124] Ibid.
[125] Rows, 'Mental Conditions Following Strain and Nerve Shock', 441.
[126] Ibid. 441–2.

about his experiences. He described not only his patient's personal story, but also how the patient tried to handle the terrible memory. Patient files generally contain no such elaborate stories of war experiences. The files are fragmentary, often without a diagnosis, and mostly they follow the same psychiatric scheme, asking about earlier mental illness or any family history of mental diseases. One example is the story of 'Private Crawford, James, age 29': 'States that he went out to France at the end of January, has been in the trenches. States that he became broken up by the strain and that his feet became bad. Was slightly deaf in his right ear . . . became very emotional and had crying attacks when questioned.'[127] We hear only about the patient's general emotional state, perhaps for want of time to ask about the stories, or write them down.

To sum up, case studies show only fragments of the personal experiences of these soldiers. However, they give us a chance to look at some unique personal experiences during the war, even though they were selected by the doctors rather than the patients themselves. The impossibility of speaking about feelings directly and the strong recurrence of wartime emotions during dreams or psychotherapy seem to be a common feature in these case histories. Yet only the doctors who, following on from their theoretical assumptions, asked questions about emotional reactions and personal experiences were able to get the patients to talk about their individual experiences. Nevertheless, patient egos can be discovered in these case studies, particularly in patient files when they were asked to write down their story.

The patient perspective had consequences too. The first case that Charles Myers reported mentioned a private, aged 20. On 31 November 1914,

for the first time he went to the fire line. His platoon advanced to one set of trenches and then crossed the road to another. During the retirement from his trenches . . . they were found by the German artillery. Up to then he had not been afraid; he had 'rather been enjoying it' and was in best of spirits until the shell burst about him . . . Immediately after the shell had burst in front of him his sight became blurred . . . It was this shell, he says, which caused his blindness.[128]

It was this case report, published in February 1915, that coined

[127] NA: MH 106/2102 Medical Sheets 1914–1915, 402253.
[128] Myers, 'A Contribution to the Study of Shell Shock: Being an Account of Three Cases of Loss of Memory . . .', 316.

the term 'shell shock', which was disliked but nonetheless used by military and medical authorities. It could be argued that the persistence of its use indicates that the diagnosis was a sign of patient power.[129] It denoted a violent physical injury as the cause of the multiple symptoms and enabled many soldiers and their families to avoid the stigma associated with terms such as 'hysteric', 'neurasthenic', or 'neurotic',[130] and helped the notion of the 'shell shocked soldier to become iconic'.[131] Although in Germany soldiers referred to similar experiences, no such friendly patient-centred term was used.

Conclusion

All these case studies can provide insights into the war experience of doctors and mentally troubled soldiers in the First World War. Above all, they illustrate the difficult situation the psychiatrists found themselves in. Trying to help their patients and emphasizing their scientific knowledge, they were confronted with hostility from the medical and the military authorities simultaneously. Their case studies reveal contemporary views on mentally disturbed soldiers, on the impact of warfare, and on social boundaries and the contemporary language used to describe these. The psychiatrists do not reveal many personal feelings, but some questions about their personal feelings and attitudes can be answered. The motives behind their work and their reasons for writing articles are apparent. Most of them wanted to present their new methods for treating mentally troubled soldiers, or to underline their scientific research by showing their efforts. They tried to position themselves in the medical scientific community and made no critical comments about harsh therapeutic methods used by other military psychiatrists.

Personal attitudes towards the mentally troubled soldiers are also visible. The British psychologists were quite sympathetic, stressed the impact of war experiences, and showed sympathy with their patients. The German psychiatrists displayed a more distant attitude, seeing themselves as the disciplinary arm of the military. One psychiatrist even enjoyed using military discipline and electric

[129] M. Thomson, 'Status, Manpower and Mental Fitness: Medical Deficiency in the First World War', in R. Cooter (ed.), *War, Medicine and Modernity* (Stroud, 1999), 149–66, at 154.
[130] Jay Winter, 'Shell-Shock and the Cultural History of the Great War', *Journal of Contemporary History*, 35 (2003), 7–11. [131] Ibid. 7.

shocks while treating patients. The psychoanalyst Willibald Sauer was more sympathetic, asking about patients' emotions and the traumatic events which had brought them to him. It is interesting to observe that, although he used a different method from most of his colleagues, he did not encounter much resistance or criticism. All these psychiatrists had to strike a balance between their roles as doctors concerned about their patients on the one hand, and as members of the military forces providing soldiers able to fight on the other, and they positioned themselves differently between those two roles. This shaped their attitudes towards the soldiers. For example, David Eder stressed his sympathy with his patients, while Otto Schultze described ill soldiers as useless human material. However, instead of highlighting only national differences, it seems that the doctors' theoretical assumptions were the more important influence on their attitudes towards the soldiers and how they asked and responded to questions about their patients' personal feelings and war experiences. For example, Walther Poppelreuter asked his patients to write short stories about their illnesses and war experiences, althouogh he never used these in his case studies. The British and German psychologists, following the theoretical assumptions of Sigmund Freud, asked about emotional and functional symptoms during the war. They often used methods such as hypnosis to gain access to unconscious memories and emotions, because most patients were unable to talk about their feelings and anxieties, and came into contact with them only during hypnosis or through dreams or nightmares. In the right environment and with the right questions, however, they were willing to talk about their individual life stories and suffering.

The patients' perspective is always filtered through the eyes of the psychiatrists, but it is possible to gain insights into individual life stories and the mental disturbances caused by warfare. Most patients connected their mental or functional symptoms to a traumatic event, often the explosion of a shell. When questioned, many could talk about their experiences and reveal personal stories and feelings, even the joy of being part of the war.

To sum up, medical case studies and patient files are complex sources. The voices of the doctors and patients are difficult to disentangle in them, but some questions about personal feelings, attitudes, and war experiences can be answered if they are read carefully.

PART III

War beyond Europe

9

Inside the Ottoman Army: Two Armenian Officers Tell their Story

MUSTAFA AKSAKAL

'There are so many diaries and memoir type "ego-documents" [*ben-metni*] that the cliché of "we don't have memoirs" must be put to rest for ever', Hakan Erdem recently observed concerning the history of the Ottoman First World War.[1] For much of the twentieth century, the number of published self-narratives from the Ottoman Decade of War (1911–22) remained relatively modest, while the accounts that did appear largely consisted of memoirs written by the Empire's political and military male elite. In recent years eyewitness accounts from the period have appeared at an astonishing rate, particularly in Turkey but also, if fewer in number, in all the Ottoman successor states. These narrations have come from men and women occupying a range of places in Ottoman society, written in the various languages of the Middle East. The surfacing of this rich body of memoirs, diaries, letters, photographs, film footage, and even voice records (in addition to newly accessible archival collections) has already exercised an enormous influence on the study of the Ottoman First World War. As might be expected, the proliferation of such texts has also generated debates as to how such accounts are to be interpreted and contextualized. Erdem, quoted above, was himself at the centre of a much-publicized exchange among historians in Turkey about the provenance, reliability, and authenticity of some of the new diary and memoir publications.[2]

[1] Y. Hakan Erdem, *Gerçek ile Kurmaca Arasında: Torosyan'ın Acayip Hikâyesi* [*Between Reality and Fiction: Torosyan's Strange Story*] (Istanbul, 2012), quotation at 13. For Arabic sources see esp. Olaf Farschid, Manfred Kropp, and Stephan Dähne (eds.), *The First World War as Remembered in the Countries of the Eastern Mediterranean* (Beirut, 2006).

[2] Kalusd Sürmenyan, *Harbiyeli Bir Osmanlı Ermenisi: Mülâzım-ı Sânî Sürmenyan'ın Savaş ve Tehcir Anıları*. ed. and introd. by Yaşar Tolga Cora (Istanbul, 2015), 9–12; Erdem, *Gerçek ile Kurmaca Arasında*.

Mustafa Kemal Atatürk's thirty-six-hour speech, delivered over six days in 1927, is surely the most prominent of all the self-narrative accounts coming out of the Ottoman context. His address, simply known as 'The Speech' (*Nutuk*), not only described the actions of the Turkish leader himself but also provided the mould for his country's future history-writing and national memory. For decades other voices adhered closely to Atatürk's account.

In this brief essay I can highlight only a very small number of such personal accounts. Religion, ethnicity, class, gender, and age were crucial determinants that shaped the individual's war experience, and we can add to these the range of economic, military, and political conditions that characterized the Empire. Regional environmental and ecological factors, too, defined the peculiarities of the Ottoman war experience, as snow-capped mountains, torrential rains, and desert coexisted across a vast region.

The Ottoman Decade of War 1911–22

On 29 October 1914 the Ottoman Empire entered the First World War on the side of the Central Powers. Confronted with the fallout from war with Italy in North Africa (1911–12) and the two Balkan Wars (1912 and 1913), Ottoman leaders had seen the July Crisis as an opportunity to end the Empire's diplomatic isolation. In the dawn hours of 2 August 1914, after a long night of negotiation in his residence on the Bosporus, Grand Vizier Said Halim Pasha concluded a secret alliance treaty with the German ambassador.

The world around the Ottomans had been changing fast. A revolution in July 1908 led to the proclamation of a constitution and elections. The next year came a counter-revolution that toppled Sultan Abdülhamid II (r. 1876–1909). Convening for the first time since 1876, the parliament brought together political representatives from all parts of the Empire. From Thessaloniki/Selanik to Jerusalem to Elazığ/Harput in eastern Anatolia, mass rallies celebrated the Ottoman constitution as the Empire's rescue from its many troubles. Thousands paraded in a sea of flags embroidered with slogans of freedom and revolution—'liberty, equality, brotherhood'—in Arabic, Armenian, Greek, Hebrew, Kurdish, and Ottoman Turkish, and frequently in more than one language side by side. The

Ottoman spring of 1908–9 marked the high point of Ottoman civic patriotism.[3]

During the period 1914 to 1918, the state mobilized roughly 3 million men from an estimated total population of 26 million. More than 770,000 of these conscripts died in combat or of disease. Faced with increasingly unbearable wartime conditions, another half a million deserted. Some 250,000 became prisoners of war, held primarily in camps in British Egypt and Russian Siberia. As for civilians, more than one million Christian Ottomans were killed or died as a result of the state's deportation policies. In Greater Syria, half a million civilians, or one in seven of Syria's population, starved to death—a tragedy bred by military confiscation policies, the Anglo-French naval blockade sealing off the Ottoman Mediterranean, and a devastating plague of locusts arriving in the spring of 1915. The first census compiled in the Turkish Republic in 1927 listed over 30 per cent of women as widows in some regions. That census also revealed that Anatolia's population still hovered below 1914 figures, and GDP had plummeted to half of prewar rates. The First World War, in short, devastated the Ottoman lands.

The subsequent conflicts and sweeping historical changes in the war's aftermath—the end of the Ottoman dynasty, the abolition of the Islamic caliphate, the massive loss of territory along with the creation of new nation states and mandates under European rule in Iraq, Palestine, Syria, and Transjordan—all provided anything but suitable circumstances for a revisiting of this history. In Turkey, the brutality and suffering of the war years rendered the public airing of those events profoundly difficult, and debate on matters of recent history and the national narrative became rigidly circumscribed.[4]

---

[3] Bedross Der Matossian, *Shattered Dreams of Revolution: From Liberty to Violence in the Late Ottoman Empire* (Stanford, Calif., 2014); Michelle U. Campos, *Ottoman Brothers: Muslims, Christians, and Jews in Early Twentieth Century Palestine* (Stanford, Calif., 2011); Dikran Kaligian, *Armenian Organization and Ideology under Ottoman Rule, 1908–1914* (New Brunswick, NJ, 2009); Nicholas Doumanis, *Before the Nation: Muslim–Christian Coexistence and its Destruction in Late Ottoman Anatolia* (Oxford, 2013); also on this theme see Julia Phillips Cohen, *Becoming Ottomans: Sephardi Jews and Imperial Citizenship in the Modern Era* (Oxford, 2014).

[4] The state's suppression and destruction of the account by Kâzım Karabekir, who served in the Ottoman Wars from 1912 to 1922, is a well-known case in point.

Kalusd and Yervant Tell their Story

From the nineteenth century, literacy rates in the Ottoman Empire began to rise quickly, even though compared with northern Europe they were still rather low in 1914.[5] Even so, the experiences of individuals during the Italian War, the Balkan Wars, the First World War, and the Ottoman war of resistance have generated over a thousand published first-hand accounts by Ottoman soldiers and officers alone.[6] When we add civilian writings—and those in all the major languages of the Empire—that figure doubles. The number of first-hand accounts of conditions and experiences in the Empire increases even further when we include the writings by non-Ottomans who spent the war years in the Ottoman theatre.[7]

The accounts of Kalusd Sürmenyan of Erzincan and Yervant Alexanian of Sivas present the experiences of two Armenians in the Ottoman army. Both served until the end of the war—both, eventually, as officers. As such, they represent a group whose experiences have remained little known. Kalusd graduated from the Military Academy (Mekteb-i Harbiye) in June 1912, just in time to serve in the Balkan Wars as a second lieutenant. Yervant, born in 1895, had not yet reached the age of conscription in 1914. In the autumn of 1914 he entered the final year of the Jesuit-run French high school, as the candidate most likely to finish at the top of his class. In November, however, the school was closed and the building requisitioned by the military authorities. The next year, in 1915, he became a private in the very army that, around the same time, deported his family. In 1916, like Kalusd, Yervant would also attend the Military Academy, where he too earned the rank of second lieutenant. Kalusd's family was likewise deported in 1915. Yervant

---

[5] Literacy rates are difficult to establish. Across the Empire they perhaps hovered around 10 per cent, but may have been considerably higher in urban centres, especially the capital. See Benjamin C. Fortna, *Learning to Read in the Late Ottoman Empire and the Early Turkish Republic* (New York, 2011), 20–1.

[6] See the bibliography of military diaries and memoirs compiled by Mehmet Beşikçi at ⟨http://www.cihanharbihatiralari.com/⟩ [accessed 15 Jan. 2018].

[7] British, German, and Austrian accounts, in particular. For the diary of a British resident of Istanbul, Marie Lyster, see Ian Lyster (ed.), *Among the Ottomans: Diaries from Turkey in World War I* (London, 2011). The observations of the Spanish consul in Jerusalem, Conde de Ballobar, are also illuminating: Conde de Ballobar, *Jerusalem in World War I: The Palestine Diary of a European Diplomat*, ed. Eduardo Manzano Moreno and Roberto Mazza (New York, 2011).

lost fifty-one members of his family. Kalusd lost his mother to the deportation but was able to save the remaining members of his family. After the war Kalusd settled in Baghdad, Yervant in the United States.[8]

The Memoir and the Retrospective

Scholars prefer diaries over memoirs for their immediacy and the often raw, undigested manner in which events and experiences are recorded. Memoirs, by contrast, are often weighed down by the baggage of intervening events; new realities, scholars suspect, tend to be written into the past retroactively. And yet memoirs should not be considered only as second best when we do not have diaries. Memoirs can tell us a great deal about how individuals select history, how they choose to put the past back together in their own distinct ways. In the memoirs of Kalusd and Yervant, for example, their treatment of the late Ottoman period comes as something of a surprise. Despite the state's horrific policies towards Armenians in the First World War, Kalusd and Yervant have largely positive observations to make about prewar Ottoman society.

Kalusd notes that young Armenians eagerly joined the colours after the promulgation of the 1908 constitution and the opening of military careers to Armenians. He characterizes the military authorities of Erzincan, his home town, as welcoming and 'accommodating', allowing Armenian men to attend church and observe religious holidays. And he adds that Muslim Turkish officers respected Armenian soldiers and considered them 'talented and capable'.[9]

After the constitution, Kalusd says, the Turks treated the Christian peoples and especially the Armenians 'with sincerity and friendship', and continues: 'in all areas, all doors were open to Armenians within the military'.[10] Few historians would accept these statements without important qualifications. But what matters perhaps even more in this instance, however, is the rosy, upbeat way in which Kalusd, fully aware of what happened to Ottoman Armenians in the First World War, chose to describe the situation of Ottoman Armenians just before the war. Once Armenians became subject

[8] Sürmenyan, *Harbiyeli Bir Osmanlı Ermenisi*; Yervant N. Alexanian, *Forced into Genocide: Memoirs of an Armenian Soldier in the Ottoman Turkish Army*, ed. Adrienne G. Alexanian, introd. Sergio La Porta (New York, 2017).
[9] Sürmenyan, *Harbiyeli Bir Osmanlı Ermenisi*, 40–1.   [10] Ibid. 42.

to military service after 1908, Kalusd and several of his friends decided to become officers, saying: 'If Armenians are going to serve in the military, let's also enter the military and defend the rights of these Armenian soldiers [by becoming officers].'[11] But they also embraced the opportunities for advancement that came with an army career. Along with four other Armenians, Kalusd enrolled in the Military Academy in 1910 (several more also applied but did not perform well enough in the entrance examination). Of the 1,200 students at the Military Academy, around ten were Armenian, a few Greek, and one a Bulgarian.[12] According to Kalusd, when the state declared mobilization on 3 August 1914, 'everyone' rushed to register, including Armenians.[13]

Yervant Alexanian of Sivas, a city located some 250 kilometres west of Kalusd's Erzincan, depicts prewar conditions in similarly positive terms. For example, he describes the 1913 'pan-Sivas "Olympic" games', a competition among several youth scouting organizations. The Armenian sports club Bertevagoump 'took the most medals, gaining the admiration of all'. He tells the story of how during the medal ceremony 'all Armenian athletes stood and sang the Turkish anthem when the flag was raised'. Yervant here goes out of his way to point out that this was not simply a pro forma performance. He saw in this moment the Armenian athletes 'demonstrating again how loyal they actually were to the country in which they lived'. He himself was not a member of this group, however, and he does not mention whether he was well acquainted with any of the athletes or their political attitudes. But the point that Yervant, like Kalusd, aimed to make was that before 1914 'Armenians were very much part of the fabric of Sivas', and that, even more crucially, 'nobody would have believed' that the Armenians of Sivas or Erzincan 'could be annihilated so quickly'. As Yervant puts it: 'Nobody would anticipate what was to befall us, even those who had survived the many pogroms and massacres, such as the Hamidian massacres, that preceded the Genocide of 1915.'[14]

The notion that the world seemed more or less fine in 1914 is expressed fairly regularly in Ottoman memoirs. Demetrios Theodore, born in 1904 in Maden, then a town of some 500 Greek Orthodox families 280 kilometres south of Erzincan, made a similar point. He surmised that the 'spirit of friendship and co-operation in a

[11] Ibid.   [12] Ibid. 42.
[13] Ibid. 45.   [14] Alexanian, *Forced into Genocide*, 29–30.

social order where both the Greeks and the Turks had found their respective places and were learning to live together in harmony was torpedoed during the four years [of] war.'[15]

Inside the First World War: Fighting for Survival

But as it turned out, the greatest, most persistent danger Kalusd and Yervant faced during the war came not from foreign troops but from the Ottoman military in which they served. Both men narrowly escaped deportation. Kalusd was perhaps saved by the intervention of an officer in Erzurum, Fuad Ziya Bey. Yervant also survived thanks to a benevolent commander, who used first Yervant's rudimentary sewing skills and then his ability to play the bugle to keep him employed and thereby exempt from working with the road crews. In order to survive, Yervant eventually converted to Islam, after which he became known as Zia. As the excellent introductions by the editors of both texts point out, Kalusd and Yervant found themselves serving the very army that deported their families. At the same time, their survival depended to a great extent on their membership as officers in that institution. Kalusd and Yervant were distinct from the general Ottoman Armenian population because of their privileged role in the army. Their Armenianness, in turn, rendered them distinct from their fellow soldiers and officers with whom they served.

A few weeks after Yervant's school was shut down in early November 1914, the governor, Ahmet Muammer, along with the police commissioner, led a 'bloodthirsty mob' to the school and 'violently removed the cross that sat atop the small chapel and replaced it with a crescent'. Shortly thereafter, in late 1914, Kalusd tells us, the government had the priest Sahak Odabashian killed, sending shockwaves throughout the Armenian population. He had been on his way from Bursa to assume his new post at Erzincan when he was murdered. Another worrying sign, according to Kalusd, was the fact that Armenian conscripts were being employed as porters, carrying military matériel on foot across long distances, such as the road through the mountains between Erzincan and Erzurum.[16]

---

[15] D[emetrios] E. Theodore, *The Sacrificials: Part of an Autobiography Depicting the Life of Minorities in a War Torn Country* (Boston, 1970), 47.
[16] Alexanian, *Forced into Genocide*, 33–4; Sürmenyan, *Harbiyeli Bir Osmanlı Ermenisi*, 50–1.

In January 1915 the Ottoman Third Army, led personally by War Minister Enver Pasha, suffered a devastating defeat at the hands of Russian forces. In the aftermath of that rout, nearly all Armenian conscripts were disarmed and put into labour battalions. Over the course of the next few months, Enver and Talat, the interior minister, issued orders for the deportation of the Armenian population from Anatolia southward to Syria. Kalusd notes that on 18–21 May 1915 the Armenian notables of Erzincan were ordered to prepare for departure. The next day, Kalusd was dispatched to Erzurum, forced to leave his family behind. Inhabitants of the roughly 'forty Armenian villages of Erzurum' had been deported already, and Kalusd found the roads filled with deportees.[17] A month later the authorities issued instructions for the deportation of Armenians in Yervant's Sivas. Yervant heard the announcement in church from his priest, Father Kalemkerian: 'The government has been told that some people have stashed weapons in this Church. I'm to stay here while they tear it down and look for them.'[18] Yervant was saved by conscription, 'just weeks before my family was forcibly made to take the road of deportation'. As a result, 'the only Armenians left in Sivas' were 'soldiers, apostates, and [those] who knew crafts that were valuable to the Ottoman government'.[19]

Yervant tells us further that officials issued a formal deportation order on 15 June 1915, and that residents of 'the Bezia neighborhood, the first to be deported, went on the death march' on 22 June 1915.[20] Yervant's use here of the phrase 'death march' raises the question as to whether Sivas deportees thought of their removal in these terms already or whether that designation was applied retrospectively. Yervant says they did know what lay in wait for them:

Eventually came the turn of my neighborhood, on July 3, 1915. Like everyone else, the Armenians were told they would be taken to a peaceful, stable region, where they would be able to establish their own communities. They were told to leave their belongings behind [and] that they would be sent after them. However, we all knew what was going on, so most Armenians sold most of their belongings at dirt cheap prices.[21]

---

[17] Sürmenyan, *Harbiyeli Bir Osmanlı Ermenisi*, 57–61.
[18] Alexanian, *Forced into Genocide*, 43.
[19] Ibid. 49.
[20] Ibid. 51.
[21] Ibid. 52.

'... *like the last day of the world* ...'

Yervant lost fifty-one family members in the deportations. Aware of the charges brought against Armenians as revolutionaries, he added quickly that 'none of these innocent victims were a member of any political party or were involved in any type of political activity'. They had not done anything to undermine the Ottoman war effort, and '[t]heir only crime was being Armenian'.[22] Kalusd saw the immediate cause behind the deportations in Enver's defeat in the Caucasus. Under Enver's direct command, the Third Army had suffered a crushing defeat at the Battle of Sarıkamış in January 1915. Upon his return to Istanbul, Enver had ordered all Armenian soldiers and officers into positions away from the front, but, Kalusd writes, most were killed before reaching their new assignments. According to Kalusd, Enver and Talat planned the destruction of the Armenians and put in charge of this policy Governor Muammer of Sivas, District Governor Memduh of Erzincan, and Bahaddin Şakir, a leading member of the Committee of Union and Progress. Then, Kalusd continues, 'from jails they released murderers and robbers [*haydut*] to form gangs to carry out this "holy business"'.[23] In fact, as one top officer (and later war minister) recorded in his diary, the army had already begun to form 'a militia and a national organization [*teşkilât-ı milliye*] against Armenian gangs' in March 1915.[24]

Before the deportation order came instructions to collect all weapons in Armenian hands and to search Armenian homes to ensure that the collection was complete.[25] Upon learning of the deportations in Erzincan, Kalusd rushed back to find his family. The trip was harrowing. A man Kalusd encountered told him of 'rumours that all Erzincan Armenians have been deported and massacred in the valley and that none survived'. Kalusd remembers: 'I sat down on a large rock and watched the sky and the sun ... I could not see anything around me. That day seemed like the last day of the world to me, nothing made sense.'[26] Arriving in Erzincan, he found that his family had been deported two weeks earlier. Entering

---

[22] Ibid. 54.   [23] Sürmenyan, *Harbiyeli Bir Osmanlı Ermenisi*, 52.
[24] *Mareşal Fevzi Çakmak ve Günlükleri*, ed. Nilüfer Hatemi, 2 vols. (Istanbul, 2002), i. 309, diary entry for 16 Mar. 1915/2 Mart 1331.
[25] Sürmenyan, *Harbiyeli Bir Osmanlı Ermenisi*, 53–4.   [26] Ibid. 62.

his empty home, he recalled the joyous celebration of his wedding just ten months ago: 'it was as if the walls were going to collapse on me'.[27]

Survival became more and more precarious for both Kalusd and Yervant. Yervant was one of a few Armenians remaining in Sivas. He was summoned by his commander and told there were orders 'from the top' that Armenians could no longer serve in the army, that they had to convert or be deported, and that thus they had to 'choose between life and death'. Yervant notes that he and six others initially refused while the majority of Armenain conscripts there agreed to convert.[28] In the end Yervant, too, converted, taking the name Zia. As Zia he received officer training and learnt how to operate a machine-gun. Promoted to second lieutenant, he served at Gallipoli and Izmir/Smyrna.[29]

Kalusd sought to hide his Armenian identity from his soldiers and fellow officers as the war went on. When he objected to soldiers boasting of attacking Armenians, they replied: 'The sultan ordered the killing of the unbelievers—who are you to hold us back?'[30] Later, as he listened to accounts by a fellow officer of the way in which Armenians had been killed, unaware that Kalusd himself was Armenian, Kalusd felt 'as though the entire world had become a cemetery'.[31] Among Kurdish fighters who had carried out raids on deportees, Kalusd thought of himself as 'a sheep in wolf's clothing hiding in a pack of wolves.'[32] Following the route of the deportees to locate his family, Kalusd bandaged his face, feigning toothache, so fearful was he that some of the deportees might recognize him and thereby expose his Armenian identity.[33]

Having abandoned his command and searching for his family, Kalusd encountered hundreds of bodies at Kemah, near the Euphrates river, 'swollen, disfigured, unrecognizable'.[34] He finally found his family, alive, some 160 kilometers south of Erzincan. His identity revealed, Kalusd was immediately arrested and charged with distributing weapons to deportees and inciting rebellion.[35] He then spent the next three months under arrest, but through another officer was able to secure a safe place for his family in Arapgir. How

---

[27] Ibid. 70–1.
[28] Alexanian, *Forced into Genocide*, 65.
[29] Ibid. 66 and 70–2.
[30] Sürmenyan, *Harbiyeli Bir Osmanlı Ermenisi*, 64.
[31] Ibid. 65.
[32] Ibid. 66.
[33] Ibid. 66–7.
[34] Ibid. 74.
[35] Ibid. 80–2; the deported members of his family were his wife, mother, sister, brother-in-law, and nephews.

exactly he managed to rescue his family, and himself, remains somewhat unclear. In any case, after his three months in jail Kalusd's uniform, weapon, missed pay, and officer status were restored to him. He was reunited with his family in Arapgir, though by then his mother had succumbed to illness.[36]

Both Kalusd and Yervant reported having encountered, at one time or another, high officials, on whom they were both tempted to exact revenge. When Yervant was in charge of the mess hall at Menemen, General Liman von Sanders and Enver Pasha came on a visit and ate there. Yervant considered poisoning them:

> Oh, how I was anxious to serve them a good meal. . . . Perhaps their last one. . . . When I realized I would come into close contact with their food, I thought of poisoning the meal, and I almost put that plan into motion, but I had to remind myself that if I had assassinated Enver Pasha, I would not have been the only one paying the price for the act.[37]

Similarly, Kalusd considered killing Memduh Bey, the district governor (*mutasarrıf*) of Erzincan. Only the knowledge that if he killed Memduh he would not be able to see his family again prevented him from going through with the plan.[38]

Conclusion

The accounts by Kalusd and Yervant reveal the lives of Armenians serving in the Ottoman army, the very institution that deported their families. Although the two texts are not diaries, and thus do not record change incrementally, they are nonetheless compelling attempts to interpret the events in which these men found themselves and their own roles in them. They describe their experiences even though, as both maintain, during the war years the world no longer made any sense to them and the unimaginable was happening. As the excellent introduction by Cora points out, Kalusd Sürmenyan's political attitude changed fundamentally over the course of the war, as did that of Yervant. Before the war Kalusd had eagerly pursued a career in the Ottoman army. In the First World War his service earned him a medal for merit (*liyakat*). In 1915 he was still surprised to learn that some Armenians were fighting alongside Russian troops. By 1919, when he went to the new Armenia, he spoke with

[36] Ibid. 84–91. [37] Alexanian, *Forced into Genocide*, 76.
[38] Sürmenyan, *Harbiyeli Bir Osmanlı Ermenisi*, 72.

satisfaction of the Armenian volunteer units he encountered there.[39] Yervant emphasized his own loyalty and that of Armenian Ottomans generally to the Empire. Their characterization of the prewar Empire—closely mirrored in Demetrios Theodore's account, as we saw—could be put down to nostalgic romanticism, but recent scholarship cautions against such a ready conclusion.[40] We do not need to accept uncritically Theodore's insistence that the First World War 'destroyed the peace and harmony that had prevailed among people of different nationalities and religions living together in peace'.[41] And yet diaries and accounts written during the war or in its immediate aftermath give voice to transitional attitudes concerning empire, religion, and nationality still in formation. Those transitional perspectives often stand in stark contrast to the new political lines that began to be laid down by the late 1920s. Theodore's remark and the stories that Kalusd and Yervant tell us go against the grain of historiography on the First World War in the Middle East, where the demise of the Ottoman Empire, with its alleged unsustainability, its ethnic and religious hatreds, is frequently taken for granted. Both Kalusd and Yervant lived the remainder of their lives far away from their place of birth and homeland. Neither fully planned this. After the war, Yervant intended to settle in Adana but was held back by news of poor job prospects there. He ended up accompanying his brother's future wife to the United States, where he remained and started his own family. Kalusd escaped Soviet Armenia for Baghdad, 'constantly remembering our home [*memleket*] in the deep belief that one day we will see our homeland [*vatan*] again'.[42]

[39] Ibid. 27 and 112.
[40] Doumanis, *Before the Nation*.
[41] Theodore, *The Sacrificials*, 42.
[42] Sürmenyan, *Harbiyeli Bir Osmanlı Ermenisi*, 115.

10
Uncovering the Colonial Cultures and Encounters of the British Empire during the First World War

Anna Maguire

In a letter he wrote in January 1915, Alexander MacGregor recalled an unusual musical performance: 'Some time ago there was a big sing song at Fort Tanskyne, and one of the men brought down the house completely by getting up and singing in a regular shrill native chant "Tipperary" in Hindustani. But I am afraid "Bwa-kutcha Tipperary ko-hai" will not catch on at home as much as one might wish.'[1] Lieutenant Colonel MacGregor served with battalions of the Mountain Battery Frontier Force during the war, travelling from India to Mesopotamia, Egypt, and Palestine.[2] The wartime letters of this white, middle-class Englishman reveal the diversity of contact that could be had between different peoples, cultures, and places. The army barracks became a site of cultural exchange as the Indian man performed a British music hall standard, which had reached global popularity, in his own language. The space of intercultural and interracial interaction was archived within the papers of the British officer. Encounters between imperial troops recorded in ego documents allow the researcher to go inside the colonial experience of conflict. The First World War and its military clash of empires created fresh spaces for encounters as diverse groups—soldiers and civilians, men and women, white and non-white people—were thrust together. In this essay I look at the historically specific colonial encounters at war as presented in the ego documents of those who experienced it. Encounter as a theoretical framework for understanding and recovering the experiences of colonial troops will be explored; how can it be used to read the archive? I will then

---

[1] Imperial War Museum (IWM), Documents 13421, Private Papers of Lieutenant Colonel A. MacGregor, Letter, 27 Jan. 1915.   [2] Ibid.

ask what the moments of encounter tell us about war experiences in the British Empire and how the First World War is commemorated and remembered.

Colonial encounters and cultural exchange during the First World War, particularly between different nationalities and races, were made possible by the Allied forces' vast and varied mobilization of troops from their empires. Estimates place the number of non-white men, combatants and non-combatants, mobilized in the European and American armies during the First World War at well over 4 million.[3] Britain drew heavily from its Empire as war demanded manpower, and sent these men across the world. India contributed the largest number, approximately 1.4 million. Another 1.3 million were recruited from the dominions: Australia, New Zealand (which had the highest proportion of enlistment to national population), Canada, South Africa, and Newfoundland. Further troops would come from the West Indies and China, as well as those Africans mobilized during the fighting in German imperial territories. British colonial troops saw service across the world, including on the Western Front, in the Dardanelles, Salonika, Egypt, Palestine, and West Africa.

What constituted a colonial encounter? Colonial encounters, as understood and employed here, were interactions and intersections involving individuals deemed 'colonials', from the British Empire, during the First World War. The idea of intersection is taken from Mary Louise Pratt's *Imperial Eyes* (2008). Pratt's 'contact zone' 'invokes the space and time where subjects previously separated by geography and history are co-present, the point at which their trajectories now intersect'.[4] The First World War's mobilizations breached geographical and historical boundaries, creating military trajectories that facilitated personal intersections. By using 'contact zone' rather than frontier, the perspective shifts from one of European expansion to one in which the geographical location and the activity creating the contact become much more flexible, allowing a range of experiences to become possible, a space for subjectivity.[5] Contact zone counteracts the idea of a binary division between colonizers and colonized and allows a more complex pic-

---

[3] Santanu Das (ed.), *Race, Empire and First World War Writing* (Cambridge, 2011), 4.
[4] Mary Louise Pratt, *Imperial Eyes: Travel Writing and Transculturation*, 2nd edn. (New York, 2008), 8.
[5] Ibid.

ture of colonial relations to develop.[6] Paths crossing, lives touching together, however briefly, and the provocation of a response—an observance, the investment of reflection, a change in perspective, or the affirmation of an imagining—constituted an encounter. In the ego documents of the colonial troops, these were trajectories created by war, patterns of mobilization affecting roles served and destinations sent to, but these trajectories carried on past the point of encounter to further war service, to returning home to civilian status or, frequently, to death. Encounters, therefore, were sites of interaction, and frequently this was interracial interaction.

Recent historical research has paid increasing attention to imperial participation in the First World War and has begun to explore the experiences of individual racial groups and the contribution of the former colonies.[7] There are archival discrepancies, though, in the ego documents available for the range of troops who served on behalf of the British Empire. While collections of First World War ego documents held by the Imperial War Museum and other archives are undeniably rich, typically, the majority of the private papers are written from white perspectives. Diaries and letters written by Pakeha New Zealanders or the 'Springboks' of the South African Infantry are abundant, whereas those by their compatriots of colour are not—a result of dominant oral cultures, non-English speakers, loose literacy requirements at enlistment, documents lost or not kept, and the absence of a tradition of donating to museums and archives, traditionally white spaces. Encounters recorded in ego documents of various forms—diaries, letters, memoirs—could be seen as 'sites' where interracial interaction has been mediated by one of the actors, recorded and archived in the cultural productions of the First World War.

The central question of colonial *encounters* allows the ego documents of people who came into contact with men from the colonies to be used by historians both to consider and to navigate the absences and silences of the archive. The difficulty in using this material, employing encounter as a theoretical framework, is a reliance on white accounts of black and ethnic minority experience. Does it allow

[6] Antoinette Burton, *At the Heart of Empire: Indians and the Colonial Encounter in Late-Victorian Britain* (Berkeley, 1998), 22.

[7] David Killingray was a leader in this field: see Killingray, *Africans in Britain* (London, 1994); David Killingray and David Omissi (eds.), *Guardians of Empire: The Armed Forces of the Colonial Powers c. 1700–1964* (Manchester, 1999); Richard Fogarty, *Race and War in France: Colonial Subjects in the French Army, 1914–1918* (Washington, 2008).

the subaltern to speak only on the terms of the colonizer?[8] I argue that the ego documents of colonial troops, white and black, serve as 'epistemic traces mediated by bodily actions and enmeshed in the materiality of colonial situations'.[9] Encounters serve as these colonial situations, where the troops interacted and came together; ego documents are the textual remnants and representations produced by these physical meetings. Using Ricardo Roque and Kim Wagner's third reading technique for European archives—'the exploration of the actual cross-cultural encounters and material practices in which colonial knowledge is grounded and embedded'[10]—this essay uses First World War ego documents to gain access into historical colonial experience. Reading for encounters in these writings insists on the presence of other racial groupings within the context of individual war experience and allows us to complicate our narratives, a method of recovery and inclusion.[11]

In the introduction to his edited volume *Race, Empire and First World War Writing* (2011), Santanu Das called for more thinking about the social and cultural history of the war and the experiences of individual ethnicities and colonies 'in a comparative and cross-disciplinary framework'.[12] A thematic focus on encounters makes comparison a necessity as the contact zones created interaction between the different forces mobilized by the British Empire and their allies, as well as with civilians and the locations encompassed by the war's extensive geographical reach. Theoretical analysis of the encounters presented in ego documents relies on an interdisciplinary approach: social and cultural history, literary theory, spatial theory, and geography. The reading technique outlined stemmed from developments in historical anthropology in the 1980s and 1990s, particularly histories of travel and exploration in the eighteenth and early nineteenth centuries.[13] This essay positions the First World War as a time of transnationalism and mobility as well as conflict in a later period to draw on this interdisciplinary work. Encounter

---
[8] Gayatri Chakravorty Spivak, 'Can the Subaltern Speak?', in Cary Nelson and Lawrence Grossberg (eds.), *Marxism and the Interpretation of Culture* (London, 1988), 66–111.
[9] Ricardo Roque and Kim A. Wagner (eds.), *Engaging Colonial Knowledge: Reading European Archives in World History* (Basingstoke, 2012), 5.
[10] Ibid. 19.
[11] Antoinette Burton, *Brown over Black: Race and the Politics of Postcolonial Citation* (Gurgaon, 2012), 30.
[12] Das (ed.), *Race, Empire and First World War Writing*, 3.
[13] Roque and Wagner (eds.), *Engaging Colonial Knowledge*, 19.

enables a more collective focus that begins to take into account the war experiences of the British Empire as a whole, allowing the operation of empire during wartime to be unpicked, as it was forced to function in different spheres.

More than an inclusionary technique, though, encounters had their own importance within the context of war. The First World War's patterns and military mobilizations meant that those who served were consistently and continually exposed to other parts of the British Empire, not just the other men serving, but the places and peoples of the Empire more generally. The consistency of cross-cultural interactions between peoples and places, even when expressed in the simplest terms, is instantly apparent when reading the ego documents of the colonial troops. New Zealander William King wrote home from Egypt in September 1918 that 'two British West Indian battalions and a Jewish battalion are here with us. We haven't seen the Jews yet I don't know what sort of soldiers they will make.'[14] When taken prisoner by the Germans from the Western Front in 1916, South African Corporal Edward Dotish described how when he 'awoke from the effects of the operation, I found myself lying next to two French Senegalese Negroes'.[15] When Reverend John Ramson arrived in England with his battalion of the British West Indies Regiment in the spring of 1916, he recorded that they 'stopped at one station where there were ladies ready with steaming tins of coffee, and cups to serve it out to the men who were very grateful for it'.[16] Alfred Horner, another padre who served with the 9th Battalion of the British West Indies Regiment, described his experience in *From the Islands of the Sea: Glimpses of a West Indian Battalion in France* (1919). He observed the men

> fraternizing in a wonderful way with the French civilians, telling them of their sunny home in broken French, which they pick up quickly, making themselves useful, and generally, by their quiet and respectful demeanour, earning for themselves the sobriquet which I have mentioned above, 'the friendly (or amiable) coloured soldiers.' Nor is that all: there will be scarcely a canteen belonging to the troops quartered there which does not contain a few of our men establishing friendly relations and exchanging experiences.[17]

[14] IWM Documents, Private Papers of W. A. King, 8 Sept. 1918.
[15] Corporal E. Dotish, *The First Springbok Prisoner in Germany* (London, 1917), 95.
[16] J. Ramson, *'Carry on'; or, Pages from the Life of a West Indian Padre in the Field* (Kingston, Jamaica, 1918), 7.
[17] A. E. Horner, *From the Islands of the Sea: Glimpses of a West Indian Battalion in France* (Nassau, 1919), 4.

The diverse spaces of encounter and exchange—on the journey to war, in military barracks and canteens, civilian hubs, prisoner-of-war camps—indicate how deeply encounters infiltrated the experience of the First World War for the troops from the British Empire.

The concentration of encounter as a recurring trope in the ego documents of British colonial troops allows closer examination of the dynamics of empire during the war, beyond the immediate 'charms' of the cross-cultural encounter. How did interactions vary across racial lines, between Europeans and non-Europeans, or between 'Others' and other 'Others'? The global crisis of war was a time of heightened emotional anxiety as life became increasingly vulnerable and death happened en masse; racial mixing would add a further dimension of concern as much for the individual soldier as for national and imperial governments. This was particularly pertinent in the British case, where anxieties about the declining birth rate in the Edwardian period were intensified by broader fears that the race was deteriorating, exemplified by the poor health and fitness of recruits in the Boer War.[18] The global nature of the First World War unavoidably juxtaposed insular domestic British concerns with the physical condition of the races of the Empire, which had been built and sustained upon the premiss of British masculinity, strength, and superiority. The imperial order was explicitly patriarchal and reliant upon strong masculinities.

War was the most obvious test of these masculinities, pitting male bodies in competition against other nations and empires. With the reluctant mobilization of black colonial troops, white British masculinity was threatened by its conflict with Germany and by its own empire. The First World War was an opportunity for individual nations not only to survive, but also to flourish and to prove themselves, if not in direct competition with the British, then in securing their rank in the imperial order. The dislocation of men from the colonies and dominions into new spaces disrupted the operation of empire and created new spaces for colonial encounter. Rather than the relationship between centre and periphery, suddenly the periphery would encounter other peripheries, and the metropolis multiple colonies at once. There was a need for a clear sense of identity and proof of position within this empire on the move. In his history, *The Maoris in the Great War* (1926), James Cowan, a noted non-fiction

---

[18] Richard A. Soloway, *Demography and Degeneration: Eugenics and the Declining Birthrate in Twentieth-Century Britain* (Chapel Hill, NC, 1990), 38.

writer at the beginning of the twentieth century, established the martial qualities of the Maori men in direct comparison to the martially renowned Gurkhas and Scottish Highlanders:

> Not merely were the native New Zealanders superior to all the coloured troops—a distinguished General said that the famous Ghurkhas were but children as compared with the Maoris—but they proved superior to many of the white troops in directions, which suited the genius of the race. They were as grim and thorough as any Highland regiment in attack work with the bayonet, and they proved themselves equal to the tremendous nerve-test of sustained shellfire, the greatest test of all.[19]

Cowan established not only that the Maoris belonged to a collective New Zealander identity, but that there was a specific 'genius of the race' that put renowned fighters of colour to shame and challenged white men's martial ability too. Alfred Horner's account of West Indian stretcher-bearers validated the work they were doing in France as essential and dangerous, and suggested that the contacts made through their labour could change the imperial order after the war:

> Often and often did our lads make the trip from regimental aid post to dressing station, working all the time with a most exemplary cheerfulness, conscious that they were at any rate doing valuable, necessary, dangerous work, and—who knows?—probably forging another link in that brotherhood of empire, for possibly some lad from a far distant clime, of another race, may remember with sympathy and affection the day when our West Indian coloured lads carried him out of danger to life and to health.[20]

Horner's writing about West Indian non-combatants' war work was an important promotion of their identity as servicemen during the war and the potential of this service to effect change. The ego documents reveal the important negotiations of colonial hierarchies through military participation and ability during a period when the British Empire had been dislocated by war.

Why, though, were these colonial hierarchies important? British governmental anxieties about the perceived inferiority of people of colour and a desire to maintain a racial hierarchy restricted the military status permitted to imperial subjects, and not all colonial troops served as combatants.[21] A ranking of colonial masculinities

---

[19] James Cowan, *The Maoris in the Great War: A History of the New Zealand Native Contingent and Pioneer Battalion: Gallipoli, 1915; France and Flanders, 1916–1918* (Auckland, 1926), 2.   [20] Horner, *From the Islands of the Sea*, 36.
[21] Soloway, *Demography and Degeneration*, 38.

was already in place, more complicated than a binary opposition between white and black. According to the theory of martial races, specific nations and ethnicities were endowed with superior fighting ability. The belief that some men were 'biologically or culturally predisposed to the arts of war' had been constructed during the nineteenth century, drawing on biological theories about racial order.[22] Shifts in the biological and human sciences during the late eighteenth and early nineteenth centuries made the culture and social behaviour of man a biological concern.[23] Thus, 'evolution' and 'biology' could determine behaviour and prowess, and were fluid in their application; Heather Streets has emphasized the 'historical instability of conceptions of "race"'.[24] The 'savage representations of masculinity' at the heart of martial race ideology privileged the perceived barbarism of some non-white men, while the racial profile of others rendered them unfit for martial activity. In particular favour as the British Empire's most manly and fiercest soldiers were the Scottish Highlanders, Punjabi Sikhs, and Nepalese Gurkhas. The necessary strategy of imperial rule required complex, inconsistent, and frequently contradictory uses of scientific, biological understandings of race; it is no surprise that Indian men were endowed with perceived superiority when this was useful to British control there. Much was made of the camaraderie that developed between the British and the Indian 'martial races' in military and civilian discourse, which would further separate these men from other colonial groups.

The rhetoric of martial races would have a bearing on the mobilization of non-white colonial troops and their military status during the First World War. There were clear concerns from the War Office and Colonial Office about mobilizing non-white men to fight white men in Europe and the destabilizing impact on the imperial order. These concerns persisted despite the utilization of colonial troops of colour in previous conflicts, not just the Indian Army but also, to take one example, the West India Regiment that was deployed in the Napoleonic Wars. Arming non-white men to fight alongside and against white men indicated some semblance of racial equality, which undermined the operation of empire at its core.[25] How else,

[22] Heather Streets, *Martial Races: The Military, Race and Masculinity in British Imperial Culture, 1857–1914* (Manchester, 2004), 1.
[23] Nancy Stepan, *The Idea of Race in Science: Great Britain, 1800–1960* (London, 1982), 4. [24] Streets, *Martial Races*, 1.
[25] Richard Smith, *Jamaican Volunteers in the First World War: Race, Masculinity and the Development of National Consciousness* (Manchester, 2004), 59.

though, could the British Army garner enough manpower to support the war on all its fronts, including Mesopotamia and Africa, without relying on colonial troops? Indian troops, including the martially superior Punjabi Sikhs and Gurkhas from Nepal, were among the first forces from the Empire to begin travelling to the front after war was declared, a process enabled by the existing Indian Army, which had its basis in martial theories. But not all of the non-white men were mobilized as quickly, nor did they serve as combatants. Black West Indians were not enlisted by the War Office until October 1915, and though they were involved in front-line combat, including manning machine-guns, in Palestine, they did not fight in Europe, where the British West Indies Regiment (BWIR) was used for labour duties, such as the stretcher-bearing already mentioned, though they retained soldier status.[26] Similarly, the South African Native Labour Contingent (SANLC) was restricted to labouring rather than combat duties when it was mobilized along the Western Front, as well as having further restrictions on its movements while in France.[27]

Hope was expressed, though, that the war would challenge the inequalities of empire, and that new bonds of friendship could be facilitated through the encounters between the different colonial groups. Some of this came in appeals to enlist that were published in newspapers: an article 'The West Indies and the War' in the *Federalist and Grenada People* asked: 'Why has not England utilised in the same manner the services of her black warriors? Because of the nasty cowardly skin prejudice characteristic of the Empire. This war however will end that.'[28]

The anticipation of the ability of encounters to enact change, beyond demonstrations of martial strength, surfaced within the ego documents written by those who were witnessing encounters at first hand. Alfred Horner noted in his published account of the war that 'many happy hours were spent cementing a friendship with the British Tommy which should bring forth its fruit yet in the great reorganization of Empire which must take place after the war'.[29] The fruits of encounters—knowledge, awareness, friendship—were invested with much wider significance than mere occasions of interracial

---

[26] Ibid. 80.
[27] Norman Clothier, *Black Valour: The South African Native Labour Contingent, 1916–1918, and the Sinking of the* Mendi (Pietermaritzburg, 1987), 12.
[28] 'The West Indies and the War', *Federalist and Grenada People*, 19 June 1915.
[29] Horner, *From the Islands of the Sea*, 21.

contact: they had the potential to challenge the imperial order and ensure equality between different colonial peoples.

Yet, more frequently, representations of encounters in ego documents concentrated on the intimacy of the contact between different groups and how enduring these relationships could become. This intimacy could be both physical and emotional. William Barry was an Australian soldier whose service took him to Sri Lanka, Egypt, and France, and who was taken prisoner during the Battle of Fromelles in July 1916.[30] In his diary, Barry wrote about meeting Jamaican men away from the front line in Egypt:

> We used to be on parade by nine am, and some days would march easy to one of the salt lakes connected by the Suez Canal, and have a swim and it was alright. One day when having a swim, two companies of troops from Jamaica came down and it looked funny to see these fine bodied coloured men, for they were as black as coal, in the water with us chaps, and it wasn't very long before we were the best of friends. Other days we would have a picnic as they called it. We would go over to one of the sweet water canals and lay under the shade of the trees, telling yarns or playing card till evening time and then we would come back to camp.[31]

The First World War literary trope of a British officer watching his men bathe, as established by Paul Fussell, was subverted in this vignette of black and white bodies mingling in the water.[32] What Barry's diary revealed was the initial shock of seeing these black men in the water with the white Australians, and undertones of homoerotic appreciation for them. It also showed how swiftly the racialized bodies of the Jamaican men became irrelevant as the men became 'friends', able to communicate and get along well. The white account does not acknowledge where the power lies in this asymmetric relation and the brokering of 'friendship', but suggests instead that from this moment of intimacy, the men were able to understand each other, confronted with their naked physicality, vulnerable but playful in the water together. Where army movements would determine when this 'friendship' would end, the intensity of this evocative moment, tactile, affective, and aesthetic, was made permanent in the physical act of writing. Multiracial friendships were developing in numerous spaces and times. Stimela Jason Jingoes, who served with the South African Native Labour Corps, gave an

---

[30] IWM, Documents 15006, Private Papers of William Barry.
[31] IWM, Barry, p. 27.
[32] Paul Fussell, *The Great War and Modern Memory* (Oxford, 2013), 299.

oral testimony of his experience in the 1970s. He described meeting William Johnstone of Folkestone as the two worked on the docks at Dieppe, France. 'We hit it off at once and spent our breaks drinking tea and talking about our two countries, until at last we were close friends. After the war we corresponded for many years, but at last we lost touch and I do not know what became of him.'[33]

Though the friendships between the white British man and the black South African, or the Australians and Jamaicans, could be portrayed as a stepping stone to restructuring the British Empire, neither Jingoes nor Barry chose to emphasize this in their representations. Instead, it was simply the moment of origin for a longer-term friendship. But more can be read about the dynamics of these moments of encounter than what is presented on the surface of these ego documents.

In accepting the encounters presented in ego documents as archives of interracial interaction during the First World War, an acknowledgement must be made of the complexity of the racial framework in which these occurred. The perceptions being discussed were not solely those of Europeans about non-Europeans or a straightforward form of Orientalism. Emotional responses to encounters, where insights were drawn and judgements were made, did, of course, shape and reflect the image of the 'Self' in reaction to the 'Other'.[34] However, Eastern/Western, European/non-European, white/non-white binaries were not the sole planes on which this process occurred. Colonial encounters during the war entailed that the 'Other' frequently met another kind of 'Other': Maoris encountered Sri Lankan 'natives', West Indians encountered Chinese labourers, black men from Jamaica met black men from Ghana. It is important, then, to recognize the complexity of self-representation and identification that was in operation, a constant activity of maintaining and reinforcing racial and social hierarchies, rather than strict binaries that are undermined by integrating ego documents into our readings. These hierarchies could draw on a myriad of symbols, cultures, and behaviours: physicality and masculinity, perceived levels of 'civilization', and army rank.

Much like Orientalism, the defining and positioning of the 'Self',

---

[33] *A Chief is a Chief by the People: The Autobiography of Stimela Jason Jingoes*, ed. J. Perry and C. Perry (Oxford, 1975), 93.
[34] Patrick Porter, *Military Orientalism: Eastern War through Western Eyes* (London, 2009), 13.

if not directly in opposition to but in separation from the various 'Others' encountered, was reliant upon the anxieties and fears of that same 'Self'. Rikihana Carkeek, a Maori member of the New Zealand Expeditionary Force, described the arrival of the First Maori Contingent in Ceylon, present-day Sri Lanka:

> We arrived in Colombo at 5 am on a lovely morning. At six we dropped anchor. There were native boats all around our ship and the other transports. The coolies coaling our boat made a great commotion. They are a very scraggy looking people with poor physique. We threw pennies into the harbour for the coolies to dive after.[35]

Myths about Maori origins as descendants of a lost Caucasian tribe allowed Maori people to be seen as a 'higher order coloured people', and images of the superior Maori or 'best black' were adopted and disseminated in New Zealand literature.[36] Encounters of white Australians and New Zealanders with 'natives' in ports 'reflected their racial assumptions and their belief in the essential superiority of what they thought of as the White Race', and the kind of language employed by Carkeek is familiar from the ego documents of white dominion troops.[37] Carkeek defined and maintained the 'otherness' of these other non-white men in relation to his own assumption of superiority, founded in this discourse of Maori being 'best black'. It guaranteed that his Pakeha counterparts would not associate the Maori with non-white men of what he considered a lower type. Carkeek's preoccupation with the 'coolies' and their physicality enabled him to define the natives as inferior, using their 'scraggy' bodies. The way the New Zealanders threw pennies for the 'coolies' to dive for was a further reflection on the poverty, naivety, and 'primitiveness' of the land they had arrived in and their own comparatively 'Western' wealth. Carkeek's construction of difference between himself and the 'coolies' of Ceylon was an active process and heavily invested in emotion; 'otherness' was 'neither inherent nor stable' and drew on his own sense of anxiety in defining himself as racially normative in the face of a racial 'other'.[38]

---

[35] Rikihana Carkeek, *Home Little Maori Home: A Memoir of the Maori Contingent, 1914–1916* (Wellington, 2003), 11 Mar. 1915.

[36] James Bennett, 'Maori as Honorary Members of the White Tribe', *Journal of Imperial and Commonwealth History*, 29/3 (2001), 33–54, at 37.

[37] Peter Stanley, 'He was black, he was a White man, and a dinkum Aussie': Race and Empire in Revisiting the Anzac Legend', in Das (ed.), *Race, Empire and First World War Writing*, 213–30, at 223.

[38] Ann Laura Stoler and Frederick Cooper, 'Between Metropole and Colony:

Those who witnessed the coalescence of perceived differences into a constructed racial order reinforced it through their representation of these moments in their ego documents. Marjorie Thomas was a Voluntary Aid Detachment (VAD) nurse, who served between April 1916 and April 1919 in India and Mesopotamia.[39] Writing in 1917, she articulated the difficulties the nurses had in organizing seating for their patients at mealtimes:

> The British Tommies did not want to sit with the 'blacks' and the 'blacks' did not want to sit with each other . . . These were negroes. Some, from the West Indies, were cultured, educated men, more fastidious than many a British soldier with their array of toilet articles in their lockers—toothbrushes, sponges, talcum powder, etc. But others, from the Gold Coast or Nigeria, were much less sophisticated. They had been brought in to work on the Inland Waterways, and had never seen things like cups, saucers and cutlery before and their table manners were non-existent.[40]

Thomas's assumption of a binary distinction between the Tommies and 'the blacks', who, to her, looked the same and were therefore of the same 'type', was challenged by the men's desire to have their separate identities and inequalities recognized. By deciding which group was more civilized, in this case determined by levels of sophistication and cleanliness, and aligning the West Indian men with the actions of British soldiers, she cedes to them the superior position. The West Indians were deemed to have qualities of whiteness over the Nigerians, whose inappropriate manners fulfilled the stereotype of the uncivilized 'native': of course the two groups could not be forced to sit together. The account reveals how colonial discourse could be drawn into encounters as they occurred during the war. Though these drew on complicated hybrids of thought, there was clear understanding of how racial order could be determined and how even 'the Other' could define another as different or inferior.

As established, the British Army's organization of non-white troops fell within a preconceived racial hierarchy, firmly embedded in the colonies: assumptions, including martial races theory, determined who would be sent to the front and what they would do once there. The enactment of racial hierarchy within army rank had clear

---

Rethinking a Research Agenda', in Ann Laura Stoler and Frederick Cooper (eds.), *Tensions of Empire: Colonial Cultures in a Bourgeois World* (Berkeley, 1997), 1–56, at 7.

[39] IWM, Documents 8236, Private Papers of Marjorie Thomas.
[40] IWM, Thomas, Diary, p. 171.

implications for how these non-white groups would encounter each other. Alfred Horner described how

> With the ordinary native labour corps, particularly the Chinese, our men do not agree very well. A good deal of this is probably our own lads' fault, for they have, I must confess, a somewhat irritating habit of rubbing in the fact that being soldiers they are on an immeasurably higher social scale than a mere labourer who is working for a wage. I distinctly remember the difficulties which we used to have when quartered with Chinese labour companies. The B. W. I's used to accuse 'John' of having committed various depredations amongst their kit, their belongings and their rations; whilst 'John' in his turn was wont to make remarks, which hardly tended to amicable relations, upon the appearance and general condition of our men. The native labour people, too, with some show of justice, were given to objecting to the B. W. I's freedom in the use of cafes and estaminets, and were frequently the cause of trouble by standing outside such places and making rather heated remarks as our boys, with, I daresay, an unnecessary amount of gusto, retired from their refreshment.[41]

Horner's paternalistic assertion, as a white British man, of West Indian superiority to non-white labour forces and their relative freedom, though written for a West Indian audience, was an important statement. The distinction between combatant and non-combatant status bestowed subjective elitism on those who were looked upon more favourably. While the West Indian men were subject to institutional racism, segregation on certain parts of the Western Front, and were soldiers only in name, this elevated them above the Chinese labourers and the 'native labour people', from either the French Empire or the South African Native Labour Corps, in terms of social standing, wages, and access to facilities such as cafés, which were hugely important during wartime. As Carkeek relied upon physicality and Thomas used civilized behaviour as distinguishing factors, here Horner reflected the fact that army rank's reliance on racial hierarchy led to this hierarchy's perpetuation through associated status.

Reading for these moments of encounter in the ego documents of colonial troops and other participants in the First World War, therefore, reveals the operation of empire and its racial hierarchies in the changing spaces of war, where they would intersect with other factors, such as army rank. Antoinette Burton has promoted histories that 'acknowledge racial difference and conflict as full bodied dimensions of the postcolonial condition in all its worldly, combative

[41] Horner, *From the Islands of the Sea*, 51.

variety, and that, frankly, resist conscription by narratives of overcoming, salvation and redemption as well as of solidarity per se'.[42] Close analysis of encounters such as those which Carkeek, Horner, and Thomas described draws out the operation of racism beyond a white/non-white binary that does not necessarily guarantee a sense of fraternity or alliance between non-white people as a result of colonialist structures in operation during the conflict. Equally, narratives of solidarity are not prohibited. However, they should be viewed in context and by comparison with friendships or alliances between white and non-white individuals and groups under similar circumstances as well, in order fully to understand racial difference.

Scrutinizing encounters illuminates the emotional complexity of meeting the 'Other' during the war, and the information exchanged and recorded in written, oral, and visual accounts of interaction is important in the challenge these can pose to established narratives of the war. This could range from additional details that nuance the existing history to more explicit counters to the imperial order that went beyond occasions of multiracial interactions and friendships. New details emerge through encounter that can tell us more about war experiences in the British Empire. This serves to reposition colonial troops within the dominant narrative, placing them at the centre rather than on the periphery. Encounters can further underline the diversity of experience shaped by war's contingent circumstances.

The potential challenge to remembered narratives is nowhere clearer than in the diary of one South African soldier, in relation to the service of men from Egypt on the Western Front. William St Leger, of British origin, recorded a mutiny by some men of the Egyptian Labour Corps (ELC), stationed in Boulogne.[43] The ELC is generally remembered for its service in the Sinai and Palestine Campaign, where they worked on the construction of roads and railways. Often admired by those who served with them for their stoicism and endurance, the men were subject to racial 'Othering', particularly being infantilized by the white soldiers with whom they served because of their non-whiteness and their lack of military status, being categorized as labourers rather than soldiers. The treatment of non-white men as children implied an inferior version of white Western maturity and masculinity. By dubbing them either 'uncivilized' and 'irresponsible', or 'playful' and 'naive', infantilizing rhetorics al-

[42] Burton, *Brown over Black*, 7–8.
[43] IWM Documents 20504, Private Papers of William St Leger, 6 Nov. 1917.

lowed these men to be patronized and controlled. Alexander Briscoe Moore, a New Zealander serving with the Auckland Mounted Rifles in Egypt, described the ELC 'going down the line singing and waving flags like children', and later 'their weird chant and laughing brown faces remind[ed] one of so many big children'.[44] Moore articulated the perceived racial inferiority of the ELC through his comparison to children, reducing their masculinity, agency, and intellect, informing the constructed elitism of the white New Zealanders during their time in Egypt. St Leger's diary entry immediately contests the narratives of Moore and others: the ELC's service was relocated to France, mutiny and anger replaced laughter, and their agency as masculine actors was reinstated.

This was an encounter within an encounter; St Leger was recalling what he himself was told by a friend who was an officer of the ELC, rather than what he had witnessed at first hand. It reveals the importance of ego documents as a place for hearsay and anecdote to be recorded and archived where they would not be included in official histories:

> The Egyptians, he said were raving with fury and, had they known that he was inside, would have put an end to the hut and its occupants. Next morning, just after the relief of the party in the hut had taken place, the row had begun. The Egyptians seized hold of poles, buckets, anything and everything within reach and began wrecking everything. For some absurd reason the British troops opened fire from three sides of a square, and had nearly twenty casualties among themselves. The Egyptians simply melted away—they had about twenty men killed, and crawled under the huts. In the afternoon their white officers had no difficulty in parading them and making them work.[45]

Heavily reliant on the army because of their distance from home and knowing the high potential cost of military punishment, the Egyptian men must have been aware of the dangers of such a mutiny. St Leger concluded by agreeing with this officer that force 'is often, if not always, the only authority that a native will recognize'.[46] In many ways, St Leger was just as 'Othering' as Moore; the Egyptian men were presented as uncontrolled and uncivilized 'natives', struggling to keep their emotions in check and weak in the face of white imperial control. His account retained the framework of imperial order: commending the power of the British Empire in controlling its imperial

[44] IWM, Books 16768, A. Briscoe Moore, *The Mounted Riflemen in Sinai and Palestine: The Story of New Zealand's Crusaders* (Auckland, 1925), 55, 139.
[45] IWM, St Leger, 6 Nov. 1917.
[46] Ibid.

subjects. Yet the encounter reveals the multiplicity of imperial experience during the First World War; the story concerning the ELC is no longer singularly based on childlike obedience but recognizes the maltreatment and coercion of colonial groups and their own resistance to the imperial order. The ELC stands alongside those from the British Empire forces who took part in the series of mutinies at Étaples in 1917, and the West Indian men who mutinied at Taranto in December 1918. The South African man's diary serves the same purpose as the poem 'The Black Soldier's Lament' in articulating colonial grievances with the war:

> Stripped to the waist and sweated chest
> Mid-day's reprieve much needed rest.
> We dug and hauled and lifted high
> From trenches deep toward the sky—
> Non-fighting troops and yet we die.[47]

In the absence of voices of the Egyptian men to recount this act of rebellion, St Leger's account allows both the mistreatment of the ELC during their time in France and the subsequent mutiny to be recorded and remembered.

Crucially, encounters also illuminate the less exceptional, more everyday experiences at the heart of ego documents that might otherwise be lost, the interpersonal relationships that challenged the operation of the imperial order. While the deeply individual focus of recording friendships that crossed rhetorical racial bounds has already been discussed, those that explicitly countered policy and regulation from the government and army have implications for how the history of the British Empire's experience of war is written. Where official records speak of segregation, limits placed on contact and racial mixing, and efforts to ensure that the imperial hierarchy would not be breached, encounters in ego documents sit outside these narratives, undermining such attempts. To rely solely on governmental or army records in these circumstances or leave them unchallenged or unquestioned would reveal only part of the story. This is particularly evidenced in two examples: Maori relationships with women during the war and the contact the South African Native Labour Corps was able to have with civilians while serving on the Western Front.

[47] George A. Borden, 'The Black Soldier's Lament', ll. 16–20 ⟨http://iwvpa.net/borden_ga/the-blac.php⟩ [accessed 31 July 2015].

In a letter in *The Times* of 2 February 1918, New Zealand High Commissioner Thomas MacKenzie addressed the subject of war marriages and explicitly stated that 'in no instance is permission given to Maori members of the New Zealand Expeditionary Force to contract marriages [in Britain]'.[48] While there were also problems with British women marrying Pakeha New Zealanders, a review process existed and marriage licences could be granted. For Maori troops, as men of colour, this would not be the case. The representations of Maori interaction with women in ego documents, however, challenged the projected experience of the enforcement of racial boundaries by official sources. Rikihana Carkeek of the First Maori Contingent wrote in his diary, when he was hospitalized in England following the Gallipoli campaign, about taking 'the train back to Trent Bridge together with two ladies who showed us the sights along the Trent River' and about meeting a lady friend in Hyde Park.[49] John Williamson, a Pakeha New Zealander, wrote about retrieving a Maori man imprisoned on the Isle of Wight for two weeks after he had 'been out with an English girl instead of being on night operations'.[50] Alexander Prebble from Auckland wrote home from hospital in Weybridge:

A wounded Maori was engaged to an English girl and just before the wedding he was put wise to the fact that he needed a 'best man'. He got another Maori to act in that capacity and the wedding was a success. The best man took a fancy to the bridesmaid (whom he had never seen before) and within a week he was married with the previously married Maori as his best man.[51]

Though meant as a humorous anecdote about how quickly marriage could take place in wartime, the result of fleeting exchanges, Prebble's letter was also about official wedding ceremonies for Maori soldiers and British women, with the usual traditions of best man and bridesmaid, that were in no way unusual. Regardless of what Thomas MacKenzie was writing in *The Times*, the lived experience of Maori men as recorded in these ego documents showed that these men were entering into marriages with English women, as well as engaging in more flirtatious interactions or romantic liaisons, much the same as their Pakeha counterparts from the New Zealand Expeditionary Force.

[48] *The Times*, 2 Feb. 1918. [49] Carkeek, *Home Little Maori Home*, 6 June 1916.
[50] IWM Documents 11515, Private Papers of J. Williamson, p. 50.
[51] Alexander Turnbull Library (ATL), MS Papers 2416, A. Prebble, 1 Nov. 1918.

The South African Native Labour Corps faced much stricter regulations than those preventing them from marrying British women: strict orders were in place about the spaces these men could inhabit in Europe. Forming its policy in the midst of imperial anxiety about the mobilization of people of colour as the need for labour on the Western Front increased with growing casualty rates, the South African government wanted to ensure that no black men fought together with white men on equal terms.[52] This would, it was hoped, preserve the colour bar that was essential to South African governance, and that had implications for how the British Empire was organized. When sending black men to serve in France, the South African government and army officials aimed to segregate the men from other troops at work and in camp to ensure that they could not draw comparisons between their own duties and treatment and those of other battalions.[53] War Office documents held in the National Archives at Kew uncover how complex this was in operation: when the SANLC were at Rouen, the army removed the Cape Coloured Labour Battalion: 'The latter were treated as soldiers, the former were segregated; it would have been impossible to enforce the rules by which the South African natives were restricted to compounds if they had seen the Cape Boys alongside them allowed practically unlimited freedom.'[54] Segregation would ensure that order could prevail in the upheaval of war: the logical response in reaction to the assumed inferiority of the black South Africans.

Yet it would prove too difficult to enforce complete segregation of the black South African men of the SANLC. As well as his meeting and friendship with William Johnstone, Stimela Jason Jingoes remembered arriving in the docks in Calais: 'met by French people, men, women and girls. All were laughing and shaking our hands.'[55] This set the precedent for their treatment while in France:

You see we liked our stay in France. It was our first experience of living in a society without a colour bar. When the time came for us to leave, some of us hid in the houses of our French friends. The military police caught most of us, but there were others who never went back to South Africa.[56]

[52] Albert Grundligh, *Fighting their Own War: South African Blacks and the First World War* (Johannesburg, 1987), 100.
[53] Ibid.
[54] The National Archives, Kew (TNA), WO 107/37, War Office Papers, A History of Labour Battalions during the First World War, 25.
[55] *A Chief is a Chief*, ed. Perry and Perry, 82.
[56] Ibid. 93.

The 'colour bar' and racialized inequalities relied upon by the South African government were comparatively absent in France. Further, the black South Africans remembered being able to experience and benefit from this more equal society. They made friends with the French people to the point of seeking refuge in their houses when forced to return to South Africa. Just as Richard Fogarty's work has pointed to French imperial troops, particularly from Indo-China, who tried to remain in France after marrying French women during the war, it seems that black South African men had been able to build strong enough relationships to rely on French civilians for refuge initially, though most were caught.[57] Jacob Koos Matli, one of the survivors of the *SS Mendi* sinking, reported that while in Rouen towards the end of their service, 'We got word that General Botha had stated that he did not want the natives who were in England back in South Africa as they were going about with English women. I do not know as to whether this was the truth or just rumour, but we came back and left many in England.'[58]

While the consequences of black South Africans mixing with white British women had more complicated ramifications than when they had relationships with French civilians, given that these white women were symbolized as the boundary-keepers of empire at home, once again the projections of the official policy of segregation were challenged by these represented lives.[59] These personal and small-scale interactions had wider implications. They subverted a hierarchy that officials had attempted to transfer from the dominion to the front line. By using encounters in ego documents to read for the experiences of the British Empire at war, we can go beyond the narrative articulated in War Office documents or army records to trace the implications of such policies for the lives of those they governed.

Encounter has been demonstrated to be a revealing theoretical approach to understanding ego documents of the First World War in the context of the experience of troops from the British Empire. Ego documents as sites of archived encounter expand the documentary evidence open to researchers of colonial troops during the war, particularly those for whom little or no first-hand written material has been preserved, by offering an alternative point of access in how

---

[57] Fogarty, *Race and War in France*, 203.
[58] Jacob Koos Matli in M. D. W. Jeffreys, 'The *Mendi* and After', *Africana Notes and News*, Mar. 1963, 188.
[59] Wendy Webster, *Englishness and Empire, 1939–1965* (Oxford, 2007), 10.

those they met, worked with, and lived alongside perceived them and their experience. Though the use of white voices articulating black experience has to be carefully deconstructed and contextualized, reading for encounters informs our understanding of how colonial troops experienced their military service. War was a time for travel, exploration, and exposure to new peoples and places, where the serving men were confronted with the unknown and the 'Other'. The consistency and recurrence of encounters in ego documents show how deeply these interactions shaped the articulation of colonial experience. Ego documents about the war—letters, diaries, and memoirs—are individual and personal reflections, and are as diverse and multifaceted as those who wrote them. Encounter proves to be a dominant feature of all spaces away from the front line and battlefield: in camps, civilian homes and social spaces, prisoner-of-war camps, hospitals, and while exploring villages, towns, and cities. These moments were not sideshows but formative in the construction of remembered experience, the everyday in contrast to the exceptional occasions of battle.

The intimacy of encounters and the endurance of the relationships formed across racialized and gendered divisions reveal the legacy of interactions on an individual level, long after war's end. Stimela Jason Jingoes spoke fondly of his friendship with William Johnstone; Prebble's Maori grooms found love with British brides during their war service. Yet these personal moments reveal the complex reality of the operation of encounters during the war. This was not simply a confrontation between white and non-white, European and non-European, the West and the rest. Instead the dynamics of encounter saw race intersect with nationality, with class, with gender, with army rank, and with war's contingent circumstances to create sites of interracial intersection that depended on hierarchies rather than binaries in an active emotional process of making distinctions between groups. These encounters provide us with different ways of knowing and understanding war experience in the British Empire. Reading encounters sees troops of colour included within the narrative, often as a peripheral feature to be commented upon, creating a diverse scene to be reported to those at home. But encounters also recentre the narratives around colonial troops, making them actors and agents in their own experience—mutineers, husbands, and friends—rather than isolated, marginal, or homogeneous groups.

PART IV

Uses of Ego Documents

11
Publishing Ego Documents as War Propaganda

GERD KRUMEICH

For years ego documents have been experiencing a boom in research on the First World War. Above all, the documents of the 'little man', of the ordinary soldier, have become an almost indispensable part of any description of the war experience.[1] They are a mark of the postmodern description of the 'war as experienced' that argues for and focuses on the individual: an individual no longer situated in his social group or context, as 'structural' historiography has understood it from Georg Lukács and Franz Borkenau through to Maurice Halbwachs and Lucien Goldmann.[2] Postmodern interest focuses, indeed, on the vital experience of individuals, which is a value in itself and, heuristically speaking, for a whole imagined group, without any cross-check concerning 'representativity'.[3]

One may make impressive arguments about the heuristic value and the methodological problems of this category of sources. For with 13 million German soldiers and an estimated 28 billion letters sent during the war,[4] one can find a counter-argument for any critical statement about the war made by a soldier. Quotations taken from individual letters about the feelings of the soldier in the field are thus only 'snapshots', and any further generalization appears to be problematical.[5]

Translated by Richard Bessel.

[1] The most recent comprehensive survey is Veit Didczuneit, Jens Ebert, and Thomas Jander (eds.), *Schreiben im Krieg — Schreiben vom Krieg: Feldpost im Zeitalter der Weltkriege* (Essen, 2011).

[2] See Georg Lukács, *Geschichte und Klassenbewußtsein: Studien über marxistische Dialektik* (Berlin, 1923); Franz Borkenau, *Der Übergang vom feudalen zum bürgerlichen Weltbild: Studien zur Geschichte der Philosophie der Manufakturperiode* (Paris, 1934); Maurice Halbwachs, *Das Gedächtnis und seine sozialen Bedingungen* (Frankfurt a.M., 1985); Lucien Goldmann, *Recherches dialectiques* (Paris, 1959).

[3] See Stéphane Audoin-Rouzeau, *Cinq deuils de guerre 1914–1918* (Paris, 2001).

[4] Bernd Ulrich, *Die Augenzeugen: Deutsche Feldpostbriefe in Kriegs- und Nachkriegszeit 1914–1933* (Essen, 1997), 22.

[5] Bernd Ulrich, 'Feldpostbriefe im Ersten Weltkrieg: Bedeutung und Zensur', in

Researchers have paid much less attention to collections of war letters published during and after the war than to the 'Field Post', the Military Postal Service, itself.[6] The first discussion and evaluation of this genre can be found in the work of Hanna Hafkesbrink, a German who had fled to the USA. In 1948 she published a rather slim but innovative reflection on the collections of soldiers' letters from the field, in which these were evaluated as sources for the 'better Germany'.[7] Hafkesbrink was concerned to alter the very negative image of Germans held in the United States after the Second World War, since, according to the author, a good peace could not be constructed if one approached the former enemy in a very negative manner, as had been the case after the First World War. Hitler had undoubtedly also been a product of the Treaty of Versailles. The editions of soldiers' letters from the field evaluated by Hafkesbrink are not quantitatively significant. She assigned the greatest importance to Witkop, to the collection by Pfeilschifter of the letters of Catholic soldiers, letters mostly published by the grieving relatives. According to Hafkesbrink in conclusion, German soldiers' main motivation for fighting was not a desire for annexations or a sense of German arrogance. On the contrary, the majority of the letters bore witness to a genuine spirituality and a 'devotion to the ideas of peace and democracy'.[8]

In his authoritative work on the soldiers' letters from the front, Bernd Ulrich dealt with the collections of such letters only relatively at the margins. Letters from the front are an essential medium not only of private correspondence but also of the public representation of the war. Ulrich also shows that very often 'private' letters from the front had been written in the knowledge or hope that they might

Peter Knoch (ed.), *Kriegsalltag: Die Rekonstruktion des Kriegsalltags als Aufgabe der historischen Forschung und der Friedenserziehung* (Stuttgart, 1989), 40–83; Klaus Latzel, 'Vom Kriegserlebnis zur Kriegserfahrung: Theoretische und methodische Überlegungen zur erfahrungsgeschichtlichen Untersuchung von Feldpostbriefen', *Militärgeschichtliche Mitteilungen*, 56 (1997), 1–30; Klaus Latzel, 'Feldpostbriefe: Überlegungen zur Aussagekraft einer Quelle', in Christian Hartmann, Johannes Hürter, and Ulrike Jureit (eds.), *Verbrechen der Wehrmacht: Bilanz einer Debatte* (Munich, 2005), 171–81, 216–19.

[6] A first attempt at an overview may be found in Wolfgang G. Natter, *Literature at War 1914–1940: Representing the 'Time of Greatness' in Germany* (New Haven, 1999), ch. 3: 'The Use and Abuse of *Feldpostbriefe* for Cultural Life', 78–121.

[7] Hanna Hafkesbrink, *Unknown Germany: An Inner Chronicle of the First World War Based on Letters and Diaries* (New Haven, 1948).

[8] Ibid. 161.

be published, or read out or posted in the village pub.[9] Very often it is possible to determine 'conversational maxims' in them that demonstrate an intent to have them published, as well as the need of many soldiers to show that they were mentally and emotionally in accord with the optimism and 'war enthusiasm' at home. In this way, the letters from the front were 'part of the public representation of the war'.[10] And this applies even more so to the published collections of letters. Altogether they are 'documents of mobilization as well as of loyalty to the state at war'.[11] Unfortunately Ulrich has not really extended his valuable research to these collections. He merely states that they played an important role in the debate about the 'true' war experience in the late 1920s.[12]

It is therefore apparent that their importance and heuristic value for German war propaganda and, over and above this, for a cultural history of the First World War has yet to be covered adequately. This essay is to be understood as a step in that direction.[13] The collections of war letters undoubtedly have great value as a source for the question of what people on the home front wanted to know about the reality of war, and especially about the soldiers' 'war experience', what they could learn publicly, and how this information was structured.

According to the official 'Directory of German Books' (*Deutsches Bücherverzeichnis*) for the years 1914 to 1918, there are twenty-four different 'collections of letters from the front' for the period of the war. These are set expressly against the very much greater number of 'collections of diaries and reports of war veterans', the total number of which is 170.[14] This a priori distinction made at the time between special 'collections of letters from the front' and other published ego documents is interesting and requires interpretation. How 'new' the

[9] Ulrich, *Die Augenzeugen*, 112. According to Natter, soldiers' letters from the field were frequently read out in school lessons: Natter, *Literature at War*, 79.
[10] Ulrich, *Die Augenzeugen*, 25. [11] Ibid. 137.
[12] Ibid. 28–9.
[13] For my understanding of 'cultural history' see Gerd Krumeich and Gerhard Hirschfeld, 'Wozu eine "Kulturgeschichte" des Ersten Weltkriegs?', in Arndt Bauernkämper and Elise Julien (eds.), *Durchhalten! Krieg und Gesellschaft im Vergleich, 1914–1918* (Göttingen, 2010), 31–53. See also Gerd Krumeich, 'Kriegs-(Un-)Kultur? Zur deutschen und französischen Forschung über eine Kulturgeschichte des Ersten Weltkriegs', in Christoph Cornelißen (ed.), *Geschichtswissenschaft im Geist der Demokratie: Wolfgang J. Mommsen und seine Generation* (Berlin, 2010), 99–114.
[14] *Deutsches Bücherverzeichnis: Eine Zusammenstellung der im deutschen Buchhandel erschienenen Bücher, Zeitschriften und Landkarten. Mit einem Stich- und Schlagwortregister 1915–1920* (Leipzig, 1921), 1654 ff.

writing of letters by ordinary soldiers must have seemed at the time should not be underestimated. Of course, there had already been soldiers' letters in earlier wars,[15] but not until the First World War did they become a mass phenomenon. Literacy among the Germans had become (almost) total in the meantime, and many millions of people now had the need and, for the first time, the opportunity to exchange views in letters about the war as an extreme situation. Probably for this reason it seems that right from the outset, collections of soldiers' letters directly from the front laid claim to, and were granted, a very special status in memorial culture. Unlike other ego documents, they could, by gathering experiences, obviously claim to allow the *Heimat* a collective and exemplary experience of the war, and to provide a much more direct portrayal of it than did other collections that nonetheless could contain a mass of letters from the front from the ranks, for example, of a single company or regiment.

It is striking that the actual collections of letters from the field are often very thin, consisting of only twenty to thirty pages, and were also issued as periodicals. For example, 'Letters from the Front and Accounts from the People's War in 1914, Concentrating on Southern and Western German Regiments'[16] was continued in 1915 as 'German Letters from the Front: Accounts and Reports of the War of the Peoples 1914', and had thirty-two pages each.

The political, social, and religious spectrum of the collections of letters is substantial. During the first two years of the war all sorts of groups in German society tried to point out that they had spared no effort and sacrifice to heed the call of the fatherland—indeed, that their group had made especially great efforts in this respect, and would let no one outdo them with regard to patriotism. Already in 1915 there were two collections of letters from Jewish soldiers.[17] By contrast, Pfeilschifter's three-volume collection of the letters of Catholic soldiers appeared only in 1918.[18] There was also a small collection of sixteen pages about 'Our Christian Working-Class Youth in the Field'.[19] Many collections, such as 'The Transylvanian

---

[15] See Natter, *Literature at War*, 79 ff., on prewar collections of letters.

[16] *Feldpostbriefe und Schilderungen aus dem Völkerkriege 1914, mit Bevorzugung süd- und westdeutscher Regimenter*, vols. 1–8 (Freiburg, 1914), continued as *Deutsche Feldpostbriefe: Schilderungen und Berichte vom Völkerkrieg 1914* (Freiburg, 1915).

[17] Ulrich, *Die Augenzeugen*, 114.

[18] *Feldbriefe katholischer Soldaten*, ed. Georg Pfeilschifter (Freiburg, 1918).

[19] This was published in 1915 by the Vaterländische Verlags- und Kunstanstalt in Berlin.

Saxons in the World War' (1916), consist of a selection of letters specifically from regions outside of Germany.[20] In 1915 two volumes of 'Wandervogel Letters from the Field' appeared.[21]

From the outbreak of the war onwards, collecting and editing letters from the front was regarded as an important patriotic duty and was, apparently, financially profitable. Letters were the most important link between 'front and *Heimat*'. For example, in Stuttgart the coffee-roaster Ludwig Frank had already begun systematically to collect documents of the war in August 1914 (from which the World War Library and today's Library of Contemporary History have arisen in Stuttgart).[22] Throughout Germany a large number of individuals and institutions began to 'collect the war'. It is of particular importance for our subject that already in 1914 the Märkisches Museum in Berlin established the Central Office for the Collection of Letters from the Front. At the end of 1915 this Central Office brought out a collection, chronologically organized and sorted by theatres of battle, of nineteen booklets entitled 'Letters from the Field 1914/15'.[23] According to a statement dated November 1914 and prefixed to the first seven booklets:

Alongside official documents, war diaries and letters from the front always were the richest and most indispensable sources for the history of the war. They will play this role to an even greater extent in the war that Germany today is forced to conduct against enemies on all sides. It will be infinitely difficult to represent the entire war, whose individual campaigns have taken place in the most diverse countries and continents and that has sent huge masses of men into many different armies. The brief and factual reports of the General Staff arguably inform in general terms about the course of events: they convey the results. But in a sense they form only the frame for the huge picture of the labour, sacrifice, and heroism that this war presents; only reports by the individual fighters give colour and content. The importance of letters from the field and war diaries as documents of our great epoch therefore cannot be emphasized enough, and their systematic collection cannot be started soon enough if much is not to be lost. The Central Office for the Collection of Letters from the Front has therefore set itself the task of bringing together

---

[20] *Siebenbürger Sachsen im Weltkrieg: Feldbriefe und Kriegsskizzen*, ed. Adolf Hoehr (Vienna, 1916). [21] *Kriegs-Fahrt: Wandervogel-Feldpostbriefe* (Leipzig, 1915).

[22] See Gerhard Hirschfeld (ed.), *75 Jahre Bibliothek für Zeitgeschichte, 1915–1990* (Stuttgart, 1990); Aibe-Marlene Gerdes, *Ein Abbild der gewaltigen Ereignisse: Die Kriegssammlungen zum Ersten Weltkrieg* (Essen, 2016).

[23] *Briefe aus dem Feld 1914/15: Für das deutsche Volk im Auftrage der Zentralstelle zur Sammlung von Feldpostbriefen im Märkischen Museum zu Berlin*, ed. Otto Pniower *et al.* (Oldenburg, 1916), totalling 798 pages.

such documents into its archive, of preserving them in a manner worthy of their importance, and of preparing the publication of selected examples.[24]

The series of booklets, however, was not continued beyond the end of 1915.[25] Public interest in the 'soldierly experience of war' seems to have declined dramatically by 1916 at the latest—an early example of the ever deepening rift between 'front and *Heimat*' over the course of the war.[26]

The majority of the texts listed, namely thirteen publications, appeared in 1915. In 1916, six publications appeared; in 1917 there were none at all; and in 1918 there were only three. For the postwar years no new collections have been detected. Great interest arose again beginning with the 'revival' of memory of the world war in 1928, symbolized by the Remarque scandal.[27] Here collections of letters, as opposed to the literary transformations in Remarque, Renn, *et al.*, became the main sources of the 'true' war experience.

Information about life in the field and propaganda concerning the meaning and purpose of the 'War of the World' were mostly inseparable. Generally, it is methodologically problematical to distinguish between real reports of experience on the one hand and collections published for propaganda purposes on the other. This had already been pointed out by Bernd Ulrich, who demonstrates how much the propaganda, as opposed to the report, resulted from the forms of selection of war experience for the individual publications.[28] The following examples from the early phase of the publications may illustrate this relationship.

As early as 1914 a collection edited by the Berliner Charité was published with a circulation of 5,000 copies.[29] In the introduction to this ninety-four-page volume the point of such a publication is described as follows: it wanted to show those who did not participate

---

[24] ⟨https://www.kriegssammlungen.de/index.php/popup?datensatznr=027⟩ [accessed 11 Sept. 2015].
[25] Today this work is almost impossible to obtain second-hand.
[26] Benjamin Ziemann, *Front und Heimat: Ländliche Kriegserfahrung im südlichen Bayern 1914–1923* (Essen, 1997); Gerd Krumeich, 'Kriegsfront—Heimatfront', in Gerhard Hirschfeld, Gerd Krumeich, Dieter Langewiesche, and Hans-Peter-Ullmann (eds.), *Kriegserfahrungen: Studien zur Sozial- und Mentalitätsgeschichte des Ersten Weltkriegs* (Essen, 1997), 12–19.
[27] Harold Bloom, *Erich Maria Remarque's* All Quiet on the Western Front (New York, 2009); Erich Maria Remarque, *Im Westen nichts Neues und die Folgen*, ed. Thomas Schneider (Göttingen, 2014). [28] Ulrich, *Die Augenzeugen*, 32 ff.
[29] *Kriegsdokumente: Erzählungen der Verwundeten der kgl. Charité aus den Schlachten im Osten und Westen 1914*, ed. Ernst Pütter (Leipzig, 1914).

actively in the fighting 'how our warriors have fought and suffered on the battlefields of the East and the West'. Testimonies were collected intentionally from soldiers of all ranks and 'from all circles'. The collection was to show contemporaries and posterity the 'high moral seriousness' of the Germans, on whom 'perfidious Albion has forced the war against their will as a result of its policy of encirclement. . . . It is to be hoped that it is not too late for this little book to fight successfully against the lies of our enemies, who want to label the German people and the German army as barbarous Huns.' Thus, in this volume there are also reports of atrocities committed by Germany's enemies, organized chapter by chapter with, for example, the following headings: 'The Russians Raised their Hands High and then Fired', 'Russian Atrocities', 'The Fountain Contaminated', and 'In Russian Captivity'. For the experiences on the Western Front, the episodes selected here are even more conclusive: ch. 1: 'The Belgians Bombard the Red Cross'; ch. 2: '*Francs-tireurs*'; ch. 3: 'Street Fight'; ch. 4: 'Harmless Civilians'. Here a clear emphasis is placed on war atrocities allegedly or in fact experienced by German soldiers. These eyewitness accounts that in part sound very truthful even today may have been all the more convincing back then, since they came from soldiers of all ranks who had themselves been wounded in these attacks by '*francs-tireurs*'.

Thus, a 'reserve lieutenant H. H. 24 years old, from Berlin' describes, in a laconic military tone typical of the time, the atrocities that took place in the Belgian Ardennes and that even today still stand as a portent of the German 'atrocities' at the beginning of the war.[30] The city had already been occupied. 'While the units stood by the guns and chatted, vigorous rifle fire suddenly opened up on us from the houses that even before had seemed suspicious.'[31] 'Bayonets were fixed and the house from which the shooting came was entered forcibly. The residents were shot, the house set on fire. In this way, very soon we were masters of the street fighting.'[32] It is interesting that in these early publications German atrocities were reported openly as defensive, yet cruel.

Also completed in 1914 was the collection of William Sparr, which appeared in 1915: 'Letters from the Field in 1914: Reports and Pic-

---

[30] See John Horne und Alan Kramer, *Deutsche Kriegsgreuel 1914: Die umstrittene Wahrheit* (Hamburg, 2004), 53–7, now questioned by Ulrich Keller, *Schuldfragen: Belgischer Untergrundkrieg und deutsche Vergeltung im August 1914* (Paderborn, 2017).

[31] *Kriegsdokumente: Erzählungen der Verwundeten der kgl. Charité*, 55. This sentence is set in letter-spaced type in the text.   [32] Ibid. 55.

tures of the Morale of Fellow Combatants and Witnesses.' According to the preface, the edition had the aim of compiling 'in a clear grouping the most valuable and most characteristic . . . from the inexhaustible wealth of "letters from the front" and similar communications'. Again it is emphasized that soldiers of all categories had the chance to speak. In fact, this volume has an important special feature: it gathers together soldiers' letters printed sporadically in various daily newspapers throughout the German Reich. The criteria that can be seen from the chapter divisions are also clearly of both an informative and a propagandistic nature—for example, the chapter entitled 'In the Land of *Francs-tireurs*'. On more than fifty pages, letter documents are linked together which tell of the fighting in Belgium quite explicitly as part of this central aspect of the illegitimate Belgian resistance. The narrative has the advantage of an uncommon directness, from the pen of genuine eyewitnesses. It is not sparing of gruesome details:

The spectacle was horrible. Every corner of the city was burning. Then inhabitants still found to be carrying weapons were summarily executed in front of our eyes. Now and then gunshots rang out. Barrels of spirits were exploding in the inns, there was such a dreadful roar that I am still half deaf from it today. The following day brought horrific images. Here lay those court-martialled and shot, there new sinners were dragged along. Here came crying and praying women and children. Despite all the anger at the treacherous attack that had kicked off systematically at 8.00 exactly, no German heart could resist feeling compassion for these innocent victims.[33]

The battles in France are portrayed with the same intensity and drama, before another long chapter gathers soldiers' letters from the fight 'against the murderous Russian arsonists'. The book was obviously very widely distributed, as it is still easy to purchase cheaply today from antiquarian booksellers.

Other early collections of war letters were quite similar in structure. One example is the collection by Hans Leitzen, 'The Great War 1914/15 in Letters from the Front',[34] published in 1914 and achieving a second edition in the same year. In this volume the letters are sorted according to the different armed services, a feature absent from later collections: this shows how strong the differentiation according to traditional military terms, as well as the importance

---

[33] Ibid. 32.
[34] Hans Leitzen, *Der große Krieg 1914/15 in Feldpostbriefen* (Leipzig, 1914).

accorded to 'technical' details, still was at the beginning of the war. Such distinctions, however, became obsolete as the 'Great War' turned into a war of the masses.

So obviously profitable was the business of publishing letters from the field at the beginning of the war that already from the start of 1915 what eventually became a ten-volume collection, 'The German War in Letters', appeared with the Georg Müller Verlag in Munich. Since the individual volumes dealt with specific theatres of the war (for example, the first volume covered Liège, Namur, and Antwerp), detailed subdivision was no longer necessary. Lined up here in an almost endless and completely anonymized form are report after report on the various phases of the war.[35] Some of these volumes show up en masse with antiquarian booksellers while others cannot be found at all; why this may be is not yet known in detail. There is a high probability, however, that the emotions stirred up by specific events could not be maintained long enough to interest consumers. As quickly as the places of battle changed, so the interest in past heroic deeds rapidly evaporated. Who in 1916 could be interested in the battles along the borders of August–September 1914, in the light of Verdun and the Somme? How distant, both for publishers and for readers, may the 'enthusiasm' of the first phase of the war have become in 1916, now that it had turned into a war of machines and attrition?

In this context a further, but as yet hardly studied, problem came to the fore, namely, that the collections of war letters published in 1914 were evidently not affected significantly by the barely developed process of censorship. Only in 1915 does it appear that the individual deputy commanding generals, who alone were concerned with censorship but had failed to act in a co-ordinated manner, began to intervene systematically. Thus, in 1915 the deputy commanding general of the 13th Army Corps (Stuttgart) forbade the description of hand grenades, mortars, and flamethrowers, and even accounts that went into too much detail in their depiction of bloody events.[36] As a result of such 'propagandistic' interventions, the descriptions of war experiences were trimmed back, and certainly as a consequence public interest in them quickly flagged.

[35] Joachim Delbrück, *Der deutsche Krieg in Feldpostbriefen*, 10 vols. (Munich, 1915–17). The tenth volume, on the battles in Russia, appeared in 1917: Joachim Delbrück, *Der deutsche Krieg in Feldpostbriefen*, x. *Die Durchbruchsschlacht in Westgalizien mit einer Einleitung von Oberst a.D. Duvernoy* (Munich, 1917).

[36] See Natter, *Literature at War*, 86 ff.

As already mentioned, alongside these collections of letters emphasizing the location of the battle there were those published by various religious communities—for example, by Jewish or Catholic groups. The three-volume collection of letters from Catholic soldiers edited by Pfeilschifter became particularly well known.[37] This would give a signal both internally and externally, since with the flagging of patriotic consensus (*Burgfrieden*) there soon resurfaced disputes, not only over war and peace, but also over a compromise peace vs. an annexationist peace. In addition, from the end of 1914 antisemitism raised its head, which had grown even uglier as a result of the war. Nor could there be any question of a supra-denominational Christian character. Just as the question was raised whether Jews really were loyal Germans or rather war profiteers, so also the old debate re-emerged as to whether the 'Ultramontane' Catholics really were to be trusted.[38] Pfeilschifter's collection was aimed explicitly against French publications that attempted to demonstrate, in their own contribution to war propaganda, that the barbarism of bellicose Germans was not only a product of Prussian German and national Protestant origin, but was unique to the Germans,[39] so much so that even Catholics now had to renounce any Christian brotherhood across national borders. For good reasons there were doubts that all or even a majority of these letters were genuine, so great is the evidence of the use of these 'sources' for propaganda. War propaganda therefore had an impact from the outset on the religiosity and the 'international relations' of the Christian churches.[40]

The most important collection of war letters, which was also the only collection published again during the Weimar Republic and the National Socialist dictatorship, was brought out by the Freiburg German professor Philipp Witkop. Witkop's 'War Letters of German Students' (from 1918 onwards: 'War Letters of Fallen Students') was a work that certainly loomed large during the war. Especially in the late 1920s, however, it would experience an astonishing career with the resurgence of the memory of the world war.

---

[37] See above, n. 18.

[38] Roland Haidl, 'Ausbruch aus dem Ghetto? Katholizismus im deutschen Heer 1914–1918', in Gerd Krumeich und Hartmut Lehmann (eds.), '*Gott mit uns*': *Nation, Religion und Gewalt im 19. und frühen 20. Jahrhundert* (Göttingen, 2000), 263–71.

[39] Alfred Baudrillart, *La Guerre allemande et le catholicisme* (Paris, 1915).

[40] See Claudia Schlager, 'Feldpostbriefe in der kirchlichen Propaganda des Ersten Weltkriegs: Zur Instrumentalisierung von Selbstzeugnissen in Deutschland und Frankreich', in Didczuneit, Ebert, and Jander (eds.), *Schreiben im Krieg*, 481–90.

There is little research about Witkop, essentially only an article by Manfred Hettling and Michael Jeismann,[41] and the recent general account of world war literature by Wolfgang G. Natter. This includes a valuable chapter on Witkop and appraises the Witkop literary estate in the German Literature Archive Marbach for the first time.[42] The problem of the Witkop letter collection is that today we can no longer determine the criteria according to which Witkop chose which letters to publish, and whether he really published them in precisely their original form. Today it cannot be ascertained whether the letters were abridged or altered, as they are no longer present in the Witkop literary estate—only a residual amount of correspondence with the publisher is there. It may be that after transcription Witkop returned most of the letters to the relatives of the students concerned, as he had promised to do in the brochure of 1915. Unfortunately, it is unlikely that any further information will come to light.[43]

The first edition of these letters was published in 1916 by the Perthes Verlag in Gotha under the title 'War Letters of German Students'. It is a fairly small book of 114 pages, which, however, already had a predecessor, namely a thirteen-page special edition of the Leipzig journal *Der Panther*.[44] In this short text, which is a kind of brochure, Witkop first explicitly presented the grounds for his selection. Such a flood of letters had already been published, he said, that it had become important to preserve 'an epic general view', which was why he had singled out the fallen students, 'a group that, while lacking cohesion and special character, possesses a general symbolic power'. Students were best suited for this purpose because they represented 'a plethora of vocations and of social classes'. In addition, this group was really capable of writing. Among students, he felt, 'the past

---

[41] Manfred Hettling and Michael Jeismann, 'Der Weltkrieg als Epos: Philipp Witkops "Kriegsbriefe gefallener Studenten"', in Gerhard Hirschfeld, Gerd Krumeich, and Irina Renz (eds.), *Keiner fühlt sich hier mehr als Mensch: Erlebnis und Wirkung des Ersten Weltkriegs* (Essen, 1993), 175–98. Ulrich's *Die Augenzeugen* does not go beyond the article by Jeismann and Hettling.

[42] Natter, *Literature at War*, 90–121. See ⟨http://www.nachlassdatenbank.de/viewsingle.php?category=W&person_id=35301&asset_id=40120&sid=29497d1456ddd174e3dd1⟩ [accessed 23 Nov. 2016].

[43] Here I am following the findings by Natter, *Literature at War*, 90–1. When I enquired in 1991, Witkop's wife informed me that she had no original letters whatsoever in her possession.

[44] Philipp Witkop, *Kriegsbriefe deutscher Studenten* (Leipzig, 1915). A copy is located in the Freiburg University Library, GW 684 U. This is noted by Ulrich, *Die Augenzeugen*, and by Natter, *Literature at War*, 94. The 114-page edition of 1916 is *Kriegsbriefe deutscher Studenten*, ed. Philipp Witkop (Gotha, 1916).

and future, subjective emotion and objective knowledge, alertness of the senses and agility of the mind intersect'. Thus, from the outset, with his 'epic' claim Witkop differentiated himself from the huge number of existing collections, whose political and propagandistic nature contemporaries had long since seen through.[45] This selection would appear all the more consistent and dramatic as only letters from students who had already died were presented, so that here death for the fatherland was always directly linked to authentic war experience.

Witkop's students were real people. From the second edition of 1918 their names, places of birth and death, and academic disciplines (e.g. 'stud. Theol') were indicated. The Panther Verlag brochure of 1915 also contains, alongside the referenced programme and a few examples of letters, a request to send letters of fallen students to the editor, with the promise that these would be returned again when needed.[46] Interestingly, in 1915 Witkop was actually planning to create an edition to appear after the war. Like everyone else, at this time he obviously still believed in an early end to the conflict. Because the war dragged on, however, Witkop then presented the first edition in book form, and it was published in 1916 by the Perthes Verlag in Gotha.

This, in a nutshell, is the structure of the text that later became so famous. It contains only letters generated in extreme situations by apparently intelligent, cultivated young men capable of writing well and who, the reader knows, all died 'for the fatherland'. This is about the experience of war in itself; even gruesome details are not left out. However, the letters do not involve themselves with the political; they are in the best sense of the time 'above politics', expressing views about God and the nature of war, impressions of nature, and a willingness to sacrifice for the fatherland—an idealistic collection, therefore, in which representatives of Germany's intellectual elite have the opportunity to speak collectively and posthumously.[47]

The book had considerable resonance, probably because it was so free of the usual realist-propagandist character. It also reflected the altered reality of war in so far as Witkop's protagonists did not at

---

[45] See also Natter, *Literature at War*, 102, with reviews of Witkop that emphasize precisely this.

[46] This probably explains why only very few remain preserved in the collection of his papers in the Marbach archive.

[47] This 'epic' dimension of the collection has been explained very well by Hettling and Jeismann.

all appear as 'heroes' or narrators of 'heroic deeds', as had mostly been the case in the letter collections of the years 1914–15. These are thoughtful, cultivated young men whose accounts of the war could be quite realistic, but whose writing always lay beyond heroic phraseology. They have a view of the war that corresponded more to the realities of the industrial war of attrition from 1916 than to the old enthusiasm of soldiers in 1914.[48] Witkop's method of selection thus reflected the changed understanding of war. As he noted in a later edition, after his call for letters and the publication of the first edition, more than 20,000 letters were sent to him. He wrote in the preface to the 1928 edition that ministries and universities also stepped in to provide him with material.

At the end of 1918, an abbreviated edition appeared, published 'in conjunction with the German education ministries', that for the first time bore the title 'War Letters of Fallen Students' (instead of 'War Letters of German Students'). It was 155 pages long, and in the preface Witkop wrote that, given the war's end and its mass of victims, the individual sacrifice for the fatherland might be forgotten, which was why this collection of letters should be 'a living memorial', 'an example . . . of performing one's duty, of victims' courage, of love for the people and the *Heimat*, which was faithful unto death'. These letters were to be 'a spur to a new world law of reconciliation and sympathy in the life of nations. Then the legacy of these young tragic idealists will be honoured and their death will not be in vain.' In the years after 1919, however, it became increasingly difficult to maintain the assertion that these millions of young men had not fallen 'in vain'. This probably explains why Witkop's collection was given no new edition during the first ten years of the Weimar Republic but was reissued only in the wave of identity-focused war memoirs after 1928, when, as is shown below, it contributed very successfully to the new emphasis on a collective sense of meaning.

Witkop's letter collection was probably the most widely received and actually 'non-partisan' heroic song of the German soldier. The letters reproduced are highly authentic: had there been any systematic or consistent falsification, that certainly would have come to public attention. Thus far no corrections or protests have been reported, as was so often the case in the heated debate over the meaning and purpose of the war during the 1920s.[49] There is scarcely a single

[48] Thus also Natter, *Literature at War*, 104.
[49] e.g. the controversy over *All Quiet on the Western Front*, or the question of the

trace of political polemic or extreme sentiment in this collection of letters. *Pro patria mori*, confident devotion to the fatherland, is the motto, which is accompanied by a 'thick description' of the war. In a sense the war is present predominantly as 'inner experience', to take up a later work by Ernst Jünger, who adopted the same position but maintained a soldierly pose. Admittedly, rather propagandistic comments are also interspersed repeatedly, and are hardly separable from the reports of experiences and metaphysical reflections that constitute the main themes of the letters, for instance, when it comes to the characterization of savage Russians or when the Serb stereotype is brought up to date: 'We are full to the brim with desire to look the Serbs in the face, to smash our fist into their face. Should we receive the order tonight to move our position forward, we will feel as if we are going to heaven'—thus the last letter in the 1916 edition.

From 1928 Witkop's book became one of the publishing successes in the course of the sudden reawakening of interest in the world war, a reawakening that is usually associated with the name of Erich Maria Remarque and the sensational success of *All Quiet on the Western Front*. Yet Remarque was just at the apex of a veritable volcano of war memories that erupted everywhere in 1928 (and not earlier). In February 1929 Witkop came out with a 354-page volume, which by 1933 had gone through six editions with at least 100,000 copies. Not infrequently the National Socialists featured Witkop's collection of letters as a repostiory of authentic sources as opposed to Remarque's war narrative. Witkop's soldiers, in the elegant formulation by Hettling and Jeismann, are not victims of war but have all consciously sacrificed themselves for everlasting values.[50] Witkop's collection, in accordance with the publisher's intention, was stylized as a veritable 'heroes' graveyard' of German soldiers.[51]

This glorification, that now clearly represents the main weakness of the collection for us, was then, quite surprisingly, capable of generating consensus. Jeismann and Hettling, who systematically mined the reviews of the 1928 edition, have concluded that this may well be the only case of a literary production in the Weimar Republic for which all reviewers, from the far right to the extreme left, were full of praise: a most amazing fact. The only critical statement, from

authenticity of Hitler's war experience. On this theme see Thomas Weber, *Hitler's First War: Adolf Hitler, the Men of the List Regiment, and the First World War* (Oxford, 2010).

[50] Hettling and Jeismann, 'Der Weltkrieg als Epos', 191.
[51] Thus Natter, *Literature at War*, 109.

the pen of Veit Valentin, noted that the vast majority of the letters selected did not stem from the final period of the war in 1918, and that the serious frictions within the army during the last year of the war, including the so-called 'officer hatred' among the soldiers, were not to be found in the selection.[52] Indeed, the 'true war experience' thus flowed into National Socialist propaganda directed against the disillusioned or accusatory view of the war, which had been a major feature of the new general interest in the Great War from the late 1920s onward.[53]

In the autumn of 1933, after Hitler's seizure of power, an apparently unchanged 'popular edition' appeared,[54] which differed only in the preface's minimal kowtow to the new rulers: 'In these days of national soul-searching we bow before them [= the fallen students] and swear to their memory that they shall not have fallen in vain, that we honour their legacy, that we will work unceasingly so that we and the nation as a whole are worthy of them.' The editions of 1935 and 1937 were essentially unchanged, even though it has been assumed that the individual letters of Jewish students were removed as a result of determined pressure from the new rulers.[55]

Specifically, it is hardly possible to check accurately the extent of the changes introduced in the editions brought out during the National Socialist era. Those issued in 1935 and 1937 are in reality not new editions, but rather 'extrapolations' of the 1928 edition, without any indication in the existing books of when the copies were actually printed. Despite many efforts through interlibrary loan, I have not yet managed to see copies of the book that actually derive from the years 1935 and 1937. However, a very interesting documentary clue can be found in Witkop's correspondence with his friend Wilhelm Schäfer. On 4 December 1937, he wrote:

Yesterday we had the ceremonial enrolment of 1,000 new students. The new student leader, inherently certainly a likeable fellow, also spoke but in a chronically overextended voice and with nothing but slogans that he had picked up. The inner *Sturm und Drang* of youth was absent. It fits that someone has deleted three letters from the new edition of my 'War Letters' (the 10th to the 20th thousand of this year), letters in which the outcry against the war

[52] Hettling and Jeismann, 'Der Weltkrieg als Epos', 192–3.
[53] Thomas F. Schneider, '"Realität" vs. "Fiktion": Feldpost in der Diskussion um Erich Maria Remarques "Im Westen nichts Neues" 1928/29', in Didczuneit, Ebert, and Jander (eds.), *Schreiben im Krieg*, 393–402.
[54] The edition was still being reprinted in the 1950s: see Natter, *Literature at War*, 111.
[55] On this see, in detail, Natter, *Literature at War*, 116–17.

just breaks through (pp. 107–8 of the Popular Edition) or in which during the wildest trench warfare a sergeant drives people forward with his pistol (p. 249). They want a chemically pure heroism.

Korfiz Holm wrote that this censorship indeed came to the publisher from the War Ministry but emanates from party officials, and that Lieutenant Colonel Jost resisted further objections, referring to the age, the distribution, and to what is already to some extent the classic status of the book.[56]

The censored letters are available in an unaltered form in the many copies of the 'popular edition' of 1933 which I have been able to see. As yet, I have been unable to find a copy in which these cuts were actually made. The first letter is by one Kurt Petersen, writing from Dixmuiden on 25 October 1914. A cry of distress is in the man, thoughts of defiance and even of ferocity: 'Down with the war, the most terrible miscarriage of human vices! People slaughter one another en masse, without knowing each other, to hate, to love. Cursed be the few who provoke war without having to experience its horrors. Destruction to them all! For they are beasts, predators.' The other passage that was 'criticized', and perhaps actually removed in the editions that appeared from 1938 onwards, is in a letter by Friedel Oehme 'At the Somme, 21 August 1916', which reads (p. 249): 'Another sergeant drives people forward from the rear with his pistol, until finally for our section of 200 metres we have about 40 soldiers forward.'

Here another publication by Witkop, one that previous research has overlooked, should be noted. It is a 46-page excerpt from the book that was issused in booklet form by the Munich publisher Albert Langen/Georg Müller as volume 16 of the series 'The German Episode: Contemporary Literature in School Editions, editor Dr Walther Linden'. It is clear from the list of published titles in the series printed on the back cover that this volume appeared in 1936. However, no National Socialist influence can be detected, either in the preface or in the selection of letters. In contrast to the popular edition of 1933, the preface even omits any reference to 'Leader' or 'Reich'. And the content of the volume also appears not to have been systematically 'cleansed'. It even prints a letter from the Kurt Petersen who was publicly condemned in 1937.

Altogether it is possible to say with certainty that the basic tenor

---

[56] Witkop's correspondence with Wilhelm Schäfer is located in the Heinrich Heine Institut Düsseldorf, folder Phil Witkop. I thank Thomas Gerhards (Düsseldorf) for examining and transcribing the material.

of the Witkop collection was not modified at all and that the interventions remained essentially marginal—another indication of the sensitivity of National Socialist politicians towards 'traditional' views and values of 'real soldiering'.[57]

It seems interesting to me that within the spectrum of the war literature of the 1920s, Witkop's book had a virtually unique position because hardly any new collections of letters from the front appeared. According to the 'Directory of German Books in Print', just four collections of letters came out during the period from 1926 to 1930, including the repeatedly issued 'War Letters of Jewish Soldiers', which occupied an important place in the never-ending discussion about Jewish 'service at the front' that followed from the 'Jew census' at the end of 1916. How this could be reissued once again in 1935 remains a complete mystery.

The only 'competition' to Witkop was the documentary collection 'We Fighters in the World War: Personal Testimonies of German Soldiers at the Front', first published by members of the staff of the Reich Archive in 1926. The four-volume original version is quite rare today. It was a decidedly militaristic work, which again aimed to document the individual theatres of the war through personal testimonies. Only in 1933 did the book achieve some success with an abridged one-volume popular edition, and the editors proudly saw Hitler's seizure of power as the completion of their own work:

> As a result of the great achievement of our Leader, the German people has again become a nation able to defend itself. . . . Nothing can provide better and more effective encouragement for the education and training for this lofty present and future task than to look at the shining example of the powerful race that endured the world war at the front.[58]

This work, however, does not appear to have been a great publishing success. Only Witkop had lasting success, because in presenting experience he invariably based his work on letters that were 'challenging' in terms of style and content, and which enhanced

---

[57] On this thesis see Gerd Krumeich (ed.), *Nationalsozialismus und Erster Weltkrieg* (Essen, 2010). For a case study see Gerd Krumeich, 'Zwischen soldatischem Nationalismus und NS-Ideologie: Werner Beumelburg und die Erzählung des Ersten Weltkriegs', in Wolfram Pyta and Carsten Kretschmann (eds.), *Burgfrieden und Union sacrée: Literarische Deutungen und politische Ordnungsvorstellungen in Deutschland und Frankreich 1914–1933* (Munich, 2011), 295–312.

[58] *Wir Kämpfer im Weltkrieg: Selbstzeugnisse deutscher Frontsoldaten in Feldpostbriefen, Kriegstagebüchern und Aufzeichnungen, vornehmlich aus dem Material des Heeresarchivs Potsdam*, ed. Wolfgang Foerster (Berlin, 1937), 8.

the metaphysical dimension of 'front experience'. The selection exclusively of 'fallen' soldiers contributed to its authenticity and exemplary nature, which, for a public saturated with propaganda of all kinds, was probably quite a special attraction.

It is not easy to draw a general conclusion from this study of collections of letters from the field. The following points seem to me to be noteworthy and to merit discussion. With the exception of the work by Witkop, the published collections of letters from the field appeared mostly during the first two years of the war. In general, the descriptions of experiences and propaganda are intermingled. The great majority of early collections presented the front soldiers' war experience along with legitimations of the war: encirclement, the mendacious Englishman, the savage Russian, the *franc-tireur* Belgian. The crucial qualitative difference, however, probably lies in the extent to which the propaganda typical of the time dwarfed the described 'war experience'. It is not by chance that the collection which was the least oriented as propaganda, Witkop's 'War Letters', had the greatest and most enduring success among the public during the war and in the postwar period.

12

A *Vita Nova*: The Construction of a War. Life Experience in Italian First World War Autobiographical Writing

Marco Mondini

War Stories by an Illiterate Nation

In many respects the literary narration of Italy's Great War is a paradox. While fighting was still in progress, and still more after it ended, written accounts by combatants were extolled as a spiritual legacy of the people on which future generations would be brought up. Anthologies of published memoirs and collections of correspondence harped on the example and the lesson to be learnt from the words of those who had seen combat. As a veteran of the front with literary ambitions, Pietro Gorgolini enjoyed a certain postwar success in occasional journalism and special-feature writing. In introducing the anthology *Pagine eroiche della Grande epopea*, published in 1923 and destined for pupils in middle school, he reminded his readers how many of the authors had fallen for their country and should be regarded by schoolchildren with 'gratitude and veneration'.[1] This was also true of Francesco Formigari, who edited one of the rare literary collections of tales by those who fought from 1915 to 1918; writing under the Fascist regime, he claimed that these stories by 'Italian literary men' demanded a 'tribute of gratitude' from the reader. In those written accounts the Italians could find the deep-seated meaning of that great national adventure, that war 'for a greater Italy'.[2] Such insistence should hardly surprise us. Fascist Italy publicly claimed descent from the 'healthy part of the nation' that had opted for war in 1915. To remember the sacrifice of those who fought (and by implication their victory in 1918) was tantamount to singing a hymn to the foundation of Fascism itself.

[1] Pietro Gorgolini, *Pagine eroiche della Grande epopea 1915–1918* (Turin, 1923), p. xv.
[2] Francesco Formigari, *La letteratura di guerra in Italia 1915–1935* (Rome, 1935), 5–6.

It saw the trenches as the ideal birthplace for a better nation; from its earliest days the regime's cultural policy devoted great efforts to building a triumphal collective memory of the event.[3]

And yet that literary account of the Italian war can hardly be said to have come from any broad swath of the nation under arms—those who bore the brunt of the fighting—or have voiced the memories and emotions of any significant part of military (or civilian) society engaged in the war effort. It was a tiny minority of those taking part in the 'fourth war of the Risorgimento' who saw fit to commit their images of the conflict to paper. A recent census of First World War publications has come up with a wide and heterogeneous galaxy of works in print: no fewer than 1,500 published titles in the period 1919 to 1940 alone.[4] To these should be added an extraordinary mass of works commemorating the fallen from 1915 onwards: a host of pamphlets commissioned by the widest range of 'grief-stricken communities' (primarily families, but also schools, firms, associations, and political movements) amounting to something like 2,300 titles.[5]

In actual fact, though, most such publications, in either category, do not belong to the real corpus of works circulating among the public as a memorial to the war. Many titles devoted to the war, especially those that came out from 1919 to the early 1920s, fell under the heading of freelance and polemical journalism that was common in a country emerging from war, when opinion was explosively divided over the whys and hows of armed conflict, before the Fascist regime muzzled all debate and imposed the official view of a united nation proudly called to the sacrifice.[6] As for printed obituaries, the genre had a patchy circulation and individual examples were often short-lived. For although a good fifth of them (devoted to 'martyrs and heroes' such as Cesare Battisti, Enrico Toti, or Francesco Baracca) were intended for public consumption and sometimes edited by professionals, most had a tiny circulation designed for readers from the same 'grieving community' that had prompted the work to be written. In the main, then, such publications had nothing to do with

---

[3] Emilio Gentile, *Le origini dell'ideologia fascista 1918–1925* (Bologna, 1996).

[4] Enrica Bricchetto, 'La Grande Guerra degli intellettuali', in Domenico Scarpa (ed.), *Atlante della letteratura Einaudi*, iii. *Dal Romanticismo ad oggi* (Turin, 2012), 477–89.

[5] *Non omnis moriar: gli opuscoli di necrologio per i caduti italiani nella Grande Guerra*, ed. Fabrizio Dolci and Oliver Janz (Rome, 2003).

[6] Roberto Vivarelli, *Storia delle origini del fascismo*, vol. i (Bologna, 1991); Giorgio Rochat, *L'esercito italiano da Vittorio Veneto a Mussolini* (Bari, 1967).

the genre of fighting men writing their own memoirs which was to dominate Italian publishing between the wars. This was a small, if important, output, therefore, comprising somewhat fewer than 300 titles, only about forty of them achieving any lasting success.[7]

That Italy's First World War literary output was so limited in range stemmed from many factors. First, of course, was the low level of schooling and the sketchy degree of literacy among Italians in 1915, especially among adult males called up to fight. According to the 1911 census, illiteracy across the peninsula had fallen to 38 per cent of the population: a comforting result when compared with 62 per cent thirty years earlier, but still higher than the official rates in other European countries, without reckoning the great disparity between north, where illiteracy was less than 10 per cent, and south, where it still affected half the population.[8] Again, school attendance was extremely uncertain in country areas, where, until the beginning of the twentieth century, the existence and upkeep of primary schools depended on the goodwill of the rural community with its often limited resources. The result was that even in northern regions, illiteracy rates in the countryside tended to be double those in the towns, in a country, it should be noted, where half the population were classified as agricultural workers.[9] In short, the Italian society called upon to fight in 1915 was far from a 'nation of readers', still less a nation of writers, unlike the British and French armies that marched to the front in 1914 primed with several decades of extensive education policy and a sharp rise in reading habits.[10] For although compulsory conscription had boosted primary education among Italian males ('regimental schools' in barracks had been functioning effectively for some years and were compulsory for conscripts), the army in the field was largely composed of farmhands who could still barely read or write. Out of 4 million Italians sent to the front, some 2.6 million probably came from rural areas (meaning virtually all the infantry, Bersaglieri, and Alpine regiments).[11]

---

[7] Marco Mondini, *La guerra italiana: partire, raccontare, tornare 1914–1918* (Bologna, 2014), 163–211. For the phrase 'theatre of memory' see Jay Winter, *Remembering War: The Great War between Memory and History in the Twentieth Century* (New Haven, 2006).

[8] *Censimento della popolazione del Regno d'Italia al 10 giugno 1911*, vol. iii (Rome, 1914).

[9] *Sommario di statistiche storiche dell'Italia 1861–1975* (Rome, 1976), 14.

[10] Paul Fussel, *The Great War and Modern Memory* (Oxford, 1975; rev. edn. Oxford, 2000), esp. 155–90; Benjamin Gilles, *Lectures de poilus: livres et journaux dans les tranchées, 1914–1918* (Paris, 2013), 74–97.

[11] Arrigo Serpieri, *La guerra e le classi rurali italiane* (Bari, 1933), 105–14; Gianfranco

Nevertheless, that initial gap in the schooling of the popular masses should not be overstated. Between 1915 and 1918 Italy did feel some of that thirst for writing that made the First World War the most written-about 'wartime experience' in the history of Europe.[12] Even the half-illiterate Italian army in 1915–18 found the Great War overwhelming enough to require written narration, and a host of occasional writers gave vent to their urge to bear witness in a spate of notes, diaries, and letters. In some respects, indeed, the war gave new impetus to the acquisition of primary learning, such that by the end of hostilities the percentage of soldiers able to read and write rudimentary Italian had risen to 70.[13] According to the most reliable estimates drawn up in the immediate aftermath, about four thousand million missives (letters, pre-franked postcards, picture postcards) had been exchanged between the war zone and the interior.[14] Naturally, that flood of writing conveyed wildly different emotions and images depending on whether the pen was wielded by a subaltern fresh from university or a conscript from the ranks of the people who needed his captain, chaplain, or a more cultured comrade to read the family news: 'Sir, lieutenant sir, might I trouble you to read me this letter?' falters Carlo Salsa's batman Cuccuru in *Trenches*, one of the many literary sources in which that common trench scene is depicted.[15]

Given the length and conditions of the conflict, even the lowliest farmhand in uniform had to reckon with the need to keep in touch with his family and friends.[16] Uprooted from civilian life, far from home for years on end with only a few days' leave to look forward to, and daily risking their lives, those fathers/husbands/sons in arms

Mastrangelo, *Le scuole reggimentali 1848–1913: cronaca di una forma di istruzione degli adulti nell'Italia liberale* (Rome, 2008).

[12] Nicolas Beaupré, 'Soldier-Writers and Poets', in Jay Winter (ed.), *The Cambridge History of the First World War*, iii. *Civil Society* (Cambridge, 2014), 445–74.

[13] Quinto Antonelli, *Storia intima della Grande Guerra: lettere, diari e memorie dei soldati al fronte* (Rome, 2014), 3–56.

[14] Beniamino Cadioli and Aldo Cecchi, *La posta militare italiana nella Prima Guerra Mondiale* (Rome, 1978), 11–15.

[15] Carlo Salsa, *Trincee: confidenze di un fante* (Milan, 1924; repr. Milan, 1995), 167. On this topos see Marco Mondini, 'Papierhelden: Briefe von der Front während des Ersten Weltkriegs in Italien und die Schaffung eines männlich-kriegerischen Bildes', in Veit Didczuneit, Jens Ebert, and Thomas Jander (eds.), *Schreiben im Krieg — Schreiben vom Krieg: Feldpost im Zeitalter der Weltkriege* (Essen, 2011), 185–92.

[16] See Antonio Gibelli, *L'officina della guerra: la Grande Guerra e le trasformazioni del mondo mentale* (Turin, 1991; 2nd edn. Turin, 1998), 51–6.

from 1915 to 1918 found writing to be a vital link with home news and dear ones, and a welcome break from the mournful routine of the trenches. The ritual arrival of mail forms one of the commonest and most important memories of life at the front. Plodding back from the line beside the corporal postman one summer's day in 1916, Lieutenant Mario Quaglia noted that none of his soldiers had eyes for him but only an eager interest in the 'inscrutable satchel-bearing messenger': 'he was home, family, the beloved, the voice of those distressed on our behalf'.[17] Within the strict limitations of the censor, a letter was an outlet for fears and emotions and the need for the consoling reassurance that bonds of love and friendship still survived the test of distance. War was a 'scene of uncertainty'; a sense of precariousness gripped all combatants, and prolonged absence jeopardized all bonds, from friends to workmates and wives. Writing was a lifeline stretching between the self in uniform and all of life beforehand.[18]

The need to voice an alien ordeal found an outlet in more than just correspondence. Even the simplest soldier, let alone the more cultured officer cadres, might keep a diary or notes destined for future enlargement.[19] Some of those chronicles of daily life stemmed from a long-established tradition of *libri di famiglia*. At the turn of the century the practice of keeping a register of accounts and family highlights was still common among families of smallholders and artisans.[20] Anyone setting off for the front might take a notebook in which to jot down expenditure; this might then map their continual postings and become a record of impressions and situations. The melancholy occasional jottings of infantryman Federico Adamoli and the memoirs of corporal Ciro Fania that were worked into strident nationalism in the early 1920s both began on the day of call-up as notepads to record petty expenses or journeys.[21] In other

[17] Mario Quaglia, *La guerra del fante* (Milan, 1934), 145.
[18] Christophe Prochasson and Anne Rasmussen, 'La guerre incertaine', in eid. (eds.) *Vrai et faux dans la Grande Guerre* (Paris, 2004), 9–35; Frédéric Rousseau, *La Guerre censurée: une histoire des combattants européens de 14–18* (Paris, 1999; rev. edn. Paris, 2003), 56–64; Michael Roper, *The Secret Battle: Emotional Survival in the Great War* (Manchester, 2009), 47–84.
[19] Fabio Caffarena, 'Le scritture dei soldati semplici', in Stéphane Audoin-Rouzeau and Jean-Jacques Becker, *La Prima Guerra Mondiale*, ed. Antonio Gibelli (Turin, 2007), 633–47.
[20] Angelo Cicchetti and Raul Mordenti, 'La scrittura dei libri di famiglia', in Alberto Asor Rosa (ed.), *Letteratura italiana*, iii/2. *Le forme del testo: la prosa* (Turin, 1984), 1117–59; Raul Mordenti (ed.), *I libri di famiglia in Italia*, ii. *Geografia e storia* (Rome, 2001), 100–11.
[21] Federico Adamoli, *Se mi salvo la vita è un caso: diario di guerra (1916–1918)* (Teramo, 2012); Ciro Fania, *La mia vita in guerra* (Vicenza, 2000).

cases, diaries had a target reader in mind from the outset, usually a wife or parents. The journal that some soldiers carried on their person would thus open with a plea that it be sent to those relatives if it were found on the author's corpse.[22]

In all cases the personal stories of ordinary soldiers expressed far more complex and varied sensations than national memoir curators such as Adolfo Omodeo may have expected (Omodeo dismissed them as 'insignificant' records of daily trifles). The idea of ever-present death was often recalled, as was the need to leave some account of one's own part in the great event taking place; again, chafing at discomfort and bafflement at the pros and cons of war were frequently couched in scathing terms.[23] The problem is that this welter of voices from Italians at the front has long been banished from the reconstruction of the war and its imagery. It was different with the cultured young men straight from university or high school. Sons of 'good families' in which a patriotic education blended with the tradition of male heroism based on tales of Risorgimento exploits, they would leave for the front aware of the historic moment (for themselves and society) and might well decide to set the record down on paper (some already with an eye to publication). But the writings of common soldiers largely languished as private mementoes, gradually forgotten, lost in family archives until recent decades, when they have gradually (and still incompletely) resurfaced.[24]

With minor differences, the same goes for female writing in First World War Italy. Though fewer girls went to school than their brothers, female education at the turn of the century had made great strides and overcome some of the traditional reservations about the wisdom or ethics of educating girls. Not that it had really

---

[22] Antonietta Di Vito, 'Scrivere per non impazzire: la difficile alterità', in Quinto Antonelli and Anna Iuso (eds.), *Vite di carta* (Naples, 2000), 225–36.

[23] Adolfo Omodeo, *Momenti della vita di guerra* (1934; repr. Turin, 1968), 271.

[24] Marco Mondini, 'Scrivere della guerra, scrivere in guerra: appunti per uno studio sulla letteratura della prima guerra mondiale in Italia', in Marco De Nicolò (ed.), *Dalla trincea alla piazza: l'irruzione dei giovani nel Novecento* (Rome, 2011), 123–33. Besides the anthologies dating from the 1980s and 1990s, a large-scale systematic publication project being undertaken by the Archivio Diaristico Nazionale at Pieve di Santo Stefano has brought to light some 400 integral diary texts (more rarely examples of memoirs worked up after the war but left unpublished) or fragments of correspondence. Cf. Pier Vittorio Buffa and Nicola Maranesi (eds.), *La Prima Guerra Mondiale in Italia: le voci*, 4 vols. (Rome, 2015).

opened doors to the intellectual professions (except for primary teaching, which had quickly turned feminine), but a potential public of women readers had formed in the main urban centres, and this bore on the success of dailies, periodicals, and mass-oriented literature.[25] This state of still partial integration into public life was heavily affected by the Great War (though precisely to what extent is still debated). Full-scale mobilization of the country speeded up women's expectations of emancipation, for one thing.[26] Yet women counted for little in written accounts of war. It was not just reluctance to credit their writing as believable evidence of the facts. Volunteer nurses and Red Cross professionals at the front served near the line (some being taken prisoner or dying during the retreat from Caporetto). This gave rise to some of the few feminine memoirs in the corpus of wartime autobiographies.[27] Yet with few exceptions, the feminine viewpoint on Italy's war was given marginal representation, in contrast to what would happen in British and Anglo-American literature.[28] In terms of impact on the market and on public opinion, Italian literature produced nothing comparable to *Testament of Youth* by Vera Brittain. This partly perpetuated the low importance of women in the Italian intellectual market, and was partly inevitable given the Fascist 'return to order' policy and its attempt to repress any hankerings after female emancipation, even in the cultural field.[29] Besides, the few established women authors (whose apprenticeship had largely been served before the war) did not take war for their subject, either to glorify its significance in

---

[25] David Forgacs, *Italian Culture in the Industrial Era 1880–1980: Cultural Industries, Politics and the Public* (Manchester, 1990); Perry Willson, *Women in Twentieth-Century Italy* (London, 2010), 3–38.

[26] Allison Scardino Belzer, *Women and the Great War: Femininity under Fire in Italy* (London, 2010); Emma Schiavon, *Interventiste nella Grande Guerra* (Florence, 2015).

[27] Maria Bianca Mojoli Barberis, *Dal taccuino di una infermiera della Croce Rossa* (Bologna, 1917); Maria Luisa Perduca, *Un anno di ospedale (giugno 1915—novembre 1916): note di un'infermiera* (Milan, 1917); Maria Antonietta Clerici, *Al di là del Piave, coi morti e coi vivi* (Como, 1919); Maria Andina, *La mia prigionia in Austria: ottobre 1917–maggio 1918* (Como, 1921); Mercedes Astuto, *I vivi: diario di guerra di Mercedes Astuto infermiera volontaria della Croce Rossa* (Rome, 1935); Ina Battistella, *Memorie* (Udine, 1952). On the mobilization of women as health workers see Stefania Bartoloni, *Italiane alla guerra: l'assistenza ai feriti 1915–1918* (Venice, 2003).

[28] Harriet Blodgett, *Centuries of Female Days: Englishwomen's Private Diaries* (New Brunswick, NJ, 1989), 233–48; Sharon Ouditt, *Fighting Forces, Writing Women: Identity and Ideology in the First World War* (London, 1994).

[29] Silvana Patriarca, 'Journalists and Essayists 1850–1915', in Letizia Panizza and Sharon Wood (eds.), *A History of Women's Writing in Italy* (Cambridge, 2000), 151–63.

generating the new Italy, or to criticize it.[30] The few autobiographies to appear in wartime gained little circulation. Even Matilde Serao, who did play a leading part in building patriotism as early as the Libyan War, as well as contributing to cultural mobilization with a set of articles entitled *Parla una donna*, was a secondary voice in the construction of a collective memory.[31]

Great War Literature in Italy: Demarcating a Cultural Field

Italy's literary war authors thus had a similar social, cultural, and military profile, besides being a small band. This was partly because the Italian publishing market between the wars was far from free. Once the dictatorship got a hold, between 1922 and 1925, the government extended, perfected, and centralized the system of preventive censorship. Under that discipline there would be many cases of self-censorship in the culture market, involving writers, playwrights, and directors. As novelist Corrado Alvaro would admit, under Fascism everyone had 'a censor inside himself'.[32] The result was a mushrooming ideological ostracism that drastically limited what could be said or published.[33]

Foreign works suspected of being offensive to the image of the army or harmful to the militant upbringing of youth were banned, which meant that literature tended to become impermeable to international input. The most striking examples were *All Quiet on the Western Front* by Erich Maria Remarque in 1928, and Ernest Hemingway's *Farewell to Arms* in 1929. In the first case the influential (and pro-Fascist) publisher Mondadori asked Mussolini for his permission to translate the book, which was already a European best-seller, and was met by a flat refusal. The Duce's advisers thought the work unduly inclined to criticize the beauty of wartime sacrifice, which was a linchpin of youth education under Fascism. Only in 1931 was Mondadori able to get round the ban by obtaining permission to put an Italian edition on the market with the proviso

[30] Lucia Re, 'Futurism and Fascism', in Panizza and Wood (eds.), *A History of Women's Writing*, 190–203.

[31] Elisabetta Rasy, '"Parla una donna": il diario di guerra di Matilde Serao', in Emmanuelle Genevois (ed.), *Les Femmes écrivains en Italie (1870–1920): ordres et liberté* (Paris, 1995), 243–54.

[32] Corrado Alvaro, *Quasi una vita: giornale di uno scrittore* (Milan, 1951; repr. Milan, 1968), 414.

[33] Ruth Ben-Ghiat, *Fascist Modernities: Italy 1922–1945* (Berkeley, 2001), 67–96.

that it should circulate only abroad. The clause was promptly infringed, producing the curious case of an above-board publication circulating clandestinely.[34] Hemingway's book broke the taboo on describing the defeat at Caporetto (not lifted until quite recently). The ban was strictly enforced until Republican times, and the first edition of *Addio alle Armi* did not appear in bookshops until 1946.[35]

Any Italian author whose story clashed with the glorious martial value of Vittorio Veneto would be obstructed or even removed from circulation. The glaring example was, of course, Curzio Malaparte's *Viva Caporetto!*, a political pamphlet that gloried in the defeat of Caporetto as a revolt by the proletariat against exploitation as cannon fodder. This had the questionable honour of three editions in a row being censored by the last liberal governments and by the Fascist regime. In vain did the author keep unwisely revising the text to make it more palatable to the climate of patriotic zeal that followed Mussolini's rise to power.[36] As it was, over the years the censor's axe would fall on writers guilty merely of undue realism about the conduct of the war, or irreverence towards the military caste. In 1932 Carlo Salsa's *Trincee* was denied a reprint, and even Paolo Monelli, whose *Le scarpe al sole* was the most widely read book of war memoirs for thirty years, got into difficulties over obtaining the right to translate it in France, that enemy country and refuge of anti-Fascists.[37] In such a climate, small wonder that relatively few war novels, memoirs, and diaries were published and sold in Italy (and nearly all by Italian authors). One marvels, indeed, at how those few managed to slip through the net of the regime's paranoid censorship.

It was fairly common for war veterans writing up their experiences of fighting to use language quite different from the overblown triumphalism of official communications. Even within the narrow ideological confines imposed by the regime, what went down best with the reading public was not the kind of overtly edifying patriotism that revelled in the 'great national ordeal', but the memoirs of those who had seen action on the front, the first-hand account of fighting and the fallen, related in gory detail. It was such autobiographical

[34] Guido Bonsaver, *Censorship and Literature in Fascist Italy* (Toronto, 2007), 50–3.
[35] Mondini, *La guerra italiana*, 167–70.
[36] Curzio Malaparte, *Viva Caporetto! La rivolta dei santi maledetti* (1921), ed. M. Biondi (Florence, 1995).
[37] Maurizio Cesari, *La censura nel periodo fascista* (Naples, 1978), 72.

writing that made the 'war story' genre so successful both on the general mass market and in specialist collections (see Table 1).[38] Clearly not all the soldier author titles launched on the market had the same degree of good fortune. Many of those published by minor publishing houses in limited editions soon vanished from the catalogues, generally hamstrung by the poor marketing skills of a disorganized book industry. But about forty titles (and their respective authors) enjoyed an intense publishing life, being reprinted or republished several times by home publishing houses during the 1920s and 1930s. Most such cases even outlived the next war and the fall of Fascism.

The main distinguishing feature of these best-sellers was the profile of the author (see Figure 1). Almost invariably they were young men who bore arms and lived out the war on the front line. Among them were a handful of orderlies serving in forward-lying military hospitals, chaplains serving in the field, and medical officers. But the classic market leader in the genre was the young subaltern (warrant officer, second or full lieutenant) or at most captain, aged from 20 to 30, whose war experience came from full-time fighting in infantry or special detachments. Often (though not invariably) he would be an *interventista* with the writing skills of a literary profession behind him, or one who had read newspapers and cultural reviews, perhaps as a student. The Italian war-story writer came from a restricted generational bracket and a well-defined social and cultural background.[39] That he had spent the war, or most of it, commanding a platoon or a company was the result of the High Command's deliberate recruiting policy; by tradition, the High Command rejected any type of volunteer service. It was practically impossible for a young, urban, middle-class student or high-school leaver to begin and end the war without being drafted into an officer cadre course.[40] Some soldier writers would leave for

---

[38] See Gigliola De Donato and Vanna Gazzola Stacchini (eds.), *I best seller del ventennio: il regime e il libro di massa* (Rome, 1991); Enrico Decleva, 'Un panorama in evoluzione', in Gabriele Turi (ed.), *Storia dell'editoria nell'Italia contemporanea* (Milan, 2004), 225–98; and Giancarlo Ferretti and Stefano Guerriero, *Storia dell'informazione letteraria in Italia dalla terza pagina ad internet* (Milan, 2010), 27–36.

[39] Mondini, *La guerra italiana*, 123–44.

[40] Marco Mondini, 'Ufficiali grigio-verde', in Mario Isnenghi, Daniele Ceschin, and Eva Cecchinato (eds.), *Gli italiani in guerra: conflitti, identità, memorie dal Risorgimento ai nostri giorni*, iii/1. *La Grande Guerra: dall'intervento alla 'vittoria mutilata'* (Turin, 2008), 201–7.

TABLE 1. *War Stories: Best-Seller Titles*[a]

Author, title, year of first edition	No. of new editions or reprints (1915-68)
Monelli, *Le scarpe al sole* (1921); D'Annunzio, **Notturno** (1921)	13
Pastorino, *La prova del fuoco* (1926); Locchi, **La sagra di Santa Gorizia** (1919)	12
Ungaretti, **Allegria di naufragi** (1919)	11
Mariani, *Sott'la naja* (1918)	9
Salsa, *Trincee* (1924); Mussolini, *Il mio diario di guerra* (1923)	8
Borgese, *Rubè* (1921)	7
Soffici, *Kobilek* (1918); Frescura, *Diario di un imboscato* (1919); Stanghellini, *Introduzione alla vita mediocre* (1920); Alvaro, *Vent'anni* (1930); Comisso, *Giorni di guerra* (1930)	6
Gasparotto, *Diario di un fante* (1919); Soffici, *La ritirata del Friuli* (1919); Marpicati, *La coda di Minosse* (1925); Lussu, *Un anno sull'Altipiano* (1945); Jahier, **Con me e con gli alpini** (1919)	5
Serra, *Esame di coscienza di un letterato* (1915)	4
Campana, *Un anno sul Pasubio* (1918); Marini, *Da Gorizia al Grappa* (1918); Reina, *Noi che tingemmo il mondo di sanguigno* (1919); Rossato, *L'elmo di Scipio* (1919); Malaparte, *Viva Caporetto! La rivolta dei santi maledetti* (1921); Sironi, *I vinti di Caporetto* (1922); Donati Petteni, *Nella luce del sacrificio* (1928); Bartolini, *Il ritorno sul Carso* (1930); Stuparich, *Guerra del '15* (1931); Landi, *Il muro di casa* (1935)	3
Agnoletti, *Dal giardino all'Isonzo* (1917); Rosai, *Il libro di un teppista* (1919); Marinetti, *L'alcova d'acciaio* (1921); Pasini, *Diario di un sepolto vivo* (1921); Marconi, *Battaglione Monte Berico* (1923); Puccini, *Il soldato Cola* (1927); Pollini, *Le veglie al Carso* (1928); Garaventa, *In guerra con gli alpini* (1934); Muccini, *E ora andiamo: il romanzo di uno scalcinato* (1938).	2

[a] Titles in bold are partly or entirely in verse; underlined titles are novels.

Source: CUBI: *Bibliografia Nazionale Italiana 1886–1957* and BNI: *Bibliografia Nazionale Italiana*.

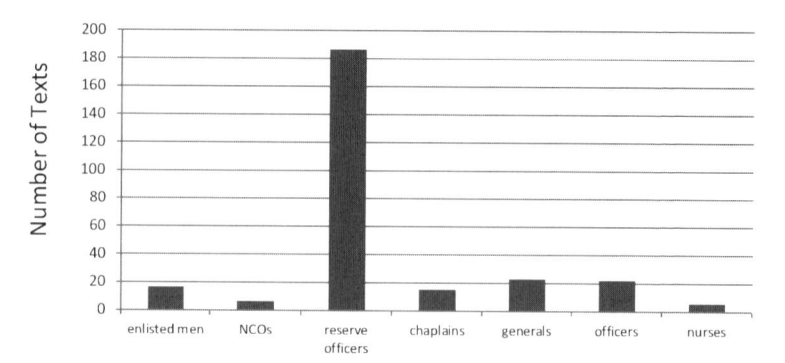

FIG. 1. Authors of War Memoirs: Italian
Literary Texts on the Great War (1915–68)

Source: Survey of 263 autobiographical texts devoted to the Great War and published in Italy between 1915 and 1968, based on the *Bibliografia Nazionale Italiana*.

the front as privates or NCOs, but few remained so beyond 1917.[41] For different reasons, Giuseppe Ungaretti and Lorenzo Viani did, but Curzio Malaparte, Giovanni Comisso, Mario Mariani, and Giani Stuparich began the war as serving infantrymen, only to be promoted later. Willy-nilly, anyone who wrote, or could write, in civilian life was bound to become an officer in the war.

Brothers, Enemies, Skivers: Themes of the Italian War Story

Brothers? Why, of course. . . . I am content with what we have in common, stronger than all division. I'm content with the road we shall travel together carrying us onward all alike: and it will be one pace, one breath, one rhythm, one destiny for all. After the first miles on the road, differences will fall away like sweat, drop by drop . . . Onward together . . . toiling in silence, together.[42]

The director of the illustrious Biblioteca Malatestiana, Renato Serra, was one of the first drafted intellectuals to put his military experience down on paper. In March 1915 he set about writing what was meant to be a summary of his view of the war as a 'generational opportunity', explaining what drove an academic and intellectual to take part. From this sprang his 'Examination of Conscience', a short work

[41] See Giorgio Rochat, 'Gli ufficiali italiani nella Prima Guerra Mondiale', in Giuseppe Caforio and Piero Del Negro (eds.), *Ufficiali e società: interpretazioni e modelli* (Milan, 1988), 231–53.

[42] Renato Serra, *Esame di coscienza di un letterato: edizione dell'autografo*, ed. Enzo Colombo, afterword by Guido Guglielmi (Bologna, 2002), 52.

hurriedly jotted down, yet destined soon to become one of the most widely read accounts of the Italian war.[43] War, argued Serra, served neither to redress the wrongs of history ('war does not change civilization . . . and in the end everything will be back more or less in its old place') nor to satisfy some urge for power: all political objectives could have waited 'another fifty years' and the destiny of the nation would not have changed.[44] The true benefit of the operation lay in its quality as a challenge and discovery, an opportunity for a generation to prove itself at long last, to recognize itself as a community able to suffer and, if necessary, die together: 'one learns to suffer, hold out, make do with little, live more worthily. . . . In that, Italy struck me as deaf and empty when I just looked on; but now I feel it may be full of men like me . . . able to rely on one another, live and die together, even without knowing why.'[45]

The image of war aiding the discovery of a sense of community was far from unusual among European volunteers of the '1914 generation'. But in Italy, the 1915–18 brotherhood in arms was much more than one piece of the story: it was the key to the war experience. The political reasons for fighting—Trento and Trieste, opposing the tyranny of the Central Empires, gaining new prestige for the country at the Council of Great Powers—soon dropped away. The soldier writers fêted their entrance into the nation under arms as an experience of birth (or rebirth) into a new existence; their unit became a community of destiny described with the emotions and in the language of a family group.[46] It was an experience of redemption (another word in vogue among war authors), though that tended not to refer to the Catholic faith. The '1915 generation' was the first to have come up through the secular schools of the Kingdom of Italy. Of course, their language reflected their school background (with Dante's *Divine Comedy* in pride of place); and the war itself served the Church as a stage in the reconquest of Italian society and culture. But Catholic authors referring explicitly to the religious sphere were

---

[43] Carlo Bo, 'La religione di Serra', in id., *La religione di Serra: saggi e note di lettura* (Florence, 1967), 25–52; Mario Isnenghi, *Il mito della Grande Guerra* (Rome and Bari, 1970; repr. Bologna 1989), 142 ff.; Giuseppe De Robertis, 'Dichiarazione', in Renato Serra, *Esame di coscienza di un letterato: ultime lettere dal campo*, preface by Barbara Tonzar (Pordenone 1994), 1–15; and Enzo Colombo, 'In debito con se stesso', in Serra, *Esame di coscienza di un letterato*, ed. Colombo, 7–34.

[44] Serra, *Esame di coscienza di un letterato* (1994 edn.), 21, 33.

[45] Ibid. 37, 53.

[46] Mondini, *La guerra italiana*, 170 ff.

thin on the ground.[47] Giosué Borsi and Carlo Pastorino were the only ones of that ilk to enjoy a certain success.[48] The absence of Catholicism from such autobiographical pieces was odd, especially as propaganda and patriotic journalism drew heavily on the language of the Church: fallen heroes were depicted as 'martyrs', and God's blessing was always being invoked on the nation's weapons.[49]

The war writers were largely immune both to the language of power politics and to religious arguments. The period 1915–18 stood out chiefly, to them, as an ethical experience, the discovery of a community in which to grow and be regenerated via discovery (or rediscovery) of the classic warrior values: courage and strength, the yardsticks of being (or becoming) a man in the masculine sense, but, above all, loyalty, friendship, and self-sacrifice—in short, camaraderie.[50] The literature of Italy's Great War took on the quality of a collective *Bildungsroman*, or of a community-building novel, in which the narration of events and even the reconstruction of the fighting paled beside the description of the small band of companions with whom the narrator shared the fortunes of war: 'great family in which we spent years that seemed like centuries, we will miss you . . . I have seen so many young men weep when they had to leave the brigade', as Michele Campana put it in winding up his memoir of war on the Pasubio front.[51]

The small band was what enabled one to survive, but it was a fragile shield. On every front of the war, his trench (or squad or platoon) became the fighting man's entire known world, a microcosm in which male friendship was the be-all and end-all of relationships and the main psychological prop: 'Enough to look in our companions' eyes to read all there was to know, to grasp their hand was an act of confession as much as before the Lord.'[52] In the end, those who

[47] See Elena Papadia, *Di padre in figlio: la generazione del 1915* (Bologna, 2015). On recourse to Dantesque vocabulary in landscape descriptions see Marco Mondini, *I luoghi della Grande Guerra* (Bologna, 2015), 63–74.

[48] 'Giosué Borsi', in Cesare Padovani (ed.), *Antologia degli scrittori morti in guerra* (Florence, 1929), 75–91; Carlo Pastorino, *La mia guerra: la prova del fuoco — la prova della fame* (Genoa, 1989).

[49] Oliver Janz, 'Lutto, famiglia e nazione nel culto dei caduti della prima Guerra mondiale in Italia', in Oliver Janz and Lutz Klinkhammer (eds.), *La morte per la patria* (Rome, 2008), 65–80.

[50] Marco Mondini, 'The Construction of a Masculine Warrior Ideal in the Italian Narratives of the First World War', *Contemporary European History*, 23 (2014), 307–28.

[51] Michele Campana, *Un anno sul Pasubio* (1918; repr. Valdagno, 1993), 177.

[52] Gino Cornali, *Un fante lassù* (Rome, 1934), 282. See also Sarah Cole, *Modernism, Male Friendship and the First World War* (Cambridge, 2003), 138–89.

wrote about their war were simple survivors, or wished to be seen as such: they were survivors of the 'generation of fire'. In return for that good luck their job was to lay bare the war exactly as it had been; an amalgam of suffering, sacrifice, and pain, but also affection, passion, and brotherhood.[53] To sing in memory of one's 'brothers in the field those who lived those who died' was the rationale for writing, as Vittorio Locchi would maintain in the prologue to his *La sagra di Santa Gorizia*. Virtually forgotten nowadays, in its day it sold 50,000 copies of its fourth edition. It was one of the most widely read works and a rare example of a rhapsodic best-seller.[54] To tell the story was a duty since the tragic adventure of war could be related only by one who had been through it.[55] In Italy, as elsewhere, the idea of someone who had not fought appropriating the memory and meaning of the experience was intolerable to a war veteran. 'Those who did not suffer, those who worshipped the fatherland from their homes, I do not accord the right to cast the first or the last stone', inveighed Carlo Salsa against the race of false, vainglorious witnesses, whether society journalists or other officers who stayed snugly behind the lines:

Why naturally; the first to hold forth were the journalists, megaphones of hearsay, binocular-brandishing lookouts in some staff officers' mess; oh, the tales we would hear . . . altered by bragging or riddled with lapses of memory, from men bailed out of the front line after a few rounds of fire . . . in which our heroic infantry—heroic in a manner of speaking, poor sods—were standing in perfect order before their embrasures, in comfortable trenches festooned with dead enemies.[56]

Whoever made it back from the trenches was the natural audience for the memoir, as well as the subject of the story, for it was *his* memory, the down-at-heel soldier's tale, that would be told in words and images remote from the fashionable celebrations and patriotic oleographs—irreverent vulgarities to those lacking first-hand experience. In *Le scarpe al sole*, Paolo Monelli neatly depicts the ideal recipient of his book, the audience he would prefer: 'there must still

---

[53] Quoted in Cornali, *Un fante lassù*, 297; on the figure of the surviving witness see Carine Trevisan, *Les Fables du deuil: la Grande Guerre. Mort et écriture* (Paris, 2001), 149–72.

[54] Vittorio Locchi, *La sagra di Santa Gorizia* (1917; repr. Trieste, 2008), 16–17.

[55] Léonard V. Smith, 'Ce que finir veut dire', in Pierre Schoentjes (ed.), *La Grande Guerre: un siècle de fictions romanesque* (Geneva, 2008), 251–63.

[56] Salsa, *Trincee*, 15. On the risk that war memoirs may be monopolized by non-combatants see Kate McLoughlin, *Authoring War: The Literary Representation of War from the* Iliad *to* Iraq (Cambridge, 2001), 21–50.

be some bewildered soul amid the drab monotony of civvy street or some hermit in these years of warfare without gloss or glory, whose heart is still heavy with recollection. To him I offer my book in all simplicity, much as we would offer some passing guest at our friendly repasts a glass for the road and a song.'[57]

It was not just mentally impossible for anyone who had not seen action to capture the essence of the front line, but those who wrote their own accounts refused to believe that anyone else could grasp the ambiguous nature of military life, death and suffering, horror and repulsion, but also ties of loyalty, devotion, courage, even joy: 'war wasn't only about people dying. War is like nature ... war is ugly and beautiful.'[58] It is ambiguity that animates Carlo Pastorino's *Ordeal by Fire*, something thought to elude most people's understanding: 'let him not be reproached for conjuring up by his book years afterwards what some would like to forget. Why? There's so much comfort in suffering what one suffered all over again and enjoying what one enjoyed.' 'The poet' (and narrator) could hardly not dedicate his memoirs to the companions with whom he had shared not only suffering, prison, and death, but also an indissoluble bond of brotherhood. Though 'they walk separate paths' now that they are back on the normal road, they still 'remember together'.[59] Thus Mario Mariani would dedicate *Sott'la naja* to his 'comrades in arms' while the war was still on. Had he not done so, the real combatants would have remained unknown and silent: 'amongst you I chewed the cud of my pain and amongst you I champed through the last of my youth. I found myself. This I owe to you, comrades. Not having any other way of expressing my gratitude, I offer you this book.'[60]

War: Vita Nova *and Homecoming*

The expression of war as an experience of redemption and access to a new life followed a recurrent narrative pattern: first a descent to hell (enlistment and despatch to the front) heralding the discovery of a new human community (trenchmates or messmates) in which some characters stand out as future mentors. Only at the end of a long

---

[57] Paolo Monelli, *Le scarpe al sole: cronache di gaie e tristi avventure d'alpini, di muli e di vino* (1921; repr. Milan, 1971), 5–6.
[58] Luigi Bartolini, *Il ritorno sul Carso* (Milan, 1930; repr. Milan, 1934), 24.
[59] Carlo Pastorino, *La prova del fuoco: cose vere* (1926; repr. Trento, 2010), 10.
[60] Mario Mariani, *Sott'la naja: vita e guerra d'alpini* (Milan, 1918; repr. Milan, 1925), 5.

'novitiate' of suffering, danger, and death is the author welcomed into the brotherhood of the combatants, marking his initiation into a morally higher state. The epilogue proves more tormented, for the end of the story does not always coincide with a return to order; exit from war need not restore the hero to a condition of peace, in the manner of a classic story plot.

'Those who have seen the atrocities of battle, one and all, have a change of heart from where they started out . . . Something new has developed in our breasts: pain has worn smooth the sensibility of our souls . . . We have come together as men without the deceit of convention and etiquette. I feel quite different now from before, midway through life . . . I have even wondered many times whether I didn't die on 25 May 1915, to be reborn', wrote Michele Campana in his meditation on war as a new life.[61] That the pattern is a recurrent one is well illustrated by the similarities between two soldier writers, Salsa and Pastorino, who are not so different in sensibility and narrative style. Subalterns in an infantry regiment on the Isonzo front, they both went through the trauma of defeat and capture. But whereas for Pastorino even prison was a positive opportunity to savour the 'fraternal love' of a close-knit band of friends, a bond that would outlive captivity and the end of war (as is far from uncommon in prisoner-of-war memoirs), Salsa found his long incarceration unmitigated torture, 'an interminable cloistering . . . which it seems must cleave a void of madness in our craniums'. It was made worse by the wretched prison conditions and the state of defeat, (self-)branded with the label of coward and hence devoid of all hope of redemption.[62] Yet the memoirs of Pastorino, edifying and often cloying, and of the caustic, disillusioned Salsa have almost the same structure: war serves as a *viaticum* to a *vita nova*. No sooner appointed second lieutenant, Pastorino yearns to get to the front with his friend Terzani. The two fledgling warriors seek the 'ordeal by fire' to show their manly scorn for danger and thus win their soldiers' and fellow officers' trust ('Then came the feeling of having taken my first step in a new life; truly, I had crossed the threshold').[63]

Likewise, in *Trenches* the gradual approach to the fire zone and war proper is marked by a Dantesque parade of premonitory signs,

---

[61] Michele Campana, *Perché ho ucciso?* (Florence, 1918), 25, 89.
[62] Pastorino, *La prova del fuoco*, 7–8. Captured in spring 1917, he was not released until the war's end. He relates his prison experience in the volume *La prova della fame* (Turin, 1940); Salsa, *Trincee*, 226. [63] Pastorino, *La prova del fuoco*, 23.

bizarre personages, and moments of bewilderment. In the Prelude Salsa leaves his first garrison post and is despatched to the front with a few colleagues. At the town of Palmanova behind the lines the friends share a meal with an officer fresh from the front, wounded and embittered, who warns them to abandon all illusion about what awaits them: a Charon figure on the threshold between war and the outside world. At the transit camp an officer 'strutting and decked out like a turkey-cock' coldly sets them on their way to another forlorn 'funereal hamlet', where the group spend a few days suspended in an apparently tranquil limbo of quiet broken only by the premonitory signs of their impending future (the sound of gunfire, stupefied soldiers newly invalided out of the front line). It is the last circle of a pre-hell which ends when the author is suddenly catapulted into a trench in pitch darkness to take command of a sector of front under enemy fire. Without the slightest idea of what is going on, the dazed young subaltern wonders how many men are his, where they are, and even whether they are still on the line. 'Have you seen?—nothing—any idea of what the line's like?—No', he confesses to a colleague in what is perhaps the truest Italian account of the front-line combatant thrown into the maze of the trenches.[64]

Their Dantesque archetype is not the only feature shared by the memoirs of Pastorino and Salsa. Pitched painfully unprepared into the whirl of combat, both authors quickly come to identify with the tiny trench community allotted to them; they pick up its habits, speech, blinkered world-view, and indifference to the daily spectacle of death around them. Much the more lyrical portrait of the front comes from Pastorino's unconventional background as a rustic scholar, poet, and schoolmaster with a deeply Catholic calling. Over these 'sons of our own people' he yearns to set a moral lead akin to a secular priesthood. The pages of *Ordeal by Fire* drip with tears of emotion, pain, nostalgia, hugging, and kissing in the set mould of his school upbringing and its prescribed reading (De Amicis and Dante above all).[65] The family spirit that imbues the grey-green folk around him is revealed during the first battle, 'a great ordeal and the peak moment of life', when the soldiers find

[64] Salsa, *Trincee*, 57. For trenches as the 'tactical reality of chaos' see Eric Leed, *No Man's Land: Combat and Identity in World War I* (Cambridge, 1981), 94–105.

[65] On Dantism in Pastorino see also Fabio Todero, *La Grande Guerra tra modernità e tradizione* (Udine, 2002).

they are bonded like brothers ('our family') and the colonel, 'gruff and bearlike but good-hearted', hugs his surviving officers 'like children'.[66] This small military world focuses the writer's attention, even to the point of obsession, on a sequence of edifying portraits of friends, colleagues, and lower ranks. Pastorino's community of fighting men is a close-knit web of ties of solidarity, acts of generosity, and personal acknowledgement between officers and soldiers in which modern discipline and hierarchy count for little.[67]

But in Salsa, too, 'platoon spirit' keeps an ethical view of war alive. For all the blunt condemnation of the tragic living conditions in the trenches, where death is always futile and inglorious ('if only we snuffed it for something at least!'), the subaltern knows he can survive only within a community of destinies coinciding with his small unit, an 'us' made up of companions in arms. They are 'my lousy . . . good comrades', who welcome their lieutenant when he walks out of military hospital, and provide a haven after a spell of leave, that trauma for any veteran.[68] It was the same for most war writers, not just the Italian ones. Behind the lines (military hospital above all) was the refuge of skivers in uniform, creatures despised as cowards and envied because they lived in safety (Pastorino's 'clean-shaven young sergeants' who emerged like mice from their holes only when there was a ceremony to attend).[69]

But for ignorance and insensitivity to the 'trench boys' the town's the thing, the true homeland of the incorrigibly different. Towns are populated with one-time warmongers who got themselves recycled behind the lines, warriors out of an operetta, and sons of string-pullers in a cushy sedentary posting, pub strategists complete with fast floozies, leading a comfortable modern life which goes on unabashed, whatever the squalor of the trenches. Half-men gone to seed (the 'fat slob' whom Fresura meets in Milan, the 'pot-bellied' colonel who punishes Salsa before he leaves for the front), these figures of scorn have a cathartic function: they sum up all that the fighting man is not (cowardly, unmanly, cunning) and cannot do (enjoy life, consort with women); they point to the noble contrast of those sacrificed on the front, the difference between those for whom

---

[66] Pastorino, *La prova del fuoco*, 87–90.
[67] Mario Isnenghi, *Le guerre degli italiani: parole, immagini, ricordi 1848–1945* (Milan, 1989), 236–7.
[68] Salsa, *Trincee*, 193, 200–13.
[69] Pastorino, *La prova del fuoco*, 119.

the war means fighting and those for whom it is just words, or even good for business.[70]

Wounded and convalescent, Luigi Tonelli winds up at a New Year's Eve party and is overwhelmed by the impact of that endless world of merry, colourful (civilian) life pressing on regardless of suffering and death (soldiers). Hypocritically, for form's sake, the fallen are extolled and acclaimed on the proper occasion in tones of patriotic duty, but in the end no one remembers them, except (perhaps) their mothers:

Elegant and bantering, the city clatters and bangs and laughs. The theatres teem with people, the cafés are under storm, the streets glitter with jewels and smiles . . . It's Christmas, time for frolicking! It's New Year's Eve! No one speaks of death or enjoins morality. And why should a soldier back from the muddy enemy-battered trenches go bitterly muttering? Does he want contrite faces, drapes of mourning, simple garb, a dignified mien? . . . There's money around, with which to pay and have a jolly time. That's the way life is. Life dictates that . . . a fiancée bereft of her paramour should smile at her renewed hopes of youth; that the young widow resign herself swiftly to the joys of the world. Only the mothers . . . in bitter solitude stifle an unnamed grief.[71]

On his few days' leave Mario Quaglia turns in solace from the unbearable hypocrisy of the patriotic bourgeois clubs and the stiff barrack-room manners of his superiors to a brothel he frequented in his student days. There, however, he meets one of those 'behind-the-lines cavalry officers', elegant and dandified, who holds forth on the tedium of garrison life and the need to organize a good track for horse-racing: 'trembling-lipped I yelled—here we are at war and no one appears to know! I've seen more than one such cluttering these halls of prosperous amusement ever since the days of call-up. May I remind you there are people who have shed their blood several times . . . and without whining gone back up there where men weep and die.' But the odd man out is the convalescent on home leave who is forced to flee a town that is no longer his. 'Don't talk like that, young master Mario', says one of the prostitutes, 'why, you've grown so sharp making war.—I'll say I've grown sharp. What on earth possessed me to come down here?'[72]

In this sense the Great War writers are clearly disillusioned. Dis-

---

[70] On the skiver as a cathartic figure see Charles Ridel, *Les Embusqués* (Paris, 2007), 48–59.
[71] Luigi Tonelli, *L'anima e il tempo: stazioni spirituali d'un combattente* (Bologna, 1921), 63.
[72] Quaglia, *La guerra del fante*, 196.

illusionment is the gap between the naive picture of war many harboured before seeing action and experience on the front line, and still more the unbridgeable gulf between fighting men and the rest of society, military or civilian, who go on denying the reality of warfare and ignoring the sacrifice of the men at the front. This stark truth is usually borne in on the veteran precisely when home on leave. 'I've seen too many young men in mufti or townie-style military uniform pacing the pavements of the Corso or wearing out the café seats; I've seen too many jostling at the theatre or cinema door.'[73] But there is no disillusionment when it comes to portraying the band of brothers at the front, a haven of good feeling for the trench veteran who has 'lost all memory of that other life' and has no patience with anything except the little family of his unit. The pathos of group feeling rivets attention on portraying the trenches as a place of triumphant camaraderie, solidarity, and honest emotion—a state of contentment that may lapse into rhapsodic moments of narrative hymning military life.[74]

On the worst European front, and even amidst the shambles of the Caporetto retreat depicted in Ardengo Soffici's sombre epic *La ritirata del Friuli* (1919), war is still the sublime adventure of 'splendid heroic youth' daily facing death in the serene awareness that theirs is an extraordinary time of testing. They will pine for the days spent in the trenches as 'something open and pure', never to be repeated. Likewise, when the retreat is over, the beauty of that lost land, 'the serene Alps and the Carso crimson . . . with blood and glory', will cause the diarist a pang of melancholy: there, he confesses, he spent the best part of his youth.[75] Such topoi are common to Soffici, the national interventionist, to a populist democrat such as Mario Puccini (*Il soldato Cola*), to dégagé novelists and diarists such as Giovanni Comisso (*Giorni di guerra*) and Corrado Alvaro (*Vent'anni*), and disenchanted veterans such as Arturo Stanghellini (*L'introduzione alla vita mediocre*) or Luigi Bartolini (*Il ritorno sul Carso*). Though differing in their background, ideology, and life patterns, all these found their wartime days an extraordinary human (male) community experience amidst which, and thanks to which, they shared a season that was grandly tragic, unrepeatable, and unforgettable.

---

[73] Riccardo Pizzicaria, *Fra una pallottola e l'altra* (Florence, 1931), 57.
[74] Fulvio Senardi, 'Scrittori in trincea', in id. (ed.), *Scrittori in trincea: la letteratura e la Grande Guerra* (Rome, 2008), 7–52.
[75] Ibid. 203; see also Fulvio Senardi, *La ritirata del Friuli* (Florence, 1920), 258.

In *Giorni di guerra* (*Wartime Days*), one of the most eccentric war memoir narratives, the ethical code of the little band provides an anchor of moral safety. The soldier author Commisso is a rare monument of egocentrism; the recollection of his time as a combatant is a voyeuristic description of the natural beauty and fascinating bodies of his comrades. Few pages in the entire corpus of Italian war literature afford such a bold description of the potentially homoerotic trench community as Commisso gives of his fellow soldiers.[76] But when the rout of Caporetto shatters this idyllic 'war game' and military hierarchy collapses, it is the common destiny of his companions in arms, 'my soldiers' tied by bonds of 'affectionate obedience', that enables a sense of duty and resolve to survive.[77] With a handful of companions Commisso embarks on a daring anabasis towards the Italian lines, during which the responsibility of command will steady the carefree hedonism of the foregoing months and change the boy in uniform into a brave and prudent leader.[78]

The memories of many who returned would revert insistently to that community of their twenties. Civilian life proved a disappointment; they pined for a war now remembered for its mythical courage, loyalty, and friendship. 'Nostalgia for the front' would find its way into the pages of writers for many years to come. That 'impossible return' and trench nostalgia are the guiding theme of Luigi Bartolini's pilgrimage to the memorial places, the war zone where once he fought. Bartolini's is the paradigm contrast between the heroic, glorious myth of wartime experience and the flatness of civilian life. Prolific and versatile, painter and best-seller writer, the intellectual Bartolini's *Return to Carso* conjures up the battles, the months in the trenches, the shared risks of his brothers in arms as 'our high point', and peace as regression to a state of drabness. At every station of his memorial Via Crucis the memory of daring deeds, adventures of love and war, friends lost and found is set against the disenchantment of the ensuing phase of life.[79] For Gino Cornali, demobilization would

---

[76] Renato Bertacchini, 'Le tre redazioni dei "Giorni di guerra"', in Giorgio Pullini (ed.), *Giovanni Comisso* (Florence, 1983), 115–39. On the textual variants see also Rolando Damiani and Nico Naldini, 'Notizie sui testi: Giorni di guerra', in Giovanni Comisso, *Opere*, ed. Rolando Damiani and Nico Naldini (Milan, 2002), 1647–60; Giovanni Comisso, *Il porto dell'amore* (Treviso, 1924).

[77] Giovanni Comisso, *Giorni di guerra* (Milan, 1930; repr. Milan, 2009), 406.

[78] Ibid. 448–9.

[79] Bartolini, *Il ritorno sul Carso*, 163, 200–9. Among other things, he was the author of *Bicycle Thieves*, on which the film of the same name was based.

not arrive until autumn 1919, and it meant returning to a civilian life offering various aspects of promise (a fiancée awaiting him, home and creature comforts, university to finish, and the prospect of a good job). But it also presaged the end of a marvellous adventure in which he discovered the only friendship possible, that between men who have looked death in the face together, have protected one another, and together won each battle for survival. Peace is goodbye to all that, to an exceptional situation coinciding with being in one's twenties and discovering a better self:

> Yes, we should meet up dressed in mufti; we should hug one another in emotion and then find some hidden nook to swap memories. But it would be different: each of us would have his own life, family, and other friends in need, other duties, other responsibilities. The way we were up until that day, with our proud 20-year-old's serenity, would linger as a ghostly past that we would lack the courage to pine for aloud, but leave it shut away in the cupboard with our crumpled uniform.[80]

Youth protracted by war with its apparently endless shelving of responsibility (finishing education, a family, a definitive job, the arrival of adult duties), and one's companions in arms: these two linchpins of wartime life proved hardest to shake off. Arturo Stanghellini's famous memoir has its fair share of front-line horrors and the victory of the sublime over the mediocrity of peace. He is no rootless survivor, and not a fanatical nationalist either, but an intellectual and civil servant with a solid career and considerable success as a novelist. Yet his, too, is an 'unachieved return' from the front, a *nostos manqué* from a war that included 'illustrious, grandiose ideas', while civilian life offers only derision from the old skivers, pettiness, and calculating self-interest:

> the inebriation of sacrifice, the purity of every gesture made in the face of death, contemplation of death in the face of fallen friends, the joy brought by news of our distant families, the rapt marvel of a fresh morning bird call during a lull in the bombardment. That was the war we shall continue to love in the silence of this peace where hatred, egoism, and envy seem fiercer than the necessary ferocity of war.[81]

[80] Cornali, *Un fante lassù*, 282.
[81] Arturo Stanghellini, *Introduzione alla vita mediocre* (Milan, 1920; repr. Milan, 1924), 242–3.

13

Alloying Dissent with Patriotism: Dragiša Vasić in Yugoslav Siberia

JOHN PAUL NEWMAN

*Introduction: Ego Documents and Serbia's
Wars of 'Liberation and Unification'*

The use of ego documents to cast light on the Serbian experience of war (which in this case spans the two Balkan Wars of 1912–13 and the First World War itself, which in the interwar Serbia/Yugoslavia period was usually termed collectively the war of 'liberation and unification' of all South Slavs) begs a number of urgent heuristic questions. On the one hand, the conflicts of 1912 to 1918 are undoubtedly examples of 'total war' experienced across the entire society, encompassing occupation, privation, violence, mourning, and death; but on the other, high levels of illiteracy (that is, well over 50 per cent of the population) in what was an essentially pre-modern society have left scant written records that could rightfully constitute a corpus of 'ego documents' whose size and significance match those of the wars themselves. Historians of Britain's First World War have noted how the output of the 'war poets' has had a distorting effect on subsequent understandings of the broader impact of war on British society because of the war poets' garrulity, but also because the literary merits of Siegfried Sassoon, Wilfred Owen, Edmund Blunden, *et al.* have preserved their works down the years, whereas lesser writers have faded from memory.[1] There is a similar situation in Serbia: a cadre of glittering literary talents—poets, novelists, memoirists—have largely defined the story of Serbia's war. Indeed, some of the finest poetry and modernist art of the interwar period took as a theme the wars of 1912 to 1918.[2] But beneath these rarefied

[1] See Rosa Maria Bracco, *Merchants of Hope: British Middlebrow Writers and the First World War, 1919–1939* (Providence, RI, 1993).
[2] e.g. the work of Miloš Crnjanski, Miroslav Krleža, Rastko Petrović, Stanislav Vinaver, and Dušan Vasiljev.

planes we have very little to go on: even diaries and letters, ego documents that abound in western Europe, are in short supply in the case of Serbia, to say nothing of published memoirs or literary outputs.

This, of course, does not entirely rule out the use of ego documents from research into Serbian history. In fact, it was the very disjunction between a literate and articulate minority and an apparently silent majority that moved people to talk about and record the war in interwar Yugoslavia. In the context of nineteenth-century Habsburg east central Europe, Pieter Judson has shown how 'nationalist activists' in imperial frontier lands were moved to action precisely through fear of the grass-roots 'indifference' of the larger population.[3] There is a similar phenomenon in territories with Orthodox Slav populations in the Habsburg and Ottoman Empires at the turn of the twentieth century: Serbian 'national workers', educated, literate, nationally conscious, expended much energy in 'unredeemed' lands such as Bosnia, Kosovo, and Macedonia precisely because they believed there was much work to be done towards the nationalization/Serbianization of these parts. These sentiments survived the ordeals of 1912 to 1918. Despite the 'liberation' of the lands in question and their incorporation in 1918 into the new South Slav state, the Kingdom of Serbs, Croats, and Slovenes, so-called 'national workers' remained an active presence in the interwar period. This was partially because of the sense that the national work begun in these territories at the beginning of the twentieth century was incomplete, that full 'nationalization' could not be achieved through military victory alone, but would need to be shored up also by cultural work, education, the building of infrastructure, and so on. Many of the ego documents of Serbia's wars are infused with this sense of an ongoing mission and of the longer trajectory of Serbia's national arc in the first decades of the twentieth century.

The creation of the South Slav state, and the state's political and social problems in the interwar period, brought new concerns and anxieties, however, because it diluted the purity of Serbia's national revolution. Veterans had to address the question of whether their war sacrifice and continuing activism were for the Serbian or the Yugoslav cause. In fact there had been a certain ambiguity on this

---

[3] Pieter M. Judson, *Guardians of the Nation: Activists on the Language Frontiers of Imperial Austria* (Cambridge, Mass., 2006).

matter since the middle of the nineteenth century, and this Serbian/ Yugoslav dilemma continued to cleave Serbian national identity in the interwar period.[4] The war compounded this divide. The Balkan Wars of 1912–13 were clearly waged for the advancement of the Serbian national revolution, which was reflected in the patriotic pronouncements and poetry of Serbian elites in the brief euphoria following the victories of 1912–13 (most notably in the poetry of Aleksa Šantić). But from almost the very beginning the First World War had been presented as a struggle (in the event successful) for the liberation and unification of all South Slav lands: that is, the final move not just in the emancipation of the Serbs themselves, but also in that of the Croats and Slovenes. An uneasy and restless relationship existed between these two planes in the interwar period, and as the years went by, the growing sense that the South Slav state was not consolidated and was, in fact, failing led to an increasing amount of soul-searching on the part of many former soldiers, men who were troubled by the amount of blood and treasure spent on a lost cause.

And like many other nations after 1918, the Serbs were haunted by the notion that a generation had been lost to the First World War, or, in the case of Serbia, lost to the Balkan Wars of 1912–13 and the First World War itself. So to the political and economic problems of Yugoslavia we could add an ever more pronounced sense of a generational gap dividing the 'wartime generation', those who had served or fought in the wars of 1912 to 1918, and a 'postwar generation' who came of age in its aftermath. This expanding chasm was also a source of anxiety for many who wrote about their experiences in war, for the coming of age of a new generation meant a cohort of men and women who had not experienced directly the trials of war itself, and had therefore not been animated by this pure sense of the Serbian nationalizing mission. This, too, raised the importance of continued cultural and national work, a sense that the values of the war needed to be asserted more vocally and insistently lest they be lost to a new generation of South Slavs who had grown up not knowing the war.

Thus, although the conflict ended in triumph, the terrible pity of

[4] On this see Mark Biondich, 'The Historical Legacy: The Evolution of Interwar Yugoslav Politics, 1918–1941', in Lenard J. Cohen and Jasna Dragović-Soso (eds.), *State Collapse in South-Eastern Europe: New Perspectives on Yugoslavia's Disintegration* (West Lafayette, Ind., 2008), 43–74.

it weighed heavily on the new state: the catastrophic loss of civilian and military life, the ordeals of occupation and invasion, the perilous flight of government, army, and civilian refugees across Albania in the winter of 1915, the so-called 'Golgotha' of the Serbian nation, followed by its 'resurrection' in the victory of September 1918. The South Slav state of the interwar period had much to live up to, for its failure threatened to invalidate the Serbian blood sacrifice of 1912 to 1918: the war years were a frame of reference for the successes and (more often) failures of the South Slav state during the interwar years. The sacrifice of the war years was a standard against which the postwar years of political and social crisis could be contrasted. Understandably, it was felt that the many tens of thousands of Serbian war veterans were most qualified to measure the new state against the war. Their frequent commentaries, in speech or writing, carried considerable authority.

These veterans did not constitute a single social caste, nor did they possess a unified political vision. But we can say of them, in broad terms, that they supported the integrity of the South Slav state, were great admirers of the crown and especially King Aleksandar Karadjordjević (r. 1921–34), but were fiercely critical of the country's political parties and the parliament. We could also say, in passing, that the veteran slant towards Aleksandar and against the parliament created a considerable 'authoritarian potential' which was fulfilled by the king with his royal dictatorship of 1929 that he would neither have dared nor been able to introduce without support from the army and war veterans.

Dragiša Vasić

There were but a few Serbian war veterans who bucked this trend towards patriotic statism and support for the crown in the interwar period. Dragiša Vasić (1885–1945), prominent Serbian author, journalist, and republican, was one such.

Vasić fits well the biographer's trite description of a 'man of contradictions'. He served in the Serbian army during the Balkan Wars and the First World War, demobilizing at war's end and entering civilian life as a lawyer in Belgrade, a city for which he had deeply ambivalent feelings. During the interwar period Vasić also turned his hand to journalism, editing the republican newspaper *Progress* and regularly contributing to the *Serbian Literary Herald*, one of Yugoslavia's leading literary journals that featured the works of the brightest of Yugoslav authors in the interwar period. Vasić was himself a talented and versatile author, essayist, novelist, and writer of short stories. His reputation, which is undergoing a minor renaissance in contemporary Serbia, is based primarily on his works about Serbia during the wars of 1912 to 1918, the most important of which are the long essay *The Character and Mentality of a Generation* (1919), a collection of short stories *The Glowing Lamps* (1922), and the novel *Red Fogs* (1922).[5]

In his own time, *bien pensant* intellectuals and the literati of Yugoslavia acknowledged Vasić as one of the country's most important 'war writers', an appellation that meant essentially an author who had served or fought in the war and whose literary output was marked by war themes. This was quite an honour. Many of the most important writers in the interwar kingdom, especially those from Serbia, had experienced war at first hand, and the war became a central theme in their prose, poetry, and dramaturgy in the 1920s and 1930s. Vasić managed to distinguish himself in a very large field. There were many such authors, but a quartet stands out: Vasić himself; Communist author Miroslav Krleža, author of a series of short stories dealing with the lot of Croats in the Habsburg army entitled *The Croatian God Mars* (1922); Serbian Fascist author, journalist, and film-maker Stanislav Krakov, responsible for the first feature-length film about Serbia's war, *For the Honour of the Fatherland* (1929); and Miloš Crnjanski, considered to be the father of Serbian modernism, author of the lyrical and dreamlike masterpiece *The Diary of Čarnojević* (1921). These were four talented and original artists and, tellingly, all had an abiding interest in politics, albeit of a maverick kind. This should not surprise us too greatly: maverick art and maverick politics often went hand in hand in postwar eastern Europe,[6] and the war itself was an inherently political theme.

Discussion of Vasić's political attitudes introduces the first of his many contradictions. A stalwart Serbian and Yugoslav patriot (the two did not necessarily rule each out immediately after the war), Vasić was also a vocal critic of the Karadjordjević dynasty and

---

[5] On Vasić's biography see Nikola B. Milovanović, *Dragiša Vasić: od Gradanskog buntovnika do kontrarevolutionara* (Belgrade, 1986).

[6] See e.g. Marci Shore, *Caviar and Ashes: A Warsaw Generation's Life and Death in Marxism, 1918–1968* (New Haven, 2006); Thomas Ort, *Art and Life in Modernist Prague: Karel Čapek and his Generation, 1911–1938* (New York, 2013).

the Belgrade regime, and especially the latter's military campaign against the Albanian uprising in the 'newly associated' territories in the south of the country (incorporating parts of what are today Kosovo and Montenegro). The 'uprising' and the regime's attempts at its 'pacification' scorched the south of the country immediately after the war (1918–20) and continued to smoulder thereafter until the mid 1920s. 'Pacification' efforts on the part of the army and government tended to enjoy the support and even participation of Serbian war veterans (especially those who had served in the anti-Ottoman guerrilla units, the 'Chetniks'). Many former soldiers saw the campaign against the Albanians as a continuation of the military struggle that began against the Turks with the First Balkan War (indeed, many war monuments in the south of the country were inscribed with the dates 1912–1920, incorporating the Balkan Wars and the postwar conflicts into the story of Serbia's First World War). King Petar and his son Crown Prince Aleksandar also held huge prestige for war veterans as the 'liberator' (Petar) and 'unifier' (Aleksandar) of the Serbs and the South Slavs.

Vasić had no such esteem for the crown. He was a vocal opponent of both the 'pacification' campaign and the crown itself, vividly expressing his outrage at the regime in his journal *Progress*. As editor of and contributor to *Progress*, Vasić railed against the corruption and misrule of the Belgrade government, often presenting a binary opposition between the sacred and selfless sacrifice of the soldiers during the war years (including, of course, his own) and the profane and egotistical behaviour of politicians since 1918. That, in fact, was the habit of many Serbian war authors in the interwar period. They tended to contrast the dignity of their own service in the wars of liberation and unification with the perceived squalor and corruption of politics. But Vasić took this to risky extremes. He also used the journal to polemicize against the violence of the army's campaign against the Albanian insurgency in the south of the country. In these volatile months immediately after the war, such open criticism was bound to be short-lived. *Progress* was one of many publications censored and eventually banned by the regime after a run of just a few months.

There are, in fact, straightforward explanations for Vasić's hostility. His political ideas were strongly influenced by Serbian socialist Dimitrije Tucović, the only prominent political figure in prewar Serbia who raised a voice against the dwarf imperialisms battling for supremacy in the Balkan Wars. Tucović hoped that instead of war and aggrandizement the Balkan peoples would find a solution that allowed them to live together in peace. He saw class and socio-economic factors where most others saw ethnicity and nationalism. Vasić was of the same mind. Importantly, and like Tucović himself (who had been a veteran of the Balkan Wars and had died fighting in the First World War), Vasić had served and fought in Serbia's wars of liberation and unification. This was an essential component of his oppositionist critique of the government, one that he never abandoned throughout the interwar period. The apparent contradiction of fighting for the Serbian government and army and simultaneously railing against its abuses in reality reflected two parts of the same polemical move. Vasić's criticism carried weight not *in spite of* but *because of* the fact that he had played his role in the sacrifice and resurrection of the Serbian nation in the war years. The voice of the war veteran carried considerable authority in the interwar kingdom, and it must be taken into account when reading all of Vasić's journalistic and literary output. This was the self as warrior, as higher authority than the civilian leaders of the country, and as an equal of the military's highest command.

As for opposition to the crown, Vasić was a prominent supporter (although not a member) of Unification or Death (known to its opponents as 'The Black Hand'), the Serbian militarist society whose members had played such a decisive role in Serbia's history since the beginning of the twentieth century. Unification or Death had suffered irrecoverable losses during the First World War, culminating in the rigged trial and execution of their leader, Dragutin Dimitrijević 'Apis', at Salonica in 1917 (Vasić's relative Ljubomir Vulović was also executed). The trial was the dynasty's and the wartime government's checkmate against Apis, a powerful and ambitious rival to their authority. After the war, the scattered remnants of Unification or Death nursed a deep grudge against the new regime and the crown.

This affiliation was also a feature of Vasić's writing, most directly in his book *Nineteen-Hundred-and-Three: Contributions for a History of Serbia from 8 July 1900 to 17 January 1907* (1925), a remarkable literary-historical account of the preparation, execution, and aftermath of the 1903 palace coup, which had been masterminded by Apis. In this work Vasić presents the coup as a defining episode in contemporary Serbian national history, an epic whose actors were raised to the level of archetype. Apis and the 'regicides' were like Furies dispatched to bring justice to a wayward and corrupt monarch. In the aftermath of the coup, Vasić told of the debasement of the regicides' 'ideals' by the new (and still present) rulers. Here, Vasić presents a wilier critique of the regime than his direct attacks in the *Progress* articles. Although making no direct mention of the rigged trial at Salonica, Vasić suggests that the death of Apis in 1917 was also the death of a crusading and vengeful military agent at the hands of a corrupt civilian class that, not incidentally, was still in power. The lessons for the present-day state were clear. In spite of its evident biases, *Nineteen-Hundred-and-Three* remains one of the best historical accounts of the Serbian palace coup.

There is, then, a peculiar tension in Vasić's biography, one that can be detected in his many writings of the interwar period, and especially those of the 1920s. Vasić is a veteran of Serbia's wars of liberation and unification who in many respects represents the conventional figure of a Serbian war hero, quite familiar in interwar Yugoslavia and much admired, too. But Vasić is also a Black Hander and a republican with socialist sympathies. What makes this author and public figure so unusual is that he combines these apparently antithetical positions, the war hero and patriot with the anti-monarchy, anti-regime dissenter. There are two Vasićs existing alongside each other, and there is considerable tension between them. Vasić's attempt to resolve this tension between his two social selves is what makes him and his work so compelling.

Two Months in Yugoslav Siberia

This tension can be further explored by looking at one of Vasić's early works, the political pamphlet *Two Months in Yugoslav Siberia* (1921). The provenance of this work is remarkable and deserves explanation at length. It went back to Vasić's writing in *Progress*. Vasić had crossed an important line in a series of articles in which he harshly criticized the approach of the minister of the army and the navy, Branko Jovanović, an attack that prompted the army and the government to take action against Vasić. It was not just a matter of defending the honour of the army and its officers, however. Jovanović, like all ministers of the army and the navy during the 1920s, was the crown's man, a member of Aleksandar's 'White Hand' faction that had helped bring about the demise of Apis and his supporters at Salonika in 1917. Men like Jovanović served as Aleksandar's praetorians in the 1920s; they brooked no challenges from Black Handers such as Vasić.

What happened to Vasić next speaks to the perverse and gratuitous behaviour that passed for retributive justice in 1920s Yugoslavia. Not only was *Progress* banned outright, but also, by way of punishment, Jovanović saw to it that Vasić was remobilized from the kingdom's reserve list and sent on a two-month military tour in the south of the country; sent, that is, straight into the eye of the insurgent storm. Perhaps it was hoped that Vasić would see for himself the important work being undertaken in the south; perhaps that Vasić would experience an epiphany and be converted from sideline critic to vocal supporter of the army and the government; or perhaps merely that Vasić would be killed in this dangerous assignment. None of these things happened. Vasić served out his two-month tour and then returned to Belgrade. Ever enterprising, he wrote a first-hand account of his service in the south, publishing it with the independent Jewish bookseller and publisher Geca Kon, in Novi Sad in 1921. This, then, is the story behind the book.

Two Months in Yugoslav Siberia is a remarkable literary achievement and an important 'ego document' of Serbia's war. But it would perhaps be reductive to start generalizing the writer's social selves and the discourses to which they belong without first acknowledging the work's originality and its literary merits. 'Yugoslav Siberia' was a much-used derogatory term for the 'southern regions' of the South Slav state (today's Kosovo and Macedonia, parts of Montenegro), a term used by soldiers and civil servants sent there, and often also by the press (including those parts of it loyal to the government and crown). It gave a sense of the wilderness and internal exile associated with these parts. But in the pamphlet the landscape and atmosphere of Yugoslav Siberia is entirely Vasić's own creation: wild and desolate, a terrain and peoples blasted bare by the war years. The history of war is ubiquitous, not just etched on the landscape itself but also in the experiences of the people that Vasić meets during his two-month tour. The author frequently soliloquizes on the nature of mortality and the fear and expectation of death in the wake of the mass killing seen here during the war (and after). Vasić gives his readers some remarkable images, including one in which the author dozes in a trench and imagines a vast army of anthropomorphic rats coming at him: an allusion to the waves of armies that have ravaged these parts over the years, and also to the columns of Yugoslav soldiers now active there.[7] There are the glimmerings here of a literary imagination that would make Vasić one of the most famous Serbian fiction writers of the interwar period.

Below the plane of high literature, the pamphlet is also very obviously an oppositionist's tirade against the government and its policies in Yugoslav Siberia. Vasić the republican polemicist is in evidence on every single page, and *Two Months in Yugoslav Siberia* can be usefully read alongside his earlier articles in *Progress*. The pamphlet picks up the same themes started in his journal: party political corruption, military blundering on the part of the army's top brass, excessive and self-defeating violence whose targets are always non-Serbs. Like Thucydides, Vasić uses the rhetorical device of enacting his own ideas and exposition by putting long speeches into the mouths of other 'characters'. The people he meets in *Two Months in Yugoslav Siberia* are given carefully blocked-out entrances and exits and well-rehearsed lines. Most representative of this technique is the functionary of the Ministry of Agrarian Reform who explains to Vasić at length the real motives behind the agrarian reform: simply to curry political favour and to gerrymander districts so that they return loyal party affiliates to Belgrade.[8] For Vasić this was a signal failure of the regime, since the agrarian reform and Belgrade's policies of internal colonization were supposed to serve as a means of rewarding the wartime sacrifice of the Serbian soldiers (who were entitled to tracts of land in the reform), not of earning political capital. Other people complain about various forms of political corruption practised by 'them above' (that is, in Belgrade), and the poor pay and equipment of the Yugoslav soldiers are contrasted with the caches of weapons used by the insurgents, a disparity attributed again to Belgrade corruption and to Italian meddling in the 'rebellion'.

Two Months in Yugoslav Siberia also belongs to the genre of opposition political polemic, and in this reading it is not different from other left-wing or socialist critiques published around the same time. These critiques are generally hostile to the royal government but evinced especial animosity for the army and the regime's attempts violently to quell the Albanian uprising. Vasić the gifted littérateur and Vasić the Serbian war hero disappear almost entirely from view

[7] Dragiša Vasić, *Dva meseca u jugoslovenskom Sibiru* (Novi Sad, 1921), 31.
[8] Ibid. 51.

at this level. He becomes just another of a small number of left-wing polemicists trying to provide the minority report against the elite census that says the government and army are doing the right thing in the south. He could even be any one of the contributors to his own journal *Progress*, who wrote in similar terms about the problems of the south.

What we do see at this level are the defining features of Vasić's socialism. Unlike nationalist authors, but very much like his mentor Tucović, Vasić is at pains to break down the ethnic contours of the battle in the south. He presents Albanian militias fighting *against* the Albanian uprising, introduces a sympathetically portrayed Turkish peasant who has lost much in the war and its outcome, and embarks on a lengthy and rather plaintive monologue about how he does not understand the general animosity felt by many of his countrymen against the 'Turks'.[9] It is thus also fascinating to approach *Two Months in Yugoslav Siberia* by way of the new scholarship of east central Europe and the Balkans that seeks to break down static notions about nationalism and national identity at grass-roots level and replace it with the 'indifference' of the broad masses, or the 'situational' factors that produce an alternative identity in these parts.[10] Vasić seems to testify to the existence of such factors here. But this is clearly the interested voice of Balkan socialism, whose proponents had long dreamt of a class-based, cross-ethnic alliance to break down the petty imperialisms of the various Balkan nation states (and would continue to dream in this way throughout much of the twentieth century).

And yet Vasić was not just another socialist pamphleteer taking shots at the government and the army. As we journey further into the text the tensions between the various authorial identities resurface. Vasić was also a patriot who believed in the ennobling effects of the Serbian sacrifice during wartime and of the honourable role played by Serbian soldiers in the period 1912 to 1918. On this point, the author was forced to confront the government's own line regarding the small war being fought against the rebellion: that is, that it was simply the continuation of the struggle for liberation and unification

[9] Ibid. 11–12.
[10] Judson, *Guardians of the Nation*. See also Tara Zahra, *Kidnapped Souls: National Indifference and the Battle for Children in the Bohemian Lands, 1900–1948* (Ithaca, NY, 2008); Florian Bieber and Erin K. Jenne, 'Situational Nationalism: Nation-Building in the Balkans, Subversive Institutions and the Montenegrin Paradox', *Ethnopolitics*, 13/5 (2014), 431–60.

that had begun with the Balkan Wars of 1912–13 and gone on without pause into the First World War. This was emphatically not Vasić's understanding of the government's post-1918 military campaign, and *Two Months in Yugoslav Siberia* is also an attempt to wrest the dignity of the Serbian wartime sacrifice back from the politicians and generals of the postwar period.

To this end, Vasić was able to use the tension between his two identities, the veteran patriot and the socialist dissenter, to good effect. He drew upon his own background as a veteran of the wars to refute the official line about the legitimacy of military action against the rebellion. In *Two Months in Yugoslav Siberia* Vasić continually reminds his reader that his experience as a soldier during the wars of 1912 to 1918 entitles him to speak authoritatively about the nature of the post-1918 action. In this way, Vasić the war hero bestows insight and authority upon Vasić the oppositionist, and dissent is alloyed with patriotism. The tension between Vasić's two social selves is thus resolved, albeit only temporarily.

Throughout the text, Vasić's war experiences are brought to bear upon the present and grave situation in the south of the country. This begins in the preface of the book, a poignant dedication to a 'Celestial Brother'—an unnamed comrade of Vasić's killed during the war. Vasić's loyalties lie with the fallen; they are the true heroes of liberation and unification, not the politicians and top brass of the postwar period. Later in the text, on learning of his punishment tour of Yugoslav Siberia, Vasić scoffs that the real punishment would be to stay in civilian life: 'I'll admit that I felt really good. I'm someone who loves change. It seemed to me that the greatest punishment would be if I was made to stay in a regular job for a whole year.'[11] The contrast here is between the dignity of military life and the lassitude of its civilian counterpart, although Vasić also wonders why *he* should be sent south, he who knows the terrain so well (having served there during the war), and not one of the many civilians who had not fought during the preceding years, but who nevertheless clamour for military action now.[12] For Vasić there are both real and phoney patriots: the former, like him, actually fought; the latter merely called for others to fight.

The bonds Vasić forms with other soldiers are typically based upon a common experience of serving in the wars of 1912 to 1918. There is an immediate and intimate understanding between Vasić

[11] Vasić, *Dva meseca u jugoslovenskom Sibiru*, 5.   [12] Ibid. 6.

and his commanding officer in Bircana ('the centre of all Albanian conspiracies') because both men are veterans, and they both discern the contrast between the war they fought and the war being fought now.[13] This is in stark contrast to a group of raw recruits conscripted by the government who have not experienced combat before. Vasić treats them to a much-needed lecture on military hierarchy and discipline, something he learnt from his own experience in the wars of liberation and unification. To the uninitiated, the fresh conscripts and the civil servants and functionaries serving here, Yugoslav Siberia is just a political and career wilderness of malarial swamps and constant danger from Kaçak raids. Vasić sees much more than this—he remembers visiting these parts in 1913 (the Second Balkan War) and 1915 (the First World War, during the great retreat across Albania). Yugoslav Siberia is a historical palimpsest whose many layers depict a long history of war and violence, and national and imperial hubris. Again, this is the fusion of Vasić's two identities of war hero and political dissenter: the author can see the fatal flaws of the most recent military campaign only because he has experienced the previous conflicts.

Thus it was that Vasić turned the tables on the government and the army. Ingeniously, he used his considerable literary talents to transform a punitive military tour into a potent critique of the government's postwar military campaign, charging the country's political leaders and military top brass with betraying the finest traditions of the nation and the blood sacrifice of the war years, exposing the many instances of corruption and back-room dealing that undoubtedly marked the Serbian state-building project in these parts. And in turning the tables, Vasić also found a way to quiet his own restless and competing spirits. The veteran spoke on behalf of the political dissenter, his attacks on the government carried the weight of experience and therefore, also, authority.

Pressed into service by a government he hates and for a cause he does not believe in, Vasić finds a way to assert his ideas. The alloy of Vasić's various identities holds, I think, but it is a precarious one, and the tension between Vasić the patriot and Vasić the oppositionist is only alleviated temporarily, not fully resolved. This we see quite clearly in the final pages of the pamphlet when, having completed his tour of duty, the author returns to Belgrade and civilian life, to his job and his friends and family. He has mixed feelings about this.

[13] Ibid. 37–8.

Vasić is 'most alive' when in combat; civilian life seems spiritless by comparison. The war veteran is Vasić's most important social self, to which all others are subordinate.

Vasić in the European Context

Vasić had much in common not only with his fellow veterans in the South Slav state, but with those across Europe in the years immediately after the war. There were throughout the Continent a significant number of conspicuously active and productive veteran authors for whom the war and the experience of combat became a defining part of their identity and their writing. Ernst Jünger is the archetype of this kind of war writer, and while Vasić did not share Jünger's views about the spiritual and cathartic nature of combat experience, he certainly held that the military and the civilian spheres were hermetically sealed and separated from one another, and that the former, with its pure sense of sacrifice, should be elevated above the latter. These attitudes continued to loom over postwar Europe in the interwar period—the experience of war as one that should inform the nature of the peace that would hold civilian leaders to account. In this sense Vasić was one of many.

Perhaps, also, class and educational background made Vasić typical of a certain kind of author in interwar Europe. Vasić was, after all, an educated member of the bourgeoisie, still a small minority in Serbia on the eve of the war. Indeed, Vasić's political and public engagements preceded his combat experience; the war galvanized and shaped his attitudes, but it did not create them. From this angle, Vasić is perhaps more typical of the 'vanguard' nationalist elites of the Balkans and east central Europe in the nineteenth and early twentieth centuries, someone who sees himself as a guiding hand that will lead the masses out of empire and into national emancipation. This, too, compelled Vasić to write and to continue writing throughout his lifetime, and it informs much of his literary and journalistic output.

Shifting Planes: Vasić in the 1930s

Vasić continued to grapple with his two selves, the patriot and the dissenter, throughout the interwar period. But it seems that in these years the former calcified, while the latter withered away. As the

1920s wore on Vasić became gradually estranged from his left-wing friends and colleagues. The 1930s saw him ever more concerned about the fate of Serbs in the South Slav state and the fate of Yugoslavia in a Fascist Europe. Both of these concerns spoke more urgently to the patriotic war veteran in Vasić than to the critical intellectual. At the end of the 1930s he became vice-president of the Serbian Cultural Club, a nationalist association committed to upholding what they saw as the Serbian national interest in Yugoslavia, supposedly trammelled by the country's other national groups. The patriot in Vasić was by this stage ascendant.

Vasić, an experienced journalist and polemicist, edited the club's journal *The Serbian Voice*; his articles on the need for Serbian nationalist mobilization are difficult to reconcile with the fulminating critic of the government and army who wrote for *Progress* and who penned *Two Months in Yugoslav Siberia*. Indeed, it is worth comparing the firebrand criticisms of government and ethnic violence written by the young Vasić with his no less vocal and aggressive calls for Serbian unity in the face of domestic and foreign adversaries in the late 1930s. It is like reading two completely different writers, two entirely detached social selves. How to account for this startling transition? We could see this through the lens of generational history, an undoubtedly important and still neglected area of research with regard to veterans of the First World War. Vasić was no longer a young man at the end of the interwar period, and there is a discernible shift towards conservatism and nationalist chauvinism amongst many of his fellow veterans of 1912 to 1918. Perhaps, as Milovan Djilas, the Montenegrin Communist and former ally of Vasić, remarked, he had merely 'lost his fire'.[14]

Perhaps, but if we accept that Vasić's 'self' was defined 'socially', then we could posit instead that the transformations in the South Slav state and in Europe in the twenty years since the end of the First World War were also dramatic and far-reaching, and that these may have impacted on Vasić's ideas. But at the end of the 1930s there seems to have been a consensus throughout the country that the Yugoslav project was failing. Ironically, this was one of the few areas in which South Slavs of all ethnicities were united. The country had lurched from one political crisis to another, from democracy to dictatorship, back to partial democracy. To these political crises we can add acute agrarian depression and economic

[14] Milovan Djilas, *Wartime* (New York, 1977), 252.

paralysis, terrorism, violence, assassination (including that of the king himself, in 1934). This played back to the ambivalence in Serbia between Yugoslav and Serbian national causes; not only was the former failing, it also seemed to be damaging the latter. This was not a problem men like Vasić would have had to confront in the years before the unification. The social frame of reference therefore needs to be considered alongside the personal shifts in Vasić's politics and ideas as inseparable. And the objective problems that Yugoslavia faced undoubtedly also shaped Vasić's thinking.

Finally, there is the international context and its bearing on the legacy of the war, highly important factors in the 'successor states' of central and eastern Europe. For Serbian veterans such as Vasić, much more than their French and British counterparts, an important legacy of the war, one of the causes for which they fought, was the protection of the Versailles settlement. The war was worthwhile because it resulted in the creation of new nation states, in this case Yugoslavia, but there were also Czech Legionaries who saw the First Czechoslovak Republic as the prize for their blood sacrifice, and there were similar figures in Poland and Romania, 'victor states' of the First World War. As the forces of revisionism became more vocal and stronger in the 1930s (especially after the Nazi seizure of power in 1933), so the notion that the territorial and national gains of the war were now in jeopardy became ever stronger. For men like Vasić, the canary in the cage was the annexation of the Sudetenland from Czechoslovakia by Germany at the end of 1938, a shocking example of the sacrifice of a 'victor state' of the First World War and therefore a betrayal of the values of the war itself. When, less than a year later, the appeasing leaders of Yugoslavia reorganized the state to allow for large-scale autonomy in the Croat lands, Vasić saw this as part of the same trend, declaring it the 'Serbian Munich'.[15] This, too, hardened his attitudes for the future.

Conclusion

Another biographer's bromide: nothing in Vasić's life became him quite like the leaving of it. In 1941, with Yugoslavia invaded by Axis forces and divided between them, Vasić remobilized into the ranks of Dragoljub 'Draža' Mihailović's Chetniks, the Serbian nationalist and royalist (!) resistance movement. He was for a time one of

---

[15] Cited in Branko Petranović, *Istorija Jugoslavije 1918–1988* (Belgrade, 1981), 148.

Mihailović's leading ideologues, responsible for drawing up the blueprint for a 'Greater Serbia' whose creation depended upon the 'ethnic cleansing' of non-Serbs in parts of Bosnia and Croatia. The socialists' calls for cross-ethnic alliances are not at all evident here. The world had changed and so had Vasić: from a leftist and maverick patriot to a nationalist zealot. There would be no chances for further transformation. Vasić was captured and executed by the Croat Fascists, the Ustashe, in Bosnia, in 1945, and little mourned by the Partisans, who took power in Yugoslavia after the war.

Had the struggle between Vasić's two social selves decisively played out in these last days? Fascinatingly, Milovan Djilas, the Montenegrin Communist and later party dissenter, who had known Vasić in his leftist days, wondered if, after all, the lapsed republican had exerted a moderating and progressive influence on the chauvinism of the Chetniks. Djilas wondered whether Vasić had not actually tried to rein in the nationalist excesses of Mihailović's brutal lieutenants.[16] It could be that Vasić is an important key to understanding the ideological programme and strategies of the Chetniks during the Second World War. It could also be that Vasić's various selves continued to grapple in him until the very end.

Veterans who had fought in the period 1912 to 1918 were a great presence in the interwar state. Although they did not constitute a single social caste or present a unified political vision, when they spoke or wrote about the war they were presumed to do so with an authority that civilian commentators lacked. They also had a reciprocal bond with the South Slav state, for which they had fought during the wars of liberation and unification. This meant that the state owed them a return on their blood sacrifice, to be paid out in social welfare, land, or more generally effective and good governance (on the part of the political class). Veterans, in turn, maintained vigilance over the state, which they had won in war and handed over to civilian leaders only on the understanding that they should govern effectively—or else. Warriors once, warriors always, Serbian veterans were ever ready to defend the state, even, if necessary, from its own leaders. Many of their ego documents carried this admonitory charge: it was we who shed blood for this state; it is you who must respect our values. Vasić was part of this *soi-disant* generation. He, too, carried the authority of experience on account of his service during the war years.

[16] Djilas, *Wartime*, 252.

14

The Apotheosis of the Unknown Soldier: Officers, Soldiers, and the Writing of the Great War in Russia

JOSHUA SANBORN

In the wake of the devastation of the Great War, governments and publics in western Europe built large stone cenotaphs to honour the fallen and constructed Tombs of the Unknown Soldier.[1] Why? At face value, these monuments served to represent all those who had perished without a trace and thus became an important component of a postwar necrology that had initially focused on the proper burial and recognition of corpses.[2] They served as sites for mass remembrance, by nearly all accounts powerfully so. The Cenotaph in Whitehall, originally planned as a temporary monument, drew one million people at the first Remembrance Day and inspired politicians to commission Sir Edwin Lutyens to design the stone tower that stands there today. As Jay Winter comments, 'Its simplicity and ecumenical character gave it its appeal. By saying so little, it said much about the moment of exhaustion and mourning which coincided with victory. By moving to pre-Christian notation, it announced that the imperial nation was honoring men who were not only Protestant and Catholic, but Muslim, Hindu, or Jewish—or who had no religion at all.'[3] More cynically, some contemporaries saw in the creation of these monuments a search for tourist cash, a search that served only to demonstrate the trivialization of the war and the rottenness of the capitalist system.[4]

But these tombs served a discursive purpose as well: they estab-

[1] George L. Mosse, *Fallen Soldiers: Reshaping the Memory of the World Wars* (New York, 1990), 93–8.
[2] David Crane, *Empires of the Dead: How One Man's Vision Led to the Creation of WWI's War Graves* (London, 2013).
[3] Jay Winter, *Remembering War: The Great War between Memory and History in the Twentieth Century* (New Haven, 2006), 142.
[4] Karen Petrone, *The Great War in Russian Memory* (Bloomington, Ind., 2011), 12.

lished once and for all that the regular 'soldier' had become the 'pure signifier' in the ideological field of the war. They had become, in a literally concrete way, the 'signifier without the signified', the 'element through which the signifier's non-sense erupts in the midst of Meaning—is perceived as a point of extreme saturation of Meaning, as the point which "gives meaning" to all the others and thus totalizes the field of (ideological) meaning'.[5] Put in a slightly less Continental way by Hew Strachan:

> Today Remembrance Sunday embraces not only every subsequent war in which Britain has been engaged but also more general reflections on war itself, and on its cost in blood and suffering. The annual service at the Cenotaph in Whitehall is therefore deeply paradoxical. A ceremony weighted with nationalism, attended by the Queen and orchestrated as a military parade, bemoans wars fought in the nation's name.[6]

The Cenotaph totalizes the field of meaning because it provides an 'empty' soldier and an 'empty' war, devoid of specificity but 'saturated with meaning'. All those who genuflect before the tomb— the Queen, the military, mourning families, pacifists, and Fascists alike—may enter that field of meaning once they have acknowledged the sanctity of the Soldier at the heart of the symbolic system. We can recognize this veneration of the simple infantryman as part of the ideology of war in twentieth-century Europe and North America, one that underpins demotic (if not always democratic) nationalism and promotes the constant militarization of societies even as statesmen and civilians avow their peace-loving nature.

What about societies that did not build cenotaphs or tombs of unknown soldiers? In Russia, for instance, no such monuments were built. Military graveyards were consecrated both at the front and in cities in the rear during the Great War, but they named the soldiers lying under the crosses and stones. There are many reasons for the Soviet Union's refusal to participate in the pan-European trend of empty tombs even as Russia and the Soviet Union shared the ideology of the (militarized) nation.[7] Russia's exit from the war was extended and ambiguous, and the priorities of designing public space shifted in the postwar period. Above all, the

---

[5] Slavoj Žižek, *The Sublime Object of Ideology* (London, 1989), 99.
[6] Hew Strachan, *The First World War* (London, 2003), p. xvi.
[7] For more on 'national' and militarized ideologies in the Russian and Soviet cases see Joshua Sanborn, *Drafting the Russian Nation: Military Conscription, Total War, and Mass Politics, 1905–1925* (DeKalb, Ill., 2003).

Revolution became the Ur-event that required a master signifier. Despite the centrality of the Revolution, however, the Great War was too extensive an experience and too great a trauma completely to resist representation and narration (and thus ideological aspects as well), a fact that Karen Petrone has demonstrated with clarity and vigour. Petrone investigated the literature of the interwar Soviet Union (especially fiction) and argued that throughout the 1920s and 1930s 'World War I was decentered rather than forgotten'.[8] Looking for particular themes rather than titles allowed her to trace the effect of the war on spirituality, gender, violence, and national identity and to show the profound impact of the conflict upon Russian and Soviet culture, an impact that mirrored the experience of western European belligerents in many ways. Still, as Petrone also argued, the Revolution always took precedence in the public culture of the Soviet Union, and this made the Soviet memory of the war unique within the European context.[9]

Even beyond the Revolution, the Russian case proved different. In France, at least a thousand published authors participated in the war, many of them enlisted men.[10] British and German reading publics also had no difficulty finding and reading accounts written by subalterns. This multirank participation in creating the written testimony of the war was important. As Leonard Smith has argued, '[i]n the Great War, the linchpin of authorship was firsthand experience in the war of the trenches, and the text the meeting place between that experience and the rest of society. To narrate that experience was to represent a coherent identity that has had that experience and that can properly discern its meaning.'[11] General Haig could not dominate the discursive field of the war's meaning at the expense of the men who lived in the trenches, in large part because they wrote so much about themselves and their own experiences of the war. Indeed, by the end of the process, Haig could not get a word in edgeways, with corresponding results for his reputation. The authors of war narratives mattered, not just culturally but politically. In the spirit of Petrone's excavation of the history of Russia's participation in a pan-European discourse of the war, I would like here to ask whether the simple 'soldier' served as the master signifier for Russia's

---

[8] Petrone, *The Great War in Russian Memory*, 8.
[9] Ibid. 292.
[10] Leonard V. Smith, *The Embattled Self: French Soldiers' Testimony of the Great War* (Ithaca, NY, 2007), [11] Ibid. 16.

ideological discourse on the war as well, to search, as it were, for Russia's hidden Tomb of the Unknown Soldier.

This tomb did exist, but it was found on paper rather than stone—in the many accounts of the war written by Russian army officers, narratives which relied on the figure of the 'soldier' who was to all intents and purposes 'unknown' to his military superiors. Instead of a solid foundation of accounts from combat soldiers, the narrow and shallow edifice of officer war narratives has at its base the proclamations, reminiscences, and historical analyses written by commanders who claimed to know their men, to love their men, and to speak for them. At the base of this foundation, supporting nearly the entire weight of the enormous stack of secondary works, are a mere handful of books. Pick up a work that examines the Eastern Front in any detail, and you will find them listed there: Nikolai Golovin, Aleksei Brusilov, perhaps Andrei Lobanov-Rostovsky.[12] More frequently still, you will see Alfred Knox, the British military attaché, who is cited repeatedly as an expert on the thoughts and beliefs of Russian enlisted men.[13] If you read Russian, add just a handful more—Iurii Danilov maybe, or Mikhail Lemke.[14] These men told the story of the Russian Great War for us, sometimes well. They did a less effective job, however, in describing the nature of Russian soldier subjectivity. My goal in this essay is therefore twofold. First, I want to describe how *officer* ego documents have come to substitute for *soldier* ego documents in the writing of the war, and how those accounts came to have such importance for our understanding of the conflict and the revolution that succeeded it. Second, I want to think about this process not as an act of speaking for a 'silent' majority but as an act of suppression. In order to sustain their own narrative of the war, officers had not only to represent their men in a particular way, but also to preclude enlisted men from offering their own narratives.

None of this is to suggest that the Russian officer corps was uniform in outlook during the Great War, whether on the question of 'peasant' outlooks, on the question of the meaning of the war, or, more

[12] N[ikolai] N[ikolaevich] Golovin, *The Russian Army in the World War* (New Haven, 1931); A[leksei] A[lekseevich] Brusilov, *A Soldier's Note-Book, 1914–1918* (Westport, Conn., 1971); Andrei Lobanov-Rostovsky, *The Grinding Mill: Reminiscences of War and Revolution in Russia, 1913–1920* (New York, 1935).

[13] Alfred William Fortescue Knox, *With the Russian Army, 1914–1917*, 2 vols. (London, 1921).

[14] Iu. N. Danilov, *Na puti k krusheniiu: ocherki iz poslednego perioda russkoi monarkhii* (Moscow, 1992); M. K. Lemke, *250 dnei v tsarskoi stavke (25 Sent. 1915–2 Iiulia 1916)* (Petersburg, 1920).

generally, in their political outlook. The unusually sharp schism between various types of officer can be explained in part by imperial Russia's recruiting system and the pressure that widespread illiteracy placed upon it. Ever since the institution of 'universal' conscription in 1874, military reformers had sought to develop mass education in an effort to modernize the civic base from which they drew their soldiers and officers. The main incentive, ironically, was to excuse teachers and other educated draft-aged men from peacetime service by enrolling them directly into the reserves as junior officers, thereby not only giving a much-appreciated deferment to well-connected but non-belligerent elites, but also providing concrete reasons for Russians lower down the social scale to attend to their education while they were young. As with much of the rest of the educated elite in Russia, the men ultimately excused from basic training and three years in the barracks were more likely to hold oppositionist views. In contrast, those who chose to volunteer for officer careers were frequently criticized for being indifferent to books and advanced training of any kind. The concerted effort of reformers prior to the war to make officers more intellectual and intellectuals more patriotic did not substantially change this situation, even in places like the General Staff Academy, where book learning and tactical training ought to have formed the core experience for students. Pedagogy was problematic in these officer training programmes. As John Steinberg has noted, the Academy was plagued by 'boring and irrelevant lectures, accompanied by cumbersome and insufferable textbooks'.[15] As a result, when members of the intelligentsia were rapidly mobilized in 1914, they joined an officer corps dominated by politically conservative careerists with little interest in the life of the mind.

Just as there was variety among officers, so too was there variety among officer ego documents. Still, most fall into one of two categories: the 'aristocratic' and the 'progressive'. Aleksei Brusilov's memoirs fit into the first category. Brusilov was a rare individual. He was both famous (as a result of his offensive in 1916) and accessible (since his memoirs were published both in the Soviet Union and, in English, abroad). As a result, he became the centrepiece of many popular treatments of Russia's war effort, most notably Orlando Figes's *A People's Tragedy*.[16] Nevertheless, we can wonder how

---

[15] John W. Steinberg, *All the Tsar's Men: Russia's General Staff and the Fate of the Empire, 1898–1914* (Washington, 2010), 58.
[16] Orlando Figes, *A People's Tragedy: The Russian Revolution, 1891–1924* (London, 1996).

often and how perceptively Brusilov communicated with the enlisted men under his command. Here is his account of one line of that conversation:

> Time after time I asked my men in the trenches why we were at war; the invariable senseless answer was that a certain Archduke and his wife had been murdered and that consequently the Austrians had tried to humiliate the Serbians. Practically no one knew who these Serbians were; they were equally doubtful as to what Slav was. Why Germany should want to make war on us because of these Serbians, no one could say. The result was that the men were led like sheep to the slaughter without knowing why . . .[17]

Brusilov's opinion of the qualities of his men did not improve with time. On the contrary, he moaned that as time went on, 'the reserve troops became worse and worse, not only in the matter of military training, but morally and politically'.[18] It was only as a mass that Brusilov praised 'the men' or 'the Army', and then only to the extent that they obeyed his orders. 'I knew that one could ask anything of the Army', he commented near the end of his memoirs, 'and that the Army would willingly do anything it was asked, provided it was well clothed in cold weather and well fed.'[19] Sheep indeed.

Brusilov never shed the proud and haughty stance of the Russian lord he was, and he must be counted as among the *most* progressive of the aristocrats at the top of Russia's hierarchy.[20] The aristocratic ethos and patterns of authority dating back to the days of serf ownership remained strong throughout the army. Another popular officer memoir, written by Prince Andrei Lobanov-Rostovsky, shows this attitude in stark, even comic, relief. Lobanov-Rostovsky's book, again popular because it is in English, begins as follows: 'The spring of 1913 found me in Nice with a difficult problem to solve: should I carry on my studies or do my military service?'[21] Again we might wonder whether he is capable of understanding the very different lives of his men, but he does not show any doubt in the matter. Instead, he pontificates boldly on peasant attitudes. As with Brusilov, enlisted men are not individuals, they are 'the men'. 'The soldiers' attitudes to the officers were interesting', he wrote. 'They divided

---

[17] Brusilov, *A Soldier's Note-Book*, 37. [18] Ibid. 77.
[19] Ibid. 263.
[20] Brusilov 'came from an old Russian noble family with a long tradition of military service. One of his ancestors in the eighteenth century had distinguished himself in the battle for the Ukraine against the Poles' (Figes, *A People's Tragedy*, 59).
[21] Lobanov-Rostovsky, *The Grinding Mill*, 3.

them into three classes: those officers who were loved, those who were not disliked, and those who were hated.'[22] Unfortunately, this empty analysis is all he can really muster. The memoir is much more telling in what it only glimpses.[23] In the early days of the war, Lobanov-Rostovsky witnessed the court martial of a soldier who, while drunk, had struck an adjutant and was sentenced to death:

> During the whole evening we could see the unfortunate man, in a fit of frenzy, pleading for pardon. The execution took place on the same spot that night. A crowd of soldiers from his regiment assembled, and their mood was such that I thought at any moment we would face a mutiny. However, after a few cries of 'Pardon' were heard in the dark the men finally returned quietly to their tents.[24]

It is hard to create a better image of the gulf between officer consciousness and that of the individuals in the lower ranks than this one of futile cries of 'pardon' ringing through the dark to no avail.

The next year found Lobanov-Rostovsky in the midst of Russia's most significant wartime disaster. In the spring of 1915, a joint German–Habsburg force achieved a major breakthrough in the Russian lines just north of the Carpathian Mountains. The assault forced Russian troops to withdraw along their entire South-Western Front, and another massive attack in the summer in Russian Poland sent Russian soldiers (and Ukrainian and Polish civilians) into a panicked flight that became known as the 'Great Retreat'. It was only at this point, a year into the war and Lobanov-Rostovsky's memoirs, that an enlisted man is mentioned by name. This was Lobanov-Rostovsky's 'faithful batman Anton', and he is mentioned largely to show the prince's views on a 'peasant's love of order and an equal contempt for books'. For Lobanov-Rostovsky, in the midst of the Great Retreat, had stepped into a bookshop in Warsaw as the shells were flying, and had picked up some French novels and some 'bulky' historical tomes. 'Anton particularly disliked the three volumes of "Napoleon and Alexander I" by Vandal and used to pack them in such a way that they might drop out. I had to keep a close watch to see that the books were there.'[25] Even book-loving historians might have a twinge of sympathy for Anton's position here, as he was the one who had to trudge across Poland humping Vandal's history under

---

[22] Ibid. 9.
[23] Lobanov-Rostovsky is far from the only example. See e.g. Vladimir S. Littauer, *Russian Hussar* (London, 1965).
[24] Lobanov-Rostovsky, *The Grinding Mill*, 28.   [25] Ibid. 115–16.

the critical eye of his prince. Lobanov-Rostovsky, however, displayed no inclination to understand Anton's resistance as anything other than 'contempt for books'.

Nikolai Golovin would at least have recognized the problem in Lobanov-Rostovsky's interactions with Anton. Before the war, Golovin had been a leading member of the 'Young Turks' in the Russian General Staff. The Young Turks had espoused the position that Russia had to transform its political, social, and educational system substantially and rapidly if it wished to create the modern citizens necessary to win total wars.[26] They had been defeated as a group, but they remained important figures in the officer corps during the war. We can reasonably see him as a 'progressive': he wanted to modernize Russia through conscious government and civic initiatives designed to maximize the potential and well-being of ordinary citizens, and he was aware of many of the ways in which the legacies of autocracy and serfdom obstructed the fulfilment of this vision. 'Progressives' were an important part of prewar Russian politics and society, and their importance only increased over the course of the war.[27]

Golovin was critical of the aristocratic notion that peasant soldiers were ignorant and unpatriotic, taking General Iurii Danilov to task for his account of soldiers proclaiming that 'We are of Vyatka, or Tula, or Perm. The Germans won't come to our province.'[28] Golovin objected that '[i]t must not be forgotten that such words were not heard until after three years of bloody endeavors to win the War, and not before the Revolution had overthrown the Government'.[29] Still, Golovin was not quite ready to grant the soldiers a Western subjectivity. Their patriotism was a 'ritual' that 'unquestionably grew out of the bond that bound the Russian people to the Orient' and was 'of a primitive sort'.[30] The whole point of the progressive movement was that the Russian people had to be transformed in order to become modern, and their postwar criticism was that this process was thwarted before the war and helped to account for Russia's

[26] Sanborn, *Drafting the Russian Nation*.

[27] See esp. chs. 3 and 4 of Joshua A. Sanborn, *Imperial Apocalypse: The Great War and the Destruction of the Russian Empire* (Oxford, 2014). For a recent thoughtful discussion of the emergence of 'progressivism' in Russia see Ilya V. Gerasimov, 'What Russian Progressives Expected from the War', in Eric Lohr, Vera Tolz, and Alexander Semyonov (eds.), *Russia's Great War and Revolution, 1914–1922: The Empire* (Bloomington, Ind., 2014), 189–216.

[28] Golovin, *The Russian Army*, 205. Danilov's statement subsequently found its way into many later histories of the war.   [29] Ibid.

[30] Ibid. 206–7.

terrible loss and its revolution. Interestingly, the source that Golovin cites most often when discussing Russian soldiers is Alfred Knox. We should pause here to contemplate this oddity. British authors on the war do not cite the pronouncements of Russian military attachés on the nature of the English soldier with reverence, and the fact that Golovin does so points again to the unusual level of suppression of soldier voices in the literature on Russia.

The best instances of progressive officers, however, are from those lower in the chain of command. Some of these men, such as Fedor Stepun and Viktor Shklovskii, ended up pursuing intellectual careers in emigration and took the time to write interesting and valuable accounts of the war.[31] I will use a somewhat rarer source as an example here, Boleslav Vevern's account of his years as an artillery battery commander, which he self-published in Paris in 1938 with an introduction from none other than Nikolai Golovin.[32] Vevern was very conscious of the processes that obscured the subjectivity and humanity of all the participants in the war:

At the present time there are no people and no horses: there are human and equine complements. And I am also not a person: I am the Commander of the battery. I should discard all the human feelings that trouble my mind and my soul. I should forget everything, how I lived, what I strove for, what distressed me, and what gladdened me.[33]

But Vevern consciously refused this 'mechanistic' striving for a goal, saying he could not see the men in his battery simply as weapons specialists, but had to understand them as men 'with all their human feelings and desires'.[34]

When Vevern considers the 'human complement' of his battery as a whole, however, he moves quickly from the flesh-and-blood men in front of him to the realm of idealistic fantasy:

It's an excellent human complement: from the Murom and Kostroma forests. From the 'Kerzhenetskii' forests, from the Volga, Shekena, and Kliazma rivers, from the places where the folk songs of mythic heroes [*bogatyry*] were composed, these men arrived, the descendants of those mythic heroes, bold,

---

[31] See e.g. Fedor Stepun, *Iz pisem praporshchika artillerista* (Prague, 1926); Fedor Stepun, *Byvshee i nesbyvsheesiaa*, 2 vols. (New York, 1956); Viktor Borisovich Shklovskii, *A Sentimental Journey: Memoirs, 1917–1922* (Ithaca, NY, 1970).

[32] B. V. Vevern, *Shestaia batareia, 1914–197 g.g.: povest' o vremeni velikago sluzheniia rodine* (Paris, 1938). [33] Ibid. 14.

[34] Ibid.

literate, powerful, and strong . . . They have an unshakeable faith in God, in Fate, and in Divine Providence.[35]

In front of Vevern stand not sheep, but representatives of The People, and with their ascension to this higher plane, the living individuals slip through our fingers again.

For all of these officers, there was tension between the modest amount they knew about soldier subjectivity and the authority with which they spoke of it. Why did they feel compelled to offer their interpretations at all? The answer is that the attitude of the run-of-the-mill peasant soldier was central to a range of questions that emerged prior to the war, became acute during it, and then dominated the postwar discussions about what went wrong (or right) in 1917. Were the modernizers or conservatives right about the urgent need to create educated and independent Russian citizens? Who was to blame for Russian military defeats? Why did the Revolution occur? For both the aristocratic and the progressive paternalists, there was a great deal at stake in the assertion that Russian soldiers were normally good material but that their primitive nature left them prone to indiscipline and unable fully to understand what was happening to them in the war. When they fought faithfully and fatalistically, they were the epitome of the Russian national character. When they lost faith because of political seduction or other reasons, they represented defeat and revolution. In sum, victories were due to officer skill and Russian character, while defeats were the result of political chicanery either from above (as with the explanation that the defeat at Tannenberg was the result of orders from the high command to satisfy the French with a precipitous assault) or below (through liberal or Bolshevik subversion).

This narrative depended on soldier silence, or at least on officers acting as constant interpreters of soldier voices. In a certain respect, this silence was not too hard to come by. The Russian army was not wholly illiterate, but it is true that soldier ego documents are rare and many are unrepresentative. Volumes written by literate enlisted men, such as Os'kin and Pireiko, are small in number, and they bear the imprint of the Bolshevik postwar narrative to greater or lesser degrees.[36]

Russian historians have, of course, been aware of this problem for

[35] Ibid. 15.
[36] William B. Edgerton, *Memoirs of Peasant Tolstoyans in Soviet Russia* (Bloomington, Ind., 1993); see also A. Pireiko, *V tylu i na fronte imperialisticheskoi voiny: vospominaniia*

some time, in particular as historiographical attention has increasingly concerned itself with the subaltern.[37] We have therefore turned to other sources to try to get to the heart of soldier subjectivity. The most popular of these in recent years have been the reports of Russian military censors. In contrast to other belligerent armies, which set up censorship offices only as the war progressed, a Russian army that had survived a period of mutiny less than a decade before (in the wake of the Russo-Japanese War) established offices and appointed censors even before the bullets began flying. By the end of the war, thirty-three censorship branches had read more than 40,000,000 pieces of mail. As Bill Rosenberg has recently argued, this was a censorship regime unusually interested in the 'mood' of its soldiers, so they included many concrete soldier testimonies about their thoughts and feelings at various stages of the war.[38]

I shall briefly describe these reports by using a very typical example from October 1916. The report was written by the Censorship Section of the Staff of the Eleventh Army and was sent to the Chief of the Military Censorship Section of the Staff of the Commander of Armies on the South-Western Front on 21 October 1916. As with nearly all of these reports, the captain in charge begins with a summary of the army's mood:

Judging by the letters in the ranks of the army, the mood continues to be positive [*bodryi*]; the spirit of attack awaits the opportunity to present itself, and the soldiers are fully conscious of their duty to defend the Tsar and Motherland. Apparently the trenches are sufficiently prepared for winter, and the inevitable inconveniences that have resulted from constant rain are being borne with a stoic submissiveness to fate.[39]

After thumbnail sketches of other key categories of interest (views on shell supply and inflation, for instance), the censor provides several

riadovogo (Leningrad, 1926); D. Os'kin, *Zapiski soldata* (Moscow, 1929); Richard Boleslavsky and Helen Rosen Woodward, *Way of the Lancer* (New York, 1932).

[37] A. B. Astashov, *Russkii front v 1914–nachale 1917 goda: voennyi opyt i sovremennost'* (Moscow, 2014); E. S. Seniavskaia, *Chelovek na voine: istoriko-psikhologicheskie ocherki* (Moscow, 1997); O. S. Porshneva, *Krestiane, rabochie i soldaty Rossii nakanune i v gody pervoi mirovoi voiny* (Moscow, 2004).

[38] William G. Rosenberg, 'Reading Soldiers' Moods: Russian Military Censorship and the Configuration of Feeling in World War I', *American Historical Review*, 119/3 (2014), 714–40, at 718–19.

[39] 'Svodka otchetov po tsenzure v chastiakh XI-I armii za period s 11–20 oktiabria 1916 g.', 21 Oct. 1916, Russian State Military History Archive (RGVIA) f. 2067, op. 1, d. 2937, ll. 7–10ᵒᵇ.

pages of excerpts from the letters, all classed under the same headings used in previous weeks: the 'mood' of the army, 'drunkenness', 'views of internal affairs and the government', and so forth. These excerpts supported the summaries provided by the censor. Thus, Semen Opanasiuk of the 417th Lugansk Infantry Regiment testified: 'We're doing OK, though the terrible weather is beginning to affect the mood . . . It rained all day yesterday, and today it got cold and snowed. It's muddy and wet everywhere. . . It's uncomfortable to sit in the trenches now, but nevertheless God is with us and we will defeat the enemy.'[40] Occasionally letters contravening the general summary were included, but overall the censor reports were carefully constructed documents intended to demonstrate the correctness of the censor's judgement. Since censors did best when they met the expectations of their superiors and reported a fighting mood and a fatalistic tolerance of unpleasantness and disaster among their peasant soldiers, their reports almost universally reinforced these cultural preconceptions, even in periods of devastating defeat and apparent demoralization, such as the Great Retreat in 1915.[41]

A very productive debate is now emerging about how historians should read this disjuncture, but the point I would like to make in this context is much simpler: no matter how we analyse this material, we must recognize that these censor reports reflect the ways in which the Russian army replaced soldier 'ego documents' (the letters) with carefully calibrated reinterpretations written by Russian staff officers. Soldier voices were literally censored and suppressed in order to convince not others (these were classified documents) but themselves of the nature of the Russian soldiers they commanded. It is this point that even some of the most diligent readers of these censor reports sometimes miss. A. B. Astashov, in his magisterial tome on the experience of the Russian Front, uses dozens of these reports. However, he starts from the premiss that Russian peasants were, almost by definition, unmodern, and he argues that the modernizing institutions that should have transformed them (such as the army) instead became 'peasantized'.[42] As a result, when he reads reports about 'peasant' attitudes, he attributes them to the soldiers rather than the censors.

I shall conclude by making two observations, one of them as summary, the other as epilogue. First, I shall return to the idea

[40] Ibid. 9.   [41] Rosenberg, 'Reading Soldiers' Moods', 728.
[42] Astashov, *Russkii front*, 52.

promised in the title about apotheosis. It is not simply that the figure of the Russian peasant soldier was interesting or important to those who wished to build narratives about the war—that figure was absolutely central. Whether one was a conservative or a progressive, the entire interpretation of the war effort depended on how the thoughts and actions of these mysterious cloaked men were read. They could be the alternately fatalistic and chaotic primitive men of conservative fantasy, or they could be the betrayed simple heroes of progressives, but they could never be allowed to speak for themselves, or all the narratives about both the war and to a larger extent even Russia might collapse. The tomb of these unknown soldiers had to be empty and silent for the narrative monuments to exist.

As an epilogue, we might note that through a twist of historical fate, these silenced soldiers were unexpectedly able to seize their moment on the historical stage in 1917. Golovin is right to warn that we should not automatically project the mindsets of that revolutionary year backwards into the earlier years of the war, but I think it is fair to consider what they said when they not only abetted but more or less drove the Revolution for most of its early months. What aristocrats such as Lobanov-Rostovsky saw as wild anarchy in fact had a very definite logic. Call us by name, they said. Treat us as individuals, as citizens, and as important voices regarding the advisability of continuing the war effort. They repeatedly rejected the claims of officers to speak for them and insisted on making their views known through soldier committees instead. They made a bid for their own subjectivity and ability to construct a new narrative. The fact that their former taskmasters and their new Bolshevik leaders took control of the narrative once more in the postwar period should not blind us to the fact that at the one juncture at which they were able to speak, they did so in a way that firmly rejected the pieties of conservatives, progressives, and Communists alike.[43]

[43] On this see esp. Allan K. Wildman, *The End of the Russian Imperial Army*, 2 vols. (Princeton, 1980).

15

'Emplotting the Witness': Henri Barbusse and Marc Bloch

LEONARD V. SMITH

In ego documents of the Great War, the linchpin of authorship was experience, above all the experience of the war of the trenches. In a sense, ego documents are of a piece, be they daily diaries, redacted reflections written days, months, or years after the fact, or even novels. In all of these texts, the author claimed in one way or another the authentic voice of experience. To represent experience is to represent a coherent identity that has had that experience. As Joan Scott put it, 'it is not individuals who have experience, but subjects who are constituted through experience'.[1] The text thus emplots the identity of the witness as well as the experience of that witness.

Experience makes sense through narrative, through the emplotment of events in time. Following Martin Heidegger on this point, Paul Ricœur argued against what he called 'the crude conception of time imagined as a succession of instants succeeding one another in an abstract line oriented in a single direction'.[2] Rather, time as experienced by everyday people exists as complex structures understood through language. Language structures narrative, which in turn structures time. Time and narrative are thus inseparable. To Ricœur, narrative figures as prominently as it does in literature and in history because time itself exists as a lived human experience largely through narrative.[3] Narrative requires a structure commonly referred to as the plot, which situates events as they unfold. The challenge of narrative, then, is emplotting the events of experience

---

[1] Joan W. Scott, 'The Evidence of Experience', *Critical Inquiry*, 19 (Summer 1991), 773–97, at 779.
[2] Paul Ricœur, 'La Fonction narrative et l'expérience humaine du temps', *Archivio de filosofia*, 80/1 (1980), 343–67, at 349.
[3] On this see Hayden White, 'Ricœur's Philosophy of History', in id., *The Content of the Form: Narrative Discourse and Historical Representation* (Baltimore, 1987), 169–84.

in such a way as to bring them under a structure of time, with a distinct relationship to past, present, and future.

The diary, assuredly the simplest form of memoir, might seem a transparent representation of 'crude time', in the sense of a succession of 'nows' structured by the clock or the calendar. But this chronological structuring of time swiftly proved an inadequate means through which to represent the experience of the war of the trenches. The most 'accurate' rendering of experience is not necessarily the most meaningful. Immediacy and narrative are fundamentally at odds with each other.

Combatants Henri Barbusse and Marc Bloch left ego documents comprising diaries and narrative accounts. At first, the decision to compare them might seem odd. Barbusse was the most famous left-wing writer of his day. He became a committed Communist after 1920, and remained so until his death in 1935. He remains best known as the author of *Le Feu* (*Under Fire*, 1916), to this day the best-selling French novel of the Great War. Marc Bloch achieved renown in two capacities, as one of the great medieval historians of the twentieth century, and as a Resistance hero in the Second World War, tortured and killed by the Gestapo in 1944. Literally to his last breath, Bloch saw himself as a citizen soldier of France—wholly assimilated into the Republic, yet aware and appreciative of his Jewish cultural origins.

The fragmentary yet fascinating diaries of Barbusse and Bloch would probably never have been published had their authors not achieved considerable stature for other reasons. Yet the existence of two peculiar yet invaluable sets of ego documents offers historians an exceptional opportunity to see how the most literal and immediate rendering of personal experience becomes narrative. Through considering the representation of time first in the diary and then in the published versions, we can understand how narration evolved differently from similar origins.

Committed socialist and author of the *Le Feu*, Henri Barbusse left two versions of a diary, both published well after his death. The first covered a period of five and a half months (1 August 1914 to 15 January 1915) in only nine printed pages. The following footnote gives the diary in its entirety from the mobilization to Barbusse's departure for the front lines.[4] Barbusse represented his experience

[4] 'Le Carnet de notes', published as a preface to *Lettres d'Henri Barbusse à sa femme* (Paris, 1937), p. v. Here is the diary: '*1 August 1914*.—Drum Aumont. Mobilization

simply by noting time and place, sometimes indicating day and time, sometimes simply date. Even his profound transition from civilian to soldier is marked by single words: 'mobilization', 'recruitment', and 'engagement'.

Why might Barbusse, already an established writer by August 1914, tell the story of his war in such a manner? Certainly, he was not uninterested in the details of daily life, or in the broader issues of the war. His letters to his wife recounted his time in Albi, compared his 1914 encounter with military life with his life as a conscript twenty years previously, and testified to his conviction that Germany would seek peace before its destruction by the Entente.[5] Like a medieval annalist, Barbusse recounted his war in a way that appeared haphazard, inconsistent, and above all elliptical.[6] Yet if medieval annals rested on the ultimate narrative conclusion of the Second Coming, which would transform time itself, Barbusse's diary too rested on a transformative event—his arrival at the front. Before then, he could demarcate his experience simply by measured time and geographical location. His arrival at the front recalibrated time, and required a different means of narration.

Medievalist and Resistance hero Marc Bloch kept a diary from the first to the last days of the Great War.[7] Bloch's diary began in a regular notebook rather than a personal calendar, in which he transcribed the dates in his own hand. At the beginning, Bloch's diary provided more detail than that of Barbusse, though nothing seemed to combine that detail into any kind of definite narrative. With equal emphasis and explanation (or rather non-explanation) Bloch noted data as diverse as the assassination of Jean Jaurès (1 August), the contents of his pockets (2 August), and a description of a corporal as a 'neurasthenic man of the world, not much of a warrior' (23 August).

Bloch's recounting of his war in the diary appeared to have been

4h1/2; *2 August.*—Return to Paris. Recruitment. Engagement; *14 August.*—First voyage to Melun; *19 August.*—Second voyage to Melun; *Thursday, 10 September.*—5 o'clock, convocation for Albi. I leave at 9 o'clock; *Saturday, 12 September.*—Arrival at Albi; *10 October.*—Hélyonne [his wife] in Albi. Home of Juéry; *Monday, 21 December.*—Departure from Albi with the 231st—5h. 3/4 in the evening.'

[5] *Lettres d'Henri Barbusse*, 15–20.

[6] I am indebted here to the analysis of medieval chronicles in Hayden White, 'The Value of Narrativity in the Representation of Reality', in *Content of the Form*, 1–25.

[7] Marc Bloch, *Écrits de guerre, 1914–1918*, ed. Étienne Bloch, introd. Stéphane Audoin-Rouzeau (Paris, 1997), 41–68.

written in close proximity to the experience described. When his unit reached the front, his writing switched from pen to pencil.[8] He seldom wrote in complete sentences. The longest single entry in the diary recounted Bloch's initiation into combat, on 9–10 September 1914. The details he provided are intriguing, reflective, and confused. The excerpt began with the balance sheet—the total casualties suffered by his company. He then recounted the chaos that followed, the noise, the slight wound he suffered and the wounding of Corporal Scalabre, the ensuing panic. Finally, he returned to some sort of 'present', his discovery of his near miss with death, his observation that the Germans had finally been silenced, his having slept on the ground, and his departure from the battlefield.

For all its detail, the entry is as problematic as the medieval annals, a genre of writing with which the young medievalist was surely already familiar.[9] Lacking here is not so much detail as a combination of that detail into a narrative, as Hayden White puts it, 'in which endings can be linked to beginnings to form a continuity within a difference'.[10] After 1916 Bloch's diary continued in a skeletal form until 30 November 1918. Why he reduced his diary simply to measured time and place, and why he continued to keep a diary in this form at all, are among the most intriguing aspects of his war writing.

The daily diary represents experience according to chronologically measured time, demarcated either by a printed agenda or by the combatant himself. The diary is thus 'authentic' in that it was written in close proximity to the experience described. As in

---

[8] Étienne Bloch confessed to considerable difficulty reading the portions written in pencil. Below appears about half of the entry, the broken grammar preserved from the original: '. . . the next day we will count 89 wounded, killed, or missing in the company; noise, artillery, fused; case shot like a swarm of wasps—episodes I leave and find again the section, Corporal Scalbre; I am lightly wounded and in dressing the wound Oriol caught a bullet in the leg, the section panics and the horses hauling the machine-guns; the trench with Samuel and the adjutant; the colonel and the last rush, lost! no contrary a bit less bad; the next morning I will find a hole like a point in my canteen, a tear on my greatcoat on the right at the shoulder, a bullet hole in my greatcoat between the two legs; night-time, the German machine-guns (finally!) are reduced to silence by our own we turn around in the forward direction last slope of the night; the wounded, the smell, sleeping on the ground, sardines; relieved toward morning, visit of the field ambulances' (ibid. 43).

[9] As Hayden White observed of the genre: 'There are too many loose ends—no plot in the offing—and this is frustrating, if not disturbing, to the modern reader's story expectations as well as his desire for specific information' ('Value of Narrativity', 8).

[10] White, 'The Question of Narrative in Contemporary Historical Theory', in *Content of the Form*, 26–57, at 52.

the case of Marc Bloch, the diary could also mark the exceptional experience of combat. But by definition, the diary cannot provide a narrative, at least not one that properly presents experience to the public sphere. It looks inward towards the author rather than outward. Diaries, at least as Barbusse and Bloch wrote them, are essentially private ego documents. They remain of interest primarily to their author and as artefacts, not unlike debris on the battlefield found by archaeologists. Something else is needed for experience emplotted in time to reach the public domain, a different and more clearly narrative ordering of temporality.

Narrative Practice and the Pubic Sphere

War authors could write for themselves, friends and family close to them, an academic or artistic elite, or the audience of mass-market publishing. The interplay among the individual and social requirements of narration helped to determine the genre within which the 'truth' of a given memoir would reside. Barbusse and Bloch left behind enough documentation to show that this interplay occurred. The result was two very different genres of war memoirs. For Barbusse, the 'true' emplotment of time, the witness, and his experience culminated in a novel, *Le Feu*. For Bloch, paradoxically, emplotting the meaning of his experience culminated in a return to medieval history.

The two diaries of Barbusse tell their own story of the evolution of his novel, which came to supersede the diary itself. Of the nine printed pages of the first diary, six and a half cover the time from 7 to 18 January 1915. This corresponded to Barbusse's first period of service in the front lines, in a dangerous sector in miserable weather.[11] As in the first part of the diary, Barbusse scrupulously noted dates and the movements of his unit, sometimes hour by hour. These writings also avoided the gruesome description for which Barbusse became best remembered. The first diary terminated without explanation on 29 June 1915 at 3h.

Barbusse began his second diary, a much longer work published as thirty-seven printed pages, on 14 October 1915.[12] Clearly, he intended the second diary to serve as the basis for a larger work. He

[11] Barbusse, 'Le Carnet de notes', pp. vi–xii.
[12] 'Carnet de guerre d'Henri Barbusse', annotated by Pierre Paraf as an annexe to *Le Feu* (Paris, 1965), 439–76.

noted only three dates (14 October, 15 October, and 2 November), though it is clear from internal evidence that he continued to write in the diary into the autumn of 1916, after *Le Feu* had begun to appear in serialized form in *L'Œuvre*, before its publication in a single volume in December 1916.

In this second diary Barbusse embarked upon the great narratological task of *Le Feu*, linking the experienced horrors of the Great War to ideological remobilization. For Barbusse, this meant transforming the conflict into a crusade leading to a world founded on deeply felt (if confused) international socialism. In his second diary Barbusse's personal time transformed into a time that was supposed to record change on a global scale. After November 1915 Barbusse renounced dates and specific locations, filling the diary with pieces of dialogue and with reflections on the meaning of the great struggle.

By the autumn of 1916, Barbusse was out of physical danger, serving as a staff secretary. His thoughts could turn to the literary world. In the second diary he began to give himself literary and political advice.[13] The 'realism' of *Le Feu* also has its origins in the second diary, in Barbusse's fascination with torn and putrefying flesh as the physical site where global change would originate.[14] The last sections of the second diary mark the transition to the novel. The final pages include a list of 'Great Books' and a list of prominent individuals to be sent a copy of *Le Feu*.[15] Like the first diary, the second terminated without an explicit conclusion. In this respect, it has similarities to a medieval chronicle, in which a

[13] On 2 November he advised himself: 'To deepen the tragic character of the banal side of the war. It is the more shameful, because the other, the danger, the apprehension of violent death, is not completely separate. All this is emphasized in the future' ('Carnet de guerre', 446). He continued to insist that Germany had been the aggressor: 'Never had we provoked Germany, never had we spoken of revenge or hoped to take back Alsace and Lorraine. Never did we show the least hatred, the least unkind [sentiment] towards the Germans' (ibid. 451).

[14] See e.g. the somewhat disordered entry for 15 October: 'One sees a face like that of Rameses II, which emerges from a torn sack, shrivelled underneath, the tibias, the femurs, the bones and the hands or the feet tightened up at the knuckles around suspect bulges. From the ends of fraying fabrics, coated with tar, emerge the fragments of a vertebral column. These are no longer cadavers, but jumbles of desiccated filth, which seem to have been dumped out with broken equipment, quarter-litre pitchers, crates for garbage' (ibid. 442).

[15] These included works as diverse as Shakespeare's *Hamlet* and *Romeo and Juliet*, Kant's *Critique of Pure Reason*, Zola's *Germinal* and *Les Paysans*, and Kipling's first and second *Jungle Books*, and many others. The prominent individuals included Paul Adam, General Paul Maistre, Roman Rolland, Albert Thomas, and Joseph Caillaux.

clear narrator recounts at least fragments of a story, but does not tie them together into a proper ending. Rather, as White argued, a chronicle terminates when the external conditions that initially brought forth the narrative change around it.[16] The second diary of Barbusse stopped by juxtaposing a penultimate list of chapters from the integral version of *Le Feu* with a paragraph on the silent soldier, for whom Barbusse wished his novel to speak.[17] A version of this paragraph could well have served as the dedication of *Le Feu*. The diary did not need a proper conclusion, or rather, the novel itself served as the conclusion by supplanting the diary, by bringing the experience sketched out there into the public domain.

At first, little would seem comparable in the war writings of Barbusse and Marc Bloch.[18] Paradoxically, Bloch expressed the 'truth' of his experience by returning to medieval history. He began to turn his diary into a proper memoir after his evacuation from the front in 1915 for typhoid fever. Bloch never made clear the public he envisaged for this memoir, whether himself, his close associates, or a future academic audience. Certainly, there was no way to know in 1915 that the future Resistance martyr would achieve such stature that his entire life would become a text of great historical interest.[19] His stated objective is both explicit and imprecise: to prove the exceptional character of his experience. He began his memoir by presenting his thesis, asserting the fragility and unreliability of human memory.

The version in the memoir of Bloch's initiation into combat imposed a sort of narrative order on the chaotic events by proving the thesis of the academic. He began with another frank confession

[16] See White, 'Value of Narrativity', 19–20.

[17] 'For those who hardly speak at all. At each moment, he seems to have decided to speak. But he decides not to. One senses what he is going to say, then he judges that it is not worth it, he chokes it back and keeps it. The mute witness to act as a foil to certain realities, better than to speak about it' (Barbusse, 'Carnet de guerre', 476).

[18] Before his death in 1944, Bloch had published only one article on the Great War: 'Réflexions d'un historien sur les fausses nouvelles de la guerre', *Revue de synthèse historique* (1921), reprinted in Bloch, *Écrits de guerre*, 169–84.

[19] 'I intend to use this respite to fix my recollections before their still fresh and vibrant colors fade. I shall not record everything; oblivion must have its share. Yet I do not want to abandon the five astonishing months through which I have just lived to the vagaries of my memory, which has tended in the past to make an injudicious selection, burdening itself with dull details while allowing entire scenes, any part of which would be precious, to disappear. The choice it has exercised so poorly I intend this time to control myself' (Marc Bloch, *Memoirs of War, 1914–1915*, trans. Carole Fink [from the 1969 French edn.] (Ithaca, NY, 1980), 77.

of *both* the precision *and* the narrative confusion of his own memory.[20] As in the diary, events themselves resist narration, the establishment of continuity within a difference. Fittingly for the work of a careful scholar, his plotline in the memoir followed more or less the same form that it took in the diary. But he provided the continuity through his thesis. The events of that day were exceptional because he witnessed and experienced great danger, and survived. Indeed, Bloch closed his story of this extraordinary day with a moral, which revolved around the ferocious joy he took in having lived, in having won for now the bet that combat soldiers placed with violence and death.[21] He established his authority as author by mildly scoffing at those who would disparage his satisfaction on the day after the battle. He alone could discern the meaning of his experience. But Bloch would shortly interrogate this claim of authority.

The gaps and peculiarities in the war writings of Bloch prove as revealing as the writings themselves. He ceased writing his souvenirs at the end of his sick leave, but began again about two years later, when his unit was stationed in Algeria. Part of his stated reason was simple boredom.[22] He wrote a few more pages and then stopped again without comment, never to begin his souvenirs again. But he continued to write in his skeletal diary, to the end of the war. The issue is certainly not that 'nothing happened' to Bloch or his regiment after the autumn of 1914.[23]

At stake here was nothing less than a reconceptualization of time,

[20] 'It is likely that as long as I live, at least if I do not become senile in my last days, I shall never forget the 10th of September 1914. Even so, my recollections of that day are not altogether precise. Above all they are poorly articulated, a discontinuous series of images, vivid in themselves but badly arranged like a reel of movie film that showed here and there large gaps and the unintended reversal of certain scenes' (ibid. 89).

[21] 'Despite so many painful sights, it does not seem to me that I was sad on that morning of September 11. Needless to say, I did not feel like laughing. I was serious, but my solemnity was without melancholy, as befitted a satisfied soul; and I believe that my comrades felt the same. I recall their faces, grave yet content. Content with what? Well, first content to be alive. It was not without a secret pleasure that I contemplated the large gash in my canteen, the three holes in my coat made by bullets that had not injured me, and my painful arm, which, on inspection, was still intact. On days after great carnage, except for particularly painful personal grief, life appears sweet. Let those who will condemn this self-centered pleasure. Such feelings are all the more solidly rooted in individuals who are ordinarily only half aware of their existence' (ibid. 94).

[22] 'For my part, I lead a quiet life in Constantine, comfortable though somewhat empty. The moment has come to call on the past to fill up the present' (ibid. 167).

[23] His regiment returned to France in May 1917, and rotated in and out of the front lines in more and less active sectors until the end of the war. See Carole Fink, *Marc Bloch: A Life in History* (Cambridge, 1989), ch. 4.

and Bloch's own statement on the structures of time that he did and did not consider himself qualified to narrate. Bloch came to reject the authority of the witness as arbiter of experience.[24] His earlier concern with the fragility and unreliability of memory had come to the forefront. In a private letter, Bloch made a crucial statement about time, itself wrapped up in an anguished statement of his confidence in an eventual French victory.[25] To Bloch, the basic structure of historical time was something the Annales School would one day call *la longue durée* (the long run). The task of narrating time began with a confession of humility towards the position of any given individual within historical time.

Bloch's statement on narration in the Great War found its most complete expression in his 1921 article on false news stories of the war.[26] Witnesses, he concluded, could recount time only according to momentary preoccupations, which would prove disjointed and contradictory. *Ipso facto*, they would resist narration. Inevitably, stories would get better with the telling, as they got further from the empirically demonstrable truth. The temptation to invent specific knowledge when needed to complete a narrative would prove irresistible, even among witnesses most concerned with reliability. This did not mean that first-hand testimonies lacked value for historians. Quite the contrary, for Bloch's article concluded with an impassioned plea to collect as much testimony from combatants of the Great War as possible, as quickly as possible.[27] But witnesses themselves would always remain too close to this material themselves to sift through it 'scientifically', separating what was empirically 'true' from what was 'false', or rather, what mattered as folklore rather than as empirical documentation. Bloch believed that as a historian, he had established the necessary critical distance from the 'false news stories' of the Middle Ages.[28] But for himself, Bloch

---

[24] In a private letter to Georges Davy in September 1917 Bloch wrote: 'But as for formulating through writing confessions and judgements, truly I am hardly up to the task. I would have too many things to say, which would be too mixed up and sometimes too self-contradictory; plus I don't have enough distance' (*Écrits de guerre*, 117).

[25] 'I believe in victory, but it will come slowly. I still know enough history to know that great crises are long. And the poor embryos that we are can only seek their pride in resignation' (ibid. 118).

[26] See Audoin-Rouzeau, 'Introduction', *Écrits de guerre*, 22–6.

[27] Bloch, 'Réflexions d'un historien', 184.

[28] Carlo Ginzburg and Audoin-Rouzeau have noted the profound if indirect influence of the Great War in Bloch's *Les Rois thaumaturges* (*The Royal Touch*, 1924). See Audoin-Rouzeau, 'Introduction', 5.

overtly renounced the task of narrating the war and his experience in it, at least in the public domain.

But why, then, did Bloch continue his skeletal private diary until the end of November 1918? Like Barbusse, Bloch wrote various annexes to the diary, such as his list of what he read, notes on his reading, even a work schedule for his delayed doctoral thesis. In so doing, Bloch sought to normalize his intellectual life, even while he remained mobilized. In considering the diary and its annexes as a single text, we need to recall Bloch's statement of 1917: 'The moment has come to call on the past to fill up the present.' He did so as witness and historian in three forms of the emplotment of experience. His memoir narrated his personal experience, a form of narration he considered unsatisfactory, and in which he would shortly lose interest. But two other forms of emplotment continued: his scattered writings on his historical work, notably what would become his 1920 doctoral thesis, 'Roi et serfs' ('King and Serfs'); and his diary strictly speaking, the recitation of places and dates that upon first inspection seems so meaningless to historians. Surely, Bloch understood the genre of medieval annals, which his diary had come so much to resemble. In the diary, the passage of historical time *was* the narrative, the plot, and the moral of the story. The witness had only to note time, measured by date and place. Historical time would continue, whatever happened to Marc Bloch, the French army, or even France itself.[29] For Bloch as witness to the Great War, the private genre of annals sufficed as testimony. For Bloch as historian and intellectual, his encounter with temporality and narration meant returning to the writing of medieval history.

In his 1936 essay on the narrator, Walter Benjamin lamented the passing of a world in which experience as an individual and social phenomenon seemed unproblematic.[30] Stories passed orally from narrators to communities, shaping the memory of those communities. If such a world ever existed (and Benjamin seems sure it did), the Great War catalysed its demise. He contended that fighting the war of the trenches rendered silent those who survived it, their capacity as narrators diminished rather than enhanced.

---

[29] As White wrote of annals as a genre: 'the modern scholar seeks fullness and continuity in an order of events; the annalist has both in the sequence of the years' ('Value of Narrativity', 9).

[30] Walter Benjamin, 'The Storyteller: Observations on the Works of Nikolai Leskov', trans. Harry Zohn, in Walter Benjamin, *Selected Writings*, ed. Howard Eiland and Michael W. Jennings, iii. *1935–1938* (Cambridge, Mass., 2002), 143–66, at 143–4.

Indeed, experience as something uniting the individual and the community seemed defeated by the brutality of the stalemated war, its violence, its economic devastation, and the lies still told about it.

At a certain level, we can certainly prove Benjamin wrong. Thousands of combatants published ego documents of their experience, and many thousands more wrote of it privately in one form or another. I have tried here to show the ways in which something striving for 'narration' persisted in writing practices at the front, even if the results did not enter the public domain, or did so long after the fact. Historians should never consider narratives completely interchangeable, or completely disregard 'truth' in an empirical sense. But debates about that kind of truth showed their limitations long ago. Rather, historians might better devote their efforts to trying to discern why so many individuals looking for 'truth' found it in so many different genres and in what seemed so many contradictory ways. In so doing, and in seeing the diversity and disparities of narratives as an intellectual opportunity rather than as a hardship, we can perhaps begin to appreciate the persistence of the artisanal character of narration in the Great War that Benjamin thought so irretrievably lost.

Notes on Contributors

MUSTAFA AKSAKAL is Associate Professor of History and Nesuhi Ertegün Chair of Modern Turkish Studies at Georgetown University. He is the author of *The Ottoman Road to War in 1914: The Ottoman Empire and the First World War* (2008) and 'The Ottoman Empire', in Jay Winter (ed.), *The Cambridge History of the First World War* (2014).

RICHARD BESSEL is emeritus Professor of Twentieth Century History at the University of York. His most recent books are *Germany 1945: From War to Peace* (2009) and *Violence: A Modern Obsession* (2015).

ROBERT BLOBAUM is Eberly Family Professor in the Department of History at West Virginia University. His most recent book is *A Minor Apocalpyse: Warsaw during the First World War* (2017). He is also the editor of *Antisemitism and its Opponents in Modern Poland* (2005) and author of *Rewolucja: Russian Poland, 1904–1907* (1995).

PAVLINA BOBIČ has been CENDARI Project Research Fellow in the Department of History at the University of Birmingham. She is the author of *War and Faith: The Catholic Church in Slovenia, 1914–1918* (2012).

SOPHIE DE SCHAEPDRIJVER is Ferree Professor of Modern European History at Pennsylvania State University. Her most recent books are *Bastion: Occupied Bruges in the First World War* (2014); *Gabrielle Petit: The Death and Life of a Female Spy in the First World War* (2015); and (co-written with Tammy Proctor) *An English Governess in the Great War: The Secret Brussels Diary of Mary Thorp* (2017).

CHRISTA HÄMMERLE is extraordinary Professor of Modern History and Women's and Gender History at the History Department of the University of Vienna. She is managing editor of *L'Homme: Europäische Zeitschrift für feministische Geschichtswissenschaft* and the author of *Heimat/Front: Geschlechtergeschichte/n des Ersten Weltkriegs in Österreich-Ungarn* (2014).

ANDREA GRÄFIN VON HOHENTHAL is a doctoral student at the Albert Ludwig University of Freiburg. Her research project is entitled 'Zur Entwicklung der Psychologie im Ersten Weltkrieg: Großbritannien und Deutschland im Vergleich'. She is also a medical doctor and psychologist and worked for several years at a clinic for neuropsychological rehabilitation.

GERD KRUMEICH is emeritus Professor at the Heinrich Heine University of Düsseldorf. He is Vice-President of the Research Centre of the Historial de la Grande Guerre in Péronne. His most recent books are *Juli 1914: Eine Bilanz* (2014) and (with Antoine Prost) *Verdun 1916* (Paris, 2015; Essen, 2016).

ANNA MAGUIRE is a Teaching Fellow in Twentieth-Century British History at King's College London. Her doctoral research comparatively examined the colonial encounters of troops from New Zealand, South Africa, and the West Indies.

MARCO MONDINI is a Researcher at the Istituto Storico Italo-Germanico-FBK in Trento and an Adjunct Professor of Military History at the University of Padua. He is co-editor (with Massimo Rosprocher) of *Narrating War: Early Modern and Contemporary Perspectives* (2013) and his books include *La guerra italiana: Partire, raccontare, tornare (1914–1918)* (2014); and *Il Capo: La Grande Guerra del generale Luigi Cadorna* (2017).

JOHN PAUL NEWMAN is Senior Lecturer in Twentieth-Century European History at the National University of Ireland in Maynooth. He is the author of *Yugoslavia in the Shadow of War: Veterans and the Limits of State Building, 1903–1945* (2015) and co-editor (with Mark Cornwall) of *Sacrifice and Rebirth: The Legacy of the Last Habsburg War* (2016).

ROBERTA PERGHER is Assistant Professor of History at Indiana University, Bloomington. She is the author of *Mussolini's Nation-Empire: Sovereignty and Settlement in Italy's Borderlands, 1922–1943* (2017) and co-editor (with Giulia Albanese) of *In the Society of Fascists: Acclamation, Acquiescence and Agency in Mussolini's Italy* (2012).

JOSHUA SANBORN is Professor and Head of the History Department at Lafayette College. He is the author of *Imperial Apocalypse: The Great War and the Destruction of the Russian Empire* (2014) and *Drafting the Russian Nation: Military Conscription, Total War, and Mass Politics, 1905–1925* (2003).

LEONARD V. SMITH is Frederick B. Artz Professor in the Department of History at Oberlin College. He is the author of *The Embattled Self: French Soldiers' Testimony of the Great War* (2007) and (with Stéphane Audoin-Rouzeau and Annette Becker) of *France and the Great War, 1914–1918* (2003).

ALEXANDER WATSON is Professor of History at Goldsmiths, University of London. He is the author of *Enduring the Great War: Combat, Morale and Collapse in the German and British Armies, 1914–1918* (2008) and *Ring of Steel: Germany and Austria-Hungary in World War I* (2014).

DOROTHEE WIERLING is the former Deputy Director of the Forschungsstelle für Zeitgeschichte in Hamburg. Her most recent book is *Eine Familie im Krieg: Leben, Sterben und Schreiben 1914–1918* (2013).

Index

Abdülhamid II, Sultan 196
abortion 37
Abschwangen 89 n.
Adam, Paul 310 n.
Adamoli, Federico 253
Adana 206
Adriatic Sea 119
aeroplanes 128, 161
Africa, as source of troops 208, 215
Africa, colonies in 119
Africa, North: *see* North Africa
Africa, South: *see* South Africa
Africa, West: *see* West Africa
Agnoletti, Fernando 259
agricultural workers 251
aircraft 40
   see also aeroplanes
Aksakal, Mustafa 14
Albania 276, 278, 285
Albanian militias 283
Albanian uprising 282–3
Albert (Belgian king) 75
Albi 307
L'alcova d'acciaio 259
Aleksandar, Serbian King Karadjordjević: *see* Karadjordjević, King Aleksandar
Alexanian, Yervant (Zia) 198–206
Algeria 312
Allegria di naufragi 259
Allenstein 87, 91–3
   see also Olsztyn
All Quiet on the Western Front 152–3 n., 236, 243 n., 244, 256
Alma, Bernhardine 163 n.
Alpenkorps 132

Alpine front, Alpine war 5, 17, 120, 122, 127, 130, 132, 139, 141
   see also Tyrolean front
Alpine regiments 251
Alps 119–20, 269
Alsace 310 n.
Alvaro, Corrado 256, 259, 269
American Civil War 4
American Indians 127
Anatolia 196–7, 202
Anglo-American literature 255
Anglo-French naval blockade of Ottoman Empire 197
Annales School 313
Un anno sull'Altipiano 259
Un anno sul Pasubio 259
Anschluß 157
Ansky S.: *see* Solomon Zanvel Rappoport
antisemitism 37, 44, 46–7, 50, 54, 240
Antwerp 68, 239
ANZAC troops 6, 179
Apis: *see* Dimitrijević, Dragutin
Arandjelović, Natalija 62
Arapgir 204–5
Archivio Diaristico Nazionale (Pieve di Santo Stefano) 254 n.
Archiwum Akt Nowych (Warsaw) 31
Archiwum Państwowe in Olsztyn 87
Ardennes 237
Argonne 67
aristocrats:
   Austrian 157

Belgian 65
Polish 34, 42, 45, 54
Russian 295–6, 298, 300, 303
Armenia, Armenians 198–206
Armenian conscripts 201–2, 204
Armenian genocide 8, 199–200
Armenian language 196
Armenian soldiers 199–200, 202–6
Armstrong, David 177
Arnejc, Franc 115
arson, arsonists 97, 238
Arys 90
artillery 4, 8, 37, 40, 120, 123, 127–9, 161, 188, 190, 299, 308 n.
Asiago 121 n.
assassination 288, 307
Astashov, Aleksandr Borisovitch 302
Atatürk, Mustafa Kemal 196
atrocities 20, 49, 64, 83, 85–100, 237, 265
Atrocities of Russian Troops against German Civilians and German Prisoners of War ('White Book') 88, 96–7
atrocity fantasies 98–100
attrition 60–1, 239, 243
Auckland 224
Auckland Mounted Rifles 222
Audoine-Rouzeau, Stéphane 4, 160, 313 n.
Äußeres Burgtor (Vienna) 156
Australia 71, 208
Australians 217–18
Australian soldiers 216
  see also ANZAC troops
Austria 18, 21–2, 108, 114–15, 117, 119, 121–2, 132, 134, 138–40, 147, 149, 151 n., 152, 155–6, 158, 163, 166
  First Republic 135, 142–3, 153
  Fascist period 146, 156–7, 162

Austria-Hungary 109, 115–16, 119–20, 130, 132, 136, 141, 143, 145–7, 151, 166
  Italian speakers fighting for 141
  Italy declares war on 119, 132, 134–5
  see also Austria, Habsburg Empire, Hungary
Austrian Alpine Club 133 n., 138
Austrian culture of war remembrance 144, 146, 152–3, 158, 166
Austrian dignitaries 45
Austrian Emperor 43, 105–6, 115
Austrian officers 112, 125–8
Austrian parliament 116–17
Austrian soldiers 112, 125–8, 132, 135
  Italian-speaking 142
'Austrian solution' (to the Polish question) 39
Austrian War Archive 152
Austro-Fascism 155–6, 162
Austro-Hungarian army, soldiers 62, 106, 108 n., 116 n., 130, 135, 139, 157, 178
  attacks Russian army in 1915: 297
Austro-Hungarian Empire: see Habsburg Empire
Austro-Hungarian military medical service 146
Austro-Italian conflict 120–1, 124 n., 126–7, 130–2
  see also Alpine front, Tyrolean front
Austro-Serbian conflict 39
authenticity 10, 24, 31, 34, 58, 99, 127, 141–2, 153, 168, 195, 232, 243–4, 248, 305, 308
Axis forces 288
Ažman, Anton 112–13

Baghdad 199, 206

Balaklava, Battle of 131–2
Balkans 8, 14, 283, 286
  illiteracy in 12
  see also Albania, Bosnia, Croatia, Montenegro, Serbia
Balkan Wars 145 n., 166 n., 196, 198, 273, 275–6, 278–9, 283–5
Barbusse, Henri 306–7, 309–11, 314
Barmherzige Schwestern 154
Baracca, Francesco 250
Barry, William 216–17
Barth, Karl 106
Bartolini, Luigi 259, 269–70
Batocki, Adolf von 88
Battaglione Monte Berico 259
Battisti, Cesare 250
Bayet, Adrien 65–7, 70, 79 n.
Becker, Annette 61, 160
Beersheba 151
begging 48
Belgian army 63, 71
Belgian *franc-tireurs* 237–8, 248
Belgian gendarmes 75
Belgian government 73, 80
Belgian labourers 5, 76, 79, 80
Belgian refugees 73
Belgian resistance 238
Belgian soldiers 76
Belgian underground press 61 n.
Belgium 5, 19, 31 n., 57, 59–81, 85
  German atrocities in 20, 74, 85, 237
  German occupation of 59–81
  fighting in 238
  hostility towards Germany 72–3
  invasion of 69–71, 74, 77–8
  literacy in 57, 64
  unoccupied 76
Belgrade 108 n., 276, 278, 281–2, 285
Benjamin, Walter 314–15
Berlin 30, 87, 89, 109 n., 174, 235, 237

Berliner Tageblatt 72, 98 n.
Bern 143
Bersaglieri 251
Bertevagoump (Armenian sports club) 200
Beseler, Hans von 31, 34, 38, 45, 52
Bey, Fuad Ziya 201
Bey, Memduh 205
Bezia 202
Bialla 92
Biblioteca Malatestiana 260
Bildungsroman 15, 262
Bischofstein 92
Bircana 285
'The Black Hand': *see* Unification or Death
black marketeering 65
Blobaum, Robert 21
Bloch, Étienne 308 n.
Bloch, Marc 306–12, 314
blockade (Anglo-French, of Ottoman Empire) 197
Błonie 49
Blunden, Edmund 273
Bobić, Pavlina 17
Boer War 212
Bohemia 154
Bolshevism, Bolsheviks 46, 300, 303
bombing 50, 79, 161–2
Borden, Mary 161 n.
Borgese, Giuseppe Antonio 259
Borkenau, Franz 231
Borsi, Giosué 262
Bosnia 274, 289
Bosporus 196
Bossier, Herman 76 n.
Bossier, Walter 76 n.
Botha, General Louis 226
Boulogne 221
bourgeoisie 21, 80
  Austrian 126, 128
  Belgian 60, 65, 70, 75
  Italian 150, 268

Polish 42, 54
rural 64 n.
Serbian 286
Bovy, Daniel 70–1
Bovy, Élie 70
Bovy, Henriette 70–1, 79 n.
Bozen/Bolzano 135, 137 n.
Bozner Nachrichten 135
Bozner Zeitung 135
Bratniak (student fraternity) 35
Braun, Otto 23 n.
bread rations:
 in Warsaw 36, 45
Bregenz 153
Brenner Pass 137
Brest-Litovsk, Treaty of 46
Britain 13, 18 n., 19, 21 n., 131, 137 n., 145, 146 n., 151 n., 166, 167 n., 168–9, 174, 176, 208, 214, 273, 292
 hospitals in 169, 176
British Army 169, 172, 215, 219, 251
British Colonial Office 214
British colonial troops 18, 207–15, 220–1, 226–7
British doctors 169, 172, 175, 177, 180–2, 190
British Empire 207–15, 217, 221–3, 225–7
British literature 255
British military attachés 294
British reading public 293
British soldiers 5, 178, 219, 222
British War Office 214–15, 225–6
British West Indies Regiment 211, 215
British women:
 marrying Pakeha New Zealanders 224
 mixing with black South Africans 225–6
Brittain, Vera 166 n., 255
Brown, William 170, 172–3, 178, 189

Bruges 76 n.
Brusilov, Aleksei 294–6
Brussels 58 n., 61, 65–71, 73
Bulgarians 200
Buquoy, Duchess Therese von 159
Burgfrieden 240
Bursa 201
Burton, Antoinette 220–1

Calais 225
Caliphate, abolition of 197
Cambridge, University of 172
Campana, Michele 259, 262, 265
Camporosota 161
Canada 208
Cankar, Ivan 108 n., 114
Cape Coloured Labour Battalion 225
Caporetto 120, 255, 257, 269–70
captivity 112, 265
Caracal (Romania) 154
Carinthia 115
Carkeek, Rikihana 218, 220–1, 224
Carpathian Mountains 112, 297
Catholic associations 107–8
Catholic authors 115, 261
Catholic Church:
 in Austria 159 n.
 in Belgium 59
 in East Prussia 91
 in the Habsburg monarchy 106–7, 159 n.
 in Italy 262
 in Slovenia 115, 117
Catholic faith, Catholicism 106–7, 109–10, 113–14, 117, 137, 261–2, 266
Catholic groups publishing war letters 240
Catholic imagery 105, 110
Catholic newspapers 114
Catholic priests 107
Catholic soldiers 232, 234, 240, 291

Catholic war propaganda 116 n.
Catholic women's congregations 146
Catholic youth 108
Caucasus 86, 203
Cauillaux, Joseph 310 n.
Cavell, Edith 71
Cenotaph (Whitehall) 291–2
censorship 11, 30, 34, 53, 67, 72, 139, 186, 239, 246, 253, 256–7, 278, 301–2
Central Citizens' Committee (Warsaw) 32
Central Office for the Collection of Letters from the Front (*Zentralstelle zur Sammlung von Feldpostbriefen*) 235
Central Powers 18 n., 29, 32, 43, 119, 196
Ceylon: *see* Sri Lanka
chaplains: *see* military chaplains
The Character and Mentality of a Generation 277
Charité (Berlin) 236
Chetniks 278, 288–9
children 36, 42, 44, 49, 68, 71, 84, 86, 89–91, 94, 96, 98–100, 113, 134, 155, 163, 182, 213, 221–2, 238, 249, 267
China 208
Chinese labourers 6, 217, 220
cholera 50, 151
Christ 113–14
Christian Ottomans 197, 199
citizenship 57, 71, 144 n.
civil servants 41, 88, 92, 271, 281, 285
clergy 85, 113
La coda di Minosse 259
Col di Lana 134
Cologne 174 n., 176, 184
Colombo 218
Colonial Office (British) 214

colonial troops 18, 207–15, 220–1, 226–7
colonies 7, 119, 209–10, 212, 219
Comisso, Giovanni 259–60, 269–70
commemoration 53, 79, 121, 125, 141–4, 147, 150, 153, 158
Committee of Union and Progress 203
Communists 303, 306
Con me e con gli alpini 259
conscription:
 labour 33
 military 48, 198, 202, 221, 251, 295
conscripts 106–8, 187, 201–2, 204, 251, 285
Constance, Lake 153
conversion 159 n.
 to Islam 204
Cora, Yaşar Tolga 205
Cordin, Ettore 134
Cornali, Gino 270–1
corruption 39, 52, 278, 282, 285
Cortina 134
Cossacks 49, 90–3, 96–7
Council of Great Powers 261
Cowan, James 212–13
cowards 265, 267
Cracow: *see* Kraków
Crimean War 131, 145 n.
Critique of Pure Reason 310 n.
Crnjanski, Miloš 277
Croatia, Croat lands 288–9
The Croatian God Mars 277
Croats 275, 277, 289
cult of mourning 150
cultural pessimism 109 n.
culture of remembrance 146–8, 152
Cvelbar, Jože 105, 110, 112, 115
Czech hospitals 165
Czech Legionaries 288
Czechoslovak Republic 288
Czechoslovakia 288

Czech troops 139

Danilov General Iurii 294, 298
Dante (Alighieri) 261, 265–6
Dardanelles 208
Darrow, Margaret 148, 158, 164
Das, Santanu 210
Davy, Georges 313 n.
deaconesses, German 146
De Amicis, Edmondo 266
death:
  in combat 4, 13, 17–18, 23 n., 80, 108, 110–11, 113, 115–17, 126, 128, 161, 212, 243, 254, 264–9, 271, 273, 281, 308, 310 n., 312
  for the fatherland 242
  from starvation 197
  marches 202
  of Apis 280
  of Armenians 202, 204, 209
  of East Prussians 86, 94
  of Emperor Franz Joseph 115
  on the Cross 114
  sentence 297
defeat 23, 36, 99, 109, 120, 146, 202–3, 247, 265, 298, 300, 302, 315
Defregger, Franz 131
demobilization 270, 276
  of nurses 151, 152 n., 154
demonstrations (hunger) 36
deportation:
  of Armenians 198–9, 201–5
  of Belgians 5, 6, 76–7, 79
  of Germans in East Prussia 84–6, 92, 97, 100
  of Jews (in Poland) 40, 49
  of Ottoman Christians 197
De Schaepdrijver, Sophie 10, 17
desertion 197
Deutscher Ritterorden: see Knights Hospitallers
devaluation 39

diaries 34–5, 38 n., 42–3, 45, 53, 61–2, 65–75, 77–8, 80, 110 n., 120–1, 125–7, 129, 133–4, 138, 141, 151, 154–5, 160, 164, 195, 203, 206, 209, 216, 221–4, 274
  of Henri Barbusse 306–11, 314
  of Marc Bloch 306–12, 314
  discussion about 10, 11, 13, 15, 20, 22, 30, 57–9, 61, 64–5, 67, 70, 79–81, 142, 227, 253–4, 305–6, 308
  discussion of violence in 13
Diario di un fante 259
Diario di un imboscato 259
Diario di un sepolto vivo 259
The Diary of Čarnojević 277
Didier, Béatrice 64
Dieppe 217
Dimitrijević, Dragutin (Apis) 279–81
Dinsacher, Frida 105
Directory of German Books (*Deutsches Bücherverzeichnis*) 233
disabled 23, 182, 184
discourse analysis 83
disease 8, 29, 50, 52, 143, 151, 154, 165, 171, 177–9, 181, 190, 197
Divine Comedy 261
Dixmuiden 246
Djilas, Milovan 287, 289
Dluggen 96
Doberdò plateau (battles) 109, 111
doctors 9, 19, 21, 150, 165, 167–72, 175–92
  see also psychiatrists
Dolomites campaign 121, 132
domestic servants 151
Donati Petteni, Giuliano 259
Dorgelès, Roland 57–8
Dostoevsky, Fyodor 17, 108 n., 114
Dotish, Edward 211
drunkenness 302
Drygallen 90

INDEX

Drzewiecki, Ludwik 32
Drzewiecki, Piotr 31–2
Drzewiecki, Wiesław 32–3
Dunin-Wąsowicz, Krzysztof 3–5, 37, 39–40, 47, 54
Dutch language 75–6
Dzierzbicki, Stanisław 31–4, 42
Dzikowski, Stanisław 39–41

Eastern Front 5–6, 8, 18, 49, 108 n., 116 n., 122–3, 130–1, 149 n., 155, 178, 294
East Prussia 20, 83–101
Eder, Montague David 171–2, 176 n., 178–9, 181, 188, 192
Eekhoud, Georges 61, 65–6, 68, 70, 72–3, 75, 77–8, 79 n., 80
Egypt 173, 197, 207–8, 211, 216, 221–2
Egyptian Labour Corps (ELC) 221–3
Egyptians 222–3
'Eigen-Sinn' 129
Eiger, Maria: *see* Kamińska, Maria
Elazığ 196
electro-shock therapy 170, 180, 182–3, 187
L'elmo di Scipio 259
emigration 37, 299
England 171, 181, 211, 215, 224, 226
  see also Britain, United Kingdom
English people 179, 248
English women 224, 226
Entente 60, 67, 88, 115–16, 119, 137, 145 n., 307
Enver: *see* Pasha, Enver
Erdem, Hakan 195
Erfahrung: *see* experience as a concept
Erlebnis: *see* experience as a concept
erotic dreams 68
Erzincan 198–205
Erzurum 201–2

Esame di coscienza di un letterato 259
Étaples 223
'ethnic cleansing' 289
  see also atrocities, genocide
Euphrates 204
Europeana 20–21 n.
executions 71, 86, 97, 279, 297
experience as a concept 5, 9, 14–16, 24, 58, 83, 124–5, 141, 313–14
experience of war 3–4, 7, 8–23, 29, 57–9, 66, 80, 85, 105–6, 111–12, 117–18, 120–2, 124, 129, 141, 148, 151, 155, 158–61, 163, 165, 168, 171, 176–7, 180, 182–92, 196, 198, 208, 210–11, 231, 233–4, 236–7, 239, 242, 245, 248, 258, 261, 269–70, 273, 275, 284, 286, 293, 305–12, 314

factory workers 151, 153, 155
false memories 99
Fania, Ciro 253
A Farewell to Arms 120, 256–7
Fascism:
  censorship under 256–7
  fall of 258
  foundation of 249
  rise of 120
  Tyrolean German speakers under 138
  Tyroleans portrayed as victims of 140
  see also Austro-Fascism
Fascist commemoration 147
Fascist Italy:
  alliance with Germany 139–40
Fascist regime in Italy 249–50, 255–7
Fascists 292
  Croat 289
  Serbian 277
Federal Military Archives Freiburg 187, 187–8 n.

Fell, Alison 159
female emancipation 255
Fessler, Agathe 153–4, 162
Le Feu 306, 309–11
'Field Post' (German): *see* Military Postal Service
Figes, Orlando 295
First Balkan War 278
First Maori Contingent 218, 224
Flanders 74–5
  see also Belgium
Flemings 75
Flemish language 75
Flemish Movement 76
Flemish nationalism 76–7
Flemish soldiers 76
Flemish University of Ghent 77
Fogarty, Richard 226
Folkestone 217
'Folkist' party (*yidische folkspartei*, Jewish People's Party) 51
food deprivation 54
  see also hunger
food distribution 52–3
food rations 36, 41
forced labour, labourers 76, 79–80
Formigari, Francesco 249
Fort Tanskyne: *see* Tanskyne Fort
Foucault, Michel 177
France 13, 21, 30, 57, 59, 61–3, 72, 85, 137 n., 146 n., 148–9, 156, 166 n., 172–3, 180 n., 190, 213, 215–17, 222–3, 225–6, 257, 306, 312 n., 314
  battles in 238
  destruction in 6
  literacy in 57, 64
  nurses in 146 n.
  Prussian occupation of in 1870–1: 77
  war generation 57
  war literature published in 293
'*francs-tireurs*' 237–8, 248

Frank, Ludwig 235
Frankfurter Zeitung 72
Franz Ferdinand, Archduke 296
Franz Josef, Kaiser 105–6, 115, 135
Frascati 47
Frass, Wilhelm 156 n.
Fredericq, Paul 75–7, 79 n.
Freiburg im Breisgau 240
French army 99, 251, 314
French civilians 211, 226
French Empire 220
French hospitals 172
French imperial troops 226
French reading public 293
French Red Cross 146 n.
French Resistance 306–7, 311
French soldiers 3, 5, 132
French women 96, 226
Frescura, Attilio 259
Freud, Sigmund 171, 185–6, 192
Fromelles, Battle of 216
'Frontgemeinschaft' 23
Fussell, Paul 216

Galicia 8, 47, 49, 59–60, 145 n., 153, 155, 157, 161
Galli, Franz 136
Gallipoli 8, 171, 204, 224
Garaventa, Alberto 259
Gasch, Mary 157, 161
Gasparotto, Luigi 259
Gasser, Hannes 141
Gasser, Sonja 155 n.
Gause, Fritz 88, 93
Geheimes Staatsarchiv, Preußischer Kulturbesitz (Berlin-Dahlem) 86–7
General Government (Warsaw): *see* Warsaw General Government
General Staff (German) 235
General Staff (Russian) 84, 298
General Staff Academy (Russian) 295

Gendarmes (Belgian) 75
gender 15, 79, 85, 148, 160, 166, 227, 293
    as determinant of war experience 196
gender-based hierarchies 158
gender discrimination 35
gendered depictions of nurses 148
gender order, roles 22, 159–60, 164–6
genocide 8, 199–200
    see also atrocities
Georg Müller Verlag, Munich 239, 246
Gerhards, Thomas 246 n.
German ambassador to Ottoman Empire 196
German army 59, 62–3, 71, 73, 77, 84–5, 88, 98, 237, 239
German atrocities 20, 74, 85, 88
German education ministries 243
German Literature Archive (Marbach) 241, 242 n.
German nationalism 137–8
German occupation:
    of Belgium 59–81
    of Poland 30–41, 45, 51, 53
German officers 36
German police:
    in Belgium 69, 75
    in Warsaw 36
Germans:
    deported in Russian Empire 86
    literacy among 234
    in Marc Bloch's diary 308
    in Poland 32–3, 35–6, 38, 42, 44, 47, 50, 53
    taking prisoners on Western Front 211
German soldiers 3, 5, 35, 45, 90–1, 96, 98–100, 139, 178, 231–2, 237, 243–4, 247
German ultimatum to Belgium 80

Germany 5, 7, 13, 19, 21, 23, 30, 36, 48, 59–60, 72, 76, 83, 86, 89, 98, 109 n., 138–9, 144–5, 156, 168–70, 174, 179, 191, 212, 232, 235, 237, 296, 307
    annexes Sudetenland 288
    Belgian hostility towards 69, 72, 75
    censorship in 186 n.
    in the diary of Henri Barbusse 310 n.
    intellectual elite 242
    Italy declares war on 119, 132
    literacy in 64
    National Socialist regime in 22
    newspapers in 87, 238
    nurses in 146 n., 151 n.
    violation of Belgian neutrality 73
Germinal 310 n.
Gestapo 306
Gesellschaft für Experimentelle Psychologie: see Psychological Society
Gevers, Marie 68, 70, 74–5, 77, 79 n.
Ghana (Gold Coast) 217, 219
Ghent 61, 66–8, 75, 76 n., 77
Dal giardino all'Isonzo 259
Gibb, Robert 132
Giedion, Siegfried 16
Ginzburg, Carlo 313 n.
Giorni di guerra 259, 269–70
Głodowska-Sampolska, Władysława 35–7, 54
The Glowing Lamps 277
gluttony 65
Gold Coast 219
    see also Ghana
Goldmann, Lucien 231
'Golgotha' of the Serbian nation 276
Golovin, Nicolai 294, 298–9, 303
Golowitsch, Helmut 140

Gorgolini, Pietro 249
Gorizia 154
Da Gorizia al Grappa 259
Gorky, Maxim 110
Gotha 241–2
Graeffe, Constance 71–2, 79 n.
Graeffe, Otto 71
Grand Vizier Said Halim Pasha 196
graveyards 244, 292
'Greater Serbia' 289
'Great Retreat' (Russian in 1915) 6, 297, 302
Greek Orthodox families 200
Greeks 200–1
Gregorčič, Simon 114
Greyerz, Kaspar von 168
Grillparzer, Franz 111
In guerra con gli Alpini 259
guerrilla warfare, guerrillas 127, 278
Gumbinnen 87
Gurkhas 213–15

Habsburg army: *see* Austro-Hungarian army
Habsburg emperor 105
Habsburg Empire 5, 105–7, 115, 137, 145, 156, 170, 274
 collapse of 117, 138
Habsburg military administrative service (Belgrade) 108 n.
Habsburg military medical service 146
Habsburg monarchy 21, 106, 151 n., 159 n., 178
Hafkesbrink, Hanna 232
Hague, Convention of 1907: 87
Haig, General Douglas 293
Halbwachs, Maurice 231
Hall 133
Hamidian massacres 200
Hamlet 310 n.
Hämmerle, Christa 18, 22

Hanisch, Ernst 152
Harput: *see* Elazığ
Harris, Ruth 99
Hasidic religious communities 50
Hazomir literary club 49
Hegenscheidt, Alfred 77 n.
Heidegger, Martin 305
Heldendenkmal (Heroes' Monument) (Vienna) 156
Hellpach, Willi 174–5, 183–4
Hemingway, Ernest 120, 256–7
Herbst, Franciszek 40–2
heroes, heroism 12, 17, 19–20, 22, 43, 61, 97, 106–8, 121 n., 122, 128–9, 131–2, 138, 140, 143, 149–50, 156, 159, 235, 239, 243–4, 246, 250, 254–5, 262, 269–70, 280, 282, 284–5, 299, 303, 306–7
Hettling, Manfred 241, 242 n., 244
Himmelforth 90
Hindus 291
Hirschfeld, Magnus 148
Hitler, Adolf 232, 244 n., 245, 247
hoarding 72
Hofer, Hans-Georg 186
Hohenstein 94
Hohenthal, Andrea von 19
Holland 68
Holm, Korfiz 246
Holocaust survivor interviews 83
home front 4, 9, 11, 13–15, 22, 30, 63–4, 142, 233
homoeroticism 216, 250
For the Honour of the Fatherland 277
Honvéd 113, 130
Horne, John 7
Horner, Alfred 211, 213, 215, 220–1
horses 4, 47, 90, 299, 308 n.
hospitals 43–4, 46, 50, 105 n., 144, 145 n., 146, 150–1, 154–6, 161–2, 165, 169, 172–4, 176–9,

INDEX

180 n., 181, 183–5, 187, 224, 227, 258, 267
hospital staff (Warsaw) 46
Hotel Europa (Warsaw) 50, 54
housing:
  in Warsaw 35
Hrouda, Eveline 157, 162
human rights 61
Hungary 150, 154
  see also Austria-Hungary, Habsburg Empire
hunger:
  in Belgium 60
  in Warsaw 36, 45–6
Huns 237
Hutten-Czapski, Bogdan 34, 38
Hyde Park 224
hypnosis 180 n., 181–2, 185, 188–9, 192
hysteria 170, 173, 178–9, 187, 191

Ibsen, Henrik 114
illiteracy 11 n., 12, 21, 92, 94
  in the Balkans 12
  in Italy 21, 241, 251–2
  in Ottoman Empire 12, 21, 188, 198 n.
  in Poland 29
  in Russian Empire 12, 21, 285
  in Serbia 273
  see also literacy
immoral behaviour 148, 164
Imperial Military Nursing Service 146 n.
Imperial War Museum 209
India 207–8, 219
Indian Army 214–15
Indian men 214
Indian troops 215
Indo-China:
  troops from, marrying French women 226

industrialized warfare 4, 123, 146, 161, 243
Inland Waterways 219
Innerkofler, Sepp 133, 138
Innsbruck 136, 144
Insterburg 89
Institute for Clinical Psychology 184
L'introduzione alla vita mediocre 259, 269
Iraq 197
Islam 201
Isle of Wight 224
Isonzo front 8, 109 n., 111, 116 n., 120, 123, 135, 154–5, 157, 162, 265
Isonzo river 120, 123, 135
Istanbul 203
Italian army 120, 157, 252
Italian front 108 n., 130, 154, 164
Italian High Command 258
Italianization of German speakers, Tyrol 138, 140
Italian literature 255
Italian meddling in Serbia 282
Italian prisoners of war 105 n.
Italian soldiers 5, 120, 135, 254
  attitudes towards 139
Italian–Swiss border 119–20
Italy 21–2, 109, 116–17, 119–21, 123–4, 130, 132, 135, 137, 139, 150, 161, 249–52, 254–7, 261–3, 266–7
  enters war 116, 119, 130–2, 134–5
  illiteracy in 12 n., 21, 251–2
  status of South Tyrol in 140
  war with Ottoman Empire (1911–12) 196, 198
Izmir (Smyrna) 204

Jabłonna 40
Jagiellonian University (Kraków) 47
Jahier, Piero 259

Jamaica, Jamaicans 216–17
Janz, Oliver 150
Jarka, Marianne 155, 162–3
Jaurès, Jean 307
Jeismann, Michael 241, 242 n., 244
Jerusalem 151, 196, 198 n.
Jesuits 74, 198
'Jew census' of 1916: 247
Jewish authors 22, 306
Jewish groups publishing war letters 240
Jewish merchants 54
Jewish soldiers 234, 247
Jewish students 245
Jews 37–8, 40, 49, 51, 53–5, 62, 83, 211, 240, 281, 291, 306
  deported in Russian Empire 86
  emigration from Poland 37
  expelled in Poland by Russian army 40
  in British Jewish battalion 211
  in Warsaw 29, 40–2, 44, 49–50, 52
  regarded as German spies 54
Jingoes, Stimela Jason 216–17, 225, 227
Johannisburg 89, 90
Johnstone, William 217, 225, 227
journalists 34, 37, 39–40, 68–9, 263, 276–7, 279, 286–7
Jovanović, Branko 280–1
Judson, Pieter 274
July Crisis (1914) 196
Jünger, Ernst 12 n., 244, 286
Jungle Books 310 n.
Jurčič, Josip 114

Kaçak raids 285
Kaiserjäger 126, 130–1
Kalemkerian, Father (priest) 202
Kalusz 161
Kamińska, Maria 35, 37, 54
Kant, Immanuel 310 n.
Kantorowicz, Ernst 59, 60

Karabekir, Kâzim 197 n.
Karadjordjević, King Aleksandar 276, 278, 280–1
  assassinated 288
Katholisches Sonntagsblatt 137 n.
Kaufmann, Fritz 182
Kauffman, Jesse 31
Kemah 204
Kemal Atatürk, Mustafa: *see* Atatürk, Mustafa Kemal
Kerchnawe, Hugo 156, 160
Kern, Karl Ritter von 105 n.
'Kerzhenetskii' forests 299
Kiel military hospital 187
Kingdom of Galicia and Lodomeria 155
Kingdom of Italy 261
Kingdom of Serbs, Croats, and Slovenes 274
Kinsky, Countess Nora 157
Kipling, Rudyard 132, 310 n.
Klaipėda: *see* Memel
Klanßen 90
Kliazma (river) 299
Knežević, Jovana 61
Knights Hospitallers (*Deutscher Ritterorden*) 146
Knox, Alfred 294, 299
Kobilek 259
Kokosken 90
Kolomea 139
Kolomyia (Ukraine) 150
Kon Geca 281
Königsberg 86–7
Königsberg City Archive 88
Königspitze 126
Konrad, Rosine Marie 154–5, 160, 162, 164
Kościuszko, Tadeusz 43
Koselleck, Reinhart 60
Kosovo 274, 278, 281
Kostroma forest 299
Kozak, Ferdo 108, 112–13

INDEX

Kozak, Juš 108, 114
Krakov, Stanislav 277
Kraków 47–8
Kraushar, Aleksander 37–9, 41
Kreuzbergsattel 135
Kriegsbriefe deutscher Studenten 20
Kriegsneurose: *see* 'war neurosis'
Kriegszitterer, *Kriegszittern* 19, 178
Kries, Wolfgang von 32–3
Krleža, Miroslav 277
Krumeich, Gerd 20
Krzywicka, Irena 36–7
Kurjer Warszawski 39
Kutrzeba, Stanisław 47–8

labour conscription 33
labour migration 48, 57
The Lancet 172
Landesschützen 126, 130–1
Landi, Stefano 259
Landsturm 126, 130
Langen, Albert 246
Langl, Otto 133 n., 138
Łazienki palace grounds 37
Leipzig 241
Leitzen, Hans 238
Lemberg: *see* Lwów
Lemke, Mikhail 294
Lempruch, Moritz Erwin Freiherr von 127
Leopthien-Verlag 143
letters 63, 68, 71, 89, 105, 110, 112–13, 115, 132, 151, 154, 156–7, 160 n., 195, 207, 209, 231–48, 252–3, 274, 301–2, 307
  discussion about 9, 10–13, 20–2, 30, 34, 57–8, 227
Das letzte Aufgebot 131
Levstik, Vladimir 114
Library of Contemporary History (*Bibliothek für Zeitgeschichte*) (Stuttgart): *see* World War Library

Il libro di un teppista 259
Libyan War (Italy) 256
Lichem, Heinz 141
Lidwin, Johann 90
Liège 239
Linden, Walther 246
Lipovci 113
literacy 9, 57, 94, 209
  among Germans 234
  among Italians 251
  literacy courses (in Warsaw) 37
  in Ottoman Empire 198
  see also illiteracy
Liverpool 174
Ljubljana 105 n., 162
Lobanov-Rostovsky, Prince Andrei 294, 296–8, 303
Locchi, Vittorio 259, 263
Łochów 40
Lodomeria 155
Lokau 91
London 32
  Treaty of 137 n.
la longue durée 313
looting 85–6
Lorraine 310 n.
Lososice 157
Loveling, Virginie 61, 66–7, 74–7, 79 n.
Lubomirska, Princess Maria 42–7, 53–4
Lubomirski, Prince Zdzisław 33, 42, 44
Nella luce del sacrificio 259
Ludendorff, Erich 7
417th Lugansk Infantry Regiment 302
Lukács, Georg 231
Lusitania 71
Lussu, Emilio 259
Lutyens, Sir Edwin 291
Lwów 39

Macedonia 274, 281
MacGregor, Alexander 207
machine-guns 4, 40, 94, 204, 215, 308 n.
MacKenzie, Thomas 224
Maden 200
Maghull Red Cross Military Hospital 174
Maguire, Anna 14
Maistre, General Paul 310 n.
Majcen, Stanko 108–9
Malaparte, Curzio 257, 259–60
Malta 171, 176 n.
Malta Medical Conference (1916) 171
Maltese Order, *Malteserorden*: see Order of Malta
Maoris 213, 217–18, 223–4
  marrying British women 224, 227
  see also First Maori Contingent
Maoris in the Great War 212
Marbach 241, 242 n.
Marconi, Piro 259
Mariani, Mario 259–60, 264
Marienheim 153–4
Marinetti, Filippo Tommaso 259
Marini, Gian Francesco 259
Märkisches Museum (Berlin) 235
Markl, Matthias 155 n.
Marpicati, Arturo 259
marriage 45, 60, 144 n., 165, 224
Marseillaise 68
martyrdom 44, 106, 115–16
martyrs 81, 106, 250, 262, 311
masculinity 23, 98, 152, 212, 214, 217, 221–2, 262
massacres 61, 71, 74, 85, 89 n., 97, 200, 203
Masurians 92
Matli, Jacob Koos 226
Maupassant, Guy de 77–8
Max, Paul 69, 79 n.
Mayr, Erich 126

Mayr, Karl 128–9, 133, 141 n.
medical authorities 182, 191
medical care/treatment 8, 14, 92, 168–9, 171, 173, 176–8
  see also doctors, nurses, psychologists
medical centres 49
medical community 170, 181–2, 186, 191
medical courses 153
medical files 10, 192
medical journals 175, 177
medical officers 181–2, 258
medical service expedition (to Syria) 150
medical staff 154, 161
  see also doctors, nurses, psychologists
medical units 74, 156
medicine 167, 173–4, 180
Meiringen 143
Memduh, Governor of Erzincan 203, 205
Memel (Klaipėda) 84
memoirs 34–7, 40–1, 54, 57, 69 n., 97, 111, 125–7, 132, 138–9, 143, 146–7, 152–60, 162, 195, 199–200, 227, 243–4, 249, 251, 253–5, 257, 260, 262–6, 270–1, 273–4, 295–7, 309, 311–12, 314
  discussion about 8–13, 15, 20, 22–3, 30, 34, 209, 306
memorials 23, 30, 143, 153, 156, 234, 243, 250, 270
memory, memories 29–30, 69, 105, 107, 111, 120–1, 124–5, 127, 129–31, 141, 170, 189–90, 196, 236, 240, 245, 250, 256, 263, 269, 270, 273, 293, 314
  loss of 173, 178
  unreliability of 99, 100, 311–13
'memory wars' 152
SS Mendi sinking 226

Menemen 205
mental illness 144 n.
    see also shell shock trauma
mentally disturbed soldiers 116, 169, 173–7, 179–80, 182, 188, 190–2
    see also psychiatrists
Meran 136
Mercier, Cardinal Désiré-Joseph 59–61, 65, 69–70, 75
Mesopotamia 67, 207, 215, 219
Messal, Lucyna 39
Michielli, Luigi 134
Middle Ages 313
Middle East 195, 206
Mihailović, Dragoljub 'Draža' 288–9
Mihajlović, Slavka 62
Milan 267
Military Academy (Ottoman, Mekteb-I Harbiye) 198, 200
military chaplains 115, 258
military hospitals 50, 150, 155, 173–4, 181, 185, 187, 258, 267
    see also hospitals
military mental hospitals 174, 183
military police 69, 75, 225
Military Postal Service (German) ('Field Post') 232
Ministry of the Interior (Austrian) 150
Il mio diario di Guerra 259
Mittermaier, Johann 126–7
Mlakar, Albin 116
Mohrungen 90
Der Moment 51
Mondadori (publisher) 256–7
modernism, modernist art 273, 277
Mondini, Marco 22
Monelli, Paolo 257, 259, 263–4
Monte Cucca 105 n.
Montenegro 62, 278, 281
Moore, Alexander Briscoe 222

Morandini, Simone 134
Moravia 157
Mörl, Anton von 139
morphine addiction 144 n., 145 n.
mortality rates 52
Mountain Battery Frontier Force 207
mourning 6, 150, 152, 268, 273, 291–2
Muammer, Ahmet 201, 203
Muccini, Mario 259
Müller, Georg 246
    see also Georg Müller Verlag
Munich 170, 182, 185, 239, 246, 288
Il muro di casa 259
Murom forest 299
Museum for the History of Polish Jews 65
Museum for the History of the Warsaw Uprising 30, 55
Muslims 291
    deported in Russian Empire 86
    Turkish officers 199
Mussolini, Benito 256–7, 259
mutiny 221–3, 297, 301
Myers, Charles 172–3, 178, 182, 187, 190

Naepflin, Maria: see Pöll-Naepflin, Maria
Naglič, Peter 105–6
Namur 239
Napoleonic Wars 131, 160, 214
narration 5, 101, 195, 249, 252, 262, 293, 305–7, 309, 312–15
narratives 10, 12, 14–16, 54–5, 94–6, 100–1, 107, 121–2, 125–31, 133, 137–42, 146, 154, 157–8, 162, 164, 166, 195–6, 210, 221–3, 226–7, 238, 264–5, 269–70, 294, 300, 303, 305–9, 311–15
national narratives 21, 197
postwar narratives 142, 300

public narratives 23, 125, 142
'trauma narratives' 160
war narratives 8–9, 12, 14–15, 95, 119, 125, 141, 158, 221, 244, 293–4, 303
National Archives (Kew) 225
National Democrats, Polish 47
nationalism 17, 115, 117, 120, 283, 292
  in Austria-Hungary 116
  Flemish 76
  German 137–8
  Italian 253, 271
  Serbian 274–5, 279, 287–8
National Socialism 138, 155, 156 n.
  Tyroleans portrayed as victims of 140
National Socialist dictatorship 240
National Socialist era 245
National Socialist influence 246
National Socialist politicians 247
National Socialist propaganda 245
National Socialist regime 22, 144, 159 n.
National Socialists 144, 156, 159, 163, 244
National Socialist seizure of power 288
Natter, Wolfgang 241
Nazis: *see* National Socialists
Nazism: *see* National Socialism
Netherlands 70, 74
  see also Holland
Neue Freie Presse 72
neurasthenia 170, 179, 186, 191, 307
Newfoundland 208
Newman, John Paul 14
newspapers 4, 20, 45, 67, 87, 89, 95, 98, 135, 142, 149, 169, 215, 238, 258
  for individual newspapers see their titles
New Zealand 208

New Zealand Expeditionary Force 218, 224
New Zealand High Commissioner 224
New Zealand literature 218
New Zealanders:
  Native 213
  Pakeha 209, 218, 224
  white 211, 218, 222
NGOs 30
Nice 296
Nietzsche, Friedrich 17, 110
Nigeria, Nigerians 219
Nightingale, Florence 145 n., 159
nihilism 106
Nineteen-Hundred-and-Three 279–80
Noi che tingemmo il mondo di sanguigno 259
North Africa 196
North America 18, 292
Notturno 259
'Not Yet Diagnosed Nervous' (NYDN) Centre 170 n., 173
November Revolution 35, 36
Novi Sad 281
Novo Mesto 105 n.
Nowa Gazeta 41
nurses 9, 11, 14, 17–18, 21–2, 44, 71, 91, 97, 120, 143–66, 219, 255
  sexualized imagery of 148, 163–5
nursing school 145 n.
Nyst, Ray 69 n.

Ochota (Warsaw district) 37
Odabashian, Sahak 201
Oehme, Friedel 246
L'Œuvre 310
officers 18–19, 182
  Armenian 198, 200–1, 203–4
  Austrian 122–3, 125–8, 152, 165
  Belgian 75–6
  British 169, 172–3, 179, 222
  Czech 139

German 35–6, 69, 93, 99, 170
Italian 150 n., 258, 263, 265, 267–8
Ottoman 198
Russian 50, 85, 100, 284, 294–7, 299–300, 302–3
Serbian 280
Slovenian 105, 114, 116 n.
Turkish 199
Okoren, Anton 112–13
Olsztyn 87
  see also Allenstein
Omodeo, Adolfo 254
Opanasiuk, Semen 302
E ora andiamo: il riomanzo di uno scalcinato 259
Ordeal by Fire 264, 266
Order of Malta (*Malteserorden*) 146, 157, 161
Orel (Catholic sports association) 108
Orientalism 217
Orthodox Slav populations 274
Ortigara, Battle of 121 n.
Ortler massif, Ortler campaign 120–1
Os'kin, D. 300
Ostpreußische Kriegshilfe 89, 96
Ottoman Decade of War (1911–22) 195–6
Ottoman Empire 5, 8, 12, 14, 21, 195–8, 206, 274
  army 198, 201–2, 205
  constitution 196
  enters First World War 196
  government 202
  illiteracy in 12, 21
  mobilizes soldiers 197
  parliament 196
  patriotism in 197
  Third Army 202–3
  war effort 203
  wartime conditions in 197

Owen, Wilfred 273

pacifism 152, 162
pacifist interpretations of war 23, 159
pacifists 138 n., 144, 162, 292
Pakeha New Zealanders 209, 218, 224
Pajewski, Janusz 42
Pale of Settlement 49
Palestine 197, 207–8, 215, 221
Palmanova 266
Der Panther 241
Panther Verlag 242
Papillon, Marcel 3
Pardubitz (Pardubice) 145 n.
Paris 140, 299
  peace conference 124, 140
  see also Versailles
Pasha, Enver 202–3, 205
Pasha, Grand Vizier Said Halim:
  see Grand Vizier Said Halim Pasha
Pasha, Talat 202–3
Pasini, Ferdinando 259
Pastorino, Carlo 259, 262, 264–7
Pasubio front 262
patient case files 168–9, 174, 176–9, 184–7, 190, 192
Patriotic Women's Benevolent Societies of the Red Cross 153
Les Paysans 310 n.
peasants, peasantry:
  German 138
    literacy among 94
  Italian 134
  Russian 294, 296–8, 300, 302–3
  Turkish 283
pensions 169, 171
A People's Tragedy 295
Pepernik, Amandus 111
Perathoner, Julius 135
Pergher, Roberta 9

Perm 298
Perthes Verlag 241–2
Petar, King (Serbia) 278
Petersen, Kurt 246
petite bourgeoisie 21
petits bourgeois 65
Petrograd 44
Petrone, Karen 293
Pfeilschifter, Georg 232, 234, 240
photographs, photography 53, 70, 73, 105, 154, 160, 195
Piave river 120
Picard, Edmond 66, 70, 73, 75, 76 n., 77–8, 79 n.
Picard, Leo 76 n.
Pireiko, A. 300
Plan/Planá 145 n.
Podlesnik, Ivan 110
poison gas 8, 170, 178
Poland 5, 18–19, 21–2, 29–55, 87, 90, 288
  Communist regime 35
  1968 anti-Zionist campaign in 37
  Russian 'Great Retreat' in 297
Poles:
  antisemitism among 50–1
  attitudes among 52–3
  attitudes of nurses towards 44
  attitudes towards Russia 39
  enlistment in Russian army 43
  fighting against Ukraine 296 n.
  flee from fighting in 1915: 297
police:
  German:
    in Belgium 69, 75
    in East Prussia 93
    in Warsaw 36, 41, 52
  military in France 225
  Ottoman 201
police brutality/mistreatment 54, 69
police files/reports 30, 53, 65, 87
Polish Academy of Science 47
Polish constitution 47
Polish language 37
Polish legions 39
Polish soldiers 36, 139
Polish students 33, 35, 37
politics of memory 129
Pollini, Leo 259
Pöll-Naepflin, Maria 143–7, 153, 156, 159–60, 162–5
Pölzleitner, Josef 126
Pont-à-Mousson 3
Poppelreuter, Walther 174–6, 184–7, 192
Porter, Roy 177
postmodernism, postmodernists 83, 231
post-traumatic stress disorder 109
POWs: see prisoners of war
Pratt, Mary Louise 208
Prebble, Alexander 224, 227
Predazzo 134
Preporod 108 n.
Presser, Jacob 83, 168
prisoners of war (POWs) 123, 157, 197, 212, 216, 227, 255, 265
prisons, imprisonment 41, 67, 108 n., 157, 211–12, 224, 227, 264–5
profiteering 39, 65
Progress 276, 278, 280–3, 287
propaganda 16, 19, 116 n., 127, 139, 159, 233, 236, 240, 245, 248, 262
prostitutes 148, 165, 268
Protestants 92, 94, 240, 291, 299
La prova del fuoco 259
Provincial Commission for East Prussian War History 88–9, 94, 101
Prussia 87
  see also East Prussia
Prussian occupation of France in 1870–1: 77

Prylucki, Noah 51–5
psychiatric treatment 99, 172, 176–7, 184, 186, 190
psychiatrists 168–77, 179–80, 182–9, 191–2
psychiatry 172–4
psychoanalysis 171, 175, 180–2, 185, 188, 192
psychological societies 175
Psychological Society (Gesellschaft für Experimentelle Psychologie) 172, 174
psychological treatment 172–3, 175–6, 180, 183–4
psychologists 171–5, 178–83, 186–92
  see also psychiatrists
psychology 167 n., 171–5, 184
psychopathology 172
psychotherapy 169, 172, 174–5, 180, 182, 190
Puccini, Mario 259, 269
Punjabi Sikhs 214–15

Quaglia, Mario 253, 268
The Queen 292
Queen Alexandra's Imperial Military Nursing Service 146 n.

race, racial hierarchy, racial order 179, 198, 207, 209–10, 212–14, 217–27, 247
Rada Główna Opiekuńcza (RGO Main Welfare Organization) 31–2
Radkau, Joachim 186
Radziwiłł, Prince Franciszek 51–2
Radziwiłł Palace 36
railways 63, 90, 101, 156, 221
Ramson, John 211
Rapacki, Józef 53
rape 86, 92, 96–8
Rappoport, Solomon Zanvel (S. Ansky) 48–51, 54

Rastenburg 90
rationing, rations 32, 36, 41, 45–6, 48, 52
Red Cross 43–4, 145 n., 146, 149–51, 153–7, 164 n., 174, 237, 255
Red Fogs 277
refugees 6, 40–2, 45, 49, 73, 88–9, 99, 276
  see also deportation
Regency Council (Warsaw) 32–3, 42, 45
Reich Archive 247
Reina, Giuseppe 259
religion 15, 17, 117, 196, 206, 299
religiosity 159, 240
religious orders 151, 154
  see also Jesuits
Remarque, Erich Maria 152 n., 236, 244, 256
remembrance 13, 144, 146–8, 152–3, 158, 166, 291
Remembrance Day 291
Remembrance Sunday 292
Renn, Ludwig 236
Rennenkampf, Pavel 84–5
reparations 23
reservists 126, 130, 133, 135
Return to Carso: see *Il ritorno sul Carso*
Reut-Nicolussi, Eduard 138
revolution 6, 19, 21, 35–6, 44, 46–7, 54, 110, 196, 203, 274–5
  see also Russian Revolution
Ricœur, Paul 305
Riga 187
Ringstraße (Vienna) 156
Risorgimento 250, 254
rite of passage 18
La ritirata del Friuli 259, 269
Il ritorno sul Carso 259, 269
robbery 86
Rohrer, Margarete von 157
Rolland, Roman 310 n.
Romandie 145 n.

Romania 154, 288
Romanian troops 139
Romeo and Juliet 310 n.
Ronikier, Adam, Count 32
Roque, Ricardo 210
Rosai, Ottone 259
Rosenberg, William 301
Rossato, Arturo 259
Rössel 90
Rouen 225–6
Rows, Richard Gundry 174, 177 n., 180, 184, 189–90
Royal Army Medical Corps (RAMC) 171–3, 178 n.
Royal Society of Medicine 170
Rubè 259
Rudolfinerhaus (Vienna) 145 n.
Rueh, Franc 114
rumours 14, 43, 50, 53–4, 63, 87, 99, 163, 203, 226
rural population:
  diaries among 64 n.
  illiteracy among 12, 21
  observations about 74
  soldiers from 107, 251
rural–urban differences 79
Russia 18–19, 21, 48, 119–20, 123, 130, 135, 137 n., 292–5, 298–9, 303
  lack of war monuments in 292, 294
  secret Treaty of London 137 n.
Russian aristocrats 296, 303
Russian army 31, 40, 42–4, 49, 62, 83–5, 97, 302
  antisemitism in 44
  Armenians fighting alongside 205
  in Brusilov's memoirs 296
  cavalry 132
  censorship in 301–2
  defeats Ottoman Third Army 202

deportations:
  in East Prussia 83–9, 94, 98, 100
  of East Prussians 85
  of Jews 40, 49
  evacuation of Warsaw (1915) 31–2, 39, 44, 48, 51
  First Army 84
  illiteracy in 300
  Military Censorship Section 301
  Poles enlisted in 43
  recruiting system 295
  withdraws on South-Western Front in 1915: 297
  see also 'Great Retreat'
Russian educated elite 295
Russian Empire 6, 12, 21, 49, 51, 86
  deportations in 6, 8, 40, 49
  illiteracy in 21, 300
Russian Front 302
Russian front (with Austria-Hungary) 109, 113, 119, 120–1, 123, 130, 145
Russian General Staff 298
Russian General Staff Academy 295
Russian high command 300
Russian intelligentsia 295
Russian military attachés 299
Russian national character 300
Russian officer corps 84, 294
Russian officers 50, 84–5, 100, 294–5, 299–300, 302
Russian peasants, peasant soldiers 302–3
Russian prisoner-of-war camps 157
Russian progressivism 298 n.
Russian regime in Poland 29–30, 32, 35, 38–9, 42–3, 46, 53
Russian Revolution 46, 293, 298–300, 303
Russian soldiers 44, 294, 297, 299–300, 302

in East Prussia 20, 83–4, 86–99, 238
in German published testimonies 237, 244, 248
Russo-Japanese War 301
Ruthenian soldiers 139

sacrifice 18, 23, 43 n., 73, 78, 80–1, 106–7, 116, 127, 131, 138, 140–1, 151, 234–5, 242–4, 249–50, 256, 262–3, 267, 269, 271, 274, 276, 278–9, 282–6, 288–9
La sagra di Santa Gorizia 259, 263
St Leger, William 221–3
Şakir, Bahaddin 203
Salamon, Anna 90, 96
Salonica 279–80
Salonika: *see* Thessaloniki
Salsa, Carlo 252, 257, 259, 263, 265–7
Samsonov, Aleksandr 84
Sanborn, Joshua 18–19
Sanders, General Liman von 205
Sanders Van Loo, Alida Wynanda 68, 79 n.
Šantić, Aleksa 275
Sarikamiş, Battle of 203
Sassoon, Siegfried 273
Sauer, Willibald 174–5, 185, 188, 192
Scalabre, Corporal 308
Le scarpe al sole 257, 259, 263
Schäfer, Wilhelm 245, 246 n.
Scherer, Marie 151 n.
Scherer, Wilhelm 151 n.
Schimmer, Stefan 3
Schindler, Hannes 126
Schlagekrug 90
Schmidkunz, Walter 127
Schneeberger, Hans 139
schoolchildren 249
schools 18, 33, 37, 81, 133, 198, 201, 249–52, 254, 261

Schopenhauer, Artur 114
Schult, August 93–4, 98–9
Schulte, Regina 148, 156, 158
Schultze, Emil Otto 174–5, 187–8, 192
Schultze, Friedrich 182–3, 185
Schwerin 93
Schwingshackl, Johann 137 n.
Scott, Joan 305
Scottish Highlanders 131–2, 213–14
Second World War 29–30, 34, 38 n., 88, 137, 140, 157, 159 n., 232, 289, 306
Seeburg 91
Senegalese soldiers 211
Serao, Matilde 256
Serbia 8, 21 n., 62–3, 119–20, 123, 130, 135, 273–89
  border 150
  illiteracy in 12 n., 273
Serbian army 276, 279
Serbian civilians' diaries 61–2
Serbian Cultural Club 287
Serbian front 109, 121, 165
Serbian government 279
Serbianization 274
Serbian king 117
Serbian Literary Herald 276
Serbian Ministry of Agrarian Reform 282
Serbian modernism 277
Serbian national identity 275
Serbian palace coup of 1903: 279–80
Serbian soldiers 282–4
The Serbian Voice 287
Serbian wars of liberation and unification 279–80
Serbian war veterans 276, 278–9, 288–9
Serbs 273–89, 296
  in Witkop's collection of letters 244

sermons 57, 107
Serra, Renato 259–61
Sexten 133
Sexten peaks 120
sexual anxieties 98
sexual assaults 86, 96
  see also rape
sexual imagery 148, 163–5
sexuality 164
sexual morality 37–8, 164–5
Shakespeare, William 310 n.
Shekena (river) 299
shelling 40, 99, 108, 112, 170, 172–3, 183, 187–90, 192, 213, 297
shell shock, shell-shocked soldiers 19, 168–70, 172–4, 176–85, 189–91
Shklovskii, Viktor 299
shooting clubs: see Standschützen
Showalter, Dennis 63
shtetls 49
Siberia 197
  see also 'Yugoslav Siberia'
Sievers, Faddey Vasilievich 84
Sikhs 214–15
Silesia 157
Sinai and Palestine Campaign 221
Sironi, Guido 259
Sivas 198, 200, 202–4
Slovak troops 139
Slovenec 114
Slovenes 105–17, 275
Slovenia 17, 105–17
Slovenian officers 116 n.
Slovenian politicians 117
Slovenian priests 107
Slovenian soldiers 5, 105–17
Smith, Leonard 132–3, 293
Smyrna: see Izmir
snipers 71
socialism 172, 283, 310
Socialist Party (Austria) 152
Soffici, Ardengo 259, 269

Il soldato Cola 259, 269
soldiers 3–14, 16–21, 23, 25–6, 42–6, 49, 57, 72, 76, 86–7, 90–3, 96–100, 106–17, 120, 122 n., 123, 125–9, 131–5, 139, 141–3, 145 n., 146, 148–50, 152, 156, 159–64, 167–85, 189–92, 198–207, 211–16, 219–21, 223–7, 231–4, 237–8, 243–8, 252–4, 258, 261, 263, 265–8, 270, 275, 278, 281–4, 291–303, 306–7, 311–12
  Armenian 199–200, 202–6
  Australian 216
  Austrian 112, 125–8, 132, 135
  Belgian 76
  British 5, 178, 219, 222
  Catholic 232, 234, 240, 291
  fallen 156, 244, 248, 268
  Flemish 76
  French 3, 5, 132
  German 3, 5, 35, 45, 90–1, 96, 98–100, 139, 178, 231–2, 237, 243–4, 247
  illiterate 12, 252
  injured, wounded 49, 96, 115, 161–3, 172, 182
  Italian 5, 120, 135, 254
  Jewish 234, 247
  non-European 211, 213–15, 220–1, 223–7
  Polish 36, 139
  Russian 20, 44, 83–99, 238, 294, 297, 299–300, 302
  Ruthenian 139
  Serbian 282–4
  Slovenian 5, 105–17
  South African 221, 223
  unknown 291–2, 294, 303
soldiers' councils (Soldatenräte) 36
solidarity 61, 72, 78, 221, 267, 269
Somme, Battle of the 169, 173 n., 239, 246

Sonnenthal, Horaz 150
Sonnenthal-Scherer, Maria 150–1
Sott'la naja 259, 264
South Africa 208, 225
South African government 225–6
South African Infantry 209
South African Native Labour Corps (SANLC) 215–16, 220, 223, 225
South Africans 217, 223, 225–6
South African soldiers 221, 223
South-Eastern Front 171
South Slavs 273, 275, 278, 287
South Slav state: *see* Yugoslavia
South Tyrol 105 n., 137, 139–40
 annexation to Austria 140
South-Western Front (Russian) 297, 301
Soviet Armenia 206
Soviet Union 21, 292–3, 295
Spanish Civil War 111
Sparr, William 237
spirituality 232, 293
Splügen-Verlag 143
'Springboks' 209
Sri Lanka, Sri Lankans 216–18
Sroka, Jankiel 52
Standschützen 128, 130–6, 139, 141
Stanghellini, Arturo 259, 269, 271
Steinberg, John 295
Stepun, Fedor 299
Stockholm 32, 44
'Storm of Steel' (*'In Stahlgewittern'*) 12 n.
Strachan, Hew 292
'Strafexpedition' (May 1919 Austrian offensive) 121 n.
Streets, Heather 214
Streuvels, Stijn 73–5, 79 n.
strikes 33, 36, 46, 48
students 22, 33–5, 37, 76–7, 133, 200, 240–3, 245, 258, 268, 295
 Jewish 245

women 35
Stuparich, Giani 259–60
Stuttgart 235, 239
Styria 149 n., 150
subjectivity, subjective experience 9–10, 15–16, 20, 24–5, 57, 64–5, 79, 81, 208, 220, 232, 294, 298–301, 303
Sudetenland 288
Suez Canal 216
Sultan Abdülhamid II: *see* Abdülhamid II, Sultan
Sürmenyan, Kalusd 198–206
Swiss border (with Italy) 119–20
Switzerland 134, 144–5
synagogues 49
Syria 150–1, 197, 202

Tannenberg, Battle of 84, 300
Tanskyne Fort 207
Taranto 223
teachers 88–90, 95, 205
Teirlinck, Herman 77 n.
Territorial Force Nursing Service 146 n.
terrorism 288
Testament of Youth 255
Theodore, Demetrios 200–1, 206
Thessaloniki 196, 208, 281
Theweleit, Klaus 148
'thin red line' 119 n., 131–2
Third Reich: *see* National Socialist regime
Thomas, Albert 310 n.
Thomas, Marjorie 219–21
Thorp, Mary 73, 79 n.
Thucydides 282
The Times 170 n., 224
Toggenburg, Friedrich von 136
Tolstoy, Lev Nikolayevich (Leo) 108 n., 110, 114
Tombs of the Unknown Soldier 291–2, 294, 303

Tonelli, Luigi 268
torture 93, 265, 306
'total war' 7, 90, 273, 298
Toti, Enrico 250
Traba, Robert 97
Transjordan 197
Tratnjek, Ivan 113
trauma 95–6, 98–100, 109, 160, 163, 169, 182, 185, 188, 192, 265, 267, 293
Treaty of London 137 n.
trenches 5, 12–14, 17, 67, 172, 187, 189–90, 233, 252–3, 262, 266–70, 281, 293, 296, 301–3, 306, 308 n., 314
  as birthplace for Italian nation 250
  as a place to write 13
  community (Frontgemeinschaft) 18, 23, 264, 266, 269, 270
Trenches 252, 265
trench newspapers 4, 75 n.
trench warfare 17, 120, 122, 246, 293
Trent Bridge 224
Trentino 123, 137
Trento 261
Trieste 119, 137 n., 261
Trincee 257, 259
Trouillot, Michel-Rolph 30
Tsar 34, 301
Tsarist Empire 14, 21, 62, 84
  illiteracy in 12
  see also Russian Empire
Tucović, Dimitrije 278–9, 283
Tula 298
Turkey 6, 21, 197
  illiteracy in 12 n.
  publication of eyewitness accounts in 195
Turkish anthem 200
Turkish Republic 197
Turks 199, 201, 278, 283

Two Months in Yugoslav Siberia 280–4, 287
Tygodnik Ilustrowany 53
Tymczasowa Rada Stanu (Provisional State Council) 31–2
typhoid fever 311
typhus 41, 51
Tyrol 105 n., 110, 120, 122–3, 125, 130–2, 134–41
  annexation to Austria 140
  as multi-ethnic crownland 140
Tyrolean front 120–3, 125, 129–32, 135–6
Tyrolean newspapers 135
Tyrolean troops in the Napoleonic War 131
  see also Alpine front

Überegger, Oswald 152
Ukraine 36, 44, 150, 296 n.
Ukrainians:
  flee from fighting in 1915: 297
Ulrich, Bernd 232–3, 236
underground press, Belgian 61 n.
UNESCO 12 n.
Ungaretti, Giuseppe 259–60
Unification or Death ('The Black Hand') 279–80
United Kingdom 21, 30
  see also Britain
United States 155, 199, 206, 232
universities, institutions of higher education 18, 32–5, 37, 47, 54, 77, 172, 174–5, 243, 252, 254, 271
Upper Austria 155
Ustashe 289

Valentin, Veit 245
Valentini, Louise 155
Valhalla 156
Vandal, Albert 297
Van de Woestijne, Karel 77 n.

Vasić, Dragiša 276–89
Le veglie al Carso 259
Vent'anni 259, 269
Verdun, Battle of 169, 239
Vermeylen, August 77 n.
Versailles, Treaty of (settlement) 117, 232, 288
Verschaeve, Cyriel 78
Vevern, Boleslav 299–300
Via Crucis 270
Viani, Lorenzo 260
victimization 132–3, 139–40, 152
Vienna 145 n., 153 n., 155–6
I vinti di Caporetto 259
violence 7–8, 14, 23, 62–3, 69, 74, 83–9, 94, 97, 109, 112, 160, 273, 278, 282, 285, 287–8, 293, 312, 315
  relative absence of in ego documents 13
Virgin Mary 113
Vistula 45
Vittorio Veneto 257
Viva Caporetto! La rivolta dei santi maledetti 257, 259
Volga 299
völkisch publications 138
Volksgemeinschaft 140
Voluntary Aid Detachment (VAD) 146 n., 219
volunteers 13, 18, 20, 22, 24, 40, 68, 71, 92, 128, 130, 133, 135, 146, 156–7, 161, 166, 196, 255, 258, 261, 295
Vosges 3
Vulović, Ljubomir 279
Vyatka 298

Wadowice 155
Wagner, Kim 210
Wahre Soldatengeschichten 149
Wakenitz, Oskar von der Lanken 73 n.

Wallonia 75
War Assistance Office (*Kriegshilfsbüro*) (Austria) 150
'war culture' 80
'war enthusiasm' 161 n., 233
war experience: *see* experience (of warfare)
war memoirs: *see* memoirs
war memorials: *see* memorials
War Ministry (Prussian) 246
'war neurosis' (*Kriegsneurose*) 173 n., 182, 189
War Office (British) 214–15, 225–6
'war poets' 273
war profiteers 240
Warsaw 29–55
  Jewish refugees arriving in 40, 49
  Jews in 44, 50–1
  population of 35, 48
  Russian evacuation of (1915) 31–2, 39, 44, 48, 51
Warsaw Citadel 41
Warsaw Citizens' Committee 30, 32–3, 41–4
Warsaw city administration 33, 41
Warsaw city archives 40
Warsaw city council 54
Warsaw city militia 51–2
Warsaw General Government 32, 47
Warsaw Royal Castle 38
Warsaw University 33–5, 37, 54
Warsaw Uprising 30
  Museum of 30, 55
Wartel, Leopold 69 n.
Watson, Alexander 20
Weber, Fritz 138 n.
Weber, Max 4
Weibliche Hilfskräfte der Armee im Felde 149 n., 151 n.
Weil, Simone 111
Weimar Republic 240, 243–4
Wejnberg, Mordechai 51

Wels (Upper Austria) 155
West Africa 208
Western Front 4–8, 13–14, 62–3, 99, 122–3, 127, 133, 157, 161 n., 172–3, 178, 187, 189, 208, 211, 215, 220–3, 225, 237
West Indian battalions (British) 211
West Indians (BWIs) 213, 215, 217, 219–20
West Indian soldiers, mutinied 223
West India Regiment 214
West Indies 208, 219
West Indies Regiment (British) 211
Weybridge 224
White, Hayden 308, 311
white-collar workers, professions 21, 37
Whitehall 291–2
'White Hand' faction 280
widows 197, 268
Wielopolska, Countess 37
Wierling, Dorothee 58
Wilhelm II, Kaiser 34, 43
William, King 211
Williamson, John 224
Winter, Jay 5, 291
Witkop, Philipp 20, 22, 232, 240–8
women 9, 11, 14, 18, 22, 35, 57, 64, 74, 78, 100, 143, 146–53, 156, 158–61, 163–6, 197, 207, 238, 267, 275
  British:
    marrying Maoris 224, 227
    marrying Pakeha New Zealanders 224
    marrying South Africans 225–6
    deported in East Prussia 84, 86
  French marrying French Imperial troops 226
  in labour 182
  Italian 254
    authors 255–6
  'new' women 23
  relationships with Maoris 223–4
  sexual images of 163–5
  university students 35
  victims of violence in East Prussia 89, 92, 96–9
    see also rape
  in Warsaw 35, 37, 42–3, 46, 48
women's movement 149
World War Library (Stuttgart) (Library of Contemporary History) 235

Yiddish 37, 49–51
YIVO Institute for Jewish Research 55
Young Turks (in the Russian General Staff) 298
Ypres 76
Yugoslavia (South Slav nation, South Slav state) 21, 117, 273–7, 280–1, 286–9
  see also Serbia
Yugoslav idea 107, 117
Yugoslav Partisans 289
'Yugoslav Siberia' 280–5
Yugoslav soldiers 272, 282
  see also Serbian soldiers

Zallinger-Thurn, Bernhard 137
Zionism 172
Zola, Émile 310 n.
Župančič, Oton 114
Zurich 144